The Rehabilitation of Cognitive Disabilities

Mid-South Conference of Human Neuropsychology...

The Rehabilitation of Cognitive Disabilities

Edited by

J. Michael Williams
Center for Applied Psychological Research
Memphis State University
Memphis, Tennessee

and

Charles J. Long
Center for Applied Psychological Research
Memphis State University
and Neuropsychology Laboratory
University of Tennessee Center for the Health Sciences
Memphis, Tennessee

PLENUM PRESS • NEW YORK AND LONDON

Library of Congress Cataloging in Publication Data

Mid-South Conference of Human Neuropsychology on the Rehabilitation of Cognitive Disabilities (4th: 1986: Memphis, Tenn.)
The rehabilitation of cognitive disabilities.

"Proceedings of the Fourth Mid-South Conference of Human Neuropsychology on the
Rehabilitation of Cognitive Disabilities, held May 29–30, 1986, in Memphis,
Tennessee" — T.p. verso.
Includes bibliographies and index.
1. Cognition disorders — Patients — Rehabilitation — Congresses. I. Williams, J. Michael,
1954–   . II. Long, Charles J., 1935–   . III. Title. [DNLM: 1. Brain Injuries — rehabili-
tation — congresses. 2. Cognition Disorders — rehabilitation — congresses. W3 MI286 4th
1986r / WL 354 M627 1986r]
RC394.C64M53   1986   616.8   87-7948
ISBN 0-306-42594-7

Proceedings of the Fourth Mid-South Conference of Human Neuropsychology
on the Rehabilitation of Cognitive Disabilities, held May 29–30, 1986,
in Memphis, Tennessee

© 1987 Plenum Press, New York
A Division of Plenum Publishing Corporation
233 Spring Street, New York, N.Y. 10013

Printed in the United States of America

Contributors

Gerald Bennett, Spain Rehabilitation Center, University of Alabama at Birmingham, Birmingham, AL

Thomas Bergquist, Spain Rehabilitation Center, University of Alabama at Birmingham, Birmingham, AL

Tina Brown, Department of Psychology, Memphis State University, Memphis, TN

Marian B. Danse, Department of Preventive, Family, and Rehabilitation Medicine, Monroe Community Hospital, University of Rochester, Rochester, NY

Raymond S. Dean, Neuropsychology Laboratory, TC-521, Ball State University, Muncie, IN

Kathleen Fitzhugh-Bell, Department of Neurology, Indiana University Medical Center, Indianapolis, IN

Wm. Drew Gouvier, Department of Psychology, Lousiana State University, Baton Rouge, LA

Gregory Harter, Department of Psychology, Memphis State University, Memphis, TN

Donna L. Hartley, Spain Rehabilitation Center, University of Alabama at Birmingham, Birmingham, AL

Aleida K. Inglis, Department of Reading, Language, and Learning Disabilities, Harvard University, Cambridge, MA

Marsha M. Little, Department of Psychology, Memphis State University, Memphis, TN

Charles J. Long, Department of Psychology, Memphis State University, Memphis, TN

Kurt A. Moehle, Department of Psychology, Purdue University at Indianapolis, Indianapolis, IN

Sam B.Morgan, Department of Psychology, Memphis State University, Memphis, TN

Thomas A. Novak, Spain Rehabilitation Center, University of Alabama at Birmingham, Birmingham, AL

Randolph W. Parks, Department of Psychiatry, Massachusetts Mental Health Center, Harvard Medical School, Cambridge, MA

George Prigatano, Department of Neuropsychology, St. Joseph Hospital and Medical
        Center, Phoenix, AZ

Jeffrey L. Rassmussen, Department of Psychology, Purdue University at Indianapolis,
        Indianapolis, IN

Gurmal Rattan, Indiana University of Pennsylvania, Indiana, PA

Robert Sbordone, University of California at Irvine School of Medicine and Orange County
        Neuropsychology Group, Fountain Valley, CA

Cathy Telzrow, Cuyahoga Special Education, Service Center, 14605 Granger Road, Maple
        Heights, OH

Mark, T. Wagner, Department of Preventive, Family, and Rehabilitation Medicine, Monroe
        Community Hospital, University of Rochester, Rochester, NY

Mark S. Warner, Department of Psychology, Lousiana State University, Baton Rouge, LA

J. Michael Williams, Department of Psychology, Memphis State University, Memphis, TN

Lisa A. Wolfe, Department of Psychology and Social Relations, Harvard University,
        Cambridge, MA

Preface

The rehabilitation of intellectual impairment resulting from brain injury has become a major professional activity of clinical neuropsychologists. In recent years, neuropsychology has developed from a professional role stressing assessment and diagnosis to one that now includes treatment and rehabilitation activities. Such trends are also manifested in two new research interests of neuropsychologists: the study of the generalizability of neuropsychological test findings to everyday abilities, often referred to as the "ecological validity" of tests, and outcome studies of cognitive retraining treatments. Discovering the relationships between traditional neuropsychological tests and everyday behavior is important because the referral questions posed to neuropsychologists have changed. Now, the neuropsychologist is asked to comment on the patient's functional intellectual abilities as they relate to the everyday demands of home, work and educational settings. Of course, the development of cognitive retraining theory and procedures allows neuropsychologists to intervene in the treatment of the cognitive problems that the neuropsychological evaluation has documented.

Since these approaches are still in their formative stages, they have been the subject of clinical lore, great controversy and little systematic research. This situation prompted one of our presenters to lament, "Either you believe Cognitive Retraining is divinely inspired, or the work of the devil." There is apparently little middle ground.

Given this state of affairs, the program committee of the Mid-South Conference on Human Neuropsychology decided to focus on the role of neuropsychologists in rehabilitation. Such a conference would allow us to mull over all of the new problems inherent in developing new research and clinical programs. We also decided to include presentations on intervention approaches used to remediate learning disabilities. This area is also in its formative stages and shares many of the retraining techniques and controversies present in the rehabilitation of brain injuries.

The following chapters represent the proceedings of the fourth May conference on human neuropsychology. The chapters cover a broad area and we are not sure we have achieved a significant new synthesis of ideas in this volume. We can certainly claim that the present chapters are excellent current reviews of the major topics. As such, we certainly hope this book will bring some clarity to the study of cognitive rehabilitation.

J. Michael Williams and
Charles J. Long

Memphis, Tennessee

Contents

Part One: General Theories of Cognitive Rehabilitation

1.   A Conceptual Model of Neuropsychologically-Based
         Cognitive Rehabilitation... 3

         Robert J. Sbordone

2.   Neuropsychological Rehabilitation After Brain Injury: Some
         Further Reflections.. 29

         George P. Prigatano

3.   The Role of Cognitive Retraining in Comprehensive Rehabilitation................. 43

         J. Michael Williams

4.   Neuropsychological Theories and Cognitive Rehabilitation....................... 57

         *Kurt A. Moehle, Jeffrey Lee Rasmussen and
         Kathleen B. Fitzhugh-Bell*

Part Two: The Practice of Cognitive Rehabilitation

5.   The Current Status of Computer-Assisted Cognitive Rehabilitation................. 79

         Charles J. Long

6.   Methodological Issues in Cognitive Retraining Research........................... 95

         Gregory W. Harter

7.   Treatment of Visual Imperception and Related Disorders........................... 109

         Wm. Drew Gouvier and Mark S. Warner

8.   The Remediation of Everyday Memory Deficits..................................... 123

         Marsha M. Little

9.   Cognitive Rehabilitation: Psychosocial Issues.. 139

        Mark T. Wagner and Marian B. Danse

10.   Cognitive Stimulation in the Home Environment.....................................149

        *Thomas A. Novack, Thomas F. Bergquist, Gerald Bennett, and
        Donna Hartley*

Part Three: Pediatric Cognitive Rehabilitation

11.   The Neuropsychology of Children's Learning Disorders............................173

        Gurmal Rattan and Raymond S. Dean

12.   The "So What?" Question: Intervention with Learning
        Disabled Children... 191

        Cathy F. Telzrow

13.   Learning Disabilities and Hyperactivity: Implications for
        Research and Clinical Assessment... 207

        Lisa A. Wolfe, Aleida K. Inglis, and Randolph W. Parks

14.   Cognitive Training with Brain-Injured Children: General Issues
        and Approaches...217

        Tina L. Brown and Sam B. Morgan

Subject Index...233

Part One: General Theories of Cognitive Rehabilitation

1

A Conceptual Model of Neuropsychologically-Based Cognitive Rehabilitation

Robert J. Sbordone

Approximately 3 1/2 percent of the people in the United States sustain head injuries each year. Approximately 1/4 of these injuries include skull fractures and intracranial injuries, resulting in long-lasting and often permanent alterations in cognitive, emotional, and behavioral functioning (Cooper, 1982). Rehabilitation programs have traditionally been geared toward physical recovery (Bond, 1975), although recently there has been a growing effort to improve the cognitive functioning of these patients, through what has often been referred to as "cognitive rehabilitation". This paper will present a conceptual model of neuropsychologically-based cognitive rehabilitation for head trauma patients who have left the acute hospital or inpatient rehabilitation setting. It will also examine many of the myths about treatment and recovery from head trauma that have handicapped neuropsychologists and rehabilitation professionals. This paper will present the author's views (and prejudices), as well as provide a conceptual framework for cognitive rehabilitation services for the severe traumatic brain-injured patient.

Stages of Recovery from Severe Head Trauma

Cognitive deficits, emotional disturbances, and "personality change" have long been recognized as salient, and sometimes permanent, sequelae of severe traumatic brain injuries. The author has found it helpful to view the recovery process as consisting of six relatively discrete stages. Table 1 presents the stages of recovery from severe head trauma.

During the Early Acute stage, the patient is in coma as a result of their head injury. The Late Acute stage begins when the patient first opens their eyes. This stage is characterized by either severe agitation, restlessness, confusion, or a persistent vegetative state. If the patient is not in the latter, they are typically disoriented to place and time, but not to person. The third and Early Intermediate stage begins when the patient becomes oriented to place, but tends to remain disoriented to time (e.g., day of the week). During this stage, the patient exhibits confusion of moderate severity. The most salient characteristic of this stage is the patient's marked denial of cognitive deficits. These patients, however, may complain of somatic problems, particularly pain, if they have sustained orthopedic injuries. During this stage of recovery, the patient fatigues very easily and frequently displays poor judgment. Patients typically have markedly severe attentional deficits, along with severe memory, social, and problem-solving difficulties.

When the patient becomes oriented to place and time and begins to complain of cognitive deficits, the patient has entered into the Late Intermediate stage of recovery. Patients in this stage will typically display mild confusion and mild to moderate attentional

Table 1

Stages of Recovery Following Severe Head Injury

Early Acute	Injury; Patient in coma
Late Acute	Patient opens eyes; Severe agitation-restlessness or vegetative state; Severe confusion; Disoriented to place and time
Early Intermediate	Oriented to place and time; Moderate confusion; Denial of cognitive deficits; May complain of somatic problems; Fatigues very easily; Poor judgment; Marked to severe attention deficits; Severe memory deficits; Severe social difficulties; Severe problem-solving difficulties
Late Intermediate	Oriented to place and time; Becoming aware of cognitive deficits; Mild confusion; Mild to moderate attention difficulties; Poor problem-solving; Moderate to marked memory deficits; Early onset of depression; Unsuccessful attempts to return to work or school; May appear relatively normal; Moderate to marked social difficulties.
Early Late	Significant depression-nervousness; Mild to moderate memory deficits; Mild to moderate problem-solving difficulties.
Late Late	Mild memory impairment; Mild problem-solving difficulties; Acceptance of deficits; Improving social relationships; Return of most responsibilities; Generally positive self-image.

difficulties. Their memory is markedly impaired, while problem-solving skills are usually more severely impaired. During this stage, the patient's mood appears depressed with frequent displays of agitation. It is also during this stage that the patient may attempt to return to work or school (usually unsuccessfully). During this stage, patients may appear relatively normal but are frequently referred to as the "walking wounded" by rehabilitation professionals. In spite of the "normal" appearance, they will most likely encounter moderate to marked social difficulties.

The fifth stage of recovery (Early Late) is characterized by an increase in the severity of the patient's depression. During this stage, the patient will make frequent unfair comparisons to their premorbid self. They tend to underestimate their present skills and abilities and overestimate their premorbid skills and abilities. It is often during this stage that the patient is given little hope of further recovery by well-meaning rehabilitation professionals or physicians. The patient typically has returned to school or work, but is frequently taking a reduced academic load or is working at a less demanding job than prior to their injury. During this stage of recovery, the patient will exhibit mild to moderate memory and problem-solving difficulties. It is also during this stage that the patient has withdrawn from or been shunned by most, if not all, of their friends. The sixth and final stage of recovery (Late Late) is characterized by the patient's acceptance of their residual cognitive deficits. They have assumed many of their premorbid responsibilities and have begun forming new social relationships. It is during this final stage that the patient's self-image is generally positive, whereas in previous stages, it was negative. These patients continue to experience mild residual memory and problem-solving difficulties, although they typically develop a number of coping strategies that permit them to function effectively in their environment. It should be pointed out that many patients do not reach this final stage.

Obstacles to Effective Cognitive Rehabilitation

Inaccurate Prognosis

A number of obstacles exist today which undermine the neuropsychological-based rehabilitation professional's efforts and motivation in working with head trauma patients. The most difficult obstacle is the assumption that most of the recovery following head trauma occurs within the first six months and that virtually all of the recovery occurs within the first year or two post injury. This assumption appears to be largely based on studies by Bond (1975) and Bond and Brooks (1976), who assessed the recovery of patients with severe traumatic head injuries. In Bond's first study, he examined 56 patients (47 men and 9 women) whose ages range from 15 to 64 (mean = 30.9; standard deviation = 13.2). Ninety-six percent of these patients had post traumatic amnesia seven days or longer in duration. Fifty-two percent of these patients had post traumatic amnesia of more than four weeks. It is important to note that all of the subjects in this study had been referred for neurosurgical treatment. He grouped his patients according to their length of post traumatic amnesia and time since injury. He then compared the WAIS IQ scores of these groups, since he did not actually perform serial testing. He found that groups of patients with approximately the same WAIS IQ scores when he compared the length of time since injury. Therefore, he argued that the most rapid recovery occurs during the first six months, followed by a slower rate of improvement which continued steadily and reached a maximum at 24 months post injury. This study can be criticized for several reasons. For example, Bond did not use a representative sample of brain-injured patients, since each of the patients used in his study had been referred for neurosurgical treatment. He based his findings entirely on WAIS IQ test scores. He did not perform serial testing of these patients, and had no premorbid IQ scores. He did not utilize any suitable control groups and ignored the possible influence in IQ of such factors as age, sex, education, employment status, medications, physical disability, or emotional factors.

In a second study (Bond & Brooks, 1976), 40 of the patients from the first study were serially administered the WAIS at intervals of less than 3 months (4-6 months, 7-12 months, and more than 13 months post injury). Their patients were grouped according to the duration of post traumatic amnesia (PTA). They found that most of the improvement in WAIS IQ scores occurred during the first six months, with little change from six months to two years. Their study can be criticized for the same reasons listed above. They also failed to consider the influence of confounding factors that evolve over the course of recovery from brain injury, such as the deleterious effects of depression and anxiety, which begin in the fourth stage of recovery. This author has found that the fourth stage of recovery does not typically begin until at least six months post injury and generally lasts from six months to one year. It will be recalled that during this stage, patients may develop emotional problems and have usually experienced at least one major failure (usually an unsuccessful attempt to return to school or work). It will also be recalled that during the fifth stage of recovery, patients typically develop significant emotional problems (e.g., depression) which inhibit their cognitive functioning. It should also be noted that these emotional problems are rarely, if ever, displayed during the first three stages of recovery. Thus, the results of Bond and Brooks (1976) are confounded by their failure to consider the disruptive effects of secondary emotional improvement. Unfortunately, they did not evaluate their subject's emotional functioning, either clinically or psychometrically, during the course of their study.

Recently, a number of investigators and clinicians have reported findings which seriously challenge the findings of Bond (1975) and Bond and Brooks (1976). For example, Klonoff, Low, and Clark (1977) reported that 76.3 percent of head-injured children and adolescents make a marked recovery over a five year follow-up period. These investigators found a significant improvement between years four and five post injury. They also found that, in addition to improvements on neuropsychological measures, the EEG improved throughout the entire five year follow-up period. They also reported that neuropsychological, neurological, and trauma-related variables accounted for less than 50 percent of the variance in predicting outcome or residual deficits at five years post injury. They suggested that other variables (e.g., premorbid and environmental) might provide a more precise prediction, since the neurological, and trauma variables subsequent to head injury accounted for less than 50 percent of the variance in predicting outcome or residual deficits at five year post injury. They suggested that other variables (e.g., premorbid and environmental) might provide a more precise prediction, since the neurological variables accounted for only 22.7 percent of the variance. Miller and Stern (1965) followed 100 consecutive cases of severe head injury with a PTA in excess of 24 hours (an average of 13 days). The 92 survivors were reexamined on the average of 11 years post injury and the quality of their recovery was assessed. Only 10 of the 92 survivors showed evidence of persistent dementia, and only 5 of the 92 were unemployed. Despite the severity of their initial injury, half of these patients had returned to their previous occupation. They found that 28 (73.7) percent out of 38 patients had returned to work, even though their physicians, who evaluated them on the average of three years post injury, had expressed serious doubt that these patients would ever be able to work again. Thus, the overwhelming majority of these patients demonstrated a continual, gradual recovery from the initial effects of their head injuries over the course of 11 years. Thomsen (1981) reported a case involving a 44 year old male who sustained very severe head trauma, which resulted in a pronounced global aphasia. At eight months post injury, the patient exhibited signs of frontal lobe dysfunction and disinhibition, severe rigidity, and perseveration. The patient also exhibited verbal paraphasia, neologisms, and frequent perseverations. At two years post injury, he continued to exhibit signs of marked cognitive impairments. Twelve years later, followup assessment revealed that, although the patient had a number of generally mild cognitive problems, his memory and language had continued to improve for 14 years post injury.

Sbordone (in press) reported a case study involving a 22 year old male who sustained a severe closed head injury in a motor vehicle accident shortly after his 17th birthday. The patient spent nine months in coma and remained hospitalized for 18 months. Approximately two years post injury, he was evaluated at a well-known rehabilitation hospital in the Midwest. His parents were told that there was no hope of any further recovery, and that the patient would require long-term institutionalization. Prior to his injury, the patient had been an honor student in high school who excelled in writing. At two years post injury, his attentional skills and memory for recent events were profoundly impaired. He was unable to speak, although he could type very closely with his left hand on a Memo Writer. However, analysis of his typed output revealed aphasic errors. He was unable to ambulate or stand. He only had use of his left arm, which exhibited severe ataxia during volitional movements. His mood was labile without evidence of depression. An intense cognitive rehabilitation program was initiated to improve his attentional skills which required approximately 40 hours per week. Approximately half of this time included the use of computer-assisted cognitive rehabilitation programs with the assistance of his speech therapist or family member. Follow-up assessment ten months later revealed a dramatic improvement. For example, his oral skills had improved to where could speak, although with severe dysarthria. He was able to perform serial 3 addition and serial 7 subtraction without error, although in a very slow and deliberate manner. IQ testing with the Raven Colored Progressive Matrices Test revealed an IQ of 75. He was able to recall 3 out of 12 words at the end of five consecutive trials, but could not recognize any words after a 15 minute delay. The cognitive program was continued with more emphasis placed on improving the patient's language and cognitive skills. A second followup assessment one year later revealed that his IQ had improved to 115. His performance on tasks involving attention, concentration, and memory also improved significantly. For example, he was able to recall 7 out of 12 words at the end of five consecutive trials. He was able to recognize all 12 words after a delay of 15 minutes. Over the next two years, the patient continued to receive daily and extensive cognitive rehabilitation. Follow-up neuropsychological testing, as well as the observations of family members and significant others, demonstrated that the patient has continued to improve in his cognitive functioning.

Affective Disturbance

A second obstacle to cognitive rehabilitation is affective disturbances. The author has found that at least two different types of affective disturbances can occur in patients who sustain traumatic head injuries. The first has been reported by Sbordone (1985) and has been described as a "atypical bipolar depression" which typically follows right hemisphere diencephalic injuries. This consists of a manic and depressive phase, lasting for 1-2 days each, which alternate and tend to exacerbate with time. None of these patients had a previous or familial history of affective disorder. It should be noted that Cummings and Mendez (1984) reviewed the etiology of neurological disorders associated with secondary mania in 24 published studies. They found evidence of right hemisphere diencephalic injury in the overwhelming majority of the patients in these studies.

While right diencephalic brain injuries can produce affective disturbance in head trauma patients, such cases represent represent a minority. Most affective disturbances subsequent to brain injury can be more directly ascribed to a variety of psychosocial factors (Table 2).

Table 2

Contributing Factors to Emotional Problems and Depression in the Traumatically Brain-injured Patient

---

Increasing awareness of cognitive deficits.
Frequent comparisons to premorbid level of cognitive functioning.
Poor understanding of head trauma and recovery.
Unrealistically high expectations of recovery.
Pressure from family and significant others to perform at premorbid level of cognitive functioning.
Increasing criticism from family and significant others.
Premature return to work or school.
Termination from job or academic difficulties.
Loss of status within family.
Loss of friends.
Pessimistic predictions of recovery from physicians and rehabilitation professionals.
Substance abuse.
Tendency to utilize disabilities as a means of receiving attention and controlling others.

As a consequence of brain damage, the patient's problem-solving and emotional coping skills markedly diminish. Thus, brain-injured patients easily become upset and frustrated. As a result of diminished coping skills, they are more likely to become nervous or depressed. As a result of frequent unfair comparisons between their present and premorbid level of intellectual functioning, they are likely to see themselves as damaged or impaired. As their awareness of their cognitive deficits increases with time, which parallels their improving cognitive functioning, they are likely to perceive themselves as getting worse, rather than improving. Very few patients who sustain traumatic head trauma possess an adequate understanding of their injury and the recovery process. Many brain-injured patients set unrealistically high expectations of recovery. Some of this, of course, may reflect the severity of their brain injury while, in other cases, it may also reflect the unrealistic expectations of their family and significant others. Most patients with brain injuries are placed under considerable pressure from their families and significant others to perform at their premorbid level of functioning. Their failure to perform at this level often invites harsh criticisms from others. Because of a combination of pressure from family and/or significant others, and their own poor awareness of their cognitive deficits, these patients are likely to return to work or school prematurely. This author has found that approximately 95 percent of the brain-injured patients who return to work or school prematurely encounter significant problems, which often results in their termination from work or severe academic difficulties. When this occurs, they will lose status within their family and lose the respect of others. The head-injured patient's egocentricity, irritability, cognitive and social difficulties frequently result in alienation of most, if not all, of their friends by the end of the first year post injury

The overwhelming majority of head trauma patients have been told by their physicians and/or rehabilitation professionals that they will continue to recover for up to one or two years post injury. While this prospect may sound encouraging during the acute stages of recovery, it has a devastating impact on the patient when the "recovery period" elapses. Many patients have confessed to the author that they became severely depressed when the one or two year period of recovery elapsed. Many also confessed to suicidal thoughts and felt that life was not worth living any longer. Many of these patients began to abuse drugs and alcohol, and utilized their disabilities to control others or seek attention. It is no wonder why the brain-injured patient becomes depressed and remains this way for some time. Thus, the second major obstacle to overcome is alleviating the patient's poor self-esteem, depression and emotional distress.

Unwarranted Disassociation Between Cognitive and Emotional Functioning

The third obstacle in dealing with severe traumatic head-injured patients is to erroneously assume that their cognitive and emotional functioning are unrelated. The cognitive functioning of a brain-injured patient can be dramatically influenced by emotional functioning. Psychometric tests, such as the Wechsler Adult Intelligence Scale, tend to be, in this author's experience, particularly sensitive to emotional factors. Other psychometric tests, however, may be relatively insensitive to these factors. Table 3 presents information on a 51 year old male who sustained a closed head injury, which resulted in three days of coma and a PTA of 12 days. When the patient was tested at six months post injury, the patient obtained a Full Scale WAIS IQ of 97, with a Verbal IQ of 116, and a Performance IQ of 78. When retested at one year post injury, the patient's Full Scale IQ dropped to 90. Most of this was due to a 13 point drop from his previous Verbal IQ score and, more specifically, on subtests which tend to be particularly sensitive to emotional factors, such as

Table 3

Patient: E.L.	Education: 19 years
Sex: Male	Occupation: Attorney
Dominance: Right-handed	Diagnosis: Closed Head Injury
Age: 58	

Tests	Time Since Injury	
	6 months	12 months
WAIS-R		
V.I.Q.	116	103
P.I.Q.	78	77
F.I.Q.	97	90
SBORDONE-HALL MEMORY BATTERY		
Immediate Verbal	100%	100%
Delayed Verbal	100%	91.7%
Immediate Visual	93.3%	93.3%
Delayed Visual	87.5%	87.5%
WISCONSIN CARD SORTING TEST		
Total Correct	37	97
Total Errors	91	33
Perseverative Errors	70	27
Categories Achieved	0	6
LURIA-NEBRASKA		
Scales exceeding Critical Level	8	3

Digit Span, Arithmetic, and Comprehension. Little change was seen in his scores on Performance subtests. His immediate and delayed visual and verbal memory revealed no change from previous testing. On the basis of these test results, one could easily be tempted to conclude that this patient's cognitive functioning had become worse or had not improved. However, when his performance on the Wisconsin Card Sorting Test was examined, we found that he failed to complete any of the six categories and made a total of 91 errors when tested at six months post injury. However, when tested at one year post injury he completed all six categories and made a total of only 33 errors. The Luria-Nebraska Neuro-psychological Battery at six months indicated that eight of the Clinical Scales exceeded the Critical Level. Followup testing at one year post injury revealed that only three scales exceeded the Critical Level. Thus, while this patient's WAIS IQ decreased, he showed significant improvement on tasks involving problem-solving and overall neuropsychological functioning.

The above findings may appear somewhat contradictory. They can probably be explained in terms of the relationship between the patient's emotional and cognitive functioning. For example, this patient was also administered the Minnesota Multiphasic Personality Inventory (MMPI) to evaluate emotional functioning. This patient's profile at six months post injury revealed evidence of only mild levels of depression and anxiety. When tested at one year post injury, the MMPI profile, particularly the Depression and Psy-chasthenia scales, was dramatically elevated. Thus, the patient reported considerably more depression and anxiety at one year post injury. The Luria-Nebraska Neuropsychological Battery and the Wisconsin Card Sorting Test clearly reveal that this patient had significantly improved in cognitive functioning. When this occurs, it has been the experience of this author to expect that the patient will become increasingly depressed and anxious, since improved cognitive functioning in brain-injured patients usually results in a greater awareness of their shortcomings and frequent comparisons to their premorbid level of functioning. In this particular case, the patient had been a successful attorney who read voraciously and enjoyed a number of intellectual pursuits. Although he received considerable support from his family and significant others, he attempted to return to work prematurely and was assigned to handling trivial legal matters within his law firm, which upset him greatly. He also found that he was unable to pursue his previous intellectual interests and had lost many of his friends. As he became more frustrated, his depression in-creased and adversely affected his cognitive functioning. Eventually, he was asked to resign from the law firm.

Patients often exhibit significant improvement in cognitive performance when their depression begins to remit. Table 4 presents a 58 year old male truck driver who sustained a closed head injury, which resulted in a coma of two days and a post traumatic amnesia of seven days. He had only completed eight years of formal education and had been employed as a truck driver at the time of his injury. When tested at three years post injury, he obtained an IQ of 81 on the Raven Standard Progressive Matrices Test. When tested on the Sbordone-Hall Battery, his immediate and delayed visual and verbal memory was found to be markedly to severely impaired. When tested one year later, his IQ improved to 108, his memory improved dramatically. For example, when tested at three years post injury, he required 115 seconds to complete Part A of the Trail Making Test, and 185 seconds to complete Part B. One year later, he completed Part A in 80 seconds, and Part B in 143 sec-onds, and made only two errors. His most dramatic improvement was seen on the Symbol Digit Modalities Test. When tested at three years post injury, he obtained a score of only 8. When tested at four years post injury, he achieved a score of 25. A comparison of his profile on the MMPI at both three and four years post injury revealed that his scores on the Depression, Psychasthenia, and Schizophrenia Scales had significantly decreased. The major reason for this improvement is that the patient had been referred to a clinical psychologist for psychotherapy. Over the course of one year, the patient had responded well to therapy and was less depressed and anxious.

These case examples illustrate that cognitive and emotional factors interact and can often lead to changes in the patient's cognitive functioning, as measured by neuropsychological tests. This author, who has reviewed a significant number of neuropsychological reports, finds it puzzling that many of these reports make little, if any, mention of the patient's emotional functioning.

Inappropriate Therapy

The fourth obstacle that stands in the way of effective cognitive rehabilitation is the tendency to rely on traditional methods of treatment in rehabilitation of the brain-injured. For example, most clinicians who practice psychotherapy see their patients on a weekly basis for approximately 50 minutes. Other members of the family are seldom contacted, unless

Table 4

Neuropsychological Test Results for Patient T. B.

Age:	58	Education:	8 years
Sex:	Male	Occupation:	Truck Driver
Dominance:	Right-handed	Diagnosis:	Closed Head Injury

Tests	Time Since Injury	
	<u>3 years</u>	<u>4 years</u>
RAVEN I.Q.	81	108
SBORDONE-HALL MEMORY BATTERY		
Immediate Verbal	41.7%	91.7%
Delayed Verbal	33.3%	83.3%
Immediate Visual	13.3%	60.0%
Delayed Visual	31.2%	81.2%
TRAILS A	115 seconds	80 seconds
TRAILS B	185 seconds	143 seconds
	5 errors	2 errors
SYMBOL DIGIT MODALITIES TEST	8	25

therapeutic issues necessitate this. While this may be appropriate for patients with emotional problems, it may be inappropriate for the majority of patients who have sustained traumatic brain injuries. Because of their memory difficulties, limited attention span, tendency to fatigue easily, and numerous behavioral problems, psychotherapy, as it is typically practiced, may be inappropriate for many brain-injured patients. Unfortunately, very little attention has been given to the issue of psychotherapeutic treatment of patients with traumatic head injuries.

Since virtually all patients with severe traumatic head injuries have significant social, emotional, and behavioral problems, it may be necessary to include the entire family in the treatment and rehabilitation process. Rather than dealing with patient's feelings or striving to improve insight, the emphasis should be placed on improving the family's understanding of the patient's impaired behavioral functioning, as well as to extinguish their tendency to unwittingly reinforce behaviors which frequently contribute to a number of secondary emotional problems. It may be constructive for the therapist, in this particular situation, to take a problem-solving orientation with regard to specific complaints and issues which are brought up by the family and/or patient. A concerted effort should be made to treat the problem as a behavioral management issue, rather than exploring its possible psychodynamic significance. Unfortunately, many families do not wish to become involved in the patient's treatment or rehabilitation. They frequently give lip service to many of the suggestions that are given to them, and often fail to carry out many of the suggestions or behavioral intervention strategies offered by the therapist. Thus, the fifth obstacle confronting the neuropsychologist or rehabilitation professional is resistance of the patient's family.

Family Resistance

When someone in the family becomes brain-injured, it is the family that must bear this burden. Families are frequently devastated by the enormous financial, emotional and psychological burdens which are placed upon them. Rather than seeking help or appearing depressed, they frequently manifest what has been described as a "Command Performance Syndrome" (Sbordone, Kral, Gerard, and Katz, 1984). Thus, their behavior may appear relatively composed, even though they are emotionally distraught. Because of their guilt, distorted perceptions of the patient, denial, and negative experience with health care professionals, they often feel emotionally "burned out". While they need a great deal of emotional support and empathy, they are often unable to reach out for help. This author has found that ignoring the family and their need for emotional support will most likely result in the failure of the brain-injured patient to make continued improvement. In the case of the 22 year old male head-injured patient described earlier, it should be noted that during one period of his rehabilitation program, he started to show evidence of cognitive decline. A careful examination of his home environment revealed that his father had been drinking heavily and that his parents were considering divorce. While his parents had a history of previous marital conflicts their conflicts exacerbated following their son's injury. The patient became increasingly disturbed by their marital conflicts and his father's alcoholism. He blamed himself for their problems and became depressed. Individual and marital counseling sessions were held with both parents, which alleviated the stresses their son's injury had placed on them. As a consequence, the patient's cognitive status began to improve. He appeared less depressed and better motivated to participate in his rehabilitation program. This example illustrates the importance of utilizing a systems, rather than patient-oriented approach to cognitive rehabilitation.

Failure to Utilize Behavior Modification Techniques

The sixth obstacle is the reluctance and failure of neuropsychologists and rehabilitation professionals to utilize behavior modification techniques to improve the brain-injured patient's functioning. It is rare to see an outpatient rehabilitation treatment program utilize behavioral management techniques to alleviate many of the psychosocial problems exhibited by its brain-injured patients. In fact, many behaviors, such as irritability, egocentricity, temper tantrums, and aggressive outbursts, which are typically poorly tolerated by family members of significant others, are often being unwittingly reinforced by hospital staff or family members. For example, parents and other family members tend to spend time with brain-injured patients, providing them with a generous amount of attention, shortly after they have temper tantrums. Thus, the brain-injured patient's undesirable behavior is often reinforced by the family or significant others. Conversely, many socially appropriate behaviors are often ignored, or sometimes even punished, by family members or significant others. Thus, it is essential that the neuropsychologist or rehabilitation professional teach family members or significant others behavior modification techniques to extinguish inappropriate or undesirable patient behaviors and reinforce behaviors which are of benefit to the patient and his or her family.

Impatience

The seventh and final obstacle is impatience. The family frequently demands or expects changes in the patient's cognitive or behavioral functioning to occur immediately. They are often put off or disappointed when they are told that such changes may take weeks, months, or even years to attain. They frequently urge that the patient return to work or school, even though the patient has recently been discharged from the acute hospital. The impatience of family members and significant others frequently results in a number of traumatic failure experiences for the patient. Unfortunately, failures are poorly tolerated by both the patient and family members, since they produce feelings of frustration, depression, anger, and rejection. Families often assume that if two hours a day of cognitive re-habilitation is effective, four hours a day should be twice as effective, and eight hours a day should be four times as effective. Ironically, family members appear to be much more patient and tolerant of orthopedic injuries, since they are usually told by their physician that the healing process will require a specific number of weeks, and will be followed by a carefully planned physical therapy program. While the patient with orthopedic injuries may be able to assess the integrity of an injured arm or leg, this is not possible in the brain-injured patient, since the injury severely reduces the patient's capability for self-assessment. Thus, one of the roles of the neuropsychologist or rehabilitation professional must often be that of providing the patient with timely feedback to improve their capability to assess themselves accurately. For example, the decision for the patient to return to school or work should never be made by the patient's self assessment or their family's wishes. Instead, it should be made by the clinical neuropsychologist or rehabilitation professional, who is armed with test data, behavioral observations, and hopefully, experience in dealing with similar patients and issues.

Steps Toward Cognitive Rehabilitation

While cognitive rehabilitation is often perceived of or defined as training or specific exercises which are systematically administered to patients with brain injuries to improve their cognitive functioning, cognitive rehabilitation is actually a complex multidimensional process that involves the patient, their family and their physical and social environment. It is simply not done by placing a brain-injured patient in front of a computer or once-a-week supportive psychotherapy. Table 5 presents what the author feels are the necessary steps to develop an effective neuropsychologically-based cognitive rehabilitation program.

Interview Patient and Family

The first step in designing a neuropsychologically-based cognitive rehabilitation program involves obtaining a detailed list of complaints from the patient, as well as their perception of their own strengths, limitations, and the effects of their disability. In a similar

Table 5

Steps in the Cognitive Rehabilitation Process

1. Complaints and perceptions of patient.
2. Complaints and perceptions of family and significant others.
3. Patient history.
4. Review of records.
5. Demands placed on patient and family.
6. Neuropsychological testing.
7. Neuropsychological assessment.
8. Evaluate rehabilitation prognosis.
9. Plan rehabilitation goals.
10. Initiate rehabilitation program.
11. Collect data.
12. Evaluate program.
13. Modify program.
14. Achieve rehabilitation goals.

fashion, the complaints and perceptions of each family member and significant others should also be obtained. The author has found that the vast majority of patients, particularly during the first year, tend to deny or minimize their cognitive, emotional, or social problems. The discrepancy between the patient's and family's description of their respective complaints and perceptions frequently serves as a rough index of the patient's disability. During the first year, family members may also minimize the number and extent of the patient's problems. The author has frequently found it helpful to ask both family members and patients to respond in a "Yes" or "No" fashion when specific problems are named, in order to elicit information that is not spontaneously provided.

Patient History

The next step involves collecting a detailed history from the patient, which includes developmental, clinical, and social factors. The Appendix presents a list of factors which the author has found helpful in this regard. In order to obtain accurate information, it is essential that the patient be accompanied by a relative and/or significant other. At least two hours are often required to collect this information. In addition, every effort should be made to review education, medical, and rehabilitation records prior to seeing the patient. These reports should be compared to the information furnished by the patient and family. When discrepancies are found, every effort should be made to clarify or identify the basis for the discrepancy. For example, families often present inaccurate information for a number of reasons, such as faulty recollections, distorted perceptions of the patient or accident, persistent anxiety, which is rekindled whenever they discuss the accident, denial, suggestibility, or a tendency to exaggerate in cases involving litigation. The author has found that the degree of concordance between the history as obtained from the patient and family and medical charts can often provide a crude index of how the family is coping with the consequences of the patient's injury.

Neurological History

Every effort should be made to determine the patient's neurological history. Of particular importance are the duration in coma, length of post traumatic amnesia (PTA), Glasgow Coma Scale scores, type of brain injury (focal versus diffuse), elevated intracranial pressure, presence of intracranial hematoma or infection, brain swelling (edema), post traumatic seizures, use and duration and of a respirator, and medications administered. It is important to determine the family and patient's perspective on past treatments and prognostic statements. For example, many patients and their families are often told shortly after injury that the prognosis for recovery is poor or that most of the recovery will occur within six months, with little further gain after one year. By the time the patient and family present themselves for cognitive rehabilitation, the period of recovery has usually elapsed. Thus, many families have given up hold of further improvement, and are often seeking a simple remedy for the patient's poor motivation or disruptive social behavior.

Social History

A detailed developmental and social history should be obtained prior to neuropsychological testing. This history should include pertinent facts, such as: the location of the patient's birth; birth order; problems or drugs used by the mother during pregnancy; type of delivery; birth weight; achievement of developmental milestones; childhood diseases; unusual problems during childhood or adolescence; a history of possible language, learning, behavioral, or attentional difficulties; hyperactivity; or seizures. Information about lateral dominance, cultural-linguistic background and educational progress such as grades received, courses failed, remedial education, grades repeated, extracurricular activities, expulsions or conduct disturbances, and reasons for leaving school should also be obtained. Previous occupations, duration of employment, earnings, reasons for termination) and avocational factors should also be included. The author has also found it helpful to inquire about the patient's military service, as well as past and current problems with law enforcement authorities.

This history should also contain information about the patient's family, including the occupation and education of parents, evidence of substance abuse, criminal behavior, psychiatric history, and possible separation and/or divorce. The author has found that the patient's perception of the parent's marriage and relationship is often revealing. Similar information should also be obtained about the patient's siblings, spouse, and children. A sexual history is important and frequently very informative, since it may often shed light on marital or relationship strains. Sexual difficulties, particularly hyposexuality, are common in traumatic head-injured patients. Finally, information about the pattern of social relationships, including the history of ability to both make and maintain friendships and the quality of those relationships, should also be obtained.

Medical-Psychiatric History

The history obtained from the patient should include the number, duration, and reasons for any previous psychiatric hospitalizations, as well as the types of medications or other treatments received. The family's history of psychiatric difficulties should also be investigated. The patient's premorbid and post-morbid history of substance abuse should also be carefully evaluated. In addition to the current stresses impinging on the patient, information should be collected about major medical hospitalizations, specifically about a history of cerebrovascular disorders, previous head trauma, respiratory problems, previous loss of consciousness, gastrointestinal problems, vascular problems, endocrine problems, diabetes, coronary dysfunction, hypoglycemia, episodes of anoxia-hypoxia, toxic exposure, hypertension, or other conditions with potential neuropsychological consequences.

Demand Characteristics of the Environment

The physical and social environment of the brain-injured patient should also be assessed in terms of its demand characteristics, or simply the burden that it places on the patient's present level of functioning (Diller and Gordon, 1981). Similarly, the various demands which have been placed on the patient's family and/or significant others should also be assessed. The author has observed that when excessive demands are placed on the brain-injured patient, one is likely to see evidence of marked anxiety, depression, paranoia, or fearfulness. When these behaviors are not observed, one is most likely to find that the patient is apt to interact with those aspects of their environment that place few demands on their deficits.

Neuropsychological Assessment

The clinical neuropsychologist frequently utilizes a variety of tests which have been developed to investigate the relationship between particular brain functions and behavior. These tests permit the neuropsychologist to evaluate basic areas of cognitive functioning, such as (1) attention, (2) memory, (3) motor abilities, (4) sensory-perceptual abilities, (5) problem-solving, mental flexibility, and planning skills, (6) language abilities, (7) intellectual, abstract reasoning and conceptual skills, (8) spatial-perceptual and constructional skills, (9) academic skills, and (10) emotional and social functioning. The choice of specific tests which are administered to the patient should reflect the cultural, educational, and linguistic background of the patient, the particular complaints expressed by the patient and/or family, the severity of the patient's deficits, the ability of the patient to tolerate stress, tendency to become fatigued, time since injury or neurological insult, specific referral questions, the patient's cooperation and motivation to perform to the best of their ability, previous familiarity with specific tests, previous testing, length of time permitted for testing, physical disabilities, current emotional and social factors, and the training, background, and experience of the examiner. For example, patients who recently sustained severe head trauma are typically severely impaired in their attentional skills and may only tolerate ten minutes of cognitive testing before becoming extremely lethargic, confused, and even antagonistic toward the examiner. The administration of a comprehensive neuropsychological battery, such as the Halstead-Reitan Neuropsychological Battery during the early stages of recovery, will typically produce an inaccurate description of the patient's cognitive skills and abilities (Williams, Drudge, Gomes & Kessler, 1984). Similarly, the administration of an IQ test which tends to be culturally and linguistically biased to a Mexican-born male whose education and understanding of English and American culture is limited, would most likely result in a spuriously low IQ score.

Many neuropsychologists tend to rely on standardized test batteries, such as the Halstead-Reitan or Luria-Nebraska Neuropsychological Batteries to evaluate patients with traumatic head injuries. There are advantages and disadvantages to this approach. The chief advantages are that the administration and scoring of tests is standardized, and that the patient's scores can be compared to normative data, as well as to their own previous performances. The chief disadvantage is that the reliance solely upon quantitative scores may be misleading, since they may be heavily influenced by many of the factors discussed above. In addition, the scores themselves may be of limited value in planning treatment for cognitive rehabilitation (Luria and Majovski, 1978).

Quantitative scores need to be supplemented by a "qualitative" approach during test administration. This approach emphasizes the manner in which the patient goes about taking a specific test. In other words, the focus is on the process of how the patient obtained the score, not just the level of performance. The "qualitative" approach examines all factors that influence test-taking behavior. It examines the types of errors made by the patient, the patient's motivation to perform the task, the patient's ability to recognize and correct their errors, the effect of cues or prompts on the patient's performance, and the influence of such factors as anxiety, depression, bizarre thinking, fatigue, or conscious efforts to perform poorly. For example, a patient referred for memory loss after sustaining a head injury during a motor vehicle accident may do poorly on a formal memory test battery, but the examiner notices that the patient gives up easily and does not appear to be trying to perform well. Examination of the patient's responses reveals scores that are worse than chance on several tests within the battery, and the errors made by the patient are generally inconsistent with memory disorders of traumatic or neurological etiology. The examiner also observes that the patient gives an excellent recollection of the accident and continues to emphasize how severely his impaired his memory is, providing the examiner with numerous instances that occurred during the previous day of his poor memory, which he says embarrassed him. The examiner also observes that the patient performs well on tests which he believes do not evaluate his memory, and poorly on tests which he has been told test his memory. The pa-tient does not realize, of course, that many of the other tests that he performs well have underlying memory component and that many of the "memory" tests given to him have only a superficial relationship to memory, but may, instead, evaluate his attentional skills. Finally, the examiner observes that during a break, or while having lunch with the patient, the patient describes an accident which occurred on his way to his appointment earlier that morning, and when asked to describe the accident, relates an excellent description of the event. By utilizing a qualitative approach to assessment, poor scores on specific tests can be evaluated and accurately interpreted by the examiner. However, skill in qualitative assessment requires a great deal of expertise and experience on the part of the neuropsychological examiner (Sbordone and Purisch, in press).

The chief disadvantage of the qualitative approach is that it is highly subjective and, thus, may be influenced by the particular examiner-patient interaction and other biases. It also does not readily lend itself to simple explanation or reporting. Neuropsychologists who utilize this approach typically have had considerable training in behavioral neurology and the neurosciences, in addition to having examined numerous (usually hundreds and sometimes thousands) patients with similar neurological disorders. The author recommends that both quantitative and qualitative approaches be concurrently used so that any inconsistencies can be noted and the most comprehensive neuropsychological assessment of the patient can be obtained.

The emotional and social functioning of the patient should also be assessed to determine how the patient is coping with diminished or altered higher cortical functions (Sbordone and Caldwell, 1979). This information can provide the neuropsychologist with crucial data for cognitive rehabilitation planning. Table 6 lists the neuropsychological tests which are generally used by the author to assess the head-injured patient.

The patient's emotional functioning and adjustment to diminished cognitive functioning can be assessed by either the MMPI or OBD-168 (Sbordone and Caldwell, 1979), in addition to careful observations of the patient's behavior during testing. The

Table 6

Neuropsychological Tests Generally Used to Assess the Head-Injured Patient

Function	Tests
Attention	Sbordone Attention Battery; Stroop; Symbol-Digit Modality; Trail Making
Memory	Logical Memory (immediate and delayed recall); Rey-Osterrieth Complex Figure; Sbordone-Hall Memory Battery.
Motor	Grip Strength; Grooved Pegboard; Finger Tapping; Luria's Neuropsychological Investigation ; Token Test;
Intellectual	Raven Progressive Matrices; Wechsler Adult Intelligence Scale
Constructional Skills	Block Design (WAIS); Draw A Clock; Draw A Bicycle; Object Assembly (WAIS); Rey-Osterrieth Figure.

patient's social functioning can also be assessed informally by observing the patient in the presence of his family, others, and in familiar and unfamiliar social settings. The author has found that taking the patient out to lunch with his family often provides valuable information.

Prognostic Indicators

The final neuropsychological interpretation involves the integration of the patient and family's complaints and perceptions, the patient's clinical, developmental, social, medical psychiatric, and current problems, academic and medical records, the demand characteristics of the patient's social and physical environment, and the results of neuropsychological testing. When all of this above information has been collected, it may then be possible to evaluate the patient's cognitive rehabilitation prognosis. The author, in collaboration with Dr. Michael Howard (Sbordone and Howard, 1985) have developed a set of pre-injury, neurological, behavioral, and environmental predictors of rehabilitation potential and outcome from head trauma. These predictors were based on our collective experience of seeing over 4,000 patients with traumatic head injuries and a review of the head injury literature. Table 7 presents the pre-injury predictors.

While there has been no attempt to empirically demonstrate the relative effectiveness of these predictors or weigh the particular importance of certain predictors over others, patients with a pre-injury history of good achievement, high IQ scores, good academic history, without a history of substance abuse or criminal behavior, and good relationships with families and others, who were strong-willed and determined, tend to respond well to cognitive rehabilitation. On the other hand, patients who have a pre-injury history of poor achievement, poor social relationships, low intelligence (IQ below 80), poor academic history, history of substance abuse, criminal behavior, and grew up in a cold and rejecting family often respond poorly. It should also be recognized that the goal of cognitive

Table 7

Pre-Injury Predictors of Rehabilitation Outcome

GOOD POTENTIAL AND OUTCOME	POOR POTENTIAL AND OUTCOME
1. History of good achievement	1. History of poor achievement
2. Good social relationships	2. Poor social relationships
3. No history of learning difficulties	3. History of learning difficulties
4. High intelligence (I.Q.)	4. Low intelligence (I.Q.)
5. Good academic history	5. Poor academic history
6. No history of substance abuse	6. History of substance abuse
7. No criminal history	7. Criminal history
8. Good character and self-control	8. Poor character and impulsive problems
9. Good relationship with family	9. Poor relationship with family
10. Warm and supportive family	10. Cold and rejecting family
11. Intact family	11. Broken family
12. Good emotional/personality adjustment	12. Poor personality adjustment
13. Strong-willed and determined	13. Tendencies to give up easily
14. Under 21 years of age	14. Over 35 years of age
15. Similar pre-injury/post injury vocational abilities	15. Wide gap in pre-injury/ post injury vocational abilities
16. No previous brain insult	16. History of previous brain insult
17. Good stress management skills	17. Poor stress management skills

Table 8

Neurological Predictors of Rehabilitation Outcome

GOOD POTENTIAL AND OUTCOME	POOR POTENTIAL AND OUTCOME
1. Coma less than 6 hours	1. Coma greater than 30 days
2. Post-traumatic amnesia (confusion) less than 24 hours	2. Post-traumatic amnesia (confusion) greater than 30 days
3. Glasgow Coma Scale greater than 7	3. Glasgow Coma Scale less than 5
4. Localized brain damage	4. Diffuse brain damage
5. Normal intracranial pressure	5. Elevated intracranial pressure
6. Normal ventricle size	6. Enlarged ventricles
7. No intracranial hematoma	7. Intracranial hematoma
8. No brain swelling (edema)	8. Brain swelling (edema)
9. No intracranial infection	9. Intracranial infection
10. No post traumatic seizure	10. Post traumatic epilepsy disorder
11. No hypoxia-anoxia	11. Hypoxic-anoxic brain damage
12. Depressed skull fracture on impact	12. Severe closed head insult on impact
13. No psychotropic medications	13. Psychotropic medication dependency
14. No anti-consultant medications	14. Anti-seizure medication dependency
15. Fast rate of recovery of functions	15. Slow rate of recovery of functions
16. Normal EEG readings	16. Abnormal EEG readings
17. Normal evoked potentials	17. Abnormal evoked potentials

rehabilitation is to return the patient to their pre-injury level of cognitive, emotional, and behavioral functioning; not habilitate the patient (e.g., make the patient better than before their injury).

Table 8 presents the neurological predictors of rehabilitation potential and outcome from head trauma. Many of these predictors were obtained from a review of the head trauma literature and from clinical observations of brain-injured patients from the Early Acute through the Late Late stages of recovery. In general, Dr. Howard and I have found that patients who are in coma greater than thirty days, sustain hypoxic-anoxic brain damage, de - velop intracranial infections, have post traumatic epilepsy, enlarged ventricles, and continue to demonstrate abnormal EEG and evoked potentials are not likely to make as good of a recovery and generally possess less rehabilitation potential than patients with similar pre-injury and environmental factors. It should also be noted that a review of the neurological literature, which examines outcomes following severe traumatic head injuries, tends to be overly pessimistic. It is the opinion of this author, which is also shared by Dr. Howard, that the patient's pre-injury, behavioral, and environmental factors may provide a more accurate prediction of rehabilitation potential than the neurological factors taken alone. Our clinical impression has received support from the work of Klonoff, Low, and Clark (1977), who, as noted previously, found that neurological variables only accounted for 22.7 percent of the variance in predicting outcomes from patients who sustain closed head injuries.

Table 9 presents the behavioral predictors of rehabilitation potential and outcome from head trauma. Patients who demonstrate persistence, an ability to recognize their errors, good judgment and reasoning skills, mental flexibility, intact perceptual skills, self-initiation of tasks, and concern for others tend to make more progress in cognitive rehabilitation than patients who are unable to recognize their errors, deficits, or who give up easily. These behaviors can usually be observed during neuropsychological testing, particularly if the clinician utilizes a more qualitatively-based assessment process. They can also be obtained by careful behavioral observations of the patient, as well as from the patient's family and significant others. Regardless of the patient's neurological injuries, we have found that these behavioral predictors have been extremely valuable in establishing realistic goals for the patient. It should also be noted that in many instances, a discrepancy will be found between the patient's scores on neuropsychological tests and their observable behavior. When such discrepancies occur, the clinician should take whatever time is necessary to determine the basis for this discrepancy.

Table 10 presents environmental predictors of rehabilitation potential and outcome from head trauma. It is unfortunate that many of us who have been trained in either the behavioral or neurosciences tend to neglect the environment. We often ignore its significance and role in shaping the patient's behavior or placing the demands upon the patient. For example, financial, interpersonal, and community resources can make the difference between successful recovery and lasting impairment. In spite of what has been said thus far, a patient without sound financial-insurance resources will not usually be able to secure professional assistance or treatment. Unfortunately, this bitter reality has severely handicapped many patients who possessed good, and even excellent, rehabilitation potential. Interpersonal resources are also critical. The importance of a "key person" in the family of the head-injured patient and the necessity of having the family involved in the patient's ongoing treatment and rehabilitation cannot be overemphasized. A warm and supportive family who accepts the patient's limitations in a nonjudgmental, uncritical manner, while at the same time reinforcing the patient's motivation and self-esteem, is extremely important in determining whether a cognitive rehabilitation program is successful or not. Community resources should also be utilized. Through the work of such groups as the National Head

Table 9

Behavioral Predictors of Rehabilitation Outcome

GOOD POTENTIAL AND OUTCOME	POOR POTENTIAL AND OUTCOME
1. Motivated and goal-oriented	1. Unmotivated with no goals
2. Able to recognize errors	2. Unable to recognize errors
3. Aware of behavioral deficits	3. Denial of disability
4. Persistent	4. Gives up easily
5. Ambulatory	5. Not ambulatory
6. Good judgment and reasoning skills	6. Poor judgment and reasoning skills
7. Mentally flexible	7. Rigid and perseverative
8. Independent self-care	8. Dependent on others for self-care
9. Intact perceptual skills	9. Poor perceptual skills
10. Initiates tasks independently	10. Cannot initiate tasks independently
11. Concerned for others	11. Self-centered and egocentric
12. Few failures	12. Many failures
13. Active and/or agitated	13. Inactive and/or apathetic
14. Mild recent memory deficits	14. Severe recent memory deficits
15. Mild "catastrophic reaction"	15. Severe "catastrophic reaction"
16. Optimistic	16. Discouraged
17. Good communication skills	17. Poor communication skills
18. Good planning skills	18. Poor planning skills
19. Fast speed of thinking	19. Slow speed of thinking

Table 10

Environmental Predictors of Rehabilitation Outcome

GOOD POTENTIAL AND OUTCOME	POOR POTENTIAL AND OUTCOME
1. Presence of "Key Person" in family	1. No "Key Person" in family
2. Family involved in team treatment	2. Family not involved
3. Family supportive and accepting of patient and team	3. Family not supportive and accepting of patient and team
4. Family realistic about patient's deficits and outcome	4. Family unrealistic about patient's deficits and outcome
5. Interdisciplinary team treatment	5. Multidisciplinary team treatment
6. Presence of "Key Person" on staff	6. Presence of "Key Person" on staff
7. Treatment goals appropriate to expected long-term outcome	7. Treatment goals appropriate to expected long-term outcome
8. Individual treatment plans	8. Individual treatment plans
9. Continuity and coordination of treatment through stages of recovery	9. No continuity and coordination of treatment through stages of recovery
10. Structure, consistency, and repetition in daily activities	10. Unstructured, erratic, and no repetition in daily activities
11. Success-producing environment	11. Failure-producing environment
12. Good financial/insurance resources	12. Poor financial/insurance resources
13. Lots of rewards for successful progress	13. Few rewards for successful progress
14. Presence of support group and community resources for family and patient	14. No support group or community resources for family and patient

Injury Foundation and many local and community-based head injury support groups, families can receive the support they desperately need, as well as some guidance to get them through the "hard times" ahead.

The purpose of utilizing these various predictors of rehabilitation potential and outcome is to prevent the clinician or rehabilitation professional to avoid setting unrealistically high or unrealistically low goals for the head-injured patient. In the case of the 22 year old head trauma victim described earlier in this chapter, the rehabilitation professionals who evaluated him at two years post injury, apparently chose to ignore the fact that this patient had a very high premorbid IQ (140) and had been an outstanding student and person prior to his injury. He had been awarded an academic scholarship to attend college and had planned on becoming a writer. His family environment was generally supportive. He also had an excellent health insurance policy. As was discussed earlier, failure is a tragic experience for both the patient and their family, and should be avoided at all costs. Using the Tables as guidelines, and not as hard and fast predictors, may provide the clinician or rehabilitation professional with a means of setting appropriate treatment or rehabilitation goals.

The Therapeutic Process

Setting rehabilitation goals can often be difficult. Part of the reason for this difficulty is that there is often a marked discrepancy between the goals of the professional, patient, and family. When this occurs, cognitive rehabilitation will most likely fail. Thus, it is important that the same goals be shared by the professional, patient, and family. Quite often, what seems important to the professional and family can be dramatically different. The family's interest may simply be to change the patient's disruptive behavior, or to have the patient perform a relatively simple task at home (e.g., dressing himself without assistance). The professional, on the other hand, may wish to improve the patient's attentional skills or memory. Unless there are good reasons to the contrary, the author recommends that the family's goals be respected and integrated into the rehabilitation program. In this way, the family will develop a better rapport and learn to trust the professional which, in the long run, will most likely result in greater involvement from the family in the patient's cognitive rehabilitation program.

It is often best to begin the rehabilitation process by restoring hope to the patient and family. This can often be accomplished by training the patient to perform a relatively simple but meaningful task or series of tasks which demonstrate the patient's preserved ability to learn. A series of successes is, of course, highly reinforcing to the patient and family, and improves the patient's self-image, sense of mastery, as well as establishes motivation for further self-initiated activities. With time, the patient's self-esteem and image within the family will improve. As this occurs, the emotional stresses which had been previously placed on the patient will gradually diminish, allowing the patient's cognitive potential to be realized or unmasked.

Based on the results of the history and neuropsychological assessment, the neuropsychologist or rehabilitation professional can devise a specific cognitive rehabilitation program that is tailor-made for that specific patient. It has been the experience of this author that, during the early stages of recovery, the major goal of cognitive rehabilitation should be to minimize the patient's irritability and the effects of fatigue, while at the same time, trying to improve the patient's attention span. The importance of avoiding fatigue in a brain-injured patient has previously been stressed by a number of investigators (e.g., Boothe, Doyle, and Malkmus, 1980; Sbordone, 1984). The dysphoric feeling and decreased cognitive functioning that comes with fatigue serves to frustrate and punish the patient for their cognitive efforts and should be avoided at all costs. Head trauma patients, particularly in the early stages of recovery are rarely able to perform a cognitive task for more than 10-15 minutes. As a rule of thumb, time sessions should last no longer than 70 to 80 percent of the patient's maximum attention span. Since most head-injured patients have considerable difficulty estimating time, an external timing device or person must be available to provide them with cues to rest. It is unfortunate that many rehabilitation programs in the United States frequently subject head-injured patients in the early stages of recovery to lengthy therapy sessions, which may actually punish their motivation for self-initiated behavior. Many of these patients who display little motivation or initiative when they are discharged from these programs are often erroneously labeled as having a "frontal lobe syndrome". The author has observed that many of these patients, when later placed in a behaviorally-oriented program which reinforces their motivation and self-initiative, no longer function as "frontal lobe" patients. Programs composed of brief modules separated by rest periods, utilizing behavioral management strategies, allow such patients to perform up to their potential and prevent the development of secondary psychological or emotional problems, which may actually "mask" their true level of cognitive functioning.

The development of secondary emotional problems commonly occurs throughout the recovery process. It is important that the neuropsychologist or rehabilitation professional recognize the importance of this "masking" phenomenon. The development of secondary emotional problems actually inhibit the patient's cognitive functioning. Thus, one of the primary goals of cognitive rehabilitation is to minimize or eliminate the presence of these problems. Failure to work in this direction will most likely jeopardize the patient's progress in cognitive rehabilitation. It should be recalled that one of the patients described earlier (Table 4) exhibited a significant improvement in cognitive functioning, simply because many of the secondary emotional problems that had previously inhibited his cognitive functioning had been alleviated. Thus, one of the goals of the cognitive rehabilitation therapist should be to "unmask" the patient's true cognitive functioning by alleviating many of the secondary problems that serve to inhibit the patient's abilities.

Figure 1 presents what the author feels are the systems dynamics of head-injured patients and their environment. It can be seen that the patient's emotional and cognitive functioning are interrelated, according to the principle of a conditional neurological lesion. Similarly, the family and environmental demands also affect the patient's cognitive functioning because of various stresses and emotionally-inducing changes they produce in the patient. By the same token, the patient's social and behavioral functioning also effect emotional functioning, thereby serving to also influence the patient's cognitive functioning. The patient's cognitive and emotional functioning also influence the patient's family and the environmental demands which are placed on the patient. When changes occur in these areas, they influence the patient's social and behavioral functioning, which may favorably or unfavorably affect the patient's emotional functioning and subsequent cognitive functioning. Thus, one can easily see that cognitive rehabilitation involves working with an entire system, of which the patient is only one component. As mentioned earlier, the failure of the cognitive rehabilitation therapist to deal with system dynamics of the head-injured patient will most likely result in a traumatic failure for both the patient and the rehabilitation professional. Cognitive rehabilitation, if effective, requires overcoming the seven major obstacles de-scribed earlier and adhering to a systems-oriented behavioral approach that requires the therapist to have problem-solving skills, the wisdom of Solomon, and the patience of Job.

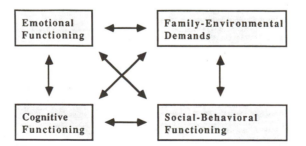

Figure 1. System dynamics of traumatic brain injury

Summary

Rehabilitation programs for head trauma patients have traditionally been geared toward physical recovery, although recently there has been a concerted approach to provide cognitive rehabilitation to these patients to improve their intellectual, memory, and cognitive functioning. Recovery from severe head trauma consists of six relatively discrete stages and occurs over many years. Effective cognitive rehabilitation involves overcoming seven major obstacles: The myth that most of the recovery following head trauma occurs within the first six months post injury; the depression and emotional distress of the head-injured patient; the myth that the patient's cognitive and emotional functioning are unrelated; the reliance on traditional methods of treatment during the rehabilitation of head trauma patients; the emotional problems and needs of the family of the head trauma patient; the reluctance to utilize behavior modification strategies when dealing with head trauma patients; and the impatience of the family and the patient.

Behavioral manifestations of a neurological insult are a function of the degree to which the patient is under stress, fatigue, emotional distress, or excessive metabolic demands. The paper also presents a conceptual model of neuropsychologically-based cognitive rehabilitation program which includes: obtaining a detailed list of complaints from both the patient and their family; their respective perceptions of the disability; a comprehensive clinical, neurological, developmental, educational, occupational, social, family, and medical-psychiatric history; neuropsychological testing utilizing both quantitative and qualitative approaches; assessment of the demand characteristics of the patient's social and physical environment; determining the patient's prognosis for cognitive rehabilitation; alleviating the patient's emotional and behavioral problems; setting appropriate rehabilitation goals; obtaining feedback from the patient and significant others; and modifying ineffective rehabilitation strategies. The importance of utilizing a systems-oriented behavioral approach was strongly emphasized to develop effective cognitive rehabilitation programs for traumatically brain-injured patients.

The author wishes to acknowledge the comments and suggestions of Drs. Michael Howard and Arnold Purisch in the preparation of this manuscript. The author also wishes to thank Christina Baker for typing and editing the manuscript.

References

Bond, M.R. (1975). Assessment of the psychosocial outcome after severe head injury. *CIBA Foundation Symposium, 34* 141-157.
Bond, M.R. & Brooks, D.N. (1976). Understanding the process of recovery as a basis for the investigation of rehabilitation for the brain-injured. *Scandinavian Journal of Rehabilitation Medicine, 8,* 127-133.
Booth, P., Doyle, M., & Malkmus, D. (1980). Meeting the challenge of the agitated patient. *Rehabilitation of the Head-Injured Adult: Comprehensive Management.* Downey, CA: Professional Staff of Rancho Los Amigos Hospital.
Cooper, P.R. (1982). Epidemiology of head trauma. In P.R. Cooper (Ed.) *Head Injury.* Baltimore, MD: Williams and Wilkins.
Diller, L. & Gordon, W.A. (1981). Rehabilitation and clinical neuropsychology. In S.B. Filskov and T.J. Boll (Eds.) *Handbook of Clinical Neuropsychology.* New York: Wiley.
Luria, A.R. and Majovski, L.V. (1978). Basic approaches used in American and Soviet clinical neuropsychology. *American Psychologist, 32,* 959-968.
Klonoff, H. Low. M.D., & Clark, C. (1977). Head injuries in children: A prospective five year followup. *Journal of Neurology, Neurosurgery, and Psychiatry, 40,* 1211-1219.

Miller, H. & Stern, G. (1965). The long-term prognosis of severe head injury. *Lancet, 1*, 225-229.

Sbordone,, R.J. & Caldwell, A. (1979). The OBD-168: Assessing the emotional adjustment to cognitive impairment and organic brain damage. *Clinical Neuropsychology, 4*, 36-31.

Sbordone, R.J. (1984). Rehabilitative neuropsychological approach for severe traumatic brain-injured patients. *Professional Psychology: Research and Practice, 15*, 165-185.

Sbordone, R.J., Kral, M. Gerard, M., & Katz, J. (1984). Evidence of a "command performance syndrome" in the significant others of the victims of severe traumatic head injury. *The International Journal of Clinical Neuropsychology, 6*, 183-185.

Sbordone, R.J. (in press). Does computer-assisted cognitive rehabilitation work? A case study. *Psychotherapy.*

Sbordone, R.J. (in press). A neuropsychological approach to cognitive rehabilitation within a private practice setting. *Rehabilitation Psychology Desk Reference.*

Sbordone, R.J. & Howard, M. (1985). Predictors of recovery following head trauma. Paper presented at conference on head trauma: From injury to independence, Kansas city, MO, October, 1985.

Sbordone, R.J. & Purisch,, A.D. (in press). Clinical Neuropsychology: Medico-Legal Aspects. *Trauma.*

Thomsen, I.V. (1981). Neuropsychological treatment and long-time followup in an aphasic patient with very severe head trauma. *Journal of Clinical Neuropsychology, 3*(1), 43-51.

Williams, J.M., Drudge, O., Gomes, F., & Kessler, M. (1984). Prediction of cognitive outcome from closed head injury using early measures of trauma severity. *Journal of Neurosurgery, 61*, 231-235.

Appendix

Elements of the Patient History

DEVELOPMENTAL

Problems or drugs during pregnancy
Place of birth
Birth order
Birth weight
Problems during delivery
Developmental milestones
Childhood diseases
Emotional problems during childhood
 and adolescence
History of learning difficulties
History of health problems
History of hyperactivity
History of physical or emotional trauma

DOMINANCE

Initial preference
Changes in preference
Familial history of sinistrality
Tasks performed with dominant
 and non-dominant hands

LANGUAGE

First language spoken
Other languages spoken
Preferred language
History of speaking or language
difficulties

EDUCATION

Highest grade completed
Grades obtained
Best/preferred courses
Worst/least preferred courses
Extracurricular activities
Awards and achievements
Courses or grades repeated
History of remedial training
History of conduct disturbances or
 expulsions
Reasons for leaving school
Additional schooling or non-academic
 training

MILITARY SERVICE

Branch and dates of service
Highest rank
Jobs held within service
Combat history

Rank at discharge
Type of discharge

OCCUPATIONAL

Present occupation
Job duties
Salary
Last worked
Previous occupations
Longest job held
History of job termination

LEGAL

Arrest history
Types of offenses
Time served in jail
Current legal problems

CULTURAL BACKGROUND

Country of birth
Ethnic background of patient and family
History of discrimination

RELIGIOUS

Religious background
Church attendance
History of religious discrimination

MARITAL HISTORY

Marital status
Number of years married
History of previous marriages
Education and occupation of spouse
Expectations placed on spouse
Expectations placed on patient
Previous and current marital difficulties
Marital stability
Number and ages of children
Effect of children on patient

SEXUAL

Sexual preference
Changes in sexual preference
History of previous sexual problems
Current sexual problems
Changes in libido
Extramarital affairs

MEDICAL

History of major hospitalizations
Previous health problems
Previous surgery

Possible history of the following problems:
    Loss of consciousness
    Head trauma
    Cerebrovascular disorder
    Coronary dysfunction
    Hypoglycemia
    Anoxia or hypoxia
    Toxic or heavy metal exposure
    Substance abuse
    Alcoholism
    Hypertension
    Diabetes
    Gastrointestinal disorder
    Respiratory problems
    Genital-urinary problems
    Headaches
    Vertigo

PSYCHIATRIC

History of previous emotional or
   psychiatric difficulties
History of suicidal behavior
Treatment history
Psychiatric hospitalization history
Psychiatric medication history
Family history of psychiatric difficulties

CURRENT STRESS

Death or loss of spouse or family member
Divorce or marital separation
Marital difficulties
Job difficulties or termination
Financial difficulties
Sexual difficulties
Loss of friends
Conflicts with others
Academic difficulties
Business difficulties

FAMILY

    Parents
        Age and education
        Occupation
        Personality
        Marital status and history
        Substance abuse history
        Psychiatric history
        Criminal history
        Health history
        Relationship with patient

    Siblings
        Number and ages of
         siblings
        Education and occupation
        Personality
        Marital status and history
        Substance abuse history
        Psychiatric history
        Criminal history
        Health history
        Relationship with patient

CLINICAL HISTORY

Complaints of patient and significant
  others
History of injury or illness
Duration of coma
Duration of post traumatic amnesia
Neurological findings
Hospitalization history
Current residual problems
Progress within past year
Effect of injury or illness on patient and others
Expectations of patient and others

2

Neuropsychological Rehabilitation After Brain Injury: Some Further Reflections

George P. Prigatano

In two recent publications, empirical observations on the efficacy of neuropsychologically oriented rehabilitation and its theoretical and clinical nature have been presented (Prigatano et al., 1984; Prigatano et al, 1986). The recently published work by Ben-Yishay et al., 1985 and a review chapter by Cotman and Nieto-Sampedro (1985) on mechanisms of CNS recovery provide an additional opportunity to further reflect on the nature and efficacy of this work.

Facilitating and Complimenting Recovery of Function After CNS Trauma

A very recent and stimulating paper by Cotman and Nieto-Sampedro (1985) summarizes their views as to the biological potential to recuperate from a lesion of the brain. Their ideas are revolutionary.

> Basic studies during the last quarter of the century on the response of the central nervous system (CNS) to injury have made it increasingly clear that, given the proper stimulus, most events necessary for the reconstruction of injured circuits in the CNS can take place in the mature adult. However, clinical evidence shows that most injuries to the mature CNS are not spontaneously repaired. We believe that a key to this paradox is the lack of temporal organization of the events in adult synaptogenesis. Perhaps the most distinctive feature of development is the strict temporal order of cellular and molecular events. The development of the nervous system depends on a complex series of steps, each of which must occur in the right place and at the right time. In our opinion, regeneration and reactive synaptogenesis, that is, synaptogenesis triggered by injury, could repair the damaged CNS in most cases if the various responses would take place in the proper ordered sequence, as they do in development. From this point of view, the role of the neurologist is to learn how to initiate and guide the steps of the repair process so as to allow each of them to occur at the appropriate moment. Intervention treatments need to be inserted into the natural repair process, complementing it when natural repair is, as in the case of neuronal cell loss, clearly insufficient." (p. 83).

This view is not only optimistic, but energizing. It suggests that various forms of "intervention" after brain injury attempt to facilitate and complement the natural recovery course. Neuropsychological rehabilitation to date has had more to offer in complementing the natural recovery course than facilitating it. We have tried to help patients compensate for residual higher cerebral deficits and learn to effectively cope with the consequences of those deficits, such as lower income, less status in a job, and loss of a spouse.

Research on present forms of cognitive retraining have not demonstrated that we can significantly facilitate rate or level of recovery of CNS function. This does not mean that the facilitory role is impossible for teaching or reeducational methods. Only, our present methodology and conceptualization of what should be done and when for a given patient is inadequate to accomplish this goal.

Obviously, the better we understand the biological mechanisms governing recovery of function, the more likely we can develop psychological models that will parallel and build upon those biological mechanisms. For example, Cotman and Nieto-Sampedro (1985) emphasize that for recovery of function to occur, a series of complicated and temporally organized events must take place for neurodevelopment to occur. Recovery of function may well mimic this pattern of neuro-development and various forms of treatment may be needed to artificially induce it or to manipulate neural events so as to produce a similar state of affairs. They also suggest that neural transplants may have a role in this regard.

In the field of physical therapy, one improves sensory-motor function by essentially reconstructing the neurobehavioral pattern necessary for ambulation seen in a child. While some neuropsychologists have applied this model to the assessment of cognitive deficits after brain injury (Eson, Yen, & Bourke, 1978), this approach has by and large not attracted much attention. There has been a bias that an adult brain injured patient's pattern of cognitive deficits are considerably different in nature than that of a child undergoing normal development. There has been perhaps, therefore, the bias that what is learned about the normal development of cognitive and affective functioning may have little to offer in the way of diagnostic and remediation techniques for brain injured adults. Obviously in light of some of the points Cotman and Nieto-Sanpedro (1985) have made, this may need to be reevaluated.

It may be too simple-minded to approach treating a traumatic brain injured adult with the insights of a cognitive and affective developmental point of view. However, would such steps work with brain injured children as they are undergoing their developmental process? Also, with appropriate biological interventions, would this model work more effectively? For example, with brain graphs or pharmacological manipulation, would the adult damaged brain respond more to tasks that are appropriate at different developmental sequences or levels?

This is clearly an important question to pursue. This field of rehabilitation needs both teachers who have experience and knowledge of normal cognitive and affective devel - opment, as well as rehabilitation therapists who have worked with brain injured adults. Direct biological intervention by neurosurgeons and neurologists may also be needed in the near future, if restitution of higher cerebral functioning is eventually going to be a reality.

At the present time, neuropsychological rehabilitation is helpful in aiding the patient to compensate for higher cerebral deficits and to complement the normal tendency of the brain to compensate for those deficits. We still lack the methodology to substantially facilitate the recovery process in terms of improving the rate of recovery or the eventual level of recovery.

Training on the Microcomputer as an Illustration of Neuropsychological Rehabilitation

Elsewhere, I have defined neuropsychological rehabilitation as consisting of two basic components: cognitive retraining and psychotherapy (Prigatano et al, 1986). Cognitive retraining is difficult to define because we have no adequate definition of the term "cognition" (see Flavell, 1977). One working definition of the term cognition is that it refers to, "the basic ability of the brain to process, store, retrieve, and manipulate information to solve problems" (Prigatano et al, 1986, p. 3).

Has research on "cognitive retraining" shown that this basic ability can in fact be improved? The answer to this rather embarrassing question appears: no, not as of yet. We are asking the same basic question that Zangwill (1947) raised after World War II. He referred to cognitive retraining at that time as direct retraining and asked whether or not it was possible. At that point he stated that he thought the answer was doubtful and at this point, I must agree with him. Yet, it is quite clear that some patients can benefit from educational efforts aimed at teaching them to improve or at least compensate for deficit areas. It is important to recognize that in cases of bilateral diffuse cerebral injury there may not be enough brain reserve to substantially foster a reorganization of a skill. Consequently, the need to teach the patient to compensate for deficits is quite important. These issues are not better demonstrated in modern times than over the issue of whether or not cognitive retraining with microcomputers "works.

Schacter & Glisky (1986) recently reviewed the lack of evidence for the effectiveness of computer programs designed to improve memory. Repetitive exercise to improve memory function--with and without computers--does not seem to "produce a general improvement of mnestic function in amnestic patients" (p. 260).

Placed in the context of this chapter, such memory retraining does not seem to facilitate recovery of CNS function. However, these authors demonstrated that some brain injured patients with amnestic impairment can be taught to use a computer. They refer to this as the acquisition of domain-specific knowledge. In a paper to be published shortly (Glisky, Schacter, & Tulving, in press), they present further data supporting this observation. The authors suggest that these findings provide, "some reason for cautious optimism about the possibilities for patients to use a computer as a substitute memory" (p. 26). Ideally, patients might be able to learn to program their own daily activities and later have access to that information via a microcomputer. This would allow the computer to truly serve as a substitute memory for at least daily activities and perhaps more. If this is accomplished, we will see a substantial utilization of the microcomputer as a complement to the recovery pro - cess. However, again, there is as yet no evidence that such use of the computer substantially facilitates the rate or level of actual recovery of brain function. For those who think that the computer can "retrain memory" the data need to be obtained to support this contention.

There is perhaps another use for the computer that we have found useful in our work with brain injured patients within the context of a neuropsychologically oriented program. The computer presents stimulating information and allows for a systematic and easy method of recording responses. With the use of innovative computer programs for "cognitive remediation," one can then use a computer as an adjunct to helping the patient become more systematic in observing their deficits and recognizing the need for strategies to compensate for deficits. This may help them become more realistically aware of residual higher cerebral strengths and weaknesses. Computer related activities also help give some patients a sense of competency when they are able to solve tasks that previously they were able to perform. This can foster a sense of hope and thereby reduce depression and raise one's self-esteem. There are no small contributions to the overall rehabilitative process of such individuals (Prigatano et al., 1986).

Current Neuropsychological Rehabilitation

The recent impetus for neuropsychological rehabilitation of young adult traumatic brain injured patients in the United States should be credited to Drs. Diller and Ben-Yishay and their colleagues at the NYU Medical Center, Rusk Institute of Rehabilitation Medicine. It should be recognized that their work stimulated very practical ideas concerning the nature of cognitive retraining and its efficacy (Diller, 1976; Ben-Yishay & Diller, 1983).

From that work evolved a model in which traumatic brain injured patients were treated from a community or milieu oriented approach. Patients were not seen only in individual "cognitive remediation" hours, but were worked with in groups to improve their thinking and interpersonal communication skills. The goal was clearly to help patients find ways of improving their adaptive abilities and re-enter, when possible a more productive lifestyle. Dealing with the patients' affective responses was also recognized and dealt with within the context of their broad therapeutic community meetings.

Ben-Yishay et al. (1985) have recently summarized this approach to treatment and their outcome data. They state:

> Based on these preliminary group analyses, we tentatively conclude that the improvements in the cognitive functions are attributable mainly to a generalized improvement to maintain focused attention and an enhanced ability to process information more efficiently. The results strongly suggest that, in the main, gains achieved by the patients in the cognitive domain through their participation in a program of systematic remedial intervention represents an improvement in the effective functional application of residual cognitive abilities, rather than an increase in the capacity levels of these underlying cognitive abilities per se" (p. 257-258).

> Approximately 50% were deemed to be competitively and gainfully employed and 25% employable in subsidized or part-time capacities only." (p. 258).

A year earlier, we presented our first outcome data with controls (Prigatano et al., 1984). The conclusions were strikingly similar:

> "The data are encouraging because they document modest, but statistically reliable improvements on standardized neuropsychological tests" (p. 511). These improvements appeared to be related to reduce cognitive confusion and teaching patients to compensate for neuropsychological impairments" (p. 511). "

> Initially, it was our impression that between 60% and 65% of the patients would work or were working shortly after their neuropsychological

rehabilitation program ended. With the passage of time, however, the percentage dropped to 50%" (p. 512).

Taken together, the collective experience of these two groups of investigators emphasizes that we may be able to teach patients to more effectively use residual cognitive skills and reduce cognitive confusion or improve ability to focus attention and process information more efficiently. and to learn to compensate for their deficits. Both agreed that about 50% of the patients chosen for this work are able to return to gainful employment.

What is similar and what is different between these two investigators' approach to treatment? The program at Presbyterian Hospital in Oklahoma City (Prigatano et al., 1984) was initially based in large part on the NYU model. In fact, Dr. Ben-Yishay served as its major consultant during its first three years of existence. In retrospect, the Presbyterian Hospital differed only in format, in the author's opinion, and probably showed really very little substantial difference in terms of topics or problems that were addressed. One formal difference in the program was the incorporation of group psychotherapy hours in the Pres- byterian Hospital program. Yet, personality issues were clearly dealt with within the NYU program in hours not called psychotherapy. The second difference was the emphasis placed on dealing with the problems of awareness of deficit after traumatic brain injury. This seemed to be especially important to the group in Oklahoma City. In reading Ben-Yishay's et al. (1985) recent paper, however, it is quite clear that they also considered this to be an important problem and one of the major stages in the rehabilitation process.

It appears, therefore, that the two programs are more similar in their content than may be obvious by how they described their various therapeutic hours. It may be for this reason that their results are quite compatible and in a sense cross validate one another. Both approaches attempt to work with the individual patient in both group and individual treatment activities and fee that the patient should be worked with within a context of a therapeutic mi- lieu or "holistic" approach to their treatment difficulties. Both emphasize that individual retraining in and of itself is necessary, but not sufficient.

Details concerning the therapeutic approaches of these two programs can be found elsewhere (see Prigatano et al, 1986; Ben-Yishay et al., 1985; and volumes entitled "Working Approaches Through Remediation of Cognitive Deficit in Brain Damage," NYU Medical Center, 1978, 1979, 1980, 1981, 1982). For purposes of this paper, however, a few points should be made. There is a great heterogeneity of the type, location, and amount of brain damage associated with moderate and severe craniocerebral trauma. Regions of the brain that are frequently affected include the anterior portions of the frontal lobes and the temporal lobes, as well as the brain stem structures. Ischemic injuries to the hippocampus and basal ganglia may also be high (Prigatano et al., 1986). This produces a true mix of cognitive and personality deficits. Limbic, paralimbic and heteromodal cortex are at high risk of such injuries (Mesulam, 1986).

The patients consequently need a fairly structured treatment program in which cognitive and personality problems are addressed. The education or reeducation process must involve both group and individual therapies. The patient needs to be taught not only how to solve problems more effectively, but how to deal with residual CNS deficits as they emerge in interpersonal interaction. Group work is vital for accomplishing these goals. Placing patients in a therapeutic community or milieu based rehabilitation program helps clarify the extent of the patient's adaptation difficulties and provides a chance to raise the

patient's level of psychosocial adjustment.   As yet, neuropsychologically oriented rehabilitation has more to offer in this regard than restitution of function per se. There are still no therapies that make a "bad memory good," but perhaps some patients can be taught to more effectively utilize residual abilities and thereby cope with life's problems more effectively. Much of neuropsychological rehabilitation is aimed at helping the patient and the family to become more aware of residual strengths and difficulties and to adjust to life accordingly.   It is interesting that the work of Oddy et al. (1985) indirectly supports the notion that impaired self awareness after brain injury can exist in some patients seven years post injury. This phenomena, therefore, is not something that necessarily spontaneously gets better with time. It is a problem that must be directly addressed in neuropsychological rehabilitation. Given the few outcome papers that have appeared (Prigatano et al., 1986; Ben-Yishay et al. 1985) it appears that some patients can in fact be helped to improve in this regard and thereby achieve a more reasonable adjustment after
significant brain injury.

The Work Trial as a Part of Neuropsychological Rehabilitation

As early as 1942, Kurt Goldstein emphasized the importance of introducing work activities into the life of the brain injured patient as soon as it was possible. The expectations that whatever patients learn in cognitive retraining and psychotherapy will automatically generalize to the workplace is indeed naive (Prigatano et al., 1984) and is not justified given what we know about the lack of generalization effects from repeated practice during memory retraining (Schacter & Glisky, 1986) and perceptual motor retraining (Weinberg et al., 1982).

The fact that only 50% of our patients, compared to 36% of controls, were able to return to gainful employment resulted in a major modification in our NRP program. The program was initially a four day a week program where patients were seen strictly on an outpatient basis and worked with approximately six hours a day. In light of our outcome data, the program was condensed. Patients continued to be worked with for four days but all cognitive and psychotherapeutically oriented activities were condensed into the morning hours. Patients were placed in work trials during five afternoons per week. Once patients were actually in a work setting, we were able to see first hand what problems patients had in being productive and how neuropsychological deficits emerged that were not observed on psychometric testing (Prigatano, Pepping, & Klonoff, 1986).

In the work trial, patients take on volunteer positions and treatment staff stay in close contact with the patient at work and his or her supervisor. The therapists who work with patients in the morning hours in various treatment activities are the very same therapists who work with the patients in the work setting. They are both therapists and "work shadows."

We have found this a very effective means of staying on top of the patient's progress in dealing with the various cognitive and interpersonal problems as they emerge in the "real world." So far work sites have been volunteer positions within the hospital or previously agreed upon work sites outside of the hospital. When the latter takes place the patient is usually a workman's compensation case and the employer is willing to allow us to work with them in their initial job environment. We have found by and large that hospital managers in various departments have been exceptionally receptive to this provided that we stay in close contact with them and troubleshoot problems which emerge for the patient on the work site.

While no formal statistical analysis has yet been done on the effectiveness of adding this component to neuropsychological rehabilitation, it has been our general impression that this has improved our capacity to return people to a productive lifestyle. Dr. Mary Pepping has continued this in the Neuropsychological Rehabilitation Program in Oklahoma City (Pepping, personal communication) and reports that it has increased the return rate about 20% over our initial 50% figure. We have not yet gathered enough experience in Phoenix to determine the effectiveness, but so far we are at about 65-70% of our patients returning back to work using this model.

We have found that patients look forward to the work trial because it is more real life in nature and less "therapeutic" in its format. Many patients are eager to get back to as close a normal living as possible. If they are in prolonged treatment programs they can start to identify more as a patient than "worker" and have a difficult time reentering a semi-normal lifestyle. Also, for the more impaired patients the work trial becomes an extremely important teaching experience. The following are two examples of this process.

The first concerns a young man who is approximately a year and a half post traumatic injury. He had an extremely severe injury and although he was devoid of any obvious motor deficits, he had profound memory loss and difficulties in abstract reasoning. He had been worked with since the time of his injury both in acute rehabilitation and was discharged to a day hospital program. After he left the day hospital program, he floundered, and was actually getting worse in terms of psychiatric status. A florid paranoid ideation emerged and this was obviously alarming to everyone. Initially the patient agreed to work in our NRP.

As we worked with him in the various cognitive and psychotherapeutic hours, we found that we were getting absolutely nowhere. He was so impaired he could not follow many of the cognitive tasks. These repeated failures actually enhanced his paranoia and he became convinced that we were trying to belittle him or make him confess that he had "brain injury." Things deteriorated and we stopped formal cognitive retraining and psychotherapy. Instead, the patient was placed into a very structured voluntary work position within the hospital and was seen individually for one hour of supportive psychotherapy per day. The meetings were spent going over his work activities and not "confronting" or "educating" him. They were simply reality based activities to see that he could maintain his work trial and to deal with any other problems as they emerged. This proved to be extremely helpful for this patient and was an important lesson for me to learn. That is, there is a point where some patients and therapists can't go any further in terms of "formal" cognitive retraining or psychotherapy. It is at that juncture that it is much better to try to find a "slot" in life for the patient and help them maintain it versus continuing "treatment." This provides a sense of productivity, self worth, and dignity, something all of us need whether brain injured or not. We also learned that this individual will most likely need a type of "spokesman", to help monitor his problems in the work environment. We project this to occur for several years to come and may well exist indefinitely. Perhaps the word spokesperson is the wrong term. It may be more like an "alter ego." That is, someone who can understand what he is going through and in a polite and appropriate manner talk with the patient, his work supervisor and coworkers, in order to maintain productivity at work. In this kind of model the patient can be given the support he or she needs in order to not deteriorate and maintain their present social adjustment. The estimated cost of this would be between $100 and $200 a month for the rest of his life. This may seem expensive, but if one does not receive this type of help, the patient would most likely need either inpatient or psychiatric treatment on some prolonged basis or a series of emergency psychiatric hospitalizations. While the cost effectiveness has not been specifically worked out, it is quite clear that if he were to be hospitalized two or three times a year for a week or two his total bill would be in excess of $20,000 per year. In light of this, we feel that this is the most efficient and humane way of working with this patient on an extended basis.

The second example of our present work trial involves a young man who had major sociopathic difficulties prior to his injury. As a result of the injury, he was able to work for the first time with psychotherapists and focused on the topic of fairness in relationships. Interpretations about his psychodynamic problems could also be discussed without needlessly upsetting or agitating him. Many of the problems centered around issues of anger and exploitation that he experienced in regards to his parents. The therapists went out of their way to be in essence "good parents" to help him. This included everything from walking with him over to a shopping mall and helping him pick out clothes, to purchasing a birthday cake which he seldom received during his eighteen years of life. This young man found that the work site allowed him to wear clean clothes and gave him some recognition and a sense of dignity. While his psychopathic and sociopathic tendencies did not disappear, a combination of continued psychotherapy with the patient and his family, as well as providing him activities which led to some sense of productivity and feeling of accomplishment, became very important ingredients in getting him back to work.

The importance of the work trial is perhaps analogous to the importance of allowing someone to feel productive again after months of dependence or "incompetency." While various treatment activities help us understand the limits of the patient and may teach them strategies for coping, ultimately the patient has to live in the real world and the sooner the patient can do this after brain injury, the better.

Outcome and Cost Effectiveness

When we examined all 44 patients who went through out neuropsychological rehabilitation program at Presbyterian Hospital in Oklahoma City, we were struck with some basic facts. First of all, patients who were deemed successful, clearly had less psychiatric problems and better cognitive functioning before treatment. This is illustrated in Table 1 and Table 2. Patients with the best outcome, were less belligerent, talkative, negativistic, more reasonable, and showed fewer overall signs of psychopathology at the very beginning of treatment. These were significant differences between successes, failures, and patients who were deemed "intermediate" or not clear successes or failures (Table 3).

The final report of the Menninger Foundation Psychotherapy Research Project (Kernberg et al., 1972), reported findings which also emphasize the importance of the patient's initial cognitive and personality status prior to treatment for determining treatment outcome. They state:

> One general finding was that patients undergoing psychoanalysis belonged to the group of high or highest improvement if they had good Initial Ego Strength and that patients undergoing supportive psychotherapy also improved if they had good Initial Ego Strength, although generally less so than patients in psychoanalysis. Patients who underwent psychoanalysis and had low Initial Ego Strength improved little if at all. Patients who

underwent supportive psychotherapy and had low Initial Ego Strength improved the least" (p. 171).

Ego strength is defined as the sum total of adaptive skills and resourcefulness the individual demonstrates in facing both internal and external reality demands. Thus patients treated in psychoanalysis, supportive psychotherapy, and neuropsychologically oriented rehabilitation have a better outcome if they are good at coping with life before they enter such treatments.

These findings indirectly suggest that people who have reasonably good coping skills before they enter treatment programs have the cognitive and personality resources to learn about themselves and to progressively modify their behavioral responses. They are likely to benefit from treatments because they have the resources to do so.

The question which will inevitably be asked is: would all of these patients with initially better coping skills have gotten better without the various forms of psychotherapy and cognitive retraining? I believe for a majority of the people the answer is no. Having the

Table 1

Mean Neuropsychological Test Scores of NRP Patients

| | Entry | | Completion | |
	Successes	Failures	Successes	Failures
Verbal IQ	100.70	91.10	104.20	95.90
Performance IQ	89.00	80.60	99.20	87.20
Vocabulary	10.00	9.20	10.10	9.50
Block Design	9.60	7.70	12.10	8.30
Digit Symbol	6.20	5.20	8.10	6.10
Memory Quotient	85.80	82.60	97.60	89.60
Logical Memory	5.60	7.30	7.60	7.70
Hard Associates	4.00	3.10	5.80	3.60
Visual Reproduction	7.80	6.70	11.00	8.80
Halstead-Reitan Tests				
Trails-A	59.70	61.90	40.60	56.20
Trails-B	167.80	155.50	128.10	158.10
Category Test	46.00	62.00	43.00	56.80
Tactual Perform (R)	422.30	562.60	486.90	534.63
Tactual Perform (L)	436.50	534.50	386.40	498.27
Tapping (R)	41.50	38.70	40.80	40.20
Tapping (L)	40.20	34.80	42.10	35.10
Ave Impairment Rating	2.12	2.75	1.94	2.56

Table 2

Mean Katz-R Test Scores of NRP Patients

| | Entry | | Completion | |
	Successes	Failures	Successes	Failures
Belligerence	0.59	2.05	-0.30	1.77
Verbal Expansiveness	0.46	1.18	-0.33	2.45
Negativism	0.26	2.17	-0.14	1.83
Helplessness	2.39	2.54	1.09	2.97
Suspiciousness	1.18	2.50	1.45	2.77
Anxiety	1.13	1.50	0.72	0.94
Withdrawal	2.93	4.04	3.23	3.45
General Psychopathology	5.03	6.65	2.73	7.44
Nervousness	2.33	1.75	0.83	1.87
Confusion	1.85	1.99	1.54	2.51
Bizarreness	0.31	0.66	0.05	0.13
Hyperactivity	1.13	1.41	0.18	1.61
Stability	-2.13	-5.09	-2.50	-5.05

Note: Scores are age-corrected Z scores. Any Z value of 1.96 is significant at the .05 level, compared with age-matched normals using Hogarty and Katz (1971) norms.

capacity to learn is different from having the knowledge and knowing how and when to apply that knowledge.

We must identify those patients who have a chance of benefiting from our present therapies and put our energies into treating them. Taking "all comers" simply because they have the money to pay for treatment ultimately produces an attitude that the effectiveness of these interventions are minimal. Until we are able to clearly document those patients who we can and cannot help, we will always be viewed with some suspicion as to the ethicalness and the scientific basis of our work.

The research on the neuropsychological rehabilitation program must also keep in mind that the present economic times forces us to consider the cost effectiveness of our work. If we do not incorporate this into our research designs, we may be in a position of showing that our treatments help some patients but not having been politically astute enough to get third party payers to fund it. It is interesting in this regard that after all of the research on the effectiveness of psychotherapy it was Cumming's (1977) work that showed that short-term psychotherapy in an HMO resulted in less utilization of more costly services. Once shown that this type of treatment saved money within a given system, it was utilized irrespective of the scientific evidence.

Present day outpatient day treatment programs for brain injured young adults range in costs anywhere from $4000 a month to as high as $10-12,000 a month. Some patients are worked with for over a year. Consequently the cost of such treatment becomes expensive, particularly if there is not adequate insurance coverage. In the face of these costs, alternative ways of caring for these patients has been sought. In fact, already in the literature, there are reports of much more cost efficient community based programs. Cole, Cope & Cervelli (1985), report on a community based program which has one staff member who is paid by a grant and the rest are volunteer staff. They describe the program as "a highly structured, supportive environment to maximize work and study habits, cognitive and academic skills, social and behavioral awareness" (p. 39). The cost of this program: "no fee is charged to the students of this program. During 1979, costs for 20 hours of instruction weekly for 15 students totaled approximately $44,000 or approximately $3/hr/student."

If traumatic brain injured patients can truly be integrated back into the community for $3 an hour, this is a major blow to all neuropsychologically oriented rehabilitation programs. In the Cole et al. (1985) paper there are no data as to the outcome of this work. There is also no data showing how effective the staff are, how much "turnover" there is in the staff, and the degree to which various interpersonal problems emerge that the staff can't handle. In any event, their paper is a challenging one because it makes it quite clear that unless those of us involved in neuropsychological rehabilitation programs can show the cost effectiveness of our work, such community based programs are going to become common and insurance carriers are going to doubt very seriously whether or not they should spend relatively large amounts of money for the types of treatment that we offer.

The report of Cole et al. (1985) is both a very positive and possibly misleading paper. It is positive because it emphasizes alternative methods of caring for young, adult brain injured people that may be cost efficient. It is possibly misleading in so far as it may convey an erroneous impression of the effectiveness of volunteers. It is reminiscent of the controversy over whether or not a good bartender who listens to your problems is as effective as a psychotherapist who charges $150 an hour. Some would say yes, others say

Table 3

Duncan Multiple-range Scores on Katz-R for NRP Patients

Belligerence	0.48	0.65	1.93	A,A,A
Verbal Expansiveness	0.15	0.63	1.71	A,A,B
Negativism	0.10	1.91	2.03	A,B,B
Helplessness	1.89	2.52	2.72	A,A,A
Suspiciousness	1.28	1.89	2.61	A,A,A
Anxiety	0.97	0.77	1.29	A,A,A
Withdrawal	3.05	3.79	3.79	A,A,A
Psychopathology	4.14	5.21	6.98	A,A,B
Nervousness	0.64	1.75	1.82	A,A,A
Confusion	1.73	1.92	2.21	A,A,A
Bizarreness	0.21	0.44	0.63	A,A,A
Hyperactivity	0.76	1.44	1.49	A,A,A
Stability	-2.43	-3.25	-5.07	A,A,B

Note: Scores are age-corrected Z scores. Letters that are different reflect a significant difference between groups ($p<.05$).

no. The effectiveness of either one depends on the quality of the psychotherapist or bartender. Until "hard" data enter the picture, we are going to be fighting for third-party reimbursement.

Summary

Neuropsychological rehabilitation after traumatic brain injury in young adults perhaps has more to offer in teaching the patient to meaningfully compensate for residual higher cognitive deficits than restitution of brain function per se. This seems especially the case several months post brain injury. The incorporation of a work trial has proven to be very important. It helps the patient regain a sense of competency and productivity and thereby adds to a sense of self-esteem. It also helps the patient become more realistically aware of residual strengths and weaknesses. This in turn helps produce some sense of meaning in life after the tragedy of brain damage. Outcome studies suggest that about one-half of the patients selected for this type of work actually show substantial re-entry into work activities. In order to advance the field of neuropsychological rehabilitation, we must formally study the effectiveness of such interventions and become embroiled in the controversy entailed in demonstrating the cost-effectiveness of our programs.

References

Ben-Yishay, Y., Diller, L. (1983). Cognitive deficits. In M. Rosenthal, E. Griffith, M. Bond, & J.D. Miller (Eds.), *Rehabilitation of the head-Injured adult*. Philadelphia: F.A. Davis Co.

Ben-Yishay, Y., Diller, L., Gerstman, L., & Gordon, W. (1970). Relationship between initial competence and ability to profit from cues in brain-damaged individuals. *Journal of Abnormal Psychology, 75,* 248-259.

Ben-Yishay, Y., Rattok, J., Lakin, P., Piasetsky, E. G., Ross, B., Silver, S., et al. (1985). Neuropsychologic rehabilitation: Quest for a holistic approach. *Seminars in Neurology, 5,* 252-259.

Ben-Yishay, Y., Rattok, J., Ross, B., Lakin, P., Silver, S., Thomas, L., & Diller, L. (1982). Working approaches to remediation of cognitive deficits in brain damage. Supplement to Tenth Annual Workshop for Rehabilitation Professionals, New York University, Institute of Rehabilitation Medicine.

Cole, J. R., Cope, N., & Cervelli, L. (1985). Rehabilitation of the severely brain-injured patient: A community-based, low-cost model program. *Archives of Physical Medicine and Rehabilitation, 66 ,* 38-40.

Cotman, C. W., & Nieto-Sampedro, M. (1985). Progress in facilitating the recovery of function after central nervous system trauma. In Nottebohm, F. (Ed.), *Hope for a new neurology*, New York: The New York Academy of Sciences, pp. 83-104.

Diller, L. (1976). A model for cognitive retraining in rehabilitation. *The Clinical Psychologist, 29,* 13-15.

Eson, M. E., Yen, J. K., & Bourke, R. S. (1978). Assessment of recovery from serious head injury. *Journal of Neurology, Neurosurgery, and Psychiatry, 41,* 1036-1042.

Flavell, J. H. (1977). *Cognitive development*. Englewood Cliffs, N.J.: Prentice-Hall.

Glisky, E. L., Schacter, D. L., & Tulving, E. (In press). Computer learning by memory-impaired patients: Acquisition and retention of complex knowledge. *Neuropsychologia.*

Goldstein, K. (1942). *Aftereffects of brain injury in war*. New York: Grune and Stratton.

Kernberg, O. F., Burstein, E. D., Coyne, L., Appelbaum, A., Horwitz, L., & Voth, H. (1972). *Bulletin of the Menninger Clinic, 36*, Nos. 1/2, Jan.-March.

Klonoff, P. (1986). Personal communication.

Pepping, M. (1986). Personal communication.

Piaget, J. (1928). *Judgment and reasoning in the child*. London: Routledge & Kegan Paul.

Prigatano, G. P., Fordyce, D. J., Zeiner, H. K., Roueche, J. R., Pepping, M., & Case Wood, B. (1984). Neuropsychological rehabilitation after closed head injury in young adults. *Journal of Neurology, Neurosurgery, and Psychiatry, 47,* 505-513.

Prigatano, G. P., et al. (1985). *Neuropsychological rehabilitation after brain injury*. Baltimore: The Johns Hopkins University Press.

Schacter, D. L., & Glisky, E. L. (1986). Memory remediation: Restoration, alleviation, and the acquisition of domain-specific knowledge. In B. P. Uzzell, & Y. Gross (Eds.), *Clinical Neuropsychology of Intervention*, Boston: Martinus Nijhoff Publishing, pp. 257-282.

Weinberg, J., Diller, L., Gordon, W., Gerstman, L., Lieberman, A., Lakin, P., et al. (1977). Visual scanning training effect on reading-related tasks in acquired right brain damage. *Archives of Physical Medicine and Rehabilitation, 58*, 479-486.

Weinberg, J., Piasetsky, E., Diller, L., & Gordon, W. (1982). Treating perceptual organizational deficits in non-neglecting RBD stroke patients. *Journal of Clinical Neuropsychology, 4*, 59-75.

Working approaches to remediation of cognitive deficits in brain damaged. Supplement to 6th Annual Workshop for Rehabilitation Professionals (1978). Institute of Rehabilitation Medicine, New York University Medical Center, Department of Behavioral Sciences.

Working approaches to remediation of cognitive deficits in brain damaged. Supplement to 7th Annual Workshop for Rehabilitation Professionals (1979). Institute of Rehabilitation Medicine, New York University Medical Center, Department of Behavioral Sciences.

Working approaches to remediation of cognitive deficits in brain damaged. Supplement to 8th Annual Workshop for Rehabilitation Professionals (1980). Institute of Rehabilitation Medicine, New York University Medical Center, Department of Behavioral Sciences.

Working approaches to remediation of cognitive deficits in brain damaged. Supplement to 9th Annual Workshop for Rehabilitation Professionals (1981). Institute of Rehabilitation Medicine, New York University Medical Center, Department of Behavioral Sciences.

Working approaches to remediation of cognitive deficits in brain damaged persons. Supplement to 10th Annual Workshop for Rehabilitation Professionals (1982). Institute of Rehabilitation Medicine, New York University Medical Center, Department of Behavioral Sciences.

Zangwill, O. L. (1947). Psychological aspects of rehabilitation in cases of brain injury. *British Journal of Psychology, 37*, 60-69.

3

The Role of Cognitive Retraining in Comprehensive Rehabilitation

J. Michael Williams

Cognitive retraining consists of a group of educational techniques ostensibly designed to remediate the impairments in cognition that result from brain injury (Diller & Gordon, 1981; Luria, 1963). For example, aphasia resulting from dominant hemisphere injury is treated using a wide array of language retraining techniques that vary with the type of aphasic symptoms (Darley, 1975). Similarly, memory disorder is treated using mnemonic techniques, such as visual mediation, or memory-assistive devices, like appointment books (Crovitz, 1979; Gianutsos, 1981; Schacter & Glisky, 1986).

The role of cognitive retraining techniques as a part of all the activities the brain injured person experiences in rehabilitation settings has not been the subject of considerable theoretical development. Recently, however, Anthony (1980) developed a comprehensive rehabilitation model that has been applied to the deinstitutionalization and rehabilitation of the chronically mentally ill. The application of this model to the rehabilitation of brain injuries might help to clarify the proper role of cognitive retraining as well as other services in the comprehensive rehabilitation of brain injuries.

The Anthony comprehensive rehabilitation model consists of six main components: skill and resource assessment, rehabilitation goal planning, skill training, resource management and plan execution (Figure 1). It will become apparent to readers already practicing rehabilitation that most brain injury rehabilitation teams practicing in hospitals or other clinic settings already engage in many of the model components. This comprehensive model is distinctive and helpful in the conceptualization of rehabilitation because it specifically defines these components of rehabilitation and attempts to explain how they interrelate. This article will discuss the application of the theory to brain injury rehabilitation in an attempt to specify the role of cognitive retraining activities within the context of this model's components and interrelating principles.

Skill and Resource Assessment

Rehabilitation of brain injury begins with the assessment of the patient's everyday functional skills (Caplan, 1982; DeJong, & Hughes, 1982; Jellineck, Torkelson, & Harvey, 1982). These range from simple sensory and motor abilities to higher cognitive functions, such as language and general problem-solving. As these are assessed, it will become clear which skills can be trained or which resources to provide in order to compensate for a missing skill. The focus of this assessment in the rehabilitation setting should be upon everyday, concrete abilities that are used at home and at work, as these are the functions that will permit the head injured person to become reintegrated into these environments. In the area of memory ability, an example of such a skill is simply to remember daily appointments

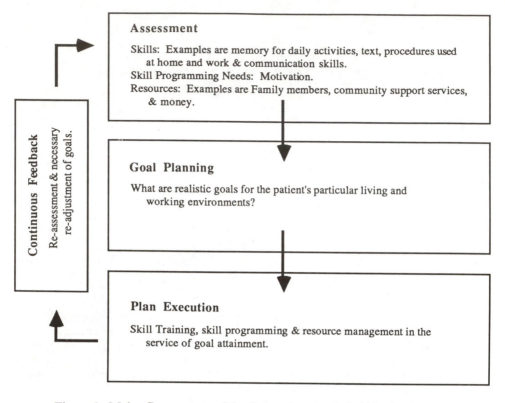

Figure 1. Major Components of the Comprehensive Rehabilitation Model.

and activities. The assessment of such a simple memory skill is extremely important in rehabilitation planning because such skills form the groundwork of successful community functioning.

It is currently unknown whether conventional neuropsychological batteries enable us to measure these abilities directly or allow us to predict everyday abilities from the test results (Heaton & Pendelton, 1981). Sbordone (1984) asserts that neuropsychological measures used in clinical practice tend to underestimate everyday ability but are still needed to properly measure cognitive abilities for diagnosis and description. If the neuropsychologist relies only on the patient's apparent everyday ability, then cognitive abilities will be overestimated. Certainly many everyday abilities can be predicted using intellectual and neuropsychological tests, and the best assessment probably derives from a combined approach (Brinkman, 1979). This is especially important in the earlier stages of recovery, when the patient's post-injury, everyday disability is unknown and has yet to be discovered.

Everyday abilities are usually assessed in an interview, using the patient's self-report or report of significant others (Prigatano, 1985; Williams, Klein, Little & Haban, 1986; Williams, 1987). Assessment should cover the full range of everyday activities, from driving the car and locating places, to cooking and accomplishing self-care activities. For the more severely impaired patient, the assessment can be summarized using many available inventories of activities of daily living (e.g., Lawton & Brody, 1969; McNair & Kahn, 1983). These inventories, which were developed for the elderly, cover much the same level of everyday impairment that the severely brain injured patient experiences and can be used for assessment of this group.

There essentially exists no formal method to summarize the everyday consequences of brain injury for the moderately to mildly disabled, especially if the patient is essentially employable. Such an inventory would be difficult to construct because each patient has a unique pattern of disability at this level which interacts with environmental demand on cognitive abilities. Because the mildly injured patient usually has no impairment of basic living skills and functions at a relatively high level, there exists no generic pattern of everyday disability as there does with dementia related illness or severe head injury. For example, a busy store manager will be greatly impaired by a subtle loss of memory ability. Such everyday memory abilities as remembering facts about inventory or payroll can be greatly impaired because they require the manager's memory to perform with complete efficiency. However, the store clerk, whose job is much more routine and does not require remembering as much new information, may not even notice a subtle loss of memory ability. The store clerk does not suffer an everyday disability comparable to the store manager even though the injury and cognitive consequences are similar. The store clerk may experience a disability when eventually promoted to store manager.

In addition to the assessment of current functioning, it is important to make some assessment or prediction of premorbid abilities because rehabilitation planning is often related to the patient's former work and educational activities. This is usually done using information provided in the interview. A rough approximation can be made from knowledge of the patient's former occupation and education (Wilson, Rosenbaum, Brown, Rourke, Whitman, & Grisell, 1978) and retrospective report of abilities made by the patient's relatives (Williams, Klein, & Davis, in preparation).

Assessment of these disabilities in a rehabilitation setting is currently very informal and relies almost exclusively on the clinician's predictions of everyday ability from screening tests, formal neuropsychological and intelligence tests and the patient's own report of the abilities needed to carry out their own everyday home and work activities. From these sources of information, the clinician forms a rough approximation of the patient's present skills and abilities. This assessment, informal as it is currently, forms the major groundwork of further planning.

The second major area of assessment is the measurement of resources available to the patient for rehabilitation. These resources include access to government personnel and agencies, money, the presence of friends and family members available and willing to contribute to the patient's rehabilitation, and health professionals and paraprofessionals. These resources vary greatly from patient to patient, almost to the extent that each patient's complement of skills are unique. However, rehabilitation efforts are very dependent upon these resources and their presence or absence will greatly determine the course of the patient's progress. For example, all cognitive retraining programs will benefit from a com-ponent that includes practice in retraining activities that are given at home by a family member. If such a family member is not available and the family does not have money to hire a tutor, then the cognitive retraining program may fail as a consequence.

Rehabilitation Goal Setting

Planning a rehabilitation intervention follows the assessment phase and represents the next necessary step in successful rehabilitation. Planning begins with the establishment of an overall rehabilitation goal. This goal represents the end point of rehabilitation that is realistically expected, given the client's profile of skill and resource assets and limitations. The rehabilitation goal is always environmentally specific, and contains some time requirement. For example, a common rehabilitation goal for the living environment is: The patient will function independently at home for the coming year. This goal establishes the framework of further skill training or resource management. The following question guides the planning of future activities in order to attain the goal: What skills or resources does this patient need in place in order to attain this goal? Once the rehabilitation goal is roughly decided and all interested parties have participated in proposing it, then planning the rehabilitation intervention becomes straightforward, but not necessarily untroublesome. The goal may be subjected to further modification as the client attempts to attain it. For many severely injured patients, independent living at home may not even be a realistic goal.

After a reasonable goal is initially established then appropriate skill training can begin. For example, many head injured clients have memory deficits early in their recovery and some degree of memory disorder may persist indefinitely. Inability to remember new information may preclude the attainment of a rehabilitation goal such as living at home. The client may not be able to manage medications, pay bills, anticipate the arrival of visiting nurses or therapists or any of a number of activities that allow for independent living at home.

In order to remedy this, the client can be trained in some mnemonic technique to remember this information or may be trained to use a memory aid, such as an appointment book or other external memory store. If the client is unable to learn this skill and it is necessary in order to achieve the rehabilitation goal, then a resource may be provided, such as a family member or paraprofessional helper assigned to monitor this information and prompt the client. In this way, resource development interacts with skill training in an effort to attain the overall rehabilitation goal.

Rehabilitation goals are often difficult to establish, both because the patients skills and resources are often largely unknown until the client actually attempts to live more independently, and because the parties involved, such as family, state agencies and health professionals, often have conflicting goals for the patient (Wright, 1980). In order to facilitate the establishment of a reasonable overall goal with which all parties can initially agree, interested parties must gather and share information and decide on a living and/or working environment and goal that the team can tentatively work towards.

Most head injured patients experience some rehabilitation planning while rehabilitation hospital inpatients. When the patient has medically stabilized after injury and is well on the road to recovery, he/she is often transferred to acute rehabilitation care for further strengthening and therapy. Throughout treatment in this setting, some rehabilitation planning is accomplished as the pattern of skills and cognitive abilities remaining to the patient become known to the rehabilitation team. At the point of discharge, many patients are medically stable and largely physically recovered.

For many inpatient rehabilitation teams, there exist two living environment goals for the discharged patient: home or extended care facility. If the patient plateaus at a low level of cognitive or physical functioning, the team usually discharges the patient to an extended care setting that can manage this level of ability. Sometimes this is home, but most often these patients are discharged to a nursing home. Other patients are discharged home usually after a meeting which includes the rehabilitation team and family members. Some rehabilitation planning is accomplished at this time. Usually the rehabilitation goal is established as independent functioning at home, although the team may not formally recognize this. Thereupon, the family and team commiserate on the resources they should provide or skills the patient should be taught in order to live at home.

This is the extent of the rehabilitation planning for most head injury cases. The remainder of the patient's recovery and rehabilitation is carried out at home with little assistance from health professionals. However, many outpatient and extended inpatient facilities have recently been developed for the head injured (Prigatano, 1985; Williams, 1986). A fully comprehensive model of head injury rehabilitation requires a strong outpatient component, to follow and guide the patient through the most active and productive phase of reintegration into home and work life. The rehabilitation program must follow the patient into the community and carry on until the patient completely recovers and attains an overall rehabilitation goal.

Skill Training

Most head injured patients will benefit from skill training of all sorts, ranging from training the memory impaired patients to use appointment books, to training the mildly injured to use visual imagery as a mnemonic tool (Godfrey & Knight, 1985; Jones, 1974). An important principle in any rehabilitation skill training is that it must be used to facilitate attainment of the overall rehabilitation goal. Without this connection, generalization of skill training will be minimal (Woods, 1983). Many rehabilitation teams do not engage in advance planning and goal setting before they begin skill training and this often results in a training regimen that has no apparent purpose. Since the therapist has been trained to administer the training program, it is implemented regardless of the client's needs or goals.

Cognitive retraining programs fall under the skill training aspects of comprehensive rehabilitation and are designed to redress a specific cognitive skill deficit. They may be used when appropriately indicated by the skill assessment and with the objective of rehabilitation goal attainment. The programs as they have been originally proposed are usually symptom oriented and may be overly specific in focus. In general, most cognitive retraining programs have loosely followed Luria's (1963) theory of functional reorganization and have the avowed purpose of reorganizing a cognitive function impaired or "disorganized" by brain injury. Most have consequently developed a very narrow focus and are directed toward specific cognitive symptoms, such as visuospatial neglect (Lawson, 1962) or memory disorder (Crovitz, 1979; Binder & Schreiber, 1980).

If the rehabilitation goal is environmentally specific, then skill training of any type should focus on everyday functional skills that directly assist in the attainment of the goal. Cognitive retraining programs can be improved by focusing on everyday cognitive skills that are needed in order to function in specific environmental settings. Put succinctly, cognitive retraining should have a goal-attainment focus instead of a symptom-reduction focus.

Resource Development

Resource management may develop independently or in conjunction with skill training. When a skill cannot be trained, then a resource can often be developed to take its place. For example, a head injured patient may not be able to overcome a unilateral visual neglect through skill training to a level enabling the patient to drive a car. Further, driving may also be necessary for a particular patient to attain an overall rehabilitation goal, such as success in a particular work environment. In this case, a resource must be developed to meet this immutable skill deficit; The patient needs a person to drive him/her to work. This driver is conceptualized as a resource within the comprehensive rehabilitation model. The driver may be a family member, who helps the patient freely, or may be provided using another important resource: money. In any event, the provision of such a resource redresses a skill deficit.

It is apparent from this example that resources also ultimately serve the attainment of the overall rehabilitation goal. It is uncommon for a rehabilitation team to err on the side of providing resources that are not related to some goal attainment. Often rehabilitation teams err on the side of providing skill training that has no overall purpose, but seldom in provid - ing resources that do not (Wright, 1980).

Most resources are developed independent of specific skill deficits. Government rehabilitation agencies include the provision of resources as one of their primary services. These resources include money, which is used to provide transportation, formal education, and other resources, information about disabilities, counseling of all sorts, and the wide range of other government and private services available to the head injured person. Most agencies, such as state departments of vocational rehabilitation, do less skill training as part of agency services, but direct the patient to available skill training and educational programs, and fund this training.

However, most resources are developed at the family level. If the patient needs someone to drive him/her to work or school, the family somehow provides that person. If the patient must have meals prepared, someone in the family usually provides that service, either by providing the services themselves, or hiring someone.

Effective resource management must therefore involve the family to a great extent. The family is the social unit that will carry through the provision of resources and much of the skill training. If people do not exist in the family who can act in this regard, then most rehabilitation plans will either fail in goal attainment or must be altered to reflect realistic expectations for resource development. Therefore, many rehabilitation programs falter because the family is not involved in planning.

Execution of Plans and Follow-up

After an overall rehabilitation goal has been devised and there is a relatively clear understanding of the skill training and resource development needed to achieve the goal, a great experiment begins. The patient will be gradually introduced to the skill training program and environment specified in the plan. It may become immediately apparent that the overall rehabilitation goal is not attainable, either because experience in the goal environment indicates that the patient cannot learn a necessary skill, or a compensatory resource cannot be developed. In this event, the rehabilitation goal must be modified to reflect this new knowledge. For example, perhaps the patient is functioning too poorly to allow for independent living in an apartment and this was originally proposed as a reasonable living environment goal. The family and patient would then be directed toward a supervised living environment such as an apartment with an attendant, or home with a family member. Such decisions involve the patient, family and rehabilitation team. The options available are very dependent upon the family's resources. If there are not sufficient funds to pay for a supervised apartment or attendants then this option is usually not available. This process of planning and experimentation continues until the patient attains some realistic adjustment in the community.

Experimentation also extends to the employment setting, for many cases of mild and moderate head injury. Employment trials are often difficult to initiate and organize (see Prigatano, this volume). The employer must be tolerant of disability and allow the patient to be less productive until some adjustment is accomplished. For many patients it is difficult to predict if they will perform adequately in their former job or one that has been proposed as part of the rehabilitation plan. This is because the skills required for individual jobs are largely unknown, and it is therefore impossible to accurately predict the fit of a patient's skill leves to a particular job. The prediction of work adjustment will improve if the patient intends to return to their premorbid occupation. In this situation, the patient and employer can describe the skills necessary for the old job and this considerably improves the prediction of future job adjustment.

It is helpful to conceptualize the transition from hospital to work and living environment as a grand experiment; sometimes the transition is easy and most predictions are verified, sometimes experiments are failures, and everyone must regroup and design another experiment. Such conceptualizations help the patients and professionals cope with the disappointments associated with even the most routine rehabilitation case. The following case illustrates a pratical, informal application of the comprehensive rehabilitation model that has been briefly discussed in this chapter.

Case Report: The Rehabilitation of Closed Head Injury

At age 23, B. W. sustained a severe closed head injury in an automobile accident. Upon admission to the emergency room, B. W. was unconscious and only responsive to painful stimuli. This corresponded to a grade IV coma on the Grady coma scale (Fleischer, Payne & Tindall, 1976). He also had multiple trauma, including fractures, lacerations, and abdominal injuries.

At this time, his wife was given the Cognitive Behavior Rating Scale (CBRS;Williams, Klein, Little & Haban, 1986) to complete. This scale allows a family member to rate the cognitve abilities of the patient. She indicated no significant premorbid cognitive problems. An estimated premorbid Full Scale IQ of 107 was computed from the CBRS and demographic information (Wilson, Rosenbaum, Brown, Rourke, Whitman, & Grisell, 1978; Williams, Klein, & Davis, in preparation). B. W. had completed high school and had worked as a warehouse forman. His duties had been to manage a section of the inventory and direct a group of workers who sorted items and filled orders.

Over the course of three weeks, he gradually recovered consciousness. Although unable to remember ongoing events, he did recognize family members and could maintain a very simple conversation. At seven weeks post injury, he became agitated and demonsrated immature behavior consisting of innappropriate language and hypersexualtity. His family reported that this was clearly inconsistent with his premorbid personality. This behavior gradually diminished over the following six months. B. W. also had three seizures during this period.

At two months post injury, B. W. was transferred to an inpatient rehabilitation setting. There he received traditional occupational, speech, physical and psychological therapies. His overall condition improved considerably over the coming weeks while he stayed at the inpatient rehabilitation service. He was discharged home after the rehabilitation team could no longer document further improvement in his intellectual abilities and everyday functional skills. Neuropsychological testing revealed a Full Scale IQ of 82, a Memory Quotient of 86, and generalized impairment on all other tests. At this point, his physical injuries had healed, he was able to remember ongoing events, easily communicate, and manage his everyday self-care. B. W. did not have a seizure while on the rehabilitation service. His seizures were apparently well controlled with medication. It was not known if he could manage his finances, drive a car, or return to his former occupation.

Although the rehabilitation team advised a much longer convelescence, B. W. decided to return to work after resting at home for two weeks. His manager agreed to test B. W. in his former role as a forman. Initially, B. W. discovered two features of his injury which almost precluded employment. First, his memory was not sufficiently recovered to allow him to consolidate and recall new information, such as new items of the inventory. Second, his employer was very reluctant to allow him to work in the warehouse if there was any possibility of a seizure. After this failed attempt, B. W. was referred to outpatient rehabilitation services by the local head injury support group.

Assessment

B. W. was given another neuropsychological evaluation at the time he entered outpatient rehabilitation. This revealed significantly improved memory (MQ=88), and overall intelligence (FSIQ=95). Performance on tests of the Halstead-Reitan neuropsychological battery were also improved. He was now much more attentive and conscientious on the tests. He was able to maintain a concerted effort on problem-solving tasks. His pattern of impairment was still diffuse, with relatively more severe impairment on memory tasks.

B. W.'s wife was interviewed and given the Cognitive Behavior Rating Scale (CBRS; Williams et al., 1986) and the Instrumental Activities of Daily Living Scale (IADL; Lawton & Brody, 1969) to complete. B. W. was also given the self-report form of the CBRS. B. W.'s wife indicated that B. W. had numerous everyday cognitive problems. In contrast, B. W. apparently denied many of the problems indicated by his performance on neuropsychological tests and his wife's responses on the CBRS (Figure 2). Responses of B. W.'s wife on the IADL scale indicated that he could manage all basic self-care in such areas as dressing, eating and ambulation.

It was not clear from these ratings and neuropsychological test results whether or not B. W. had sufficient memory and intellectual skills in order to function again as a warehouse foreman. Assessment and decision-making at this point in rehabilitation highlights one of the great weaknesses of current neuropsychological tests: The examiner cannot make valid inferences about occupational skill levels. Although these tests were valuable in

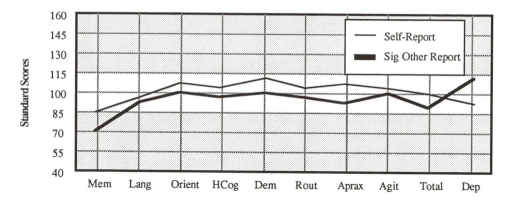

Figure 2. Responses of B. W. and his wife to the Cognitive Behavior Rating Scales.

documenting the location and severity of B. W.'s brain injury, they did not provide enough information in order to accurately determine his current functional skill levels in comparison to those needed for successful functioning in his former occupation.

Although B. W.'s original attempt to return to work had ended in failure, much was learned from this experiment. B. W.'s supervisor was contacted and interviewed. In brief, he reported that B. W. was apparently able to perform all of his former tasks except accurately remember new information. B. W. remembered all the old locations of items in the warehouse. He also remembered the old procedures used to fill an order. Former knowledge of the routine aspects of the job was intact. Such a direct analysis of job-related skills is necessary to formulate a comprehensive and accurate skill assessment. The preferred manner in which to do this is to actually construct a job trial experiment. If this is impossible, then the team should contact a former employer and informally assess job related skills in such areas as motor, sensory and social skills, abstract and verbal reasoning and memory. Needless to say, this aspect of neuropsychology and rehabilitation is poorly developed and we have much to learn from our colleagues in general vocational rehabilitation and special education (e.g., Wright, 1980).

The fact of B. W.'s relatively preserved vocational skills illustrates another important feature of occupational rehabilitation from brain injury. Most brain-injured people do not have a retrograde amnesia for their former occupational activities. Such former knowledge and skills usually constitute a considerable strength on which to build a rehabilitation intervention. As a general rule of thumb, brain-injured patients can usually re-learn aspects of a former occupation much easier than learn a completely new job. This applies to any former occupation, not just to the one the patient had immediately prior to the injury. The rehabilitation team and the patient should always carefully examine such retained job skills during the skill assessment phase.

In terms of resources, B. W. had considerable social support from his immediate and extended family. There were people in the family available to help with homework assign-ments and the like. B. W. also had financial resources, either through insurance or his own money, to pay for rehabilitation services, seizure control medications, a new car to drive to work, and a variety of other needs that emerged during the course of his rehabilitation.

B.W. also had a very tolerant employer, and this is certainly a necessary resource for attaining goals in any working environment. Many rehabilitation programs fail because resources such as these are not available. In terms of skill programming, or motivation, B. W. was highly motivated to achieve success in some occupational setting and it was not anticipated that a skill programming intervention would be needed.

In summary, B. W. had relatively preserved social, motor, sensory, and general intellectual skills, and these were apparently sufficient for successful functioning in his former work environment. The major skill deficit was in memory ability. In order to function successfully as a warehouse foreman, he must be able to remember and later recall a considerable amount of the inventory from a memory store in the brain. In terms of his home living environment, he had no apparent skill deficits. Finally, he probably had sufficient resources in order to successfully function in both these environments.

Goal Planning

During early meetings with B. W. and his wife, a set of rehabilitation goals for B. W.'s working environment were discussed. Since B. W. was functioning independently in the home, no living environment goal was established. From these discussions, a reasonable working environment goal was proposed: B. W. will independently work as a warehouse foreman for the next six months. Further planning and rehabilitation activities were then motivated by this clear, overall goal statement.

Most rehabilitation goals are stated much more vaguely, and usually in the framework of symptom reduction alone. For example, a poorly stated goal for B. W. would be, "The goal of your rehabilitation will be to remediate your memory impairment so that you can have a more productive life." This type of goal statement is inadequate because it does not necessarily result in any improvement of the patient's condition. What would be the necessary purpose of improving B. W.'s memory if it was not directly related to concrete improvements in his living or working situation? Needless to say, most rehabilitation teams operate with no goal at all, or goals so vaguely stated that the team will never know if it has been a success or a failure. With such vaguely defined goals, we will avoid defining our difficult efforts as failures, but we will also never have the satisfaction of clear success.

Plan Execution and Follow-up

B. W. was seen in an outpatient day treatment program four hours per day, three days per week. Skill training focused on B. W.'s poor ability to remember new inventory stock. We asked his former employer to send us new and old inventory listings. He was trained to remember these using visualization and organizational strategies. We learned from his employer that most inventories have a hierarchical, categorical order. B. W. was able to profit from lessons in categorizing these items, using strategies developed by cognitive retraining therapists and B. W. himself. He also practiced organizing lists with the aid of verbal memory retraining computer programs, that allow the student to enter his/her own list of words. In addition, B. W. was trained in a verbal memory compensation strategy. He was instructed to write down, on an index card, the name, date received, and distinguishing features of any new inventory item. These cards he was to keep in his pocket and then transfer to a file. Whenever he was not busy, and at home in the evenings, he was to practice remembering the contents of the new and old cards. In this way, he was to develop a memory store for inventory information that existed outside his brain.

B. W. practiced these techniques while in the outpatient program for approximately two months. We then attempted to actually implement them in the work setting. This proved difficult, as anyone might imagine. First, B. W.'s former employer did not believe B. W. should receive special help or attention. He could also not tolerate less efficient performance in his foremen. If B. W. could not keep up, he would have to be transferred to another, simpler job or continue his disability leave and find another occupation. Also, B. W.'s employer was still concerned about the possibility of seizures. What was the liability risk of having someone in the warehouse who might have a seizure and become injured?

All of these were difficult, perhaps insurmountable obstacles, that existed as part of the work environment. We were confronted with the possibility of another learning (i.e. failure) experience. However, we continued with our plan, buoyed by the simple fact that the prediction of success or failure in rehabilitation is almost impossible. The knowledge of outcome is only attainable through actual experimentation.

B. W. first attempted work by assisting another foreman for two days per week. He would then work in the outpatient rehabilitation program for the other three days. Much was learned by having B. W. attempt work while attending the program. As more specific cognitive skill deficits became known, we were able to design a training approach to cope with them. As the work trial progressed, it unfortunately became apparent that B. W.'s memory skill deficit could not be sufficiently remediated and no compensation strategy was working to bring his performance up to acceptable standards.

After meetings with B. W. and his wife, we decided to re-formulate the working environment goal. We had discovered through experimentation that the previous goal was not realistic. We decided to work toward the goal of successful functioning at a lower job position, one that more routine and did not require such a high level of memory skill. The job only required B. W. to take an order and fill it, by retrieving items from the inventory and placing them in a bin, which eventually transported them to waiting delivery trucks. B. W. responded to this new goal with some feelings of disappointment and depression. His motivation was not as great after we began working in this direction. He certainly interpreted this new job as a step down in prestige. After working for a number of years at the warehouse, he had finally been promoted to a foreman. Working at a lower level job was a demotion in his interpretation. Although he never completely accepted this new job choice, he understood his memory problems in great detail and could directly relate them to poor functioning on the job. He basically rationalized this new job as one in which he could probably perform well, and one that would provide support for his family. Also, if he continued to recover, there was always the possibility of future promotion.

Again, B. W. worked at this job part-time while attending the rehabilitation program. Almost from the first day, we realized that he had all of the necessary skills in order to perform this other job. Of course, we were unable to determine if B. W. recovered these skills, or if we actually trained him in skills necessary for this new position. The new position required some new learning ability and B. W. still used his index card system to monitor new items of the inventory. Overall, we rated B. W.'s progress as a qualified success.

This case informally illustrates the major features of the comprehensive rehabilitation model. It is typical of the substantially uncomplicated rehabilitation course of the mild to moderately brain injured person. Certainly there were numerous features of this case that especially contributed to the overall positive outcome. First, B. W. was highly motivated to return to his former occupation. This enabled him to work hard and demonstrate success in the cognitive retraining activities. B. W.'s drive and desire to succeed actually motivated the staff to continue working with him; they felt that *their* efforts were leading somewhere. Second, B. W.'s family was very supportive and he could afford outpatient rehabilitation. Many patients do not have the tangible support provided by an extended family. Also, B.W. had a largely supportive and tolerant work environment. The benefits of a supportive work environment cannot be overstated. Such work settings are a *necessary* aspect of work trials, and are often the most difficult resource to develop in the attainment of work environment re-habilitation goals.

This case also illustrates the unique qualities of goal setting and modification of goals, given the result of real-life experiences. As evaluators of treatment programs, we are conditioned by training to adopt a myopic, single-minded view of our interventions. We tend to view an intervention as having a problem formulation, such as a disease or cognitive impairment, a treatment, such as cognitive retraining, and an evaluation of outcome; either the treatment reduces the cognitive impairment in a clinically significant manner, or it does not. In the case of B. W., our first intervention was technically a failure; we did not attain our goal. However, the knowledge we gained by the initial failure prompted us to re-define a reasonable outcome and hence, our later success. This re-definition of positive outcome during the course of rehabilitation is disconcerting to evaluation-minded professionals. How is it possible to design a formal study of the effectiveness of rehabilitation, when it is possible to re-define the outcome? This is a research problem that has only been approached by Anthony and his colleagues (Anthony, Buell, Sharratt, & Althoff, 1972; Anthony, Cohen, & Vitalo, 1978). Priganto (1985, present volume) and Harter (present volume) also provide suggestions for evaluating rehabilitation outcome that may have a bearing on this issue. All of this suggests that rehabilitation interventions and outcomes are conceptually distinct from those most often used to evaluate treatment, and perhaps require a different model of evaluation, such as the single-subject designs often employed in the evaluation of behavior therapy.

Conclusions

In summary, rehabilitation from brain injuries involves the coordination of skill training and resource development in an attempt to attain a realistic, overall rehabilitation goal. This goal includes proposed work and living environments. Rehabilitation also includes execution of the plan, follow-up, and modification of the plan to include new information about the patient's skill level and resources that are derived from attempts to reach the goal. All these components work together to produce a rehabilitation experiment that may result in community adjustment immediately or only after repeated modifications and many experiments.

References

Anthony, W.A. (1980). Psychological rehabilitation: a concept in need of a method. *American Psychologist, 32*, 658-662.
Anthony, W. A., Buell, G., Sharratt, S., & Althoff, M. (1972). The efficacy of psychiatric rehabilitation. *Psychological Bulletin, 78*, 447-456.

Anthony, W. A., Cohen, M. R., & Vitalo, R. (1978). The measurement of rehabilitation outcome. *Schizophrenia Bulletin, 4*, 365-383.

Binder, L.M., & Schreiber, J. (1980). Visual imagery and verbal mediation as memory aids in recovering alcoholics. *Journal of Clinical Neuropsychology, 2*, 71-74.

Brinkman, S.D. (1979). Rehabilitation of the neurologically impaired patient: The contribution of the neuropsychologist. *International Journal of Clinical Neuropsychology, 3*, 39-44.

Caplan, B. (1982). Neuropsychology in rehabilitation: Its role in evaluation and intervention. *Archives of Physical and Medical Rehabilitation, 63*, 362-366.

Crovitz, H.F. (1979). Memory retraining in brain damaged patients: The airplane list. *Cortex, 15*, 131-134.

Darley, F. L. (1975). Treatment of acquired aphasia. In W. J. Friedlander (Ed), *Advances in Neurology*. New York: Raven.

DeJong, G., & Hughes, J. (1982). Independent Living: Methodology for measuring long term outcomes. *Archives of Physical and Medical Rehabilitation, 63*, 68-73.

Diller, L. & Gordon, W.A. (1981). Rehabilitation and clinical neuropsychology. In: S. Filskov & T. Boll, (Eds.), *Handbook of Clinical Neuropsychology*, New York: Wiley.

Gianutsos, R. (1981). Training the short and long term verbal recall of a postencephalitic amnesic. *Journal of Clinical and Experimental Neuropsychology, 3*, 143-153.

Godfrey, H.P.D., & Knight, R.G. (1985). Cognitive rehabilitation of memory functioning in amnesic alcoholics. *Journal of Consulting and Clinical Psychology, 53*, 555-557.

Heaton, R. K. & Pendelton, M. G. (1981). Use of neuropsychological tests to predict adult patient's everyday functioning. *Journal of Consulting and Clinical Psychology, 49*, 807-821.

Jellineck, H.M., Torkelson, R.M., & Harvey, R.F. (1982) Functional abilities and distress levels in brain injured patients at long-term follow-up. *Archives of Physical and Medical Rehabilitation, 63* , 160-162.

Jones, M.K. (1974). Imagery as a mnemonic aid after left temporal lobectomy: Contrast between material-specific and generalized memory disorders. *Neuropsychologia, 12*, 21-30.

Lawson, I.R. (1962). Visual-spatial neglect in lesions of the right cerebral hemisphere. *Neurology, 12* , 23-33.

Lawton, M.P., & Brody, E. (1969). Assessment of older people: Self-maintaining and instrumental activities of daily living. *Gerontologist, 9*, 179-186.

Luria, A. (1963). *Restoration of Function after Brain Injury*. New York: MacMillan.

McNair, D.M., & Kahn, R.J. (1983). Self assessment of cognitive deficits. In: T. Crook, S. Ferris, & R. Bartus (Eds.), *Assessment in Geriatric Psychopharmacology*, (pp. 137-143). New Canaan, Conn: Mark Powley Associates.

Prigatano, G. P., et al. (1985). *Neuropsychological rehabilitation after brain injury*, Baltimore: The Johns Hopkins University Press.

Sbordone, R. (1984). Rehabilitative Neuropsychological approach for severe traumatic brain-injured patients. *Professional Psychology: Research and Practice, 15*, 165-175.

Schacter, D.L., & Glisky, E.L. (1986). Memory remediation: Restoration, alleviation, and the acquisition of domain-specific knowledge. In B.P. Uzzell & Y. Gross (Eds.), *Clinical Neuropsychology of Intervention*. Boston: Martinus Nijhoff Publishing.

Williams, J. M. (1986). HORIZONS: An outpatient neurological retraining program. Unpublished manuscript, Memphis State University.

Williams, J. M. (1987). The brief and extended assessment of the elderly patient. In: L. Hartlage, P. Asken, & J. Hornsby (Eds), *Essentials of Neuropsychological Assessment* . New York: Springer.

Williams, J. M., Klein, K., & Davis, K. (in preparation). Prediction of premorbid IQ using family observations.

Williams, J. M., Klein, K., Little, M., & Haban, G. (1986). Family Observations of everyday cognitive impairment in dementia. *Archives of Clinical Neuropsychology, 1*, 183-192.

Wilson, R.S., Rosenbaum, G., Brown, G., Rourke, D., Whitman, D., & Grisell, J. (1978). An index of premorbid intelligence. *Journal of Consulting and Clinical Psychology, 46*, 1554-1555.

Woods, R.T. (1983). Specificity of learning in reality-orientation sessions: a single case study. *Behavior Research and Therapy, 21*, 173-175.

Wright, G. N. (1980). *Total Rehabilitation*. Boston: Little, Brown & Co.

4

Neuropsychological Theories and Cognitive Rehabilitation

Kurt A. Moehle, Jeffrey Lee Rasmussen and Kathleen B. Fitzhugh-Bell

According to Webster's Handy College Dictionary (1961), "rehabilitation" means to "restore to good condition or respectable position," whereas the term "retraining" means to "subject to discipline and instruction; remake proficient or fit." We see "rehabilitation" as a more global and comprehensive term, and "retraining" as applying more to specific tasks aimed at restitution of some function. Diller and Gordon (1981) have called rehabilitation, "...an active process in which services are provided to the disabled person in order to reduce impairment, to facilitate optimal acquisition of skills, and to overcome the disability" (p. 703). We would characterize this as a more generalist rehabilitation approach with patients whose primary disability happens to be of a cognitive nature, and acquired rather than congenital.

Gianutsos (1980), on the other hand, has defined CR as "a service developed to remediate disorders of perception, memory, and language in brain injured persons" (p. 36). Along these same lines, Bracy (1984) has also supplied a more specific, focused definition, calling CR "The reattainment of the mental abilities required to successfully and accurately receive sensory input, process information, and act in a manner as independently and appropriately as possible, given physiological limitations, following insult and compromise of the brain and its functions" (p. 2). We would classify these definitions as geared more specifically toward the cognitive retraining aspect of CR. Bracy's therapies, for example, are heavily computer-based and appear to emphasize restoration of cognitive skills (Bracy, 1983, 1984), although we have observed that Bracy does much planning of generalization exercises to bridge from the computer tasks to the actual home or work environment of the patient.

Thus, we perceive a difference between the more generalist rehabilitation psychologist, who also does cognitive rehabilitation, and the specifically-focused cognitive rehabilitationist. This perceived difference in outlook may account for the more focused definition provided by Bracy and Gianutsos, whereas Diller and Gordon's emphasis may be more the global rehabilitation of the individual; cognitive retraining being more clearly a secondary or adjuvant therapy.

Historically, CR traces its roots back to the realization among professionals involved in physical rehabilitation that the head-injured required more than physical rehabilitation to restore them to optimal functioning, and that cognitive deficits were not immediately apparent, but required special diagnostic study (Gianutsos & Grynbaum, 1983). As noted elsewhere in this volume, CR is, of course, only one area of rehabilitation of the brain-damaged client. Other areas of Rehabilitation of the brain-damaged client include: (1)

communication therapy, (2) behavioral self-management skills, (3) memory remediation, (4) physical rehabilitation, (5) family intervention techniques, (6) perceptual dysfunction remediation, and (7) vocational guidance (Edelstein & Couture, 1984; Rosenthal, Griffith, Bond, & Miller, 1983). Rehabilitation disciplines include: neurology/neurosurgery, neuropsychology, psychiatry, nursing, physical medicine, and many others.

As in the case of the development of clinical psychology, a major impetus for the development of CR was the large number of armed forces veterans returning from World War II with disabilities; in this case cognitive deficits secondary to head injury. Although some CR work had been going on with this adult population and with children prior to 1966, the earliest published study we were able to locate was Busse and Lighthall's (1966) article on conceptual retraining of brain-damaged adults. By the early 1970s, however, a number of articles on CR had begun to appear in the literature (Buffery, 1974; Cooke, 1973; Lewinsohn & Graf, 1973), and, by 1976 the field had begun to crystalize, as witnessed by Diller's (1976) article, in which he bemoaned the lack of technical tools and conceptual structure to guide the clinician who wished to assist a brain-damaged individual in recovering cognitive function following head injury.

Since Diller's (1976) article, the number of CR techniques available has grown exponentially. Although much of the early work borrowed heavily from the treatment of the mentally retarded (e.g., Smith & Means, 1961) and the developmental theories of Piaget (1952, 1983), the field of CR soon began to draw on the theories and techniques of Luria (1948/1963), and now appears to have begun to look to a marriage of neuroscience and cognitive psychology (Gazzaniga, 1984) for guidance in understanding cognitive function. Such understanding may come through, for example, information-processing theory and its applications to areas such as memory structures and remediation (Baddeley, 1985; Knight & Wooles, 1980).

In an effort to examine the reliance of CR on theory, we again conducted a computerized literature search of four previously-mentioned databases. The search terms used were "cognitive with retraining or rehabilitation." The results of these searches are reported in Table 1. The journals or periodicals producing two or more references are listed

Table 1

Journal Articles Devoted to Cognitive Retraining

Source	Descriptive Reports	Reviews	Experimental Studies
Cognitive Rehabilitation	48	3	4
International Journal of Clinical Neuropsychology		3	
Journal of Rehabilitation	1	2	
Journal of Clinical Neuropsychology	1	1	1
Rehabilitation Psychology			2
Clinical Gerontologist	1		1
Other	6	8	8
Totals	57	17	16
Percentages	63%	19%	18%

in order of number of citations produced. The articles were grouped into three categories: (1) opinion pieces, surveys, or descriptive "experience" reports, (2) theoretical or review articles, and (3) experimental or quasi-experimental empirical research.

As shown by the figures in Table 1, theoretical and empirical articles place a distant second place to "experience reports" or descriptive pieces. Most of the latter are found in the periodical *Cognitive Rehabilitation.* This journal appears to serve as a communication forum for CR practitioners and interested lay persons about treatment techniques or innovations, and to share experiences about working with or experiencing head injury. Unfortunately, none of the other professional journals surveyed appear to be providing theoretical or empirical research articles to keep up with the proliferation of what we will call "pragmatically developed" techniques. These techniques are usually spawned from variations on a treatment theme (e.g., adding videotaping techniques to group therapy sessions with the head-injured; Alexy, 1983).

It appears then that Diller's (1976) call for technical tools and conceptual schemes has been partially answered: New techniques are being developed monthly. But the development of new theories or conceptual schemes, or even clarifications or extension of old ones, is not being pursued with the same enthusiasm. Having noted this state of affairs, we will now examine the models or theories that appear to have been utilized in the develop - ment of the field of CR.

Major Theories Used in Cognitive Rehabilitation

Although true formal theories or empirically-validated models are rare in CR, assumptions abound. For example, an emphasis on "reeducation" of higher cortical functions (Maruszewski, 1969), is contrasted with suggestions that compensatory strategies are the "apex" of treatment (Henry, 1984). There is obviously a strong need for models in CR to sort out this confusion through organized empirical validation of some of these treat - ment assumptions.

Despite the lack of clearly validated models, a number of cognitive rehabilitation programs have developed formal treatment principles (Ben-Yishay, 1983; Craine, 1982) based roughly on a variety of theoretical models. For example, Craine (1982) developed the following treatment guidelines: (1) recovery following cortical damage is possible, (2) the cerebral cortex is an open, malleable system, (3) cortical learning comes from repeated activity, which can then become organized into a functional system, (4) activities of retraining must recapitulate cognitive development, (5) multiple modalities supplement each other in learning, (6) the primary objective is to develop the processes underlying learning, (7) training should be deficit-specific, and (8) consistent and systematic feedback is needed. Although examples such as these can serve as a starting point, programs appear to take on a life of their own through trial and error innovations and refinement of treatment techniques by the frontline practitioners (e.g., Carberry & Burd, 1983; Ensley, 1984; Wilson, 1983).

Based on our matching of published CR program treatment principles with psychological and neuropsychological theories or models, the primary models currently in use in the field of CR appear to be: (1) Luria's (1980; 1948/1963) functional systems approach, (2) the developmental models (Craine & Gudeman, 1981; Bolger, 1983), (3) learning theory models (Goldstein, 1979; Horton, 1979; Wood, 1982), and the relatively recent (4) process model (Bracy, 1984; Kaplan, 1985). Also noted are the proliferation of what we will call "pragmatic" models (e.g., Ehrlich & Sipes, 1985). These are models developed from refinement of, and experimentation with, treatment techniques or programs, and are not particularly theory-based.

Luria's functional systems theory (Luria, 1980) and its corollary model for rehabilitating brain injury (Luria, 1948/1963) is the premier applied neuropsychological approach in use today. The functional systems theory is based on a dynamic structuring of higher cortical functions in a roughly hierarchical fashion. There are three zones or "analyzers." These consist of primary sensory projection areas, secondary perception areas, and association areas. Most areas are cross-linked, providing a large array of possibilities in terms of connections necessary and sufficient to perform a certain function or behavior.

Some would argue that the entire "rationale for the rehabilitation of behavioral deficits resulting from cortical dysfunction can best be traced to Luria" (Incagnoli & Newman, 1985, p. 173). In this schema, of course, the reestablishment of defective functions through creation of new functional systems has become the goal of CR (Tsvetkova, 1972).

Other neuropsychological theories have been utilized in CR, however, including neurophysiological theories and theories about the mechanisms of recovery. Theories of recovery of function (Marshall, 1984; St. James-Roberts, 1979) have played an important part in the development of CR strategies. The major theories are summarized as follows: (1) Vicarious function theory states that other areas of the brain assume the functions of the damaged brain region; (2) In equipotentiality theory, recovery involves the mass action of the remaining parts of the neural network; (3) Substitution theory involves the utilization of analogous neurophysiological processes to achieve the same behavioral result by different means; (4) Regrowth theories, which include regeneration of axons and collateral sprouting of dendrites around the site of injury; (5) Diaschisis theory, which involves a temporary dysfunction due to "neural shock" in which edema, metabolic disturbance, and decreased blood perfusion all wreak havoc with the nervous system and shut down functions until the systemic climate returns to more normal levels; (6) Emergence trauma theory, which attributes the state of bewilderment, disorientation and negative affect to the new situation in which the organism finds itself, and in which its ability to respond appropriately is temporarily precluded.

Each of these theories has varying degrees of support, but diaschisis would appear to be the one most clearly supported by the available human evidence (St. James-Roberts, 1979). Unfortunately, diaschisis alone cannot account for the great amount of spontaneous recovery that occurs up to three years following head injury (Lezak, 1979), as most of the effects of diaschisis are considered to be relatively short-term (Marshall, 1984). Thus, other as yet unsupported theories of recovery of function must be validated to explain the remaining spontaneous recovery of function that occurs with head injury.

Piasetsky (1982), examining recovery-of-function theories from the point of view of the rehabilitationist, sees three main principles from which mechanisms of recovery have been derived. These are: (1) disinhibition, (2) compensation through redundancy, and (3) functional reorganization. The first two are seen as merely descriptive, that is, they reflect the intrinsic organizational properties of the system that may predispose it to retain its functional integrity after brain injury. The third, however, is a dynamic explanation involving active adaptation of the system to the effects of the injury. This last explanation implies an interaction with the environment and supplies the most promising potential application for intervention.

These theories have been used, in conjunction with clinical observations, to develop stage models of recovery from head injury. These typically encompass a range from coma to purposeful and appropriate behavior (Henry, 1984) and are often reduced to three stages (Szekeres et al., 1985): (1) early return of simple sensory awareness and gross motor function; (2) a middle phase involving highly structured CR techniques to aid in increasing comprehension, orientation, and return of new learning; and (3) a final phase in which greater independence of functioning is urged by gradual withdrawing of the environmental supports or structures that had been established in the middle phase.

As an example of how theory influences treatment, some cognitive rehabilitationists view the above-mentioned early phase of recovery as a period in which CR should focus on sensory and sensori-motor facilitation through increasing the patient's arousal and increasing adaptive responses to the environment (Henry, 1984; Szekeres et al., 1985). The basis of this may have been derived from regrowth and denervation supersensitivity hypotheses of neural recovery (cf. St. James-Roberts, 1979), in which new connections form or old ones have the capacity to reform if the correct stimulation is applied to the requisite pathways. Such treatment would be counter-productive or even unnecessarily stressful to the patient if viewed from the vantage point of diaschisis theory and, especially, emergence trauma theory, in which it is hypothesized that the disorienting reaction of the head trauma patient regaining consciousness is due to a combination of diaschisis and the bewilderment of re-turning to an environment full of new sensory stimuli. These latter theories would dictate an initially quiet, reassuring environment, with little stimuli to assault the "re-emerging" percetual system (Fuld & Fisher, 1977). As can be seen, the timing and type of intervention developed would vary depending on the theory of recovery of function embraced by the practitioner.

The comparative literature has also contributed much to the development of CR techniques and programs; in particular, the studies in which enviromental interventions have been shown to have an impact on lesioned or immature brain structures. Included among these studies would be Greenough's (1976) research in which gross differences in early environmental experience were associated with differences in morphological development in the brains of developing animals. Differences in rearing conditions, for example, have also been strongly related to differences in the functional physiology of the visual system (Freeman, 1979). For example, in newborn kittens, the effects on the visual cortex of up to six months of light deprivation may be reversed by environmental change (Timney & Mitchell, 1979). In these and similar studies, the maturity of the organism appears very important in recovery of brain function. Immature animals typically appear to have less functional deficit from a similar lesion than mature animals (Sharlock, Tucker, & Strominger, 1963; Wetzel, Thompson, Horel, & Meyer, 1965), although this finding has been challenged when applied to humans (Boll, 1973; Fitzhugh & Fitzhugh, 1965).

Despite the advantages of such neurophysiological and neuropsychological theories, Goldstein and Ruthven (1983) have noted a number of flaws in such approaches when applied to CR. Among them: (1) the lack of a sufficient conceptual model, (2) insufficient attention to the problem of motivation, and (3) insufficient attention to the patient's psychosocial status.

Partly in response to some of these difficulties, cognitive theories have been embraced and have recently made a huge impact on CR. Piaget's (1952; 1983) theories of cognitive development, with his stages of cognitive development, have been utilized to structure CR treatment programs. Also, Bruner (1964) has developed a hierarchical relationship for the emergence of cognitive processing systems. In the interactive motor stage, most data are processed through sensorimotor systems and primarily at the sensorimotor level, similar to Luria's (1980) primary processing zones. In the iconic processing stage, perceptual or image processing takes place. Finally, the symbolic representational stage represents experience in prototypes or categories based on function. Some rehabilitationists postulate that this sequence recapitulates in recovery from brain injury (cf. Craine & Gudeman, 1981).

Others have adopted a neopiagetian model. This model attempts to bridge the gap between Piaget's theory of learning and educational or instructional theories of learning (Case, 1978). As Bolger (1981) has stated it, in the neopiagetian model, "The cognitive retraining program is a conglomeration of various instructional programs combined according to a developmental theory to create a comprehensive therapeutic environment by which the brain-injured individual can be adequately stimulated to relearn lost information" (p.66).

In applying cognitive theory, rehabilitationists have looked at work in cognitive psychology indicating which type of cognitive strategies are often used by people, and which seem to be most adaptive or successful. Gholson, Levine, and Phillips (1972) elucidated three strategies, focusing, dimension-checking, and hypothesis-checking, and found the focusing strategy to be most efficient. These authors also found the efficiency of the strategy used to increase with age. Similarly, Bruner (1973) elucidated two strategies, focusing of a holistic strategy, in which a hypothesis is selected from all the information given, and a successive scanning strategy, in which instances are processed successively or in parts. He also found the focusing strategy to be more efficient.

Particularly important in CR has been the impact of cognitive psychology's information-processing (IP) theory. IP might be very roughly defined as the "analysis and synthesis of information in sequential steps" (Adamovich, Henderson, & Auerbach, 1985, p. 38). Humans are seen to process information in two broad modes: verbal and nonverbal or spatial-visuoconstructive. The levels of processing approach, in which it is theorized that verbal or nonverbal information must be acted upon, or processed at ever-deeper levels in order to be retained (Atkinson & Shiffrin, 1968), has become popular among rehabilitationists, as have cognitive psychology's explorations of problem-solving strategies (cf. Adamovich et al., 1985).

The learning perspective also has provided fertile ground for developing theoretically-based interventions. Besides behavior modification programs for management of inappropriate or unwanted behaviors (Edelstein & Couture, 1984), cognitive-behavioral techniques, such as the self-control strategies of Luria (1961) and Meichenbaum (1980), have been used to impart visual scanning strategies to learning disabled children (Egeland, 1974), and have been applied to generalization issues with the head-injured (Adamovich et al., 1985).

Recently, there have been efforts to combine such behavioral techniques with clinical neuropsychology (Goldstein 1979; Horton, 1979). Such "behavioral neuropsychology" would involve applying behavioral techniques to remediate behavioral deficits delineated by neuropsychological assessment. Goldstein and Ruthven (1983) would also see behavioral techniques as the answer to the nagging question of the lack of "motivation" often seen in the head-injured patient. That is, many head-injured patients do not appear to direct their behavior in a way that is understandable from the standpoint of normal learning. Individuals with frontal lobe damage in particular, are often listless, apathetic, and seemingly unmotivated (Luria, 1980). Application of behavioral principles can supply the "motivation" via external rather than internal reinforcement, as one solution to this problem.

Yet another approach to CR is the Process Approach (Bracy, 1984; Kaplan, 1985). This approach involves a careful evaluation of brain processes that have been disrupted, with a subsequent attempt to address the remediation of those processes in treatment, proceeding in a stepwise fashion. In this scheme, assessment should be directly provocative of treatment. These disrupted processes may be reduced to subprocesses and treatment may proceed hierarchically, e.g., retrain to accurately sense from the environment, then attend to sensory information in a general way, then focus on a specific sensory input, etc. (Bracy, 1984).

There have also been models derived largely from within disciplines; for example, Goldstein and Ruthven's (1983) four "philosophies of rehabilitation." These "philosophies" include: (1) the physical disability model, stressing treatment of the physical disability, and regarding the brain as just another organ system, (2) the psychiatry model, which focuses mainly on describing the illness and mental condition of the brain-damaged patient, (3) the behavioral model, which proposes an interface between applied human neuropsychology and behavior therapy, and (4) the neuropsychological model, with its heavy past reliance on assessment and brain-related behaviors. Each of these models have their problems, however, with none appearing adequate alone to face the task of rehabilitating brain-injured people.

With regard to such treatment, others have seen basically two main paradigms for treating brain-injured clients: (1) tailored treatment, in which a specific deficit is diagnosed and targeted for treatment, and (2) fixed curriculum treatment, in which all individuals receive the same instruction (Incagnoli & Newman, 1985). In addition to this, some have recommended restitution of functioning, while others have advocated compensation, or the use of preferred modalities and intact brain areas as the most sensible approach to restoring functional behavior (Hartlage, 1975; Miller, 1984).

In addition to helping guide treatment programs, however, another function of models is to organize information in such way that the practitioner will at least be able to ask the right questions about rehabilitation. Questions to be answered in CR through the application of a useful model, include Diller's (1976) original four queries: (1) What is the patient's problem?, (2) How does one diagnose?, (3) How does one treat?, and (4) Is the treatment effective? In addition to these, Lakin, Ben-Yishay, Rattok, Ross, Silver, Thomas, and Diller (1982) have produced five important areas to be explored: (1) the patient's knowledge of his situation and the program, (2) his understanding, perception, and verbalization of his specific problem, (3) specific behaviors which should be alleviated to insure patient adjustment, (4) the level of trainability , motivation, and acceptance on the part of the patient, and (5) hypotheses concerning the underlying nature of the deficit.

Given answers to the queries posed by Diller and colleagues, CR then seeks to remediate, in particular, cognitive deficits that may be leading to maladaptive behaviors. Among these deficits are: attention problems, perceptual difficulties, memory functions, etc. (Incagnoli & Newman, 1985). Added to this schema recently, has been the afore-mentioned behavioral model, in which behavioral techniques are applied to remediating maladaptive behaviors such as inappropriate social behaviors, attention and motivation problems, memory difficulties, etc. (Edelstein & Couture, 1984; Goldstein & Ruthven, 1983; Incagnoli & Newman, 1985). Among the drawbacks of the behavioral applications, however, is the fact that specialized behavioral treatment programs have not been developed and tested for the head-injured as they have been for groups such as alcoholics (Goldstein & Ruthven, 1983).

In concluding this section, Pediatric CR is presented as an example of a rapidly growing area within CR that is in need of a guiding model (see Brown & Morgan, this volume). Pediatric CR presents special challenges to the rehabilitationist, partly due to theoretical uncertainty. The pediatric cognitive rehabilitationist is confronted with a lack of informed direction as to how to proceed. This confusion is due largely to the existence of: (1) conflicting conceptions of the cognitive system, (2) varied explanations of cognitive development, and (3) insufficient information regarding brain-behavior relationships in children (Szekeres et al., 1985). Professionals are forced then to rely on a variety of theoretical frameworks, most of them borrowed from the field of special education, which involve children with congenital rather than acquired learning deficits (Szekeres et al., 1985). The CR framework that has evolved borrows from: behaviorism (Bandura, 1977; Skinner, 1969); the structural-organismic viewpoint (Flavell, 1977); information-processing models of cognitive development (Dodd & White, 1980); and theories of brain-behavior relationships (Luria, 1980).

Despite these difficulties, a number of component processes or systems have been found useful thus far in pediatric CR. These include: (1) attentionnal processes, (2) encoding, (3) permanent knowledge storage, (4) motivation, (5) search functions and executive systems, and (6) expression (Szekeres et al., 1985). Szekeres and co-workers have also found the "system" (e.g., memory) versus "process" (e.g., attentionnal processes) theoretical distinction to be helpful clinically. These rehabilitationists envision cognition as consisting of *component processes*, such as attention, perception, memory and language, *systems*, such as working memory, long term memory, and response systems, *performance variables* (e.g., "scope"--the type of situations in which performance is affected), and *functional-integrative performance* . Clearly, however, much work at the theory validation level needs to be done to provide a more solid basis on which pediatric CR may proceed.

The Science-Practice Interface

Evaluating Treatment Effectiveness

The need to develop theory-based interventions with certain attendant predictions and then to test these predictions through outcome studies is clear. For example, one might predict that the cognitive-behavioral techniques of proven effectiveness for insuring generalization of treatment effects (Meichenbaum, 1980) in other populations will not do the same for head-injured clients. For example, will a frontal lobe patient with Goldstein's (1948) loss of the "abstract attitude" be able to move from very specific strategies to more general strategies and apply them to a situation in the same general category as the one in which he was trained to use them? This is an empirical question which requires research.

Furthermore, it is predicted that the question of justifying CR from sound rational-theoretical standpoint and proving its effectiveness through empirical research studies will become an issue of paramount importance. Given the steep cost of most CR programs and of rehabilitation in general, agencies such as state Vocational Rehabilitation Divisions are asking "Given the expense, is there any evidence that it works?" Before we have even answered this question, however, such agencies are already beginning to say, "We don't care if it improves their cognitive abilities or not, the question is will it improve them enough for them to ever return to work?" This call for accountability is also spreading to the federal level (Baylor Institute for Rehabilitation, 1985). Clearly, professionals in the field of CR must begin conducting outcome studies to support the use and expense of CR techniques.

In the absence of compelling outcome studies, however, a clear theoretical rationale as to why cognitive retraining *should* work would go a long way toward buying time for such outcome studies. Findings such as those of Knight and Wooles (1980) in their review of organic amnesia, in which they conclude that it is unknown whether or not CR enhances the ability of organic amnesia patients to retain information in long term memory, are not encouraging. On the other hand, studies such as Kewman et al. (1985), in which simulated exercises significantly improved actual driving skills, lend support to rehabilitationists working on the remediation of cognitive skills.

Cost-containment procedures in many federal and state agencies may soon force rehabilitationists to decide such things as, given the limited resources, is CR with the elderly going to have enough impact on their functioning to justify the cost? The human side of such a decision is drawn into sharp focus when one is faced with the situation in which there may be enough money to cognitively rehabilitate one person and the rehabilitationist must choose between the traumatically head-injured 10 year old boy and the 50 year old stroke patient. Such choices will be extremely difficult. Hard research evidence of the relative effectiveness of CR with different etiology groups, age ranges, and even socio-economic groups, needs to be done to assist the practitioner in making these decisions.

Structuring Treatment and Developing Innovations

Although many techniques have been developed within CR in the last 20 years (Incagnoli & Newman, 1985), these techniques and the knowledge gained about CR over this time period needs a framework in which to fit, i.e., some theoretical base or means of organizing and explaining the knowledge base.

Along these lines, Miller (1984) has proposed three main practical theories for clinical application: 1) artifact theory, supported by von Monakow's, 1914, diaschisis theory, 2) reorganization theory, supported by Jackson's (1869) hierarchical model, and 3) functional adaptation theory, derived from Luria's (1980) theory of functional systems. This latter theory sets the goal of therapy as either restitution or amelioration of dysfunction, with Miller declaring that, given what we know about the limited plasticity of the central nervous system, amelioration appears the more sensible goal.

The neuropsychological theories of Luria and others have been used to develop rehabilitation program principles, such as those in use at Hawaii State Hospital. For example, Craine (1982) cites the influence of Jackson's (1869) hierarchically-arranged functions, the concept of multiple control of function (Rosner, 1970), and von Monakow's (1914) diaschisis theory in principle 1 used in their program: "The plasticity of function within the central nervous system provides the basis for structuring neurotraining activities to promote and enhance recovery from brain damage" (p. 86).

In another example, Piasetsky (1982) has applied Lurian theory with an environmentalist emphasis in discussing his conception of "functional organization." In his scheme, he argues that the "intent" of the organism is to establish organized functional units into complex behavioral activities. He further states that the "ongoing operations of processing activities becomes schematized in recognition of a set of experienced results" (p. 126). These results, of course, could also be termed "reinforcement" or "contingencies".

Forms of intervention in CR that have evolved from such models include: 1) facilitation of spontaneous neurologic recovery through graded stimulation tasks, 2) direct retraining of cognitive task components through targeted drill and practice, 3) retraining functional-integrative skills--from "component" or molecular retraining to skills that are actual functional behaviors--through practice, such as organizing a job task, 4) environmental compensation, such as adjustments in physical and social environments, and 5) personal compensation in which the patient deliberately compensates for deficits that remain despite targeted component practice. Training also exists at the "subcomponent" level, such as perceptual-motor exercises for reading maps, but this has been shown to be only marginally effective in improving the component processes and has little effect on functional-integrative skills (Kavale & Mattson, 1983).

Equally fruitful has been the application of cognitive psychology's decision-making research and problem-solving research to CR. Craik and Lockhart (1972) have outlined three basic processes in problem-solving: (1) translation of the problem into a model, (2) operating on the model to make necessary deductions, and (3) retranslation back to the problem situation. Such step-by-step cognitive strategies have been used by rehabilitationists such as Ben-Yishay (1980) in task-analyzing problem-solving behavior and breaking it down into its components in order to retrain it.

Parill-Burnstein (1981) also used information-processing theory to develop ways to remediate information-processing deficits. Among the suggestions were: (1) segment the work periods, (2) use training techniques to focus attention and facilitate rehearsal, (3) avoid the presentation of competing cues with relevant information, and (4) use instructions to increase self-monitoring skills.

The further influence of cognitive theory is seen in these rehabilitation recommendations developed from neopiagetian theory: (1) teaching should be initiated at the level of development of the patient, (3) exercises should be designed that encourage transition from one stage to the next, (3) operational structures that underlie specific tasks should be identified through a structural analysis, (4) assessment of current functioning should be done, and (5) this assessment should be followed by the establishment of an instructional design or sequence of instructions (Adamovich et al., 1985). This also means that discrimination learning should proceed by way of gradual "cognitive distancing." That is, representations of experience should proceed from the concrete to the abstract, e.g., objects to pictures to words.

Facilitating change in cognitive performance may involve a cross-fertilization from various theoretical bases (Szekeres et al., 1985). Piagetian concepts of assimilation and accommodation may serve as guidelines for controlling tasks and environmental factors in treatment, e.g., allowing the client to proceed at a pace that will not cause "overload" (resulting in withdrawal, denial, and lack of cooperation), but neither allowing such lassitude that the cognitive system is never challenged to go beyond assimilation into changing schematizations to accommodate radically-different information. Concepts of learning theory, emphasizing social, emotional, and cognitive feedback or reinforcement to motivate or direct change in the client have also been added to the armamentarium of the rehabilitationist.

As can be seen, most CR programs were given their initial structure and impetus from the application of preexisting theory. There appears to be a tendency, however, to drift from theory via innovations in practice which lack a clear careful consideration of whether the innovation makes sense theoretically for the treatment of a head-injured person. It immediately becomes an empirical question of "trying it out to see if it works." This trial and error approach has two major dangers: 1) it could conceivably have some negative effects on the individuals undergoing rehabilitation, could hurt the credibility of the field, and could cause rehabilitation funding agencies to become skeptical of CR; 2) it may remove an impetus for further investigation into and advancement of the theories and models that rehabilitators drew upon to develop the programs currently in place. This could lead to a moribund field of practice in which well-reasoned theory-based treatment innovations are not forthcoming.

Implications for Practice

Theory helps impart a "working understanding" of a phenomenon. It helps professionals and families predict and understand behavior that would be distressing under normal circumstances, and provides reference points for multidisciplinary program development and planning, and helps establish an overall focus in intervention (Szekeres et al., 1985). The ultimate implication for the practice of CR then is that clinical practice rooted in theory and buttressed by theory-driven research forms a much firmer, useful, and defensible basis than practice that has evolved from myriad trial-and-error variations on a theme.

Having said this, we reiterate that approximately 63% of the articles obtained from our computerized literature search of the field of cognitive rehabilitation had to do with promulgating CR programs, while less than one fifth were empirical studies of the treatment's efficacy and again less than one fifth were involved with theory or a scholarly review of the field. With the proliferation of techniques over the past decade, coherence and direction for the field are now needed. Noting what has happened in the field of learning disabilities with the apparently ineffective but still-popular perceptual-motor training programs (Kavale & Mattson, 1983), cognitive rehabilitationists need to evaluate CR techniques before "clinical tradition" takes hold and entrenches potentially ineffective techniques in the rehabilitationist's repertoire.

With regard to the implications of theories of brain-behavior relations for rehabilitation, Piasetsky (1982) notes two issues must be considered. These are: 1) How can recovery be understood in terms of the capacity of the central nervous system to respond to injury?, and 2) To what extent may a role for environmental influence or the recovery process be defended? Research on theories of recovery of function appears to be one area vital to the future of CR.

Rehabilitationists must also evaluate their techniques by answering these questions (Cohen, 1970): 1) Does the evidence support the conclusion that, when applied, the method results in improvement?, 2) Are there negative consequences of application of the method? For example, valuable time and money may be wasted with the ineffective treatment, or a "placebo program" may be in place when the problem requires a true remedial effort. The first step here, taking our cue from Cohen's work with perceptual-motor training with learning disabled children, is to conduct the research needed to indicate that the treatment techniques improve the very tasks that they are, e.g., perceptual motor training should improve perceptual motor tasks. Here, as in virtually all CR effectiveness studies, the most important variable to control for is spontaneous recovery.

There is also a clear need to develop treatment programs based on prominent models, such as learning theory, that are tailored to the head-injured client. As noted elsewhere (Goldstein & Ruthven, 1983), behavioral treatment programs tailored for the alcoholic exist, but no such programs are in place for the head-injured. Rather, general behavioral and learning principles have often been applied as they would be applied to any population, sometimes not taking into account that head injury frequently changes certain cognitive functions and the experience of the client such that normal learning cannot take place. "Proven" programs in other areas of intervention, with other disabilities or populations must "prove" themselves with the brain-injured, and such effectiveness data must be collected in well-constructed quasi-experimental treatment studies.

As mentioned in a previous section, cost-benefit analyses are also going to be forced upon rehabilitationists, who are going to have to produce evidence that their programs work, and answer the questions "with whom, when, and for how long" do they work. In a similar vein, follow up on treatment effects and checks on generalizability must be conducted (Incagnoli & Newman, 1985).

Another serious implication for practice is the question of whether brain functions are actually restituted or not. If indeed, functional reorganization at a neurological level occurs, then cognitive retraining exercises aimed at reinstituting or "strengthening" that "weak" functional area are justified. If in fact, no neural recovery occurs, but head-injured individuals must simply learn to do things a different way, using different modalities and brain systems, then a program emphasizing behavioral compensation would seem more sensible (Hartlage, 1975; Henry, 1983; Miller, 1984). Research on theories of recovery of function must take place simultaneously with research on the differential effectiveness of various treatments. Treatment techniques developed from belief in a specific theory of recovery of function would, of course, have implications for the validity of that theory of recovery.

There are also some new factors and populations to consider in CR. Among the areas that need to be addressed in future programs, are "secondary symptoms" of brain injury, such as depression (Brinkman, 1979), while a population that needs to receive CR services is the "silent majority" of head-injured patients; those with mild to moderate head injury. Long, Gouvier, and Cole (1984) have begun to develop a model for service delivery to this population. Another important area of growth in CR, through guidance from cognitive theories of development, should be the field of pediatric CR. As mentioned previously, there are enormous problems in pediatric CR due to the changed nature of the brain following insult, superimposed upon the natural changes in the process of the rapid cognitive development that occurs during childhood, and wide interindividual and intraindividual normal variation in that development (Ylvisaker, 1985).

Implications for Research

Further research to confirm theory is clearly needed. We have illustrated one approach to such research in an earlier section of this chapter, but such research can also take place at the neurophysiological level with biomedical tests, such as the finding that EEG studies indicate that functional neural pathways hypothesized to exist by Luria (1973, 1980) do tend to be activated during the performance of various mental operations (Thatcher & John, 1977). This research may also proceed at the neurophysiological level with human and comparative research on recovery of function mechanisms following central nervous system insult (cf. Marshall, 1984), and in sensitive controlled neuropsychological investigations of human behavioral recovery following head injury (Dikmen, Reitan, & Temkin, 1983).

Theoretical assumptions, of course, guide research. In amnesia research (Knight and Wooles, 1980), the assumption that deficits are absolute and process-specific has lead to investigations into single information-handling processes (encoding, consolidation, or retrieval) and militated against systematic concurrent study of all the processing stages. As is clear in this example, one cautionary note is that, while theory can help structure and guide research, it can also narrow the field of vision of the investigator and cause one to become "theory-bound." The question of whether cognitive processes are restituted or compensated for is another important theoretical research question that bears upon practice. It is noteworthy that, based on the results of post-injury testing on a wide spectrum of neuropsychological criterion measures, it is still not clear to researchers in one of the leading centers for cognitive rehabilitation whether systematic cognitive retraining following head injury is remediation or amelioration (Ben-Yishay & Piasetsky, 1985). This is a question researchers need to address in order to plan the types of interventions needed, i.e., whether to play to the clients's neuropsychological strengths or attempt to remediate their weaknesses.

As has been noted, there are a number of areas of growth for CR, with pediatric CR figuring prominently among them. Difficulties encountered in this area, however, include the failure of the field of child development to agree on a theory of cognitive development. Research in pediatric CR might focus on applying differential treatment strategies based on different theories of child cognitive development and comparing effectiveness. While such studies may not speak to the controversy in normal cognitive development, they would be of tremendous use in the CR of brain-damaged children.

Another important area of research is the question of motivation in the head-injured patient. Piasetsky (1982) has melded Luria's functional systems theory with a behavioral emphasis to develop the idea of "fundamental intent" of the organism. That is, the organism establishes functional brain units into complex behavioral activities based on "recognition of a set of experienced results." He further says that to change the behavior of brain-injured individuals in a broad context, rehabilitationists must devise ways for the organism to experience that context and "intend" it. This appears to us to again address the question of motivation; how to direct the person to *want* to organize his efforts toward a certain ultimate behavior. But it also delves into greater questions of a more phenomenological nature, e.g., what is worth doing?

Along these lines, it may be productive to disinter Vygotsky's original concept of socially-directed "activity" (cf. Kozulin, 1986) as the basis for consciousness and the main driving force behind human behavior. Such a theoretical basis could assist in the development of treatment efforts by emphasizing the central importance of social reinforcement and human relationship context in CR. This should lead to increased emphasis on assessment of environmental variables (social climates and perceived home, work, and hospital ward environments), thus guiding change in environments as a therapeutic or reinforcing tool to create or spur "intent" on the part of the head-injured client.

In summary, the field of CR is in need of some coherent direction and policing through a return to the scientific basis from which it began. We believe this is best done by the people who understand the field, i.e., the irehabilitationists themselves. In this respect, we feel it is incumbent particularly upon academically-trained doctoral psychologists, who have had research training, to spearhead such efforts in rehabilitation settings. As in developmental dyslexia research (Dalby, 1979), we may need to focus on theory articulation and reformulation in addition to methodological and taxonomic advances. This is especially true if none of our few current "theories" seem to fit the data particularly well (cf. Newby et al., 1983; Moehle, Rasmussen, & Fitzhugh-Bell, in preparation). But only by paying greater attention to the development of theoretical rationales for what we are doing and then testing those rationales, as well as the effectiveness of our treatments, along with followup studies and studies regarding *in vivo* generalization, will we be again moving back to placing CR in the realm of solid "science-practice" and contributing to the field and our clients at the level of which we are capable.

The authors gratefully acknowledge the extended and painstaking labors of David Hennon, whose computer skills, critical thinking, and careful analyis of the data were invaluable.

References

Adamovich, B. B., Henderson, J. A., and Auerbach, S. (1985). *Cognitive rehabilitation of head-injured patients: A dynamic approach.* San Diego: College Hill Press.

Adams, K. M. and Grant, I. (1984). Failure of nonlinear models of drinking history variables to predict neuropsychological performance in alcoholics. *American Journal of Psychiatry, 141* (5), 633-667.

Alexy, W. D. (1983). Cognitive rehabilitation: Identifying loss- related concerns. *Cognitive Rehabilitation, 1* (1), 5-6.

Armstrong, J. S. and Soelberg, P. (1968). On the interpretation of factor analysis. *Psychological Bulletin, 70,* 361-364.

Arnoult, M. D. (1972). *Fundamentals of scientific method in psychology.* Dubuque, Iowa: Brown.

Asch, S. E. (1961). Perceptual conditions of association. In M. Hendle (Ed.), *Documents of Gestalt Psychology.* Berkeley, University of California Press.

Atkinson, R. C., & Shiffrin, R. M. (1968). Human memory: A proposed system and its control process. In K. W. Spence, & J. T. Spence (Eds.), *The Psychology of learning and motivation.* (Vol. 2). New York: Academic Press.

Baddeley, A.D. (1982). Implications of neuropsychological evidence for theories of normal memory. *Philosophical Transactions of the Royal Society of London (Biology), 298,* 59-72.

Bandura, A. (1977). *Social learning theory.* Englewood Cliffs, NJ: Prentice Hall.

Barlow, D. H. & Hersen, M. (1984). *Single case experimental designs: Strategies for studying behavior change.* New York: Pergamon Press.

Baylor Institute for Rehabilitation. (1985). *Neuropsychology's role in an objective interdisciplinary treatment model.* Dallas, TX

Beaumont, J. G. (1983). *Introduction to Neuropsychology.* New York: The Guilford Press.

Ben-Yishay, Y., Ratlok, J., Ross, B., Lakin, P., Ezracki, O., Silver, S., & Diller L. (1982). Rehabilitation of cognitive and perceptual defects in people with traumatic brain damage. A five year clinical research study. In *Working approaches to remediation of cognitive deficits in brain-damaged persons* (Rehabilitation Monographs No. 64). New York University Medical Center: Institute of Rehabilitation Medicine, 127 176.

Ben-Yishay, Y. (1983). Working approaches to the remediation of cognitive deficits in brain damaged persons. *Rehabilitation Monographs,* No. 6, 113-126. New York: NYU Medical Center, Institute of Rehabilitation Medicine.

Ben-Yishay, Y. (1983). Cognitive remediation viewed from the perspective of systematic clinical research program in rehabilitation. *Cognitive Rehabilitation, 1,* 4-6.

Ben-Yishay, Y. & Piasetsky, G. (1985). Systematic cognitive retraining following traumatic head injury: Remediation or amelioration?: National Association of Rehabilitation Research and Training Centers Conference: Washington, D. C., May 6-8, 1985.

Bentler, P. M. (1980). Multivariate analysis with latent variables: Causal modeling. *Annual Review of Psychology, 31,* 419-456.

Bentler, P. M., & Bonett, D. G. (1980). Significance tests and goodness of fit in the analysis of covariance structures. *Psychological Bulletin, 88,* 588-606.

Berndt, R. S. & Caramazza, A. (1980). A redefinition of the syndrome of Broca's Aphasia: Implications for a neuropsychological model of language. *Applied Psycholinguistics, 1* (3), 225-278.

Bloom, F. E., H., Barry J., & Siggins, G. E. (1972). Norepinephrine Mediated Cerebellar Synapses: A model system for neuropsychopharmacology. *Biological Psychiatry, 4* (2), 157-177.

Bolger, J. P. (1982). Cognitive Retraining: A developmental approach. *Clinical Neuropsychology, 4* (2), 66-70.

Boll, T. J. (1973). The effect of age and onset of brain damage on adaptive abilities in children. Paper presented at the annual convention of the American Psychological Association, Montreal, Canada.

Boring, E. G. (1957). *A history of experimental psychology.* New York: Appleton Century Crafts.

Bracy, O. L. (1983). Computer based cognitive rehabilitation. *Cognitive Rehabilitation, 1* (1), 7-8.

Bracy, O. L. (1984). *Cognitive Rehabilitation: A process approach.* Paper presented at the Texas State Occupational Therapy Conference, Houston, TX, October.

Brinkman, S. (1979). Rehabilitation of the neurologically impaired patient: The contribution of the neuropsychologist. *Clinical Neuropsychology, 2,* 39-44.

Broadbent, D. D. (1958). *Perception and Communication.* London: Pergamon Press.

Broca, P. (1861). Remarques sur le siege de la faculte du language articule. *Bulletin Societie Anthropologie* 6.

Bruner, J. S. (1964). The course of cognitive growth. *American Psychologist, 19,* 1-15.

Bruner, J. S. (1973). *Beyond the information given.* New York: W. W. Norton.

Buffery, A. W. H. (1974). Clinical neuropsychology: A review and preview. In S. Rachman (Ed.). *Contributions to medical psychology. Vol. I.* Oxford, England: Pergamon Press.

Busse, T. V. & Lighthall, S. (1966). Conceptual retraining of brain-damaged adults, *Perceptual and Motor Skills, 22,* 899-906.

Carberry, H., & Burd, E. (1983). Social aspects of cognitive retraining in an outpatient group setting for head trauma patients. *Cognitive Rehabilitation, 1 ,* 5-7.

Case, R. (1978). Intellectual development from birth to adulthood: A neopiagetian interpretation. In R. Sieglar (Ed.), *Children's Thinking: What Develops?* Hillsdale, NJ: Lawrence Erlbaum Associates.

Chambliss, L. (1982). Movement therapy and the shaping of a neuropsychological model. *American Journal of Dance Therapy, 5,* 18-27.

Chaplin, J. P., & Draviec, T. S. (1960). *Systems and theories of psychology.* New York: Holt, Rinehart, & Winston.

Cohen, H. J., Birch, H. G., & Taft, L. T. (1970). Some considerations for evaluations: The Doman-Delacato "patternizing" method. *Pediatrics, 45,* 302-314.

Cooke, N. S. (1973). Neuropsychology: From theory into practice. *Newsletter for Research In Mental Health and Behavioral Sciences, 15 ,* 43-46.

Craik, F. I. M. & Lockhart, R. S. (1972). Levels of processing: A framework for memory research. *Journal of Verbal Learning and Verbal Behavior, II,* 671-684.

Craine, J. F. (1982). Principles of cognitive rehabilitation. In Trexler, L. E. (Ed.), *Cognitive Rehabilitation: Conceptualization and Intervention.* New York: Plenum Press.

Craine, J. F., & Gudeman, H. E. (1981). *The Rehabilitation of brain functions: Principles, procedures and techniques of neurotraining*. Springfield, IL: Charles C. Thomas.

Dalby, J. T. (1979). Deficit or delay: Neuropsychological models of developmental dyslexia. *Journal of Special Education, 13* (3), 239-264.

Dikmen, S., Reitan, R., & Temkin, N. (1983). Neuropsychological recovery in head injury. *Archives of Neurology, 40*, 333-338.

Diller, L. (1976). A model for cognitive retraining in rehabilitation. *Clinical Psychologist, 29* (2), 13-15.

Diller, L., & Gordon, W. (1981). Interventions for cognitive deficits in brain-injured adults. *Journal of Consulting and Clinical Psychology, 49*, 822-834.

Dixon, W. J. (1981). *BMDP Statistical Software 1981*. Berkeley, CA: University of California Press.

Dodd, D., & White, R. M. (1980). *Cognitive mental structures and processes*. Boston: Allyn & Bacon.

Edelstein, B. & Couture, E. T. (1984). *Behavioral assessment and rehabilitation of the traumatically brain-damaged*. New York: Plenum Press.

Egeland, B. (1974). Training impulsive children in the use of more efficient scanning techniques. *Child Development, 45*, 165-171.

Ehrlich, J. S., & Sipes, A. L. (1985). Group treatment of communication skills for head trauma patients. *Cognitive Rehabilitation, 3* (1), 32-37.

Ensley, G., Maclean, J., & Lewark, N. (1984). The rehabilitation care approach to cognitive retraining: A success story at Portsmouth General Hospital. *Cognitive Rehabilitation, 2* (2), 8-11.

Feeney, D. M., Pittman, J. C., & Wagner, H. R. (1974). Lateral inhibition and attention: Comments on the neuropsychological theory of Walley and Weiden. *Psychological Review, 81* (6), 536-539.

Fernald, G. M. (1943). *Remedial Techniques in Basic School Subjects*. New York: McGraw-Hill.

Finset, A. (1984). Re-integrating ou regulerings funksjonersom nevropsykologisk behandlings strategi. (Re-integration of regulatory functions as a neuropsychological treatment strategy.) *Fidsskift For Norsk Psykologforening, 21* (3), 127-135.

Fitzhugh, K. & Fitzhugh, L. (1965). Effects of early and later onset of cerebral dysfunction upon psychological test performance. *Perceptual and Motor Skills, 20* 1099-1100.

Flavell, J. H. (1977). *Cognitive development*. Englewood Cliffs, NJ: Prentice Hall.

Flourens, P. (1924). Recherches experimentales sur les prprietes et les fouctious du systeme nerveux deus les animoux nertefres. Paris: Cervot.

Freeman, R. (Ed.). (1979). *Developmental Neurobiology of vision*. New York: Plenum Press.

Fritsch, G., & Hitzig, E. (1960). On the electrical excitability of the cerebrum. In G. Van Borin (Ed.), *The cerebral cortex*. Springfield, IL: Charles C. Thomas.

Fuld, P. A. & Fisher, P. (1977). Recovery of intellectual ability after closed head injury. *Developmental Medicine and Child Neurology, 19*, 495- 502.

Gaddes, W. H. (1983). Applied educational neuropsychology: Theories and problems. *Journal of Learning Disabilities, 16* (9), 511-514.

Galton, F. (1883). *Inquiries into faculty and its development*. London: MacMillan.

Gazzaniga, M. (1984). *Handbook of Cognitive Neuroscience*. New York: Plenum Press.

German, D. (1971). Advantages and disadvantages of sub-human animal models for human neuropsychology. *Biological Psychology Bulletin, 1* (1), 24-28.

Geschwind, N. (1965). Disconnexion syndromes in animals and man. *Brain, 88*, 237-294,.

Gholson, B., Levine, M., & Phillips, S. (1972). Hypothesis strategies and stereotypes in discrimination learning. *Journal of Experimental Child Psychology, 13*, 423-446.

Gianutsos, R. (1980). What is cognitive rehabilitation? *Journal of Rehabilitation*, 36-40, July-Sept.

Gianutsos, R., & Grynbaum, B. B. (1983). Helping brain-injured people to contend with hidden cognitive deficits. *International Journal of Rehabilitation Medicine, 5* (1), 37-40.

Gilandas, A., Tauyz, S., Beumont, P. J. V., & Greenberg, H. P. (1984). *Handbook of neuropsychological Assessment*. New York: Grune & Stratton.

Goldstein, K. (1948). *Language and Language Disorders*. Grune & Stratton: New York City.

Goldstein, S. G. (1976). The neuropsychological model: interface and overlap with clinical psychology. *Clinical Psychologist, 29* (2), 7-8.

Goldstein, G. (1979). Methodological and theoretical issues in neuropsychological assessment. *Journal of Behavioral Assessment, 1*, 23-41.

Goldstein, L. H., & Oakley, D. A. (1985). Expected and actual behavioral capacity after diffuse reduction in cerebral cortex. A review and suggestions for rehabilitative techniques with the mentally handicapped and head-injured. *British Journal of Clinical Psychology*, Feb. 24 (Pt.1), 13-24.

Goldstein, G. & Ruthven, L. (1983). *Rehabilitation of the brain-damaged adult*. New York and London: Plenum Press.

Gordon, N. G. (1977). Base rates and the decision making model in clinical neuropsychology. *Cortex, 13* (1), 3-10.

Greenough, W. T. (1976). Enduring brain effects of differential experience and training. In M. R. Rosenzuelig, & E. L. Bennett, (Eds.), *Neural mechanisms of learning and memory.* Cambridge, MA: M. I. T. Press

Gummow, L., Miller, P., & Dustman, R. E. (1983). Attention and brain injury: A case for cognitive rehabilitation of attentionnal deficits. *Clinical Psychology Review, 3,* 255-274.

Guilford, J. P. (1954). A factor analytic study across the domains of reasoning, creativity, and evaluation: Hypotheses and descriptions of tests. *Reports from the Psychological Laboratory.* Los Angels, CA: University of Southern California Press.

Halstead, W. C. (1947). *Brain and intelligence: a quantitative study of the frontal lobes.* Chicago: University of Chicago Press.

Hartlage, L. (1975). Neuropsychological approach to predicting outcome of remedial educational strategies for learning disabled children. *Journal of Pediatric Psychology, 3* (3), 23-24.

Head, H. (1926). *Aphasia and kindred disorders of speech.* New York: Hafner.

Henry, K. (1984). Cognitive rehabilitation and the head-injured child. *Journal of Children In Contemporary Society, 16* (1-2), 189-205.

Honeggar, B. (1980). A neuropsychological theory of automatic verbal behavior. *Parapsychology Review, 1* (4), 1-8.

Horoszswski, B. (1983). Lurijas neuropsykologiska teori. "Science" or "Fiction." *Nordisk Psykologi, 35* (4), 255-271.

Horton, 1979. BNP newsletter. cr72

Howard, J. L., & Pollard, G. T. (1983). Are primate models of neuropsychiatric disorders useful to the pharmaceutical industry? *Progress in Clinical Biological Research, 131,* pp 307-312.

Incagnoli, T., & Newman, B. (1985). Cognitive and behavioral rehabilitation interventions. *International Journal of Clinical Neuropsychology, 7* (4), 173-182.

Jackson, J. H. (1869). *Selected writings, Vol. 2.* New York: Basic Books.

Johnston, C. W., & Diller, L. (1983). Error evaluation ability of right-hemisphere brain-lesioned patients who have had perceptual-cognitive retraining. *Journal of Clinical Neuropsychology, 5* (4), 401-402.

Joreskog, K. G., & Sorbon, D. (1984). *LISREL VI Analysis of linear structural relationships by the method of maximum likelihood.* Mooresville, IN: Scientific Software, Inc.

Kaplan, E. (1985). Overview of the process approach to adult neuropsychological assessment. Paper presented at *The Process Approach To Child and Adult Neuropsychological Assessment Sypmposium.* Dallas, TX.

Kaufman, A. S. (1984). K-ABC and controversy. *Journal of Special Education, 18,* (3), 409-444.

Kavale, K., & Mattson, P. (1983). "One jumped off the balance beam." Multi-analysis of perceptual motor training. *Journal of Learning Disabilities, 16,* 165-173.

Kephart, N. C. (1968). *Learning disability An educational adventure.* West Lafayette, Indiana: Kappa Delta Pi Press

Kerlinger, F. N. (1979). *Behavioral research: A conceptual approach.* Chicago: Holt, Rinehart and Winston.

Kershner, J. R. (1967). An investigation of the doman-delacato theory of neuropsychology as it applies to trainable mentally retarded children in public schools. (Available from Pennsylvania State Department of Public Instruction, Harrisburg, PA. SYN71775).

Kershner, J. R. & Bauer, D. H. (1966). Neuropsychological and perceptual-motor theories of treatment for children with educational inadequacies. (Available from Pennsylvania State Department of Public Instruction, Harrisburg, PA. Bureau of Research Administration and Coordination. BBB00377).

Kewman, D. G., et. al. (1985). Simulation training of psychomotor skills: Teaching the brain-injured to drive. *Rehabilitation Psychology, 30* (1), 11-27.

Kim, J., & Mueller, C. W. (1978). *Introduction to factor analysis.* Beverly Hills, CA: Sage.

Klove, H. (1963). Clinical neuropsychology. In F. M. Forster (Ed.). *Medical Clinics of North America.* New York: Saunders.

Kluve. H. (1957). *Behavior mechanisms in monkeys.* Chicago: University of Chicago Press.

Knight, R. & Wooles, I. (1980). Experimental investigation of chronic organic amnesia. A review. *Psychological Bulletin, 88* (3), 753-771.

Koukkou, M. & Lehmann, D. (1983). Dreaming: The functional state-shift hypothesis: A neuropsychophysiological model. *British Journal of Psychiatry, 142,* 221-231.

Koyulin, A. (1986). The concept of activity in Soviet psychology. Vygotsky, his disciples, and critics. *American Psychologist, 41,* 264-274.

Lakin, P. Ben-Yishay, Y., Ross, B., Rattok, Silver, S., Thomas, L., & Diller, L. (1982). Formulating and implementing the remedial treatment plan for head trauma patients in rehabilitation. In working approaches to remediation of cognitive deficits in brain-damaged persons. *Rehabilitation Mono - graph No. 64.* New York: New York University Medical Center, Institute of Rehabilitation Medicine.

Lachman, R., Lachman, J. L., & Butterfield, E. C. (1979). *Cognitive psychology and information processing: An introduction.* Hillsdale, NJ: Erlbaum, West.

Lashley, K. (1929). *Brain mechanisms and intelligence.* Chicago. University of Chicago Press.

Lewinsohn, P. M. & Graf, M. (1973). A follow-up study of persons referred for vocational rehabilitation who have suffered brain damage. *Journal of Community Psychology, 1,* 57-62.

Lezak, M. D. (1976). *Neuropsychological Assessment.* New York: Oxford University Press.

Lezak, M. D. (1979). Recovery of memory and learning functions following traumatic brain injury. *Cortex, 15,* 63-72.

Loeb, J. (1902). *Comparative physiology of the brain and comparative psychology.* New York. Putnam Press.

Long, C. J., Gouvier, W. D., & Cole, J. C. (1984). Model of recovery for the total rehabilitation of individuals with head trauma. *Journal of Rehabilitation, 50* (1), 39-45, 70.

Luria, A. R. (1961). The Role of Speech in Regulation of Normal and Abnormal Behaviour. London: Pergamon Press.

Luria, A. R. (1980). *Higher cortical functions in man.* Second Edition, Revised and Expanded. New York: Basic Books.

Luria, A. R. (1972). *The man with a shattered world.* New York: Basic Books.

Luria, A. R. (1948/1963). *Restoration of function after brain injury.* New York: MacMillan.

Majovski, L. V. (1984). The K-ABC: Theory and applications for child neuropsychological assessment and research. *Journal of Special Education, 18* (3), 257-268.

Marshall, J. F. (1984). Brain function: Neural adaptations and recovery from injury. *Annual Review of Psychology, 35,* 277-308.

Maruszewski, M.. (1973). Theoretical and practical aspects of neuropsychological research. *Studia Psycho - logiczne, 12,* 5-25.

Marx, M. H. & Hillix, W. A. (1963). *Systems and theories in psychology.* New York: McGraw-Hill.

Maruszewski, M. (1969). Neuropsychology in neurological rehabilitation. *International Journal of Psychology, 4* (1), 73-75.

McFarland, K. (1983). Syndrome analysis in clinical neuropsychology. *British Journal Clinical Psychology, 22,* 61-74.

Meichenbaum, D. (1980). Cognitive behavior modification with exceptional children: A promise yet unfulfilled. *Exceptional Education Quarterly, 1,* (1), 83-88.

Milner, B. (1970). Memory and the medial temporal regions of the brain. In K. H. Pribram and D. E. Broadbent (Ed.), *International review of research in mental retardation.* New York: Academic Press.

Miran, M. & Miran, E. (1984). Cerebral asymmetries: neuropsychological measurement and theoretical issues. *Biological Psychology, 19,*(3-4), pp 295-304.

Moehle, K. A., Rasmussen, J. L., & Fitzhugh-Bell, K. B. (1986). *Confirmatory factor analysis of neuropsychological models.* Manuscript in preparation.

Nebes, R. D. (1974). Hemispheric specialization in commissurotimized man. *Psychological Bulletin, 81,* 1-14.

Newby, R. F., Hallenbeck, C. E., & Embretson, S. (1983). Confirmatory factor analysis of four general neuropsychological models with a modified Halstead-Reitan Battery. *Journal of Clinical Neuropsychology, 5* (2), 115-133.

Orbzut, John E., & Obrzut, Ann (1982). Neuropsychological perspectives in pupil services: Practical application of Luria's model. *Journal of Research and Development In Education, 15* (3), 38-47.

Oliver, J. III, Shaller, C. A., Majovski, L. V., & Jacques, S. (1982). Stroke mechanisms: Neuropsychological implications. *Clinical Neuropsychology, 4* (2), 81-83.

Paneth, G., (1982). Rorschach B-Valaszok, A felettes-en es A mubrotalmi kus rendszer. Egy neuropzichologiai teoria, vazlater. (M answers in Roschach's test the sugeryo and the Rubrothenlamic system: The network of neuropsychological theory). *Magyar Pszichologiai Szemle, 38* (6), 541- 550.

Parill-Burnstein, M. (1981). *Problem-solving and learning dis abilities: An information-processing approach.* New York: Grune & Stratton.

Piaget, J. (1952). *The origins of intelligence in children.* New York: International University Press.

Piaget, J. (1983). Piagetian theory. In W. Kene (Ed.), *Handbook of child psychology, Vol. 1, History, theory, and methods* (pp 103-128). New York: John Wiley & Sons, Inc.

Piasetsky, E. B. (1982). The relevance of brain -behavior relation ships for rehabilitation. In Trexler, L. E. (Ed.), *Cognitive Rehabilitation: Conceptualization and Intervention*. New York: Plenum Press.

Pontius, A. A. (1984). Model of ecological (cultural) evolutionary neuropsychiatry. *Perceptual and Motor Skills, 58* (1), 143-148.

Proceedings of the symposium on primate ethopharmacology, IX congress of the International Primatological Society. Atlanta, Georgia, August 1982.

Radouco, T. S., Garcin, F., Denver, D., Gaudreault, V., & Radouco, Thomas C. (1980). A possible "eco-pharmacogenetic" model in neuropsychopharmacology. Aspects of alcoholism and pharmacodependence. *Progress In Neuropsychopharmacology , 4* (3), pp 313-315.

Rao, S. M. & Bieliauskas, L. (1983). Cognitive rehabilitation two and one-half years post right temporal lobectomy. *Journal of Clinical Neuropsychology, 5* (4), 313-320.

Reitan, R. M. (1966). A research program on the psychological effects of brain lesions in human beings. In N. R. Ellis (Ed.), *International review of research in mental retardation. Vol, I.* New York: Academic Press.

Reitan, R. (1979). *Manual for administration of neuropsychological test batteries for adults and children.* Tucson, AZ:

Reitan, R. M. & Davison, L. A. (1974). *Clinical Neuropsychology: Current status and applications.* New York: Winston/Wiley.

Rosenthal, M., Griffith, E. R., Bond, M. R., & Miller, J. D. (1983). *Rehabilitation of the head-injured adult.* Philadelphia: F. A. Davis.

Rosner, B. S. (1970). Brain functions. *Annual Review of Psychology, 21,* 555-594.

Rourke, B. P. (1982). Central processing deficiencies in children: Toward a developmental neuropsychological model. *Journal of Clinical Neuropsychology, 4* (1), 1-18.

Royce, J. R. (1973). The conceptual framework for a multifactor theory of individuality. In J. R. Royce (Ed.), *Multivariate analysis and psychological theory.* London: Academic Press.

Royce, J. R., Yeudall, L. T., & Bock, C. (1976). Factor analytic studies of human brain damage: I. First and second order factors and their brain correlates. *Multivariate Behavioral Research, 11,* 381418.

Sbordone, R. J. (1985). A model for neuropsychological rehabilitation planning. Presented at the meeting of the American Psychological Association.

St. James-Roberts, I. (1979). Neurological plasticity, recovery from brain insult, and child development. *Advances In Child Development and Behavior, 14* 253-319.

Sharlock, D. P., Tweker, T. J., & Strominger, N. L. (1963). Auditory discrimination by the cat after neonatal oblation of the trasporal cortex. *Science, 141,* 1197-1198.

Shaywitz, B. A., Wolf, A., Shaywitz, S. E., Loomis, R., & Cohen, D. J. (1982). Animal models of neuropsychiatric disorders and their relevance for Tourette syndrome. *Advances in Neurology, 35,* 199-202.

Skinner, B. F. (1969). *Contingencies of Reinforcement.* New York: Appleton Century-Crafts.

Smith, M. P. & Means, J. R. (1961). Effects of type of stimulus pertaining on discrimination learning in mentally retarded. *American Journal of Mental Deficiency, 66,* 259-265.

Spearman, C. (1904). General intelligence, objectively determined and measured. *American Journal of Psychology, 15,* 201-293.

Sperry, R. W. (1973). Lateral specialization of cerebral function in the surgically separated hemisphere. In F. J. McGuigan, & R. A. Schoonover (Eds.), *The Psychophysiology of thinking.* New York: Academic Press.

Swiercinsky, D. (1978). *Manual for the adult neuropsychological evaluation.* Springfield, IL: Charles C. Thomas.

Swiercinsky, D. P. Factorial pattern description and comparison of functional abilities in neuropsychological assessment. *Perceptual and Motor Skills, 48,* 231-241.

Szekeres, S. F., Ylvisaker, M., & Holland, A. L. (1985). Cognitive rehabilitation therapy: A framework for intervention. In Ylvisaker, Mark (Ed.), *Head Injury Rehabilitation.* San Diego: College Hill Press.

Tabachnick, B. G. & Fidell, L. S. (1978). *Using multivariate statistics.* New York: Harper & Row.

Thatcher, R. W. & John, E. R. (1977). *Foundation of Cognitive Processes.* Hillsdale, NJ: Laurence Earlbaum Associates.

Thurstone, L. L. & Thurstone, T. G. (1941). Factorial studies of intelligence. *Psychometric Monographs, No. 2.* Chicago: University of Chicago Press.

Timney, B. & Mitchell, D. (1979). Behavioral recovery from visual deprivation: Comments on the critical period. In R. Freeman (Ed.), *Developmental Neurobiology of Vision.* New York: Plenum Press

Tress, W. (1981). Perspektiven der neuropsychologie fur theorien de psychopathologie. (Perspectives of neuropsychology for theories of psychopathology.). *Zeitschrift Fur Klinische Psychologie Und Psychotherapie, 29* (1), 79-87.

Tsvetkova, L. S. (1972). Basic principles of theory of redirection of brain-injured patients. *Journal of Special Education, 6,* 135-144.

Tupper, D. E. & Rosenblood, L. K. (1984). Methodological considerations in the use of attribute variables in neuropsychological research. *Journal of Clinical Neuropsychology, 6* (4), 441-453.

Von Monakow, C. (1914). *Die Lokalisation im Grosshirn und der Abbau der Fundtionen durch cortical Herde.* Wiesbaden: Bergmann.

Usprich, A. (1976). The study of dyslexia: Two nascent trends and a neuropsychological model. *Bulletin of the Orton Society, 26,* 34-48.

Walley, R. E., & Weiden, T. D. (1973). Lateral inhibition and cognitive masking: A neuropsychological theory of attention. *Psychological Review, 80* (4), 284-302.

Warnock, J. K., & Mintz, S. I. (1979). Investigation of models of brain functioning through a factor analytic procedure of neuropsychological data. *Clinical Neuropsychology, 1* (4), 43-48.

Webster, W. G. (1985). Neuropsychological models of stuttering I. Representation of sequential response mechanisms. *Neuropsychologia, 23* (2), 263-267.

Webster's Handy College Dictionary. (1961). Albert & Loy Morehead (Eds.). New York and Toronto: Signet Reference Book.

Wechsler, D. (1955). *Manual for the Wechsler Adult Intelligence Scale.* New York: The Psychological Corporation.

Wechsler, D. (1981). *Wechsler Adult Intelligence Scale-Revised.* New York: The Psychological Corporation.

Wetzel, A. B., Thompson, V., Horel, J., & Meyer, P. M. (1965). Some consequences of perinatal lesions of the visual cortex in the cat. *Psychonomic Science, 3,* 381-382.

Wilson, P. B. (1983). Software selection and use in language and cognitive retraining. *Cognitive Rehabilitation, 1* (1), 9-10.

Wood, G. (1977). *Fundamentals of psychological research.* Boston: Little, Brown, & Company.

Wood, R. (1982). Behavioural disturbance and behavioural management. In *New directions in the neuropsychology of severe blunt head injury.* Symposium presented at the meeting of the International Neuropsychological Society, Deauville, France.

Yesavage, J. A., & Rose, T. L. (1983). Concentration and mnemonic training in elderly subjects with memory complaints: A study of combined therapy and order effects. *Psychiatry Research, 9* (2), 157-167.

Ylvisaker, M. (1985). *Head Injury Rehabilitation: Children and Adolescents.* San Diego, CA: College-Hill Press.

Part Two: The Practice of Cognitive Rehabilitation

5

The Current Status of Computer-Assisted Cognitive Rehabilitation

Charles J. Long

Millions of children and young adults suffer from brain impairment due to inborn or acquired disorders. For example, in the U.S. alone there are approximately 10 million head injuries each year. Whether due to head trama or other causes, damage to the nervous system often impairs the individual's cognitive functions. Unless accurately diagnosed and remediated, such impairment can lead to more generalized behavioral problems involving emotional, vocational, and/or social adjustment.

Most of these neurologically impaired individuals are in need of cognitive rehabilitation. In the case of head trauma, the needs are clear and are attested to by the recent development of treatment programs throughout the U.S. The majority of these programs are based on total stimulation by multidisciplinary teams of health care professionals. Such rehabilitation is a slow, laborious task which for some is prohibitively expensive. In addition to the time factor, cognitive rehabilitation is expensive because a low staff/patient ratio is required when working with patients who characteristically demonstrate impaired attention/concentration, impaired perception, slowed information processing, language problems, and/or memory problems requiring clear presentation of material in a repetitive manner. Any developments that will aid in identifying more selective treatment strategies and/or reduce direct professional contact time will reduce costs and make services available to more individuals.

At the present time, there are few published studies clearly indicating significant benefits with selective treatment strategies; however, case study reports indicate that the "total stimulation" approach often produces improved performance. The primary question is not can we augment recovery of neurological impairment, but how can we augment recovery in a cost effective manner. There are good reasons to believe that computer assisted cognitive rehabilitation is one means toward that end.

The Process of Recovery: Limiting Factors, Causes and Effects

While the "mechanics" of recovery after acquired dysfunction are poorly understood, testable changes have been shown to follow a negatively accelerated curve (Figure 1). The patient may initially be rendered comatose by the trauma. Recovery from coma frequently has no clear end point. Rather, the patient has increasingly frequent lucid periods and/or gradually lengthening periods of awareness. Recovery of awareness may progress to a period of post- traumatic amnesia (PTA). This period is generally longer than coma and is characterized primarily by impaired memory consolidation. Like coma, recovery from PTA is gradual. After PTA has cleared, the majority of patients will have normal CT Scans and EEG's and appear medically stable. However, cognitive functions may be 40% to 60% below premorbid level. It is during this time, and at this level of recovery, that the patient is at risk for developing "non-organic" complications: accordingly, it is at this time that neuropsychological assessment is most useful in determining the overall level of functioning, identifying primary areas of weakness, and educating the patient and family in understanding the problems following head injury and to assist them in formulating an effective treatment plan.

Research has shown that the parameters of the recovery curve are determined by at least six factors: 1) preinjury status of the individual; 2) damage to the brain and/or secondary insult (location, extent, and type of pathology); 3) effects of brain damage on cognitive functioning; 4) emotional adjustment; 5) social-environmental adjustment; and 6) vocational skills and demands. Since one or more of these factors may present special barriers to a favorable outcome in a given case, effective treatment planning requires an understanding of each of these six areas as well as their interrelations.

Two of the six factors -- the preinjury status of the individual as well as damage to the brain are constants in that neither can be directly modified by rehabilitation (Figure 2). These two factors co-determine the nature and severity of cognitive dysfunction, the slope of the recovery curve during the acute phase, and the maximum level of asymptotic recovery that can possibly be obtained. While specific cognitive deficits vary according to the location and extent of the pathology and pre-existing competencies, there are certain general characteristics often present with traumatic injury to the brain. These include inattention, distractibility, poor motivation, reduced speed and efficiency of information processing, inability to plan or to subdivide material, difficulty focusing on salient cues, ineffective use of feedback, and poor visual search. Within limits, in part determined by the two constant factors, these difficulties tend to resolve over time. However, the rate and level of recovery can be affected by cognitive rehabilitation treatments. Often poor social and vocational adjustment can be directly related to impaired cognitive functions.   Similarly, the development of emotional problems, though typically reactive in nature, can be related to reduced coping skills associated with impairment in cognitive functions (Long & Novack,

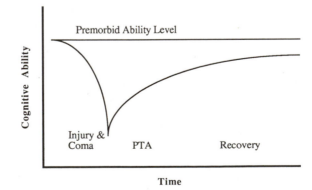

Figure 1. Time Course of Injury and Recovery

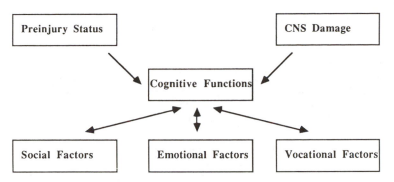

Figure 2. Factors Influencing the Course of Rehabilitation

1985). These reactive problems can, in turn, attenuate cognitive efficiency. With respect to intervention, then, we see that early diagnosis and treatment of cognitive difficulties is crucial for remediation.

Cognitive Rehabilitation

Intervention begins with a comprehensive neuropsychological assessment of cognitive deficits, competencies, and skill strengths as well as emotional/personological characteristics, social adjustment, environmental stressors and occupational demands. These data are used to outline the individual's strengths and deficits (Diller & Gordon, 1981). Rehabilitation strategies, regardless of specific orientation, ultimately are designed to reduce the impact of the deficit on the individual's life (Miller, 1980). Most strategies focus upon the consequences of cognitive dysfunction, that is, on the impact that cognitive dysfunction has on social, vocational, and emotional behavior. When the focus becomes more specific to cognitive rehabilitation, rather than involving the other aspects of behavior, the results are less convincing, perhaps attesting to the fact that most neuropsychological deficits turn out to be very complex, requiring complex treatment strategies.

Cognitive rehabilitation may involve either direct retraining of impaired function or training of alternative methods to accomplish a task. The particular rehabilitation approach should be governed by the type and extent of the deficits. As recovery progresses these deficits may change. In fact, some are not observable until demands are placed on the individual.

Initially the barriers to recovery may be largely cognitive and relate to attentional deficits, later the barriers relate more to memory deficits. As recovery progresses, the impairment in cognitive functions begins to influence other factors and new barriers to recovery may become prominent. Even after significant recovery, impaired learning and information processing continue and exert a persistent and often subtle influence on the patient's behavior. The cognitive weaknesses make it difficult, if not impossible for the patient to work or to function socially (Heaton & Pendleton, 1981; Lezak, 1978; Stein & Riessman, 1980). Finally emotional factors must be reckoned with as they are usually the most protracted and can be the most devastating (Newcombe, 1982; Oddy & Humphrey, 1980).

Perhaps the best organized approach has been outlined by Ben-Yishay (Ben- Yishay & Diller, 1973; 1981; Ben-Yishay et al., 1974; 1978; 1970). He suggests three methods to treat cognitive impairment: behavioral modification, neuropsychological retraining, or mnemonic training (Diller & Gordon, 1981). The specifics of any given program should consider the premorbid functioning, severity of injury, current deficits, etc.

Cognitive deficits following head injury may include impaired attention and/or arousal, impaired underlying skill structure, memory deficits, language and thought deficit, and inadequate feeling tone (Ben-Yishay & Diller, 1981). Problem solving is seen as involving a series of overlapping steps often involving recovery of these functions, and the overall rehabilitation process is seen as a series of steps which may take many years. The first need is to establish a consistent format for responding. Only after this is established can cognitive skills be effectively modified (Wilson, 1983). This modification or retraining, involves a carefully planned transition from motor tasks toward problem solving, from external to internal cues, from easy to hard problems, and from less to more complex stimuli.

Even with severely impaired patients, controversy exists regarding the mechanisms involved in recovery of behavioral function (Finger, 1978). Questions about neuroregen- eration, resolution of transient disturbances, functional reorganization, or behavioral compensation have yet to be answered. The behavioral compensation philosophy in cog- nitive rehabilitation assumes the patient compensates for a completely destroyed link in his/her behavior repertoire. This occurs when a functional link which hitherto has never participated in the disrupted functional system assumes a new role by replacing the destroyed components (Luria, 1963). Luria (1963) labeled this process inter-systemic reorganization. An alternative approach involves the notion of reinstitution. The implications of the reinstitution philosophy in cognitive rehabilitation involves either the reteaching of lost behavioral function or stimulation of the disrupted processes in an effort to achieve maximal functioning. Both reinstitution of function theories and behavioral compensation theories have been proposed (Horner & Rothi, 1983; Miller, 1980). Microcomputers have found application in both camps.

Regardless of the individual theory, current cognitive remediation strategies basically involve the essential components of learning; persistent study with rapid and appropriate feedback while maintaining the individual's motivation to attend to the tasks and to work toward improving their performance. The primary problems in a given case are likely to be related to time-since-injury or disease onset. In most cases of late referral, the effects of cognitive impairment on social, vocational, and emotional factors are most prominent. With early intervention, emotional complications can often be avoided by educating the patient and family and helping them establish realistic recovery expectations (Cope & Hall, 1982).

The cognitive demands of a mild head injury patient's environment are especially important to evaluate since these patients are likely to return to their former employment (Rusch et al., 1980). While they have only mild cognitive deficits, their jobs may require complete cognitive efficiency for successful performance. Often such cases are quickly discharged home without adequate preparation or education. All too often they attempt to return to work too soon and usually discover that they are unable to function in a cognitively demanding job (Ford, 1976). Subsequently they may develop post-concussion symptoms such as irritability, distractibility, severe headachesand dizziness. (Long & Novack, 1985). The recovery pattern of such patients has been poorly studied. Presumably many of these cases completely recover; however, data indicates that a large percentage of these patients experience a stormy and protracted period of recovery. Many patients continue to have some symptoms for years after their injury (Lishman, 1973).

Again, it should be noted that while such patients experience significant post-concussion symptoms as well as problems in emotional, social, and vocational adjustment, most of these problems can be related directly to impaired cognitive functions. Many remediation programs focus upon these adjustment problems and influence cognitive functions only indirectly, but there is growing interest in developing strategies to directly remediate cognitive functions.

While almost any approach to rehabilitation can aid in improving recovery to some extent, the effectiveness of any program depends upon the identification of problems or barriers to recovery and their removal. Goldstein (1984) reviewed rehabilitation strategies and identified four models of rehabilitation: (1) physical, (2) psychiatric, (3) behavioral, and (4) neuropsychological. He pointed out that chance rather than need is often the primary factor in determining not only outcome but also institutionalization. Often good alternatives are not available or programs are fragmented. Clearly the needs of patients change as recovery progresses and an integrative program holds the greatest promise. Both Goldstein (1984) and Caplan (1982) have outlined the need for rational rehabilitation -- rehabilitation treatment based upon the patient's needs rather that the availability of staff and other resources.

Regardless of the approach, the ultimate aim is to maximize the patient's recovery, that is, to aid them in developing their potential abilities to the maximum. Recovery is an active process. Professionals can aid in this process by evaluating the patient and communicating their present level of function including strengths and weaknesses. Estimates of their pre-morbid level of functioning can be made and areas of differences outlined. Perhaps the major impact that a rehabilitation facility can have is to effectively educate the patient and family as to current level of functioning, to identify barriers to recovery, and to outline strategies for overcoming such barriers.

Poor motivation represents a major obstacle to recovery and offers the greatest frustration to the staff. Motivation may be attenuated for neurological reasons, but often "poor motivation" develops in reaction to difficulty solving problems or coping with situational stress. Since motivation may decline with repeated failure, the rehabilitation staff can serve as primary motivators by helping the patient formulate short-term reachable goals so success can fuel motivation. Assistance in developing improved coping skills can further aid the patient in interacting with the environment.

To date, the major thrust of most cognitively-oriented rehabilitation programs has been toward areas where impaired cognitive functions have the greatest effect -- emotional, social, and vocational. Such approaches focus upon the barriers unique to a patient as represented in problems in their day-to-day behavior. This approach deals with the effects of cognitive dysfunction on the patient's behavior. At different stages of recovery, advantages may obtain from a more direct approach to underlying cognitive problems. However, direct intervention with cognitive weaknesses may not readily generalize to day- to-day behavior.

The assumption is, however, that as more specific strategies for direct cognitive rehabilitation are identified and tested, the overall rehabilitation process may be enhanced.

In summary, rehabilitation is a complex process that often involves an indirect attack on cognitive impairment by working with its effects on vocational, social, and emotional adjustment. Rehabilitation of mild dysfunction is carried out in an outpatient setting requiring coordination of community agents such as family and employers to facilitate and complement the patient's efforts. This is accomplished through patient, family and employer education, management of the patient's stress reactions and the building of family and social support. Through the coordinated action of these components, comprehensive rehabilitation may be accomplished.

Computers in Cognitive Rehabilitation

It is clear that individuals with neurological impairment or who are learning disabled could benefit substantially from any inexpensive computer system that can augment the efforts of the therapists and/or educators by providing feedback and by motivating individuals for sustained study (Table 1). Rehabilitation accomplishes this by maintaining a proper level of difficulty or success and by presenting a variety of tasks. Such a program needs to be flexible to compensate for sensory or motor handicaps or weaknesses. Staff or facilities need to be available for frequent training sessions. Finally, such a program needs to be designed so as to document and display the individual's progress over time.

Personal computers can fill this need. Computer applications are being made in almost all areas of human endeavor, yet some areas lend themselves more readily to computer application. Teaching and remediation of learning disabled and neurologically impaired individuals appear to be particularly fertile areas for computer application. However, the question remains as to how computers can best be applied, and how such applications will enhance the effectiveness of the area. It may be of no particular advantage to have a training program available on a computer unless such applications are either more efficient or more cost effective than traditional methods.

The primary attributes of computer are their flexibility, objectivity and speed (Kleinmuntz, 1963). Properly designed, computers can provide significant enhancement in cognitive retraining based on these attributes. A computer system can provide frequent and

Table 1

Primary attributes of computers

Flexibility, Speed, & Objectivity	Frequent and Immediate Feedback
Individualized Pacing and Programming	Motivation by
-Modular and hierarchical curriculum	-Success at level
-Speed of presentation controlled	-Stimulation of interest
-Salient cues can be emphasized	-Personalized instruction
-Complexity can be controlled	-Non-threatening
-Clarity of presentation	-Nonjudgmental
-Repetition and overlearning	-Seen as responsive T.V.

immediate feedback. Programs can be presented in a modular format and in an individualized manner in order to pace the individual through the task. Stimuli can be clearly presented in a consistent and objective manner and outcomes can be stated similarly. Computers are viewed as generally nonthreatening and nonjudgmental, and many individuals who do not perform well in a traditional instructional environment are motivated by successes insured by the computer and by stimulation of interests. The microcomputer can be used as an aid for drill and practice. Many simple drill and skill building programs exist or programs can be easily be developed to present numerous types of material. The microcomputer is able to provide extensive practice to the patient for initial learning and for newly acquired skill building. They permit extensive repetition, to the point of overlearning.

In view of the strategies for cognitive training it would appear that computers can offer a useful and effective adjunctive strategy. Lynch (1982) suggests that computers are more interesting, offer a great range of difficulty and flexibility, are generally educational and therapeutic and may be inexpensive. He designed retraining around the use of commercially available TV games (Lynch, 1983).

During the past several years numerous computer systems have become available and are advertised as cognitive retraining tools. Programs exist for memory, perceptual processes, eye-hand coordination, verbal exercise, concentration, etc. (Craine & Gudeman, 1981; Lally, 1982; Lesgold, 1982; Lynch, 1982). Many of these systems are being used by speech and occupational therapists as well as psychologists. Unfortunately, computer applications appear to be based more on speculation than hard data, with only a few case study reports documenting their effectiveness. Little is known about the overall effectiveness of computer training, much less about selecting programs appropriate for a given patient's cognitive strengths and weaknesses. A more effective system is needed to monitor the progress of the individual and new programs need to be developed which can resolve problems that arise with existing systems. A case study report of a 17 year old head injured male with 9 months coma, who received extensive computer retraining revealed significant improvement after 10 months which persisted after 2 years (Sbordone, 1985). In another study, head injured patients revealed improved attention, but the effects were highly variable (Malec et al., 1982). Bracy (1983) treated 2 patients with home computers and found improved performance on the WISC-R. In another case a 32 year old female stroke patient demonstrated improved performance on the WAIS-R after 14 months of computer training. Lynch (1983), using commercially available games, reported improved cognitive performance in 3 of 4 patients. Other studies found similar effects (Fitch & Cross, 1983; Parente & Anderson, 1983).

Overall, the findings suggest improvement in cognitive functions with computer as - sisted training of neurologically impaired patients. However, it is difficult to determine the effects of the computer instruction in the cases published thus far in view of the absence of control subjects. Bracy et al., (1985) state that the definitive study on cognitive training is yet to be done. This statement certainly summarizes the status of the literature.

We have witnessed a rapid advance of computers into education and remediation at all levels. Computer systems can significantly augment training and are available when the patient or student needs them, have the ability to shift tasks or shift level of difficulty, and give immediate feedback. A properly designed computer system can be a patient and persistent teacher.

With the extensive applications of computers in so many areas and the promising speculation regarding their use with rehabilitation, why has computer assisted rehabilitation yet to be well documented with published research? Case study reports have shown that at least some patients significantly benefit. The implication, of course, is that some do not. The trick is to identify patient characteristics and treatment characteristics which, when meshed, allow a favorable treatment prognosis.

Computers in Education

The history of computer-assisted instruction (CAI) dates back to the 1960's, with the introduction of large mainframe computer systems. With the explosive growth of personal computing in recent years it is now estimated that over 100,000 computers are in use in classrooms across the country. Given the availability of computers and a captive audience of subjects, it is not surprising that quite a bit of research has been devoted to the educational use of computers. While some studies have used gifted students or studied college students, much of the research has involved poor achievers, learning disabled and handicapped students; consequently, the results of that research may generalize to work with the neurologically impaired, since the two subject populations are known to share several characteristics, such as problems with attention and concentration.

The use of computers as educators is intuitively appealing in that the system allows for individualized instruction which is paced according to the learner and allows repetitive practice with immediate feedback. Perhaps because those characteristics are in part descriptions of an ideal teacher, quite a few educational studies have compared the effectiveness of CAI to traditional instruction (TI). Most of such comparisons have found that CAI is at least equally effective if not more effective than TI (Atkinson, 1968; Edwards et al, 1975); however, the best results are apparently obtained by using CAI as an adjunct to TI (Leiber & Semmel, 1985). This conclusion is of course consistent with the anticipated role of computers in cognitive rehabilitation. Of greater interest, however, is evidence from the educational literature indicating that the effectiveness of CAI depends upon three groups of interrelated factors - the dependent variables employed, student characteristics, and task characteristics.

When achievement test scores are used as independent variable, most but not all stud - ies have reported significant improvement with CAI (Atkinson, 1968; 1972; 1980; Brown & Alford, 1984; Campbell & Edwards, 1975; Fletcher & Hartley, 1975; Harper et al., 1986; Hasselbrain, 1982; Kulik et al., 1983; McDermott & Watkins, 1983; Silfen et al., 1984; Splittgerber, 1979; Thompson, 1980; Tsai & Pohl, 1978; Visonhaler et al., 1974; Vinson- haler & Bass, 1972). For example, Suppes and Morningstar (1969) reported significant improvement in achievement test scores with a group of grammar school students who were allowed brief, daily periods of CAI. While use of acquisition speed as a dependent variable shows a clear advantage for CAI (Jamieson et al., 1974; Kulik et al. 1980), there is evidence that measures of retention and measures of generalizability tend to favor TI over CAI. The fact that the research findings are inconsistent irrespective of the dependent variables used suggest that other factors need to be considered in evaluating CAI.

The effectiveness of CAI depends in part upon certain characteristics of the stu- dent/learner, including current ability level, educational level, and maturity (Table 2). Investigations of such student characteristics have generally been reported within the context of primary comparisons of the effectiveness of CAI with TI; consequently, the findings are

Table 2

Other Variables Influencing Computer Assisted Training Effectiveness

Grade	General Intelligence
Hyperactivity	Attention Deficit Disorder
Familiarity with Subject	Cognitive Style
Memory Span	Perceptual Skills
Persistence	Locus of Control
Knowledge vs Tactics	

as variable as those primarily concerned with comparing mode of instruction. In general, it seems that retarded or emotionally disturbed students show little or no benefit from CAI. Normal or above average individuals are likely to show significant gains but only in specific areas. While some low ability learning disabled students may benefit from CAI (Edwards et al., 1975; Brown et al., 1984), others do not (Berthold & Sachs, 1974).   Similar discrepancies are found in studies involving children with attention/concentration difficulties. Significant improvement was reported by Carmen (1982) but Brown et al. (1984), and Berthold and Sachs (1974) reported no significant difference between CAI and TI. In contrast, Douglas et al., (1983) reported that when the computer cues are too powerful they may actually be distracting. A similar observation was made by Berthold and Sachs (1974) as they describe cases in which CAI was clearly inferior to TI, apparently because the machine itself was distracting the students.

The age of the student may also be a significant consideration. Cuffaro (1984) has suggested that CAI is not likely to be of significant benefit with normal children younger than eight years. Most assuredly, the minimal effective age will vary according to developmental and neurological status in a given case. As age is generally related to achievement level, it is interesting to note that some data suggests that the effectiveness of CAI depends in part upon prior mastery of the subject matter. CAI may be an effective supplement to TI in elementary schools but with greater achievement, such as with high school and college students, CAI may be an effective replacement for TI (Jamieson et al., 1974; Bangert-Downs et al., 1985). CAI is superior to TI in college level computer pro-gramming training (Tsai et al., 1978). It has also been shown to be more effective with learning disabled students at the junior high level than with comparable students in ele-mentary schools (Chiang, 1978). In general, it seems that CAI is most effective with good achievers, even those who are classified as behavioral problems. While poor achievers may also benefit from CAI, the gains are much less dramatic (Jamieson et al., 1983).

The effectiveness of CAI is also related to certain task characteristics which are un-fortunately related to the aforementioned student characteristics in various complex and as yet poorly understood ways. Task characteristics may be subdivided into process features, materials/goals, and programming control.

For convenience, the educational process can be subdivided into tutorial efforts, sim-ulation exercises, problem solving exercises, and drill and practice routines (Gagne et al, 1981). Most research indicates a definite superiority of CAI for drill and practice exercises

(Visonhaler & Bass, 1972). Such findings seem consistent if not indistinguishable from evidence of superior speed of acquisition with CAI. While studies of simulation exercises and problem solving skills reveal no clear advantage for CAI, this may reflect to a large extent the paucity of computer programs available for such training. The effectiveness of CAI with drill and practice exercises has been shown to be related to the materials being studied or the goals of the exercises. For example, significant gains in mathematic scores have commonly been reported (Crawford, 1970; Suppes & Morningstar, 1969; Vickers, 1984). Other studies have shown significant improvement in reading scores per CAI drill and practice (Fletcher, 1972). When the goal of CAI is nonacademic, the effects of task characteristics may override certain student characteristics. For example, as previously mentioned, the results of studies on emotionally disturbed children indicate no advantage for CAI in terms of improved academic achievement scores; however, Carmen and Kosberg (1982) reported significant improvement in emotionally handicapped children in terms of improved ability to attend to task when involved in CAI.

Another important question in terms of task characteristics is that of control. That is, whether the level of difficulty and pace are controlled by the computer or if the stu -dent/learner is allowed to influence the program's processes. Some data suggests that students who control their own rate of progress may terminate too early (Tennyson, et al, 1979) or they may select problems which are not at an appropriate level of difficulty (Fisher, 1975). While those reports and others (Delland et al., 1985) question the efficacy of self-paced programs, there are no universal guidelines (Carrier et al., 1985) for other factors must be taken into consideration. For example, the less familiar the student is with the material the greater the degree of external control needed (Tobias, 1981; Ross et al., 1981). College students have been shown to be good judges (Judd et al., 1970) whereas younger, less educated students need at least moderate levels of external pacing (Delland et al., 1985). Even so, some exceptions have been reported. Whalen et al., (1978) reported that some hyperactive children do better when allowed to procede at their own pace.

In spite of considerable evidence supporting the usefulness of CAI as an adjunct to TI, some critics have voiced concerns about the role of computers in education. While several researchers have suggested that children are very receptive to CAI and tend to view the computer as a nonjudgmental and nonthreatening aid, other authors have questioned the alleged social isolation reputed to be involved in CAI (Isenberg, 1985). Obviously this is an important concern, especially when working with children, such as those with learning disabilities, who often have either developed or are at risk for developing problems in terms of their social skills. Such fears may be allayed by having students work in cooperative groups with a single computer. For example, Larson (1986) reported that students tended to be more cooperative in group sessions of CAI.

Some writers have worried about the fact that CAI tends to be much more abstract than hands-on experience such as that involved in the initial years of education. Cuffaro (1984) has argued that students need first to experience real life referents before they can deal with them symbolically as they are presented with CAI. While the benefits of CAI may be age related, Cuffaro's concerns seem exaggerated, as it seems quite clear that CAI is best employed as an adjunct to TI; that is to say, that the student learner will not be deprived of real life referents by being involved with CAI.

Another concern with CAI is the question of who develops the software. This concern seems particularly relevant to the topic at hand for as previously mentioned there is always the danger that the end user will blindly accept the product without fully understanding the rationale involved. The end user must be a critical consumer. As a side note, we may also observe that some critical consumers have tended to disparage the use of CAI, the main point being that currently CAI is primarily involved in acquiring knowledge, whereas perhaps the most important goal of the educational process is to provide the student with the skills and strat egies for acquiring and applying knowledge. It seems quite likely that this concern will be mitigated with future developments in the area. As previously mentioned, much speculation and considerable work is already underway to develop higher level computer programs which will assist the student in learning to learn.

Generalization from Education to Cognitive Rehabilitation

Our brief review of the educational research on CAI reveals several lessons. As sug- gested earlier, the educational research data may be generalizable to cognitive rehabilitation of brain injured individuals at least to the extent that such patients share common characteristics with the student studied in most of the educational research. The educational research suggests that computers are most efficient when used as an adjunct to traditional face to face human instruction. Used in this fashion, criticisms about social isolation, abstract emphasis, etc. are mitigated; rather, the student is involved in a more comprehensive teaching effort than that available by TI alone. The use of computers in cognitive rehabilitation must take into account certain characteristics of the patient. This conclusion is consistent with our belief that a comprehensive neuropsychological evaluation should be the first step in planning cognitive rehabilitation. By identifying the patient's strengths and weaknesses we can then attempt to match those with computer programs. For example, many but not all brain injured individuals have difficulty with attention and concentration. It should be obvious that the importance of attention and concentration in a given case must be empirically established.

It would be counterproductive not to mention cost. It would be inefficient to routinely force each new client in a rehabilitation program to work through a series of exercises intended to improve attention and concentration, if such training is not indicated. Similarly, objective information regarding the individual's ability structure and level of social maturity must be taken into account in order to decide the extent to which the client will be allowed to control the computer training programs.

Attention may be impaired with the more severely injured. Enhanced cueing and feedback are frequently needed and tasks need to be presented in a stepwise manner of in - creasing difficulty, depending upon performance. Finally, tasks need to be presented for more frequent but shorter periods of time. These needs closely match those of the poor academic achiever and are worthy of further investigation.

The research of educators in the application of computers would appear to serve as an ideal model for computer application with neurologically impaired. Properly developed programs can provide a cost effective, patient tutor; however, before such generalizations can be made, consideration needs to be directed toward the influence of other variables. Certainly, neurological injury often has the effect of regressing one mentally by disrupting general cognitive functions.

One advantage of microcomputer systems in cognitive rehabilitation is the presenta- tion and monitoring of individualized instruction at reasonable costs. Computer-aug mented, home-based cognitive rehabilitation programs can be designed to provide specific learning material at a pace commensurate with the learner's ability. The use of such home-based systems could serve to greatly enhance time spent by the professional. Further, when programs are designed to be interesting and challenging, therapeutic time spent in cognitive rehabilitation can be enjoyable.

At the present time, there appears to be little in the way of documentation regarding computer effectiveness in cognitive rehabilitation. In spite of this, the general consensus is that the computer represents a system ideally suited to meet the needs of neurologically impaired. Computers can perform most human tasks; the question is whether it is cost effective at any given point in time. Certainly, clinicians are wasting valuable time in performing tasks best relegated to machines.

More sophisticated applications of microcomputers for specialized computer-aided learning packages have recently emerged and have been reviewed elsewhere (Odor, 1982; Rizza, 1981). Rizza (1981) described the use of a computer as a "learning manager" rather than as simply a drill master. Based on a student's recorded performance, a computer program can produce learning activities likely to be most effective in helping the learner attain mastery of a particular skill. Concurrently, the computer monitors effectiveness of the instructional material. In a similar vein, Rizza (1981) has described the use of a computer as a "learning aid", to increase the learner's ability to comprehend a subject. This approach stresses learning by discovery, as is the case with simulation programs now used in various academic fields such as business and engineering. An underlying theory is revealed through the learner's interaction with a conceptual model or simulation of some predetermined topic area (Odor, 1982). This type of programming strategy could surely be used to create simulation programs that are relevant for cognitive rehabilitation applications.

More speculative applications involve the use of microcomputers as a personal decision-aiding system. Andriole (1982) has proposed microcomputer decision-aids as extensions of human problem-solvers in which systems are designed to be adaptive to their users, to unique problem-solving situations, and to past problem-solving experiences. An example of this type of application is the symbiotic relationship between humans and computers in lunar missions. However, the computer as a decision aid need not be limited to such esoteric applications. It may be possible to adapt microcomputers to the everyday needs of clients with limited or reduced problem-solving abilities. Andriole (1982) has argued that it should be possible to design a computer system which would interact with its human partner in a way which is consistent with specific situational problem-solving requirements. He has suggested that such a system might even monitor the physiological state of the user so as to pace the interaction or repeat sequences in order to "check" the user's coherence and logic if the user is behaving unconventionally because of emotional arousal. Weiss and Kelly (1980) have developed decision templates which free users from the model-building steps necessary to solve a decision problem. The microcomputer can then offer a means to select, organize, format, evaluate, pace, and display information for personal decision-making. This process of objectifying decision strategies and helping the user through each step could have tremendous applications in aiding neurologically impaired patients in their recovery or compensation. Applications of this type of computing for behavioral compensation of cognitive deficits are limited only by the imaginations of rehabilitation engineers, computer programmers, educational specialists, and clinical neuropsychologists. The challenge, then, is effective interdisciplinary communication and cooperation in developing systems.

References

Andriole, S.J. The design of microcomputer-based personal decision-aiding systems. *EE Transactions on Systems, Man, and Cybernetics, 12,* 463-469.

Anthony, W.Z. & Heaton, R.K. (1980). An attempt to cross-validate two actuarial systems for neuropsychological test interpretation. *Journal of Consulting and Clinical Psychology, 48,* 317-326.

Atkinson, R.C. (1968). Computerized instruction and the learning process. *American Psychologist, 23,* 225-229.

Bach-y-Rita, P. (1980). Brain plasticity as a basis for therapeutic procedures. In P. Bach-y-Rita (Ed.), Recovery of function: Theoretical considerations for brain injury rehabilitation.   Baltimore: University Park Press.

Bangert-Drowns, R.L., Kulik, J.A., & Kulik, C.C. (1985). Effectiveness of computer based education in secondary schools. *Journal of Computer-Based Instruction,* Summer, *12,* 59-68.

Ben-Yishay, Y. & Diller, L. (1981). Rehabilitation of cognitive and perceptual defects in people with traumatic brain damage. *International Journal of Rehabilitation Research, 4,* 208-210.

Ben-Yishay, Y. & Diller, L. (1973). Changing of atmospheric environment to improve mental and behavioral functioning: Application in treatment of senescence. *New York State Journal of Medicine 73,* 2877-2880.

Ben-Yishay, Y., Diller, L., Mandleberg, I., Gordon, W., & Gerstman, L. (1974). Differences in matching persistence behavior during block design performance between older normal and brain damaged persons: A process analysis. *Cortex, 10,* 121-132.

Ben-Yishay, Y., Ben-Nachum, Z., Cohen, A., Gerstman, L., Gordon, W., Gross, Y., Hofien, D., Piasetsky, E., & Rattok, J. (1978). Working approaches to the remediation of cognitive deficits in brain damaged. Supplement to the sixth annual workshop for rehabilitation professionals, New York, June.

Ben-Yishay, Y., Diller, L., Gerstman, L., & Gordon, W. (1970). Relationship between initial competence and ability to profit from cues in brain damaged individuals. *Journal of Abnormal Psychology, 75,* 278-259.

Berthold, H.C. & Sach, R.H. (1974). Education of the minimally brain damaged child by computer and by teacher. *Programmed Learning and Educational Technology, 11,* 121-124.

Bracy, O., et al. (1985). Cognitive retraining through computers: Fact or Fad? *Cognitive Rehabilitation, 3,* 10-23.

Brown, R.T. & Alford, N. (1984). Ameliorating attentional deficits and concomitant academic deficiencies. *Journal of Learning Disabilities, 17,* 20-26.

Carman, G.O. & Kosberg, B. (1982). Educational technology research: Computer technology and the education of emotionally handicapped childen. *Educational Technology,* 26-30.

Carrier, C. et al. (1985). The selection of instructional options in a computer-based coordinate concept. *Educational Communication & Technology Journal, 33,* 199-212.

Chiang, A. et al. (1978). Demonstration of the use of computer-assisted instruction with handicappped children. Final Report of the RMC Research Corp., Arlington, VA., Report No. 446-AH-60076A, 3-82

Cope, D. & Hall, K. (1982). Head injury rehabilitation: Benefit of early intervention. *Archives of Physical Medicine and Rehabilitation, 63,* 433-437.

Craine, J.F. & Gudeman, H.E. (1981). *The rehabilitation of brain functions: Principles, procedures and techniques of neuro-training.* Springfield, IL: Charles C. Thomas.

Crawford, A.N. (1970). A pilot study of computer-assisted drill and practice in seventh grade remedial mathematics. *California Journal of Educational Research. 21,* 170-181.

Cuffaro, H.K. (1984). Microcomputers in education: Why is earlier better? *Teachers College Record, 85,* 559-568.

Delland, J.C. et al. (1985). Is the self-paced instructional program, via microcomputer based instruction, the most effective method of addressing individual learning differences? *Journal of Educational Communication andTechnology, 33,* 185-198.

Derry, S. & Murphy, D. (1986). Designing systems that train learning ability: From theory to practice. *Review of Educational Research, 56,* 1-39.

Diller, L. & Gordon, W.A. (1981). Interventions for cognitive deficits in brain injured adults. *Journal of Consulting and Clinical Psychology, 49,* 822-834.

Edwards, J. et al. (1975). How effective is CAI? A review of the research. *Educational Leadership,* 147-153.

Finger, S. (1978). *Recovery from brain damage: Research and theory.* New York: Plenum Press.

Fletcher, J.D. (1972). Computer assisted instruction in reading: grades 4 - 6. *Educational Technology, 12,* 45-49.

Ford, B. (1976). Head injuries: What happens to survivors? *Medical Journal of Australia, 1,* 603-605.

Gummow, L. et. al. (1983). Attention and brain injury: A case for cognitive rehabilitation of attentional deficits. *Clinical Psychology Review, 3,* 255-274.

Harper, J.A. & Ewing, N.J. (1986). A comparison of the effectiveness of microcomputer and workbook instruction on reading comprehension performance of high incidence handicapped children. *Educational Technology,* 40-45.

Heaton, R. & Pendleton, M. (1981). Use of neuropsychological tests to predict adult patients' everyday functioning. *Journal of Consulting and Clinical Psychology, 49,* 807-821.

Horner, J. & Rothi, L. (1983). Restitution and substitution: Two theories of recovery with application to neurobehavioral treatment. *Journal of Clinical Neuropsychology, 5,* 73-81.

Isenberg, R.S. (1985). Computer-aided instruction and the mainstreamed learning disabled student. *Journal of Learning Disabilities, 18,* 557-558.

Jamieson, R.N. (1974). The effectiveness of alternative instructional methods. *Review of Educational Research, 44,* 1-67.

Jamieson, R.N. & Lovatt, K.F. (1983). Classroom delinquency, achievement, and computer assisted instruction. *Journal of Computer-Based Instruction, 9,* 145-147.

Kulik, J.A. et al. (1983). Effects of computer-based teaching on secondary school students. *Journal of Educational Psychology, 75,* 19-26.

Kulik, C., Kulik, J. & Cohen, P. (1980). Instructional technology and college teaching. *Teaching of Psychology, 7*(4), 199-205.

Lally, M. (1982). Computer-assisted handwriting instruction and visual/kinaesthetic feedback processes. *Applied Research in Mental Retardation, 3,* 397-405.

Larson, B.L. & Roberts, B.B. (1986). The computer as a catalyst for mutual support and empowerment among learning disabled students. *Journal of Learning Disabilities, 19,* 52-55.

Lesgold, A.M. (1982). Computer games for the teaching of reading. *Behavior Research Methods and Instrumentation, 14,* 224-226.

Lezak, M. (1978). Living with the characterologically altered brain-injured patient. *Journal of Clinical Psychiatry, 39,* 592-598.

Lieber, J. & Semmel, M.I. (1985). Effectiveness of computer application to instruction with mildly handicapped learners. *Remedial and Special Education, 6,* 5-12.

Luria, A.R. (1983). *Restoration of function following brain damage.* New York: Pergamon Press.

Lynch, W.J. (1983). Cognitive retraining using microcomputer games and commercially available software. *Cognitive Rehabilitation, 1,* 19-22.

Lynch, W.J. (1982). The use of electronic games in cognitive rehabilitation. In L.E. Trexler (Ed.), Cognitive Rehabilitation: Conceptualization and Intervention. New York: Plenum Press.

McDermott, P.A. & Watkins, M.W. (1983). Computerized vs. conventional remedial instruction for learning disabled pupils. *Journal of Special Education, 17,* 81-88.

Miller, E. (1980). Psychological intervention in the management and rehabilitation of neuropsychological impairments. *Behavior Research and Therapy, 18,* 527-535.

Newcombe, F. (1982). The psychological consequences of closed head injury: Assessment and rehabilitation. *Injury, 14,* 11-136.

Oddy, M. & Humphrey, M. (1980). Social recovery during the year following severe head injury. *Journal of Neurology, Neurosurgery and Psychiatry, 43,* 798-802.

Odor, P. (1982). Microcomputers and disabled people. *International Journal of Man-Machine Studies, 17,* 51-58.

Rizza, P.J. (1981). Computer-based education (CBE): Tomorrow's traditional system. *Journal of Children in Contemporary Society, 14,* 29-42.

Rusch, M., Grunert, B., Erdmann, B. & Lynch, N. (1980). Cognitive retraining of brain-injured adults in outpatient rehabilitation. (Abs.) *Archives of Physical Medicine and Rehabilitation, 61,* 472.

Schmidt, M. et al. (1985). Computer-assisted instruction with exceptional children. *The Journal of Special Education, 19,* 493-501.

Schrader, V.E. (1984). The computer in education -- Are we over our heads? *NASP Bulletin, 68,* 38-42.

Silfen, R. & Howes, A.C. (1984). A summer reading program with CAI: An evaluation. *Computers, Reading and Language Arts, 1,* 20-22.

Stein, R. & Reissman, C. (1980). The development of an impact-on-family scale: Preliminary findings. *Medical Care, 18,* 465-472.

Suppes, P. & Morningstar, M. (1969). Computer-assisted instruction: Two computer-assisted instruction programs are evaluated. *Science, 166*, 343-350.

Tsai, S.W. & Pohl, N.V. (1978). Student achievement in computer programming: Lecture vs computer-aided instruction. *Journal of Experimental Education, 46*, 66-70.

Vickers, M. (1984). Reset your button and drive into computer-assisted math. *Academic Therapy, 19*, 465-471.

Visonhaler, J. & Bass, R.K. (1971). A summary of ten major studies on CAI drill and practice. *Educational Technology, 12*, p. 29-32.

Weiss, J.J. & Kelly, C.W. BSCREEN and OPGEN: Two problem structuring decision aids which employ decision templates, Decision and Designs, McLean, VA,

Wilson, P.B. (1983). Software selection and use in language and cognitive retraining. *Cognitive Rehabilitation, 1*, 9-10.

6

Methodological Issues in Cognitive Retraining Research

Gregory W. Harter

Over the past few decades, numerous theories and procedures have been developed to remediate the cognitive impairment caused by brain injury (Diller & Gordon, 1981). These procedures have focused largely on the remediation of language and memory disorder. Some have been empirically evaluated using group outcome studies, but most are presented in the context of a narrative case report or through the use of a single-subject experimental design.

Most of these studies find that the retraining procedures are effective in remediating the problems they address. However, the paucity of well-designed group studies suggests that future research is needed to establish or dispute this trend. Also, many of the studies already published suffer from a variety of methodological weaknesses that preclude a conclusive assessment as to the effectiveness of cognitive retraining.

Evaluation strategies appropriate for investigating cognitive retraining effects are not unlike those employed in the study of psychotherapy outcome (e.g. Smith & Glass, 1977) but in many respects the methodological issues relating to cognitive retraining are more complex. These issues concern who receives cognitive retraining (subject selection issues), the setting in which cognitive remediation takes place, the selection of goals and dependent measures, the development of remedial tasks and procedures, the special problem of spontaneous recovery, and the use of between-group or within-subject comparisons in evaluating treatment effects (research design issues).

Subject Selection Issues

There is a marked heterogeneity among individuals with acquired brain injuries. In addition to varying patterns of cognitive or informational processing disturbances, such individuals differ in acute neurological factors, behavioral and emotional sequelae, premorbid personality, and demographic characteristics. The control of these subject variables is critical to an unambiguous interpretation of treatment outcomes in clinical research.

Neurological and Psychological Sequelae

Brain injured patients will vary in type of injury (e.g., trauma or vascular problem), cause of injury (e.g., motor vehicle accident or drug overdose), severity of acute symptoms/signs (e.g., mild confusion versus prolonged coma), size, locus, and density of lesions, time since injury, length of hospitalization, and various neurophysiological changes. Many of these factors have prognostic significance in the natural course of recovery. For example, head trauma cases which are associated with longer periods of coma or post-traumatic amnesia generally have poorer long-term vocational outcomes (Barth & Boll, 1981;

Levin, Benton, & Grossman, 1982). What is largely undetermined is whether cognitive retraining has any mitigating benefit on the relationship between severity of injury factors and outcome measures.

Cognitive deficits secondary to severe or moderate brain injury often exist within a context of a variety of other physical, behavioral, and emotional problems. Lezak (1983) reports that emotional dulling, disinhibition, decreased anxiety with "emotional blandness or mild euphoria," and reduced sensitivity are frequently cited effects of brain injury on personality. However, anxiety in some cases may increase, patients may become hypersensitive in social situations, and depression may be prominent. Lezak (1983) further suggests that depression as a reaction to chronic frustration and a radical change in lifestyle may be particularly influential in recovery. The potential confounding of such sequelae can be seen in a recent study of memory retraining with a closed head injured patient (Crosson & Buenning, 1984). Although improvement in this patient's memory function was attributed to a 15-day training program, the investigators also reported that the patient experienced "periodic feelings of depression related to the memory deficit and other physical injuries" which were not assessed formally either before or after memory retraining. Another plausible interpretation of their findings is that the patient's memory improved because his depression cleared.

Demographic Variables and Premorbid Functioning

In addition to neurological and behavioral sequelae, subject variables such as age, sex, education, occupation, and socioeconomic level are often important in clinical neuropsychological research (Parsons & Prigatano, 1978). The influence of such variables on cognitive remediation outcomes is largely unknown, but for head trauma patients, it might be expected that younger age and higher levels of education, socioeconomic, and occupational status could be predictive of more successful outcomes since these factors have a favorable influence on prognosis in the natural course of recovery (Bond, 1975; Jennett, Teasdale, & Knill-Jones, 1975; Rimel, Giordani, Barth, Boll, & Jane, 1981). Indices of premorbid functioning pertaining to general health, emotional stability, and intelligence, when available, may also have prognostic significance (Barth & Boll, 1981). For older stroke patients, it is important to differentiate the effects of recent brain insult from those which might be attributable to aging (Medical Research Council, 1982). Similarly, there are accumulating data on premorbid personality factors in head trauma victims which suggest that these individuals often lead socially deviant lifestyles which predispose them to greater risk of injury (Jennett, 1972; Medical Research Council, 1982; Tobis, Puri, & Sheridan, 1982). Studies of cognitive retraining in this population should attempt to assess outcome in relation to premorbid indices of functioning or a matched group of individuals with similar personality characteristics rather than normal controls.

The control of subject characteristics is critical to the internal validity of group comparison studies of treatment outcome. If groups are not equivalent prior to treatment, it is not possible to disentangle treatment effects, if any, from subject selection effects. Unfortunately, in clinical research the standard procedure for making groups equivalent, the random assignment of individuals to treatment or non-treatment conditions, is often not possible for ethical or practical reasons (Beck, Andrasik, Arena, 1984). Prigatano et al. (1984), in a study of cognitive retraining effects, dealt with this problem by matching subjects who received treatment, with individuals who mostly declined treatment, on a number of neurological (e.g., time since injury, length of coma, post trauma seizure incidence, incidence of residual paresis, residual aphasia and/or dysarthria, and clinical diagnosis) and demographic characteristics. To the extent that they were able to anticipate potentially biasing subject characteristics and demonstrate that the groups were relatively comparable on these characteristics, this approach succeeds as one of the few published group comparison outcome studies demonstrating cognitive retraining effects. There is a possible confound, however, in level of subject motivation since most individuals in the control group, who had less successful outcomes, previously turned down the opportunity to receive cognitive retraining.

Control of subject characteristics and the specification of criteria for subject selection are also important in establishing the external validity of a study. In group comparison research, when the characteristics of subjects are precisely specified, and groups are made relatively homogeneous, a study's potential for replication is enhanced, but usually at some trade-off in the generalizability of results. For example, the NYU cognitive rehabilitation program (Ben-Yishay & Diller, 1981) has fairly stringent admission criteria which should promote replicability of findings among patients with similar characteristics. Only 18 to 55 year old candidates with a diagnosis of head trauma or cerebral anoxia, at least 12 months post-trauma, who score at least 80 in either verbal or performance IQ, and do not have a history of psychiatric problems, drug abuse, or sociopathy are accepted. However, since many head trauma patients do, in fact, have such histories (Jennett, 1972; Medical Research Council, 1982; Tobis et al., 1982), it is questionable how well the findings of this program will generalize to the broader population of head trauma patients.

Similarly, a within-subject memory retraining study (Glasgow, Zeiss, Barrera, & Lewinsohn, 1977) bears on this issue of representative sampling. The investigators successfully trained two college students, who had memory complaints secondary to head trauma, in some mnemonic techniques. One subject was 3 1/2 years post-trauma and was maintaining a B average in school. The other was 2 years post-trauma and was also apparently managing in school satisfactorily; his only complaint was remembering the names of people whom he met. Both subjects improved, but both appeared to have had relatively mild memory problems. The question is, how applicable are these techniques to people with clinically significant memory problems?

Environmental Influences

The setting in which cognitive retraining occurs has an obvious impact on decisions about patient eligibility, goals, procedures, duration of training, its initiation, and its termination. In the absence of empirical data, such decisions are often influenced by institutional policies, and the availability of funding and third party payments. In many settings cost effectiveness will be a major issue (Levin et al., 1982; Miller, 1980).

Rehabilitation Settings

Cognitive retraining is often part of a larger rehabilitation program (e.g., Ben-Yishay & Diller, 1981; Goldstein & Ruthven, 1983; Prigatano et al., 1984; Rosenbaum, Lipsitz, Abraham, & Najenson, 1978) in which other services such as physical and occupational therapy, are likely to be available. When other services are provided, evaluation of cognitive remedial interventions becomes problematic since the effects of other treatments are uncontrolled. One way to solve this problem is to compare an "equivalent" control group, which only receives traditional rehabilitation services, with a treatment group, which receives cognitive retraining and the same traditional rehabilitation services. However, this can be difficult to coordinate across disciplines, and many rehabilitation centers may have policies which prohibit the withholding of any services which might be beneficial to a patient.

Analog Settings

Experimental laboratories can control for such extraneous variables, but the focus of research in such settings tends to be narrow. For example, Lewinsohn's group (Glasgow et al., 1977; Lewinsohn, Danaker, & Kikel, 1977) developed strategies to exclusively remediate memory disorders. In such an analog setting, deficits outside the target area are not treated which would exclude many individuals entirely and could leave certain treated subjects with untreated residual problems. The advantage gained in control over extraneous variables in an analog treatment setting could make studies conducted there more vulnerable to maintenance and generalization failures, but these problems often plague traditional rehabilitation programs as well. Lewinsohn's group developed *in vivo* procedures which appeared to help their clients use mnemonic strategies outside the laboratory. Ideally, any cognitive remedial intervention which requires a specialized training environment should include strategies to help clients generalize treatment gains to their natural environments.

Cognitive Retraining in the Natural Environment

According to Diller and Gordon (1981b), the quality of the environment can facilitate or undermine cognitive remedial interventions. One study (Rosenbaum et al., 1978) reported that environmental problems were among the greatest obstacles to recovery and resumption of gainful employment in 13 Israeli veterans, most of whom had received penetrating head wounds. These problems were typified by rejecting spouses, a lack of social support, and financial difficulties. Studies such as this suggest that the family, which may be supportive of intervention efforts and enhance a patient's motivation or inhibit progress by reinforcing disabilities and ignoring gains, is a particularly important variable in the recovery of a brain injured person.

Sbordone (1984) has proposed a model of cognitive retraining which has the benefits of minimizing treatment generalization problems while cutting therapy costs. In this model neuropsychologists design and monitor cognitive retraining programs for brain injured individuals which are implemented by family members or close friends in the patient's natural environment. An attempt is made to develop strategies that modify the environment so that greater demands are made on the patient's strengths while fewer demands are made on his or her weaknesses. This model lends itself well to within-subject research designs, and it is hoped that published reports of this approach will be forthcoming. One drawback, however, is the fact that many brain injured individuals have multifaceted cognitive, emotional, and physical problems which would seem to require a multidisciplinary rehabilitation approach.

Assessment Issues

Clinical neuropsychology has traditionally been concerned with diagnosing pathological conditions in the central nervous system and delineating the behavioral manifestations of such conditions. Neuropsychological test batteries such as the Halstead-Reitan Battery have been shown to be reliable and valid diagnostic instruments (Lezak, 1983). With the new emphasis on cognitive retraining of brain injured individuals, the use of such batteries is now being advocated in order to derive profiles of patients' weaknesses, and to a lesser extent their strengths, in order to plan remedial programs (Barth & Boll, 1981; Caplan, 1982; Golden, 1981; Goldstein & Ruthven, 1983; Sbordone, 1984).

A critical issue which has been raised is whether a neuropsychological test battery that was originally designed to answer neurological questions based on a deficit model is appropriate for questions concerning remediation (Horton & Miller, 1984; Horton & Wedding, 1984). Does a new battery, more sensitive to treatment issues need to be developed?

One of the problems in using standard Neuropsychological tests in cognitive retraining is the need for repeatable measures in order to assess how well a particular intervention is working. Many of the standard psychometric tests are vulnerable to practice effects, which could confound treatment effects. Although some tests come in alternate forms (e.g., the Wechsler Memory Scale), in many cognitive remedial interventions it may be desirable to obtain more than two measures of performance.

Baddeley, Meade, and Newcombe (1980) suggest that measures for assessing treatment effects should be reliable across observers, sensitive to subtle changes in perfor- mance, and valid predictors of functioning in the natural environment. While standard neuropsychological tests are generally reliable and valid for diagnostic purposes, certain tests such as the WAIS-R are relatively insensitive to subtle changes in ability over and above practice effects, and there is some question about how well neuropsychological measures predict everyday functioning (Diller & Gordon, 1981a; Newcombe, 1982).

A study recently presented at a neuropsychology conference (Weiss, 1984) illustrates the significance of this issue of valid outcome measures. The author reported that 13 head trauma patients improved their scores on 27 of 31 psychometric measures after 6 to 8 months of neurotraining and multimodal therapy. Scores such as the mean Full Scale IQ of the WAIS improved from 89 to 97, and most of the Luria Nebraska subtests improved approximately 4 points. No attempt was made to assess practice effects, but more impor- tantly, no attempt was made to assess the significance of these test score changes in the everyday lives of the patients. Were there corresponding changes in the quality of their lives? Did they enroll in the program only to improve their test scores or were they functionally better off? The author concluded that the evidence "strongly supports the viability of the treatment program," but this conclusion appears lacking in external validity.

In response to the need for more externally valid measures to assess treatment outcome, many investigators have developed their own scales of everyday functioning. The problem with this approach is that each scale is somewhat different which confounds comparisons across studies. Instead of developing yet another Activities of Daily Living (ADL) scale (there are at least 27 of them), investigators need to arrive at some consensus about which of the currently available scales are most useful, and then use these agreed upon scales in their research, so that findings across studies can be meaningfully compared (Medical Research Council, 1982).

To a great extent, the type of dependent measures employed in cognitive retraining depend on the level of intervention (e.g., a single modality treatment of a specific memory disorder versus a multidisciplinary cognitive rehabilitation program). In the former case, alternative forms of a memory recall test might be sufficient while in the second situation, psychometric test batteries, ADL scales, and various self-report measures could all be appropriate. Ben-Yishay and Diller (1983a) stress that different kinds of normative comparisons are relevant for different kinds of assessment questions. When questions pertain to employment potential, comparisons with normal persons are appropriate. When a patient's neurological prognosis is at issue, comparisons with other individuals with acquired brain damage are probably most relevant. If the patient's own goals are paramount, then comparisons with indices of premorbid functioning take on greater relevance.

Implementation Issues

Once a cognitive deficit is identified, the approach taken can vary from attempting to change "the functional structure of a given brain" via "directed stimulation" strategies (Buffery, 1977; Powell, 1981) to identifying the correlates of cognitive impairment in activities of daily living and designing training tasks that remediate functional everyday skill deficits (Ben-Yishay & Diller, 1983a; Williams, present volume). One point of view emphasizes the remediation of specific symptoms of brain injury, while the other focuses on overall behavioral functioning. It is conceivable that both approaches might use the same training task to operationalize the problem according to their particular objectives. Nevertheless, how a problem is operationalized is critical to the development of a cognitive remedial intervention.

Tasks and Procedures

Golden (1981) outlined several desirable features of remedial tasks that appear to have, at least, face validity. First, a task should be of such complexity that several skills are required, but only one, the target for training, lies outside the patient's current repertoire of behaviors. Thus, the patient has to master that skill in order to complete the task which cannot be completed in any other way. The difficulty of a training task should range from a relatively simple level to one approximating normal performance, and it should be increased as a patient's performance improves. Measures of task performance should be quantifiable, and feedback for performance should be immediate and specific. While these guidelines have a certain intuitive appeal, a number of practical issues remain concerning the order of task presentation, the manner in which levels of task difficulty are determined, the criteria for task mastery, the relationship of the task to relevant outcome measures, the number of training trials, the frequency and duration of sessions, and when training should be initiated and terminated (Barth & Boll, 1981; Diller & Gordon, 1981a).

Plateaus and Critical Periods for Retraining

An issue which especially important in therapeutic interventions with brain injured populations concerns whether there are critical periods for retraining, which end when plateaus are reached (Horton & Miller, 1984). Diller and Gordon (1981b) suggest that if a person reaches a plateau, and fails to show further improvement on a task, he should probably be dropped from training. If he improves on a task and shows improvement on external tasks as well, training should continue. If, however, he only improves on the training task, but fails to show generalization to external tasks, the decision to continue or terminate should be made on a cost-effective basis. Bach-y-Rita (1980) argues, however, that periods of no learning or plateaus may occur only to be followed by a resumption of progress, albeit at a less accelerated rate. Studies with non-brain injured subjects on perceptual and motor learning suggest that such discontinuities occur regularly. It may be that brain injured patients should discontinue training on a temporary basis when they reach a plateau in order to avoid frustration, but then should resume it at a later time. Maximal functional recovery may therefore require several periods of cognitive retraining (Bach-y-Rita, 1980).

Placebo Effects

However investigators decide to conceptualize cognitive retraining with regard to the above issues, it is important that placebo and nonspecific treatment effects be ruled out when attempting to determine the efficacy of an intervention. One way to do this is to have an equivalent control group receive an inert but credible form of "treatment" and then compare this group to the actual treatment group on outcome measures. In studies of the efficacy of EEG biofeedback training for the control of seizures, investigators often employ "sham" feedback which has the appearance of EEG contingent feedback on a subject's video monitor, but is in fact random, noncontingent information (Lubar & Deering, 1981). Conceivably, something similar could be carried out in cognitive retraining programs that are computer-based. An alternative strategy, in situations where it is difficult to devise a credible placebo, is to randomly assign equivalent subjects to two different forms of treatment and then compare them on outcome measures, to determine if one intervention is superior, i.e., produces specific therapeutic effects over and above the other treatment (Beck et al., 1984). In a rehabilitation setting this could involve a comparison of a group that receives traditional therapy, with a group that receives cognitive retraining as well as traditional therapy, to determine if there are specific, beneficial effects of cognitive retraining over and above traditional therapy.

Experimenter Effects

An additional consideration in the implementation of a cognitive retraining task is experimenter bias. The internal validity of cognitive retraining research can be enhanced by ensuring that training trials are conducted according to the established protocols for a given task. Such procedural reliability can be accomplished by periodically observing trainers and giving them objective feedback, perhaps via a rating scale. Experimenter bias an also be controlled by keeping trainers "blind" concerning patient assessment data, and in between-group comparison studies, keeping assessors "blind" concerning the group membership of patients (Beck et al., 1984).

The Problem of Spontaneous Recovery

A major threat to the internal validity of studies on the efficacy of cognitive retraining is spontaneous recovery. Natural or spontaneous recovery refers to brain function return after neurological insult, that is independent of formal, systematic intervention. If the process is ongoing at the same time cognitive retraining is implemented, it may pose a significant confound when attempting to evaluate the effects of treatment. The natural course of recovery varies depending on the nature and severity of the underlying pathology and various subject and environmental variables (Lezak, 1983). For example, natural recovery after head trauma typically follows a diminishing returns function in which changes occur fairly rapidly during the first six months but gradually slow and reach a plateau by the end of the second six months with little improvement occurring after one year (Powell, 1980). Recovery from aphasia after stroke progresses rapidly during the first three months and tends to be nearly complete in six months (Darley, 1982). Recovery from aphasia is generally faster after trauma than after stroke, but other cognitive functions typically recover more slowly after trauma than after stroke (Davis, 1983). Different functions appear to recover at different rates, with higher level, complex integrative abilities being the last to recover (Barth & Boll, 1981).

The critical questions is: does cognitive retraining make a difference in the outcome of brain injured patients over and above improvements associated with spontaneous recovery? One research strategy that has been employed to demonstrate the effectiveness of cognitive remedial interventions is the post-spontaneous recovery comparison. This approach delays initiation of treatment until after the period of maximum spontaneous recovery has transpired. The assumption of this approach, largely present in the study of aphasia therapy, is that continued improvement at a postspontaneous recovery stage would be minimal without treatment (Davis, 1983). This evaluation strategy would appear to be well suited for large-scale rehabilitation programs which are not permitted to use untreated control groups.

The NYU cognitive rehabilitation program (Ben-Yishay, 1980, 1981; Ben-Yishay & Diller, 1981, 1983b) appears to have been deliberately designed as a post-spontaneous recovery comparison study since all entrants to the program have to be at least one year post-trauma and "stable" in their recovery. To ensure that patients are stable before being allowed into the program, these investigators employ a double baseline assessment technique with a ten week interval between assessments. Preliminary data suggest that training in attention and concentration, and interpersonal skills was of significant benefit to the first 13 trainees, but the effects of training on higher level cognitive tasks yielded only mixed results (Ben-Yishay & Diller, 1981).

Incomplete knowledge of the point at which the recovery curves for different functions reach their asymptote poses significant problems for the use of the postspontaneous recovery comparison design in evaluating cognitive remedial interventions (Newcombe, 1982). The double baseline assessment technique would seem to be a necessary control in this regard. An additional practical problem in some treatment settings might be a policy that requires patients to be treated as soon as they are referred, regardless of whether the process of spontaneous recovery is complete. There is also the possibility that a critical period exists in which intensive cognitive remedial intervention may produce greater gains than would be realized by spontaneous recovery alone, but if training were delayed, these extra gains would be lost (Levin et al., 1982).

Ideally, the best way to control for the effects of spontaneous recovery is to use a randomly assigned, nontreatment control group. If a postspontaneous recovery comparison design must be used, a way to increase its logical warrant is to combine it with a within-subject experimental design and assess the effects of cognitive retraining on individuals.

Research Design Issues

Classical Between-Group Experiment

There are few published investigations of cognitive remedial interventions which use a classical experimental design with random assignment of subjects to treatment or non-treatment conditions. One notable exception is a series of studies at NYU's Institute of Rehabilitation Medicine in which Weinberg et al. (1977, 1979) used this design in a cognitive retraining program for right brain damaged stroke patients. These investigators found that a treated group substantially improved in sensory awareness and perceptual functioning compared to an untreated control group.

Aside from the fact that cognitive retraining is a relatively new field, there are a number of factors, some already discussed, which made the classic treatment versus no-treatment group comparison design difficult to implement in this kind of research. In many settings there are ethical objections to a no-treatment control condition. In rehabilitation settings, there is often the problem of overlapping multidisciplinary treatments which are beyond the control of the cognitive retraining researcher. For some patients, being placed on a waiting list may produce a different set of expectancies about treatment from those who get treatment without waiting. Finally, being placed on a waiting list may lead to greater attrition in the control group as patients seek treatment elsewhere (Beck et al., 1984).

Alternative Between-Group Comparison Designs

Alternative between-group comparison designs have been proposed in the study of psychotherapy outcome. One approach is the component control strategy (Stuart, 1973). Clients are randomly assigned to two groups and are provided with the same treatment rationale. Then one group receives the standard treatment while the control group receives only one component of the treatment or several components in therapeutically inert combinations (Beck et al., 1984). In a cognitive retraining study this might involve exposing control subjects to only the first stage of a complex, hierarchically arranged training module. In using this design, assessment of client expectancies would be necessary to make sure the groups view their treatments with equal credibility (Beck et al., 1984).

Another alternative is the comparison of two different forms of treatment for the same type of disorder. Comparable patients are randomly assigned to one or the other treatment conditions and later compared on outcome measures. While this approach does not directly address the question of whether treatment is more beneficial than no treatment, it can help determine if one treatment is more effective than the other. For example, a study (Wertz et al., 1981) of aphasia therapy compared group treatment to individual treatment and found significant differences which favored individual therapy. If it can be assumed that the effects of group treatment are no worse than the effects of nontreatment or natural recovery, then this study is suggestive that individualized aphasia therapy makes a positive difference.

Within-Subject Designs

Experimental within-subject designs may also serve as an alternative to the treatment versus no-treatment control group design. These designs offer a number of advantages for evaluating cognitive retraining effects. Such designs obviate any immediate need to find a large group of matched subjects which is often difficult within neurological populations. They permit initial testing of a treatment effect on a smaller, more cost-effective basis, and they provide information about specific individuals in treatment (Golden, 1981; Horton & Wedding, 1984; Parsons & Prigatano, 1978).

According to Kratochwill, Mott, and Dodson (1984), experimental within-subject designs, unlike the traditional case study approach, possess several methodological features which promote internal validity. First, they are characterized by repeated assessments of the dependent variable which allows for an examination of trends in the data and for assessment of client variability over time. Thus, the more pronounced a change in client behavior during

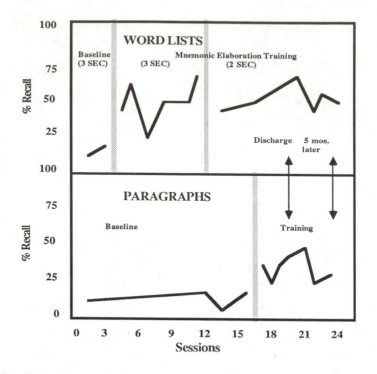

Figure 1. Recall on word list recognition task with nine interference words (top) and "gist" scoring of ideas from paragraphs (bottom). Reprinted by permission from Giantutsos, R. (1980). What is cognitive rehabilitation? *Journal of Rehabilitation, 46,* 36-40.

treatment, compared to baseline, the stronger the inference for a treatment effect. Secondly, these designs require precise specification of all of the elements in the experiment: subject characteristics, treatment setting, the therapist, and the independent and dependent variables. This information may serve to promote the external validity of a study by allowing for replication and generalization of results. A third feature of these designs is the requirement for replication of effects within the experiment in order to test the hypothesized relationship between the independent and dependent variables. Internal validity is enhanced by replications within subjects or across behaviors, settings, or subjects. Finally experimental within-subject designs can be altered during the course of an experiment in response to client behavior in different phases. For example, a therapist would probably elect to delay introducing a new phase of a study until a client's behavior had become relatively stable in the current phase.

There are many variations of experimental within-subject designs, too numerous to detail, but one which has particular merit in assessing treatment outcome is the multiple baseline design. A study reported by Gianutsos (1980) illustrates some of the advantages of this design. The investigator used a multiple baseline, across behaviors design to train a patient on two tasks: 1) memory for word lists and 2) oral reading and recall of paragraph information (Figure 1). Initially, baselines were obtained for the patient on both tasks, and then training was started in word list retention while baseline data continued to be collected on the second task. Training on the first task was discontinued when the patient's memory performance on word lists reached normal limits. At that point in time, training on the second task, paragraph recall, commenced. Following this training series, the patient's recall of paragraph information was also improved.

The patient's improvement on the first task only occurred after training was initiated. By itself, this training is comparable to an AB within-series design which is suggestive that training caused the improvement in performance over baseline, but this phase change by itself does not necessarily rule out spontaneous recovery or extraneous events. The fact that baseline measures on the second task remained stable during the training of the first task, strengthens the inference that training accounted for improved memory performance in list recall, since extraneous events, spontaneous recovery, and other training were having no ap-parent effect on the patient's baseline performance in paragraph recall. Subsequent im-provement on the second task, only after training was initiated on this task and discontinued on the first task, further strengthens the inference that training was efficacious. Thus, it can be seen that the multiple baseline design offers considerable control in ruling out alternative explanations for treatment effects by staggering phase changes within two or more simultaneous series.

Conclusion

The task of developing cognitive remedial programs and assessing their efficacy is exceedingly complex. The burgeoning field of cognitive retraining is only in its infancy, but there is a danger that the proliferation of techniques may outstrip research (Horton & Miller, 1984). Most publications in this area are conceptual, programmatic, and descriptive with little or no empirical support. While it appears that cognitive remedial interventions for brain injured patients have promise, in an age of cost/benefit analysis, there is a critical need for evaluation.

Because of the difficulties in doing controlled between-group comparison studies, practitioners are especially encouraged to test the efficacy of their techniques by using experimental within-subject designs. Once a body of data has accumulated which shows that cognitive retraining strategies work with some consistency across a diverse set of individuals, problems, therapists, and settings, some patterns will likely emerge which will suggest what kind of between-group comparison studies should be undertaken. At that time, certain treatment evaluation strategies such as constructing or dismantling different elements in a package for their relative contribution, determining the optimum parameters of a given strategy, comparing strategies for a specific problem, or matching strategies to particular pa-tient characteristics might be undertaken (Kazdin, 1983). But first studies need to be published which demonstrate that cognitive retraining has a positive impact on the brain injured client's everyday functioning over and above placebo or spontaneous recovery effects.

References

Bach-y-Rita, P. (1980). brain plasticity as a basis for therapeutic procedures. In P. Bach-y-Rita (Ed.) *Recov - ery of function: Theoretical considerations for brain injury rehabilitation*. Baltimore: University Park Press.

Baddeley, A., Meade, T., & Newcombe, F. (1980). Design problems in research on rehabilitation after brain damage. *International Rehabilitation Medicine, 2,* 138-142.
Barth, J., & Boll, T. (1981). Rehabilitation and treatment of central nervous system dysfunction: A behavioral medical perspective. In C. Prokpot & L. Bradley (Eds.), *Medical psychology: Contributions to behavioral medicine.* New York: Academic Press.
Beck, J. G., Andrasik, F., & Arena, J. G. (1984). Group comparison designs. In A. SA. Bellack & M. Hersen (Eds.), *Research methods in clinical psychology.* New York: Pergamon Press.
Ben-Yishay, Y. (Ed.). (1980). *Working approaches to remediation of cognitive deficits in brain damaged persons* (Rehabilitation Monograph No. 62). New York: New York University Medical Center, Institute of Rehabilitation Medicine.
Ben-Yishay, Y., & Diller, L. (1981). Rehabilitation of cognitive and perceptual defects in people with traumatic brain damage. *International Journal of Rehabilitation Research, 4,* 208-210.
Ben-Yishay, Y., & Diller, L. (1983a). Cognitive deficits. In M. Rosenthal, E. R. Griffith,, M. R. Bond, & J. d. Miller (Eds.), *Rehabilitation of the head injured adult.* Philadelphia: F. A. Davis Co.
Ben-Yishay, Y., & Diller, L. (983b). Cognitive remediation. In M. Rosenthal, E. R. Griffith, M. R. Bond, & J. D. Miller (Eds.), *Rehabilitation of the head injured adult.* Philadelphia: F. A. Davis Co.
Bond, M. R. (1975). Assessment of psychosocial outcome after severe head injury. In R. Porter & D. W. Fitzsimmons (Eds.), *Outcome of severe damage to the central nervous system* (Ciba Foundation Symposium 34). Amsterdam: Elsevier.
Buffery, A. (1977). Clinical neuropsychology: A review and preview. In S. Rachman (Ed.), *Contributions to medical psychology* (Vol. I). New York: Pergamon.
Caplan, B. (1982). Neuropsychology in rehabilitation: Its role in evaluation and intervention. *Archives of Physical Medicine and Rehabilitation. 63,* 362-366.
Crosson, B., & Buenning, W. (1984). An individualized memory retraining program after closed-head injury: A single-case study. *Journal of Clinical Neuropsychology, 6,* 287-301.
Darley, F. L. (1982). *Aphasia.* Philadelphia: W. B. Saunders.
Davis, G. A. (1983). *A survey of adult aphasia.* Englewood Cliffs, N.J.: Prentice-Hall.
Diller, l., & Gordon, W. (1981a). Interventions for cognitive deficits in brain injured adults. *Journal of Con- sulting and Clinical Psychology, 49,* 822-834.
Diller, L., & Gordon, W. (1981b). Rehabilitation and clinical neuropsychology. In S. Filskov & T. Boll (Eds.), *Handbook of clinical neuropsychology.* New York: John Wiley & Sons.
Gianutsos, R. (1980). What is cognitive rehabilitation? *Journal of Rehabilitation, 46*(3), 36-40.
Glasgow, R. E., Zeiss, R. A., Barrera, M., & Lewinsohn, P. M. (1977). Case studies on remediating memory deficits in brain damaged individuals. *Journal of Cognitive Psychology, 23,* 1049-1054.
Golden, C. J. (1981). *Diagnosis and rehabilitation in clinical neuropsychology* (2nd ed.) Springfield, Ill.: Charles C. Thomas.
Goldstein, G., & Ruthven, L. (1983). *Rehabilitation of the brain-damaged adult.* New York: Plenum Press.
Horton, A. M., & Miller, W. G. (1984). Brain damage and rehabilitation. In C. J. Golden (Ed.), *Current topics in rehabilitation psychology.* New York: Grune & Stratton.
Jennett, B. (1972). Some aspects of prognosis after severe head injury. *Scandinavian Journal of Rehabilitation Medicine, 4,* 16-20.
Jennett, B., Teasdale, G., & Knill-Jones, R. (1975). Prognosis after severe head injury. In R. Porter & D. W. Fitzsimmons (Eds.), *Outcome of severe damage to the central nervous system* (Ciba Foundation Symposium 34). Amsterdam: Elsevier.
Kazdin, A. E. (1983). Treatment research: The investigation and evaluation of psychotherapy. In M. Hersen, A. E. Kazdin, & A. S. Bellack (Eds.), *The clinical psychology handbook.* New York: Pergamon.
Kratochwill, T. R., Mott, S. E., & Dodson, C. L. (1984). Case study and single-case research in clinical and applied psychology. In A. S. Bellack & M. Hersen (Eds.), *Research methods in clinical psychology.* New York: Pergamon.
Levin, H. S., Benton, A. L., & Grossman, R. G. (1982). *Neurobehavioral consequences of closed head injury.* New York: Oxford University Press.
Lewinsohn, P. M., Danaker, B. G., & Kikel, S. (1977). Visual imagery as a mnemonic aid for brain injured persons. *Journal of Consulting and Clinical Psychology, 45,* 717-723.
Lezak, M. (1983). *Neuropsychological assessment* (2nd ed.). New York: Oxford University Press.
Lubar, J. R., & Deering, W. M. (1981). *Behavioral approaches to neurology.* New York: Academic Press.
Medical Research Council (1982). Research aspects of rehabilitation after acute brain damage in adults. *Lancet, 2,* 1034-1036.

Miller, E. (1980). Psychological interventions in the management and rehabilitation of neuropsychological impairments. *Behavior Research and Therapy, 18,* 527-535.

Newcombe, F. (1982). The psychological consequences of closed head injury: Assessment and rehabilitation. *Injury, 14,* 111-136.

Parsons, O. A., & Prigatano, G. P. (1978). Methodological considerations in clinical neuropsychological research. *Journal of Consulting and Clinical Psychology, 4,* 608-619.

Powell, G. E. (1981). *Brain function therapy.* Aldershot, Great Britain: Gower Publishing Company.

Prigatano, G. P., Fordyce, D. J., Zeiner, H. K., Rouche, J. R., Pepping, M., & Wood, B. C. (1984). Neuropsychological rehabilitation after closed head injury in young adults. *Journal of Neurology, Neurosurgery, and Psychiatry, 47,* 505-513.

Rimel, R. W., Giordani, B., Barth, J. T., Boll, T. J., & Jane, L. (1981). Disability caused by minor head in - jury. *Neurosurgery, 9,* 221-228.

Rosenbaum, M., Lipsitz, N., Abraham, J., & Najenson, T. (1978). A description of an intensive treatment project for the rehabilitation of severely brain-injured soldiers. *Scandinavian Journal of Rehabilitation Medicine, 10,* 1-6.

Smith, M. L., & Glass, G. V. (1977). Meta-analysis of psychotherapy outcome studies. *American Psychologist, 32,* 752-760.

Stuart, R. B. (1973). Notes on the ethics of behavior research and intervention. In L. A. Hamerlynck, L. C. Hardy, & E. J. Mash (Eds.), *Behavior change: Methodology, concepts, and practice.* Champaign, Ill.: Research Press.

Sbordone, R. J. (1984). Rehabilitative neuropsychological approach for severe traumatic brain-injured patients. *Professional Psychology: Research and Practice, 15,* 165-175.

Tobis, J. S., Puri, K. B., & Sheridan, J. (1982). Rehabilitation of the severely brain-injured patient. *Scandinavian Journal of Rehabilitation Medicine, 14,* 83-88.

Weinberg, J., Diller,, L., Gordon, W. A., Gershman, L. J., Lieberman, A., Lakin, T., Hodges, G., & Ezrachi, O. (1977). Visual scanning training on reading-related tasks in acquired right brain damage. *Archives of Physical Medicine and Rehabilitation, 58,* 470-486.

Weinberg, J., Diller, L., Gordon, W. A. Gershman, L. J., Lieberman, A., Lakin, T., Hodges, G., & Ezrachi, O. (1979). Training sensory awareness and spatial organization in people with right brain damage. *Archives of Physical Medicine, 60,* 460-477.

Weiss, R. L. (1984, October). *Impact of a multidisciplinary treatment program on the mental status of the traumatically brain injured.* Paper presented at the Annual Meeting of the National Academy of Neuropsychologists, San Diego, Ca.

Wertz, R., Collins, M., Weiss, D., Kurtzke, J., Friden, T., Brookshire, R., Pierce, J., Holtzapple, P., Hubbard, D., Porch, B., West, J., Davis, L., Matovich, V., Morley, G., & Ressureccion, E. (1981). Veterans Administration cooperative study on aphasia: A comparison of individual and group treatment. *Journal of Speech and Hearing Research, 24,* 580-594.

7

Treatment of Visual Imperception and Related Disorders

Wm. Drew Gouvier and Mark S. Warner

Spontaneous recovery of behavioral deficits following cerebrovascular accidents (CVA's) continues over a period of months and years (Hier, Mondlock, & Kaplan, 1983; Skilbeck, Wade, Hewer, & Wood, 1983) but many patients never regain sufficient adaptive skills to resume employment, or even enough independence to allow their caregivers to return to work. In many cases deficits in problem solving, social skills, memory, and visuo-perceptual processing abilities impose greater limits on occupational and interpersonal efficiency than physical limitations such as motor or speech deficits (Lewinshohn & Graf, 1973). Many of the factors limiting recovery have been recognized only in recent years, but there is a growing body of research on the remediation of these deficits (Blanton & Gouvier, 1986a, Diller & Gordon, 1981; Diller & Weinberg, 1977; Gianutsos & Matheson, 1986; Gouvier, Webster, & Blanton, 1986). This chapter will review recent studies in the area of visuoperceptual assessment and remediation strategies used to reduce morbidity among individuals afflicted with right hemisphere brain damage.

Gianutsos and Matheson (1986) have suggested that researchers and clinicians must broaden their view of visuoperceptual deficits, to allow closer attention to impairments and abberations of basic sensory functioning. Sensory based visual abberations (e.g. low acuity, poor convergence) are transmitted through the visual processing systems of the brain, and the observed behavioral deficits may represent a normal response to abnormal input. Because the mechanisms of the behavioral deficit following brain injury are not entirely clear, and the powerful negative valence of words such as "neglect", Gianutsos has recommended the use of the more neutral term, visual imperceptions, to describe a cluster of behavioral deficits that have been described under the labels of left neglect or hemi-inattention. She has also described a three-factor model which can be used to account for visual imperceptions. There is a lateral gaze factor, a peripheral spatial imperception factor, and a foveal imperception factor; these factors correspond with the anatomically distinct systems for eye movements, peripheral vision, and macular vision (Gianutsos, Glosser, Elbaum, & Vroman, 1983).

Left-sided visual imperception associated with right brain damage is a particularly appropriate target for intervention because such patients often show sparing of verbal intellectual skills and these residual abilities can be drawn upon in compensation training. If left unresolved or untreated, left visual imperceptions can place limits on the patient's functional independence. Studies in this area have focused on the identification of, 1) left spatial visual imperception, 2) hemifoveal perceptual disturbance, 3) cortical blindness, and 4) complex integrative behavior. Tables 1, 2, and 3 present summary information on 24 studies involving the assessment and treatment of acquired disorders within each of these domains (Gouvier, Webster, & Warner, 1986).

Table 1

Studies Examining Treatment For Left-Sided Neglect

Authors & Population	Methods	Results
Goldman (1966) 20 CVA patients who could not pass DDS exam	Practice on DSS trials beginning with easiest stimulus combinations and progressing through to most	Treated patients improved relative to untreated patients, and treatment gains maintained at follow-up
Gordon et al. (1985) 77 RBD CVA patients; E = 48, C = 29	35 hours of scanning + cancellation + somatosensory awareness + size est. + complex perceptual organization training vs OT, PT, & controls	Treated patients surpassed controls in all areas, but controls' recovery contiued post discharge. At 4-month follow-up, E = C.
Gouvier et al. (1986) 5 RBD CVA patients	Daily assessments of cancellation and scanning performance to assess effects of cancellation and lightboard training	Prompt gains in targeted task, but little generalization to nontrained task.
Gouvier et al. (1984) 2 RBD CVA patients	Combined scanning training with mobile scanning activities and distance estimation training	Improved wheelchair navigation promoted by additional mobile and distance estimation exercises
Lawson (1962) 2 RBD CVA patients	Reminders to "look left" and practice in using finger tracing to keep place in reading activities	Improvement noted, but limited to domain of reading
Riddoch & Humphreys (1983) 5 RBD patients	Cued patients to "look left" and required them to identify a left-sided stimulus before attempting the task	Bisection performance enhanced by left-sided scanning. Without prompting patients tended to only look to their right
Webster et al. (1984) 3 RBD CVA patients	Studied effects of stationary and mobile scanning activities on wheelchair navigation	Prompt improvement on scanning task with less pronounced generalization to wheelchair navigation task.
Weinberg et al. (1977) 57 RBD CVA patients	20 hours of training on scanning and reading tasks vs OT controls	Groups remained neurologically equivalent but E surpassed C on nearly all measures, with gains maintained at 1 year, Some generalization
Weinberg et al. (1979) 53 RBD CVA patients	Combined 15 hours of scanning and reading with 5 hours of training somasthetic localization and size estimation vs OT controls	Combined treatments appear more effective in alleviating neglect. Visuo-percetual disorders are layered and may be revealed as others resolve.
Young et al. (1983) 27 RBD CVA patients; E1 = 9 E2 = 9, C = 9	Compared scanning + cancellation + block design training (E1) vs scanning + ccncellation + OT (E2) vs OT controls	E1 surpassed E2, both surpassed C. More varied training associated with with more generalized gains

Note: DSS=Double Simultaneous Stimulation; OT=Occupational therapy.

Preliminary Sensory System Evaluation

It is important that patients who present with visual imperception receive a preliminary evaluation of their visual system, in order to identify whether there are sensory abberations in addition to whatever centrally mediated problems which are interfering with proper functioning of the overall system. Four components crucial to this preliminary assessment have been identified and discussed at length by Gianutsos & Matheson (1986). The major parameters of vision to check in a preliminary assessment are 1) near and far point acuity of each eye, 2) field of vision, 3) binocular incapacities, including problems of accommodation, suppression and diplopia, and 4) oculomotor functions.   Once this preliminary evaluation is completed, one can proceed with further investigation and assessment of the imperception problem itself.

Patients with acquired disorders of vision and perception may show a variety of specific symptoms which can appear singly or in clusters. These symptoms can represent involvement of the sensory/perceptual system, the motor/execution system, or the attentional system.   Careful assessment of the nature of a patient's disorder is crucial toward individualizing remediation strategies to match the observed deficits.

Sensory Losses and Visual Field Cuts

Patients with lesions affecting the optic radiations or occipital cortex may present with blind areas (scotoma) within their visual fields. Unless the patient is able to compensate for this loss by effective scanning with their residual vision, the result is that much of the information in a patient's frontal visual environment is not detected. Lesions affecting the primary tactile sensory areas can produce similar tactile sensory losses to the side contralateral to the lesion. The use of visual confrontation (Reitan and Davison, 1974) leaves much to be desired as a measure of visual fields, missing as many as one half of the cases who show deficits on other measures (Trobe, Acosta, Krischer, & Trick, 1981). Vision screening devices such as the Keystone VS-11 and others feature a periometer that permits controlled assessment of peripheral points along a horizontal plane. With practice, reasonable estimates of a patient's visual fields can also be mapped out using a hand held or table mounted perimeter. With information suggesting the presence of visual field defects, appropriate referral for quantitative field measurements can be made.

Hemispatial Imperceptions and Hemiinattention

Even patients without genuine sensory losses may still be unable to identify visual stimuli on their affected side when their attention is not specifically directed toward that stimulation. This fact sometimes causes patients to be misdiagnosed as having visual field defects rather than a simple tendency toward hemi-imperception. This is significant for rehabilitation planning; obviously the treatment of the former problem might be more involved than that of the latter.   Right sided CVA patients who show signs of hemiimperception often seem unaware of left-sided external space, and may fail to recognize their own left arms or legs unless cues are given. Such patients often show anosognosia as well; this refers to their unawarness of their deficits. The author (DG) has seen numerous acute cases of right hemisphere CVA patients who must be tied to their beds in order to keep them from turning over and over again, always turning toward their right sides. In effect, the patients seem to be trying to find "midline," which by their reckoning lies somewhere off in their right peripheral visual field.

Hemifoveal Deficits

While foveal or macular vision is often spared in cases with visual field cuts, differences in left and right sided foveal perception have been reported by a number of authors (Castro-Caldas & Salgado, 1984; Gianutsos et al., 1983). The presence of such deficits suggests that some patients can bring a stimulus onto the macula for detailed inspection, but still misperceive crucial aspects of the stimulus. Such deficits can often be revealed on reading tasks, either in the assessment laboratory or in the real world (e.g. misreading WOMEN as MEN on a doorway).

Computerized Assessment of Visual Perception

Advances in computer technology have had profound effects on the measurement of visuoperceptual abilities, and one can expect to see further gains in the accuracy of assessment and sophistication of computer assisted intervention strategies. Tasks employing computer displays can be made more sensitive than non-computer tasks and can often measure finer grades in performance as well (Blanton & Gouvier, 1986b). Computerized tasks have been developed for the popular "personal computers" such as the Apple II series, the TRS-80 series, and the IBM PC and its compatibles. These include programs designed to measure reaction time, peripheral field recognition tasks, and measures of foveal hemiimperception. While a thorough discussion of computer applications to the treatment of visual perceptual disorders is beyond the scope of this chapter, the reader is referred to the writings and programs of Bracy (1982, 1983), Gianutsos (Gianutsos, Cochran, & Blouin, 1984; Gianutsos & Klitzner, 1981) and Sbordone (1983) for detailed discussion of computer applications in assessment and retraining exercises.

The advantages of computer controlled tasks allow for precise control of the duration of stimulus displays and convenient measurement of response times with immediate feedback to the patient and examiner. These tasks also can be designed to reduce motor/praxic demands on the patient and allow for more efficient sensory assessment. In the future, one can expect to see further refinements in computer applications in assessment, as well as sound demonstrations of their usefulness for retraining and rehabilitation purposes.

Treatment Strategies

Spontaneous Recovery

Brain injured individuals may be expected to improve spontaneously as the recovery process progresses. Several studies have documented the spontaneous recovery of visuoperceptual abilities (Colombo, DeRenzi, & Gentilini, 1982; Hier et al., 1983; Meerwaldt, 1983), and have noted that most of the severe manifestations of hemiimperception resolve within a year of injury. Many patients recover much sooner than that, and once the acute effects of injury or infarct have passed, recovery can be likened to a negatively accelerating curve in which most recovery happens within the first 6 months, and a lesser degree in each succeeding period. Therefore, much of what is passed off as "treatment gain" may in fact be spontaneous recovery. Perhaps training can facilitate spontaneous recovery processes, but training programs that can do no more than that may offer little in treating patients with profound and lasting imperception.

Hemi-imperception and Hemi-inattention

It is not uncommon for the brain injured individual to have sustained some decrement in arousal and vigilance functions. As arousal and attention provide the "cortical tone" (Luria, 1966) upon which higher functions are supported, it is not uncommon for these patients to have extensive deficits in higher cognitive functions as well. Attentionnal remediation may improve a wide range of cognitive abilities, and is considered essential prior to the introduction of other forms of training (Luria, 1963).

Over the past two decades, there has been a growing interest in the treatment of left hemi-imperception (Table 1), also known as left neglect or left hemi-inattention. Lawson (1962) described two cases who were frequently reminded to "look to the left" and who also learned to use finger pointing as an aid to reading. Improved reading was reported, but treatment gains did not generalize to other domains of visual behavior. Luria and Tsvetkova (1964) outlined a rationale and specific techniques to use in training patients to work block designs. Goldman (1966) devised a tactile sensory training program based on the established hierarchy of double simultaneous stimulation (DSS) procedures.

The greatest amount of work in this area has been conducted at New York University Institute of Rehabilitation Medicine (NYU; Ben-Yishay, Diller, Gerstman, & Gordon, 1970; Diller, Ben-Yishay, Gerstman et al., 1974; Gordon, Hibbard, Egelko et al., 1985; Weinberg, Diller, Gordon et al., 1977, 1979; Weinberg, Piasetsky, Diller, & Gordon, 1982). The initial (1970) study demonstrated that the more intact patients were more likely to benefit from trainer provided cues than were the less intact patients, a finding common among head injury patients as well (Torkelson, Jellinek, Malec, & Harvey, 1983). Using treatment protocols described in the 1974 monograph, these investigators have demonstrated that visual scanning training and cancellation training have a greater impact on symptoms of neglect than does routine occupational therapy alone (Weinberg et al., 1977). A later study (Weinberg et al., 1979) showed that adding treatment components for size estimation and increasing accuracy and awareness in locating tactile stimulation to the body further enhances the effectiveness of scanning and cancellation training with right CVA patients. A third program (Weinberg et al., 1982) focused on perceptual organization deficits often seen in non-neglecting right brain damaged patients. Follow up reevaluation of many patients have been done, and treated patients have always tended to surpass the controls.

In the most recent work (Gordon et al., 1985), a combination of all three training programs was contrasted with a control group which engaged in either leisure activities or additional formal therapy. Treated patients performed significantly better than controls on most measures at discharge, but the control group had recovered to a level comparable to the treated group by the four month follow-up. The authors suggest that this unusually large degree of improvement among the controls may represent the influence of unstructured training experiences that all patients at NYU are likely to receive, as the institutional effects of their retraining program have become more widespread, and their procedures become more widely adopted by other therapy disciplines within the institute.

In other reports, scanning plus cancellation plus block design training surpassed scanning plus cancellation training plus occupational therapy, and both treatment combinations surpassed occupational therapy alone in promoting changes on a battery of perceptual and cognitive tasks (Young, Collins, & Hren, 1983). Training in visual scanning can help promote improved wheelchair navigation skills, but the degree of generalized improvement varies from case to case (Webster et al., 1984). Wheelchair navigation can be specifically improved by adding training exercises that focus on individual performance deficiencies which interfere with success (Gouvier, Cottam, Webster, Beissel, & Woffard, 1984). Others have shown the importance of forcing subjects to actively scan and search in their affected hemifield in order to compensate for their deficits (Riddoch & Humphries, 1983) and the need to train on a variety of tasks in order to avoid the poor generalization that is seen with limited training regimes (Gouvier, Bua, Blanton, & Urey, in press).

Hemifield Perceptual Disturbances

        The study of subtle disorders of visuo-perceptual functioning in brain damaged patients is a relatively new area (Table 2). Nonetheless, hemi-foveal deficits have been identified that can affect either left or right sided foveal perception (Castro-Caldas & Salgado, 1984; Gianutsos et al., 1983; Johnston Sablow, & Johnson, 1986), and symptoms of subtle left imperception can be revealed in non-neglecting right brain damaged patients provided sufficiently demanding assessment tasks are utilized (Blanton & Gouvier, 1986b). It is not uncommon to see perceptual distortions which are confined to stimuli that are presented in left hemispace; the same stimuli presented in right hemispace may be accurately perceived (Heilman, Watson, & Valenstein, 1985; Weinberg et al., 1979). Providing training in the use of systematic visual exploration and emphasizing careful analysis of stimuli in the left visual field has been shown to contribute to improved perceptual functioning in patients with and without gross visual imperception (Gordon et al., 1985; Weinberg et al., 1982).

Cortical Blindness and Visual Field Cuts

        While many of the previously cited studies dealt with the treatment of imperceptions in patients who also had visual field cuts, another area of investigation deals with efforts to affect the visual field cut itself. It has long been known that in the presence of lesions of the geniculo-striate visual pathways, some residual visual ability is often spared, and some recovery of the geniculo-striate system appears in about 75% of cases presenting with cortical blindness (Drymalski, 1981). While much of this improvement probably represents recovery of some geniculo-striate functions, it is believed that the sparing of some visual capabilities in the presence of areas of total cortical blindness represents the functions of the extrastriate retinotectal pathways, and although such visual information is processed outside the domain of consciousness, patients can reportedly develop a "feel" for learning to identify and use this extra-striate visual information.

        In recent studies, systematic training in form identification has been shown to promote recovery and use of residual geniculo-striate capabilities in a hypoxic adolescent (Merrill & Kewman, 1986). The actual size of a scotoma can be reduced by providing practice in light identification using stimuli presented at the margins of the scotoma according to the method of limits (Zihl & VonCramon, 1979). These authors note that other visual functions such as color and form identification skills also re-emerged concurrent with the development of light identification abilities within the inner margins of shrinking scotoma. Using a different approach, other patients have also been trained to look in the direction of visual stimuli presented within the area of their field defects even though they have no conscious experience of the stimuli (Zihl, 1980). Such training might prove useful if patients could learn to detect stimuli in their blind field, and bring them onto the fovea for conscious inspection and identification.

Table 2

Treatment Studies of Hemifield Perceptual Disturbance and Cortical Blindness

Author & Population	Methods	Results
Hemifield Perceptual Disturbance		
Blanton & Gouvier (1986b) 20 Non-neglecting RBD CVA patients	Assessed left- and right-sided reaction times, reading, and searching abilities of 10 males and 10 females	Left-sided reaction time and reading deficits noted among both groups. Males showed large L-R differences on searching tasks, females did not
Castro-Caldas & Salgado (1984) 1 LBD CVA patient	Assessed visual fields and hemifield reading and color identification	Patient could not read numbers, letter symbols, or words presented to right visual field
Gianutsos et al. (1983) 38 mixed LBD, RBD and bilateral patients versus 56 controls	Assessed left- and right-sided reading and searching abilities	Identified 3 factors associated with RBD: left spatial hemiimperception; left foveal hemiimperception; lateral scanning disturbance
Johnston et al. (1985) 30-year-old male with surgically split brain and left hemialexia	Combined training in systematic left-to-right scanning, use of left-sided anchor cues, and double checking for reading accuracy	Small improvement in daily assessment, little generalization, lower ratio of left to right-sided errors
Weinberg et al. (1982) 35 non-neglecting RBD CVA patients; E = 17, C = 18	20 hours of training in using spatial coordinates for stimulus location, organizing stimuli into patterns, and visual exploration vs OT controls	Treatment subjects showed gains in in visual analysis and organizational skills
Cortical Blindness		
Merrill & Kewman (1986) 14-year-old female with hypoxic encephalopathy	Combined verbal feedback, tracing cues and form and color identification	Prompt improvement on training tasks but little generalization
Zihl (1980) 3 CVA patients	Practice looking in direction of stimulus presented within scotomae	All patients improved in their ability to localize visual stimuli
Zihl & VonCramon (1979) 12 mixed brain injured	Practice identifying lights presented at the margins of scotomae, using	Scotoma was reduced

Complex Integrative Behavior

The human organism is routinely confronted with myriad tasks of great complexity. There have been several reported efforts to confront the molar problems encountered by train damaged patients which limit their independence in activities of daily living. An early study examined the relative usefulness of perceptual/cognitive therapy activities versus motor-practice focused occupational therapy (Taylor, Shaeffer, Blumenthal, & Grissel, 1971) but failed to reveal any differences in outcome. They attributed this to the lack of correspondence between their outcome measures of capacity for independent functioning and the perceptual-cognitive factors of Ayers' Percept-Concept-Motor Function Battery, rather than the failure of global cognitive training itself. Shifting the focus from global training to specific skills training on complex tasks, other researchers have reported the successful training of safe wheelchair transfers to a patient with profound left neglect (Stanton et al., 1983). Although gains learned in the hospital did not generalize to the patient's home setting following discharge, these gains were reinstituted in the home environment by simply providing a couple of home-based training sessions designed to promote transfer of the newly learned skill.

Loss of independence in ambulation and community mobility is a source of distress for many brain damaged individuals. In an exciting series of studies, measures that predict driving performance among brain damaged, spinal cord injured, and able bodied individuals were identified (Sivak, Olson, Kewman, Won, & Henson, 1981) and a list of those perceptual-motor domains associated with poor driving was compiled (Table 3). Subsequent training on paper and pencil perceptual-motor tasks, focusing on those domains most closely related to poor driving, has been shown to improve both closed course and open field driving abilities among the brain injured participants (Sivak et al., 1984). Furthermore, actual practice in maneuvering a vehicle through structured analog driving exercises can lead to improved actual on road driving skills (Kewman et al., 1985), and would seem to offer participants a greater measure of face validity. This might make it easier to mobilize motivation for eager involvement and learning. Further work in this domain is now underway at the Rehabilitation Engineering Center for Personal Licensed Vehicles at Louisiana Tech University. Project coordinators there have developed a video tracking task, a small scale vehicle, and a full sized van all of which have interchangeable controls. This systems would allow the identification of the appropriate prescription for assistive devices or controls early in assessment so that any further assessment or training can be done on vehicles that have the same sets of controls (Schubert & Erwin, 1985). Researchers there and elswhere (Jones, Giddens, & Croft, 1983; Timmermans, Blovin, & Reed, 1986) have demonstrated that cognitive and psychomotor tasks can be good predictors of the driving performance of brain-injured people.

An Overview of the Clinical Picture

The role of the neuropsychologist begins with the initial assessment of the patient. In order that the patient's present level of functioning might be understood from both premorbid and post injury perspectives, information from medical records, academic records, occupational history, and significant others, as well as data from neuropsychological, intellectual and personality measures should be considered. The purpose of this extensive assessment is to identify both relative strengths and weaknesses of the patient. Assessment of the brain injured patient should not just yield a litany of deficiency; relative strengths are needed to provide the foundation upon which an individualized rehabilitation program can be devised (Craine & Gudeman, 1984, Luria, 1963). Examiners should "test the limits" with their assessment procedures in order to better understand why items are passed and failed, and also to provide an opportunity for quasi-experimentation about what supports it takes to prop up a desired response. Bolger (1981) has made the point that there are three degrees of freedom in cognitive retraining. Patients can learn improved strategies for completing tasks, their capacity for task accomplishment might be improved by training and exercise, and the demands of the task might be altered in order to make it simpler to complete successfully. These are the factors that one might manipulate in order to get the most out of testing the limits of our patients' abilities.

Table 3

*Treatment Studies of Mobility Skills*s

Author & Population	Methods	Results
Jones et al. (1983) 261 mixed brain injured 39 controls	Examined ability to predict road driving with test of visual functioning, reaction time and medical & psychological appraisal	Improved screening can help reduce the need for road assessment of patients who fail. Among 38 who failed the road test and received training on the road, 15 improved.
Kewman et al. (1985) 13 brain injured with treatment, 12 brain injured controls and 11 normal controls	16 hours in analog driving exercises progressing through a hierarchy of increasingly difficult exercises versus practice driving analog vehicle without training.	Training improved analog and real-world driving, practice on analog trainer did not
Sivak et al. (1981) 23 brain-injured with treatment, 8 SCI controls and 10 normal controls	All subjects assessed on perceptual/ cognitive tests, closed course and real-world driving	Brain-injured drove the worst and poor driving among them was predicted by perceptual/cognitive tasks.
Sivak et al. (1984) 8 mixed brain injured	8 to 10 hours of training on paper and pencil perceptuomotor and cognitive tasks	All subjects improved on training tasks, 7 of 8 improved on driving. Driving improvement was related to improvement on training tasks.
Stanton et al. (1983) 44-year-old RBD CVA	Task analysis of wheelchair transfers followed by behavioral program of chaining skills with gradual fading of prompts	Patient learned safe transfers in hospital but did not at home until the program was introduced to home environment
Timmermans et al. (1986) 28 head injured	Examined ability to predict driving skills using perceutal & intellectual tests	79% of variance in on-road driving skill was predicted by night vision depth perception, auditory reaction time, WAIS-R Arithmetic and Digit Symbol.

Once the initial assessment has been completed, hypotheses are generated about why the patient's visual autonomy is impaired. Cognitive deficits revealed by the psychometric evaluation are compared with the complaints presented by the patients and their significant others. Further hypotheses are then generated about the role of other factors contributing to the patients functional deficits. Thus, case conceptualization and testing of hypotheses is conducted on an experimental basis and a specific training strategy is formulated.

The second stage in the treatment process is education. The patient and family need to be taught what is wrong by a detailed, but simple, verbal and pictorial explanation. In a case where sensory deficits exist, the patient may appear confused in instances where his sensory system failed, without giving enough information to let the patient know of this. While it is important that such patients experience the consequences of their imperception, the clinician's role is to offer the patient the opportunity to discover for himself that his sensory system is no longer functioning up to snuff. Arguing or verbal confrontation are doomed to be less effective than experiential feedback, and are likely to prove aversive to the patient. Once the patient recognizes that there is a problem of imperception, then the proposed treatment strategy is explained and discussed in detail.

We have been particularly impressed by a technique described by Diller et al (1974) in which the hemiimperceptive patient is seated at a large table and 20 or more U.S. Currency bills in varied denominations are arranged in front of and to both sides of the patient. The patient is simply told to pick up all the money he or she can find. The demonstration seems more effective when real money vs. play money is used, and also with bills of higher denominations. We often plant the largest bill available on the far left, so that even patients who find many of the bills can still be told "you missed over half of the money there." This demonstration seems most effective when used to introduce imperceptive patients to the fact and significance of their problem, and the need for treatment. Used after initial assessment is underway, when patients often do find all of the money, the demonstration is counterproductive. It can be used to validate treatment effectiveness to a patient that had previously performed imperfectly.

Step three involves repeated exercise and practice of the retraining strategy on a scheduled basis. Retraining and compensatory techniques may be developed based on the profile of strengths and weaknesses generated from the assessment data. Throughout treatment, as the patient's performance improves, case conceptualization and specific interventions should be revised to accommodate progress and continue to challenge the limits of functioning, rather than plodding along doing repetitions of exercises that have become easy. As recovery proceeds, behavioral goals become more complex and deficits may become more subtle in their manifestation. As the treatment program is modified, premorbid personality and adjustment factors should be considered in so far as they may contribute to the residual deficits. Such factors should be considered as primary problems, however, only after other hypotheses have been assessed, evaluated, and rejected. As behavioral recovery plateaus, it is often necessary to reassess performance and initiate the case conceptualization/ intervention process, but recognizing that with the passage of time, the likelihood increases for residual deficits to become permanent.

The fourth step is recovery generalization and self management. Gianutsos and Matheson (1986) recommends assisting the patient in maximizing "top down" processing when "bottom up" processing deficits exist. These terms refer to two modes of administrating the contents of consciousness. The "top down" mode represents strategically driven information processing with use of systematic hypothesis testing, problem solving, and compensatory techniques. The "bottom up" mode is driven by incoming sensory information which is interpreted, integrated and stored. The patient needs to know as much as possible about how their visual- perceptual system is operating, and how it is failing to function, to permit effective planning for situations in which compensation will be needed. External cues may be necessary and whenever possible problems should be overcome with alternatives that still permit greater independence (e.g. a patient may find it easier to learn to read a digital watch than to re-learn how to read an analog dial).

Concluding Comments

There is growing evidence that acquired visuoperceptual disorders can be treated, and that treatment gains can be related to improvements in patients' capacities for independent living. Our present level of sophistication in this area still lags far behind the "instructional psychology" for brain damaged individuals that has been called for (Diller & Gordon, 1981). While individualized assessment and treatment are currently valued approaches, the development of individual programs could be improved if more facts about general patterns of recovery from brain damage were known.

The more often we can recognize regularly occurring progressions of recovery, the more they can be related to other regular progressions in complex training activities. For example, the double simultaneous stimulation (DSS) extinction hierarchy (Bender, Fink, & Green, 1951) ranges from DSS trials least likely to show tactile suppressions (ipsilateral hand and contralateral face) to those most likely to reveal suppressions (ipsilateral face and contralateral hand).   Another continuum that influences the probability of revealing suppressions refers to the simultaneity of the left and right sided stimulus presentations (Birch, Belmont, & Karp, 1967). DSS trials in which the contralateral stimulus precedes the ipsilateral stimulus are the least likely to reveal suppressions, while those with the ipsilateral stimulus presentations first are the most likely to reveal suppressions. The breadth and depth of training exercises might be enhanced by using these known relationships to provide initial experiences in the most supportive conditions and then gradually change the values along all relevant dimensions from most to least supportive so that clients gain experience with training conditions that may be more severe than those typically encountered in the outside world.

There are other regularities affecting the expression of symptoms of brain damage as well. Deficits can be revealed as task complexity is increased by introducing new processing or memory demands, by introducing competing or distracting stimuli, by degrading the clarity of relevant stimuli, by having the patient practice under conditions of fatigue, reduced oxygenation, or illness. We can manipulate some of these factors to minimize patient's deficits early in training when patients need the most help. For example, changes in body position can be used to help overcome a tendency to keep the head turned to the right following a right sided CVA. By invoking the asymmetric tonic neck reflexes, positioning the patients arms and legs appropriately can help allow the patients to maintain better head coordination. These and other factors can influence task demands, degree of environmental support for the response, and patient variables in such a way that training exercises emulate characteristics encountered in the criterion setting, the outside world.

Further investigation into the factors affecting generalization is also warranted. Since no effective technology for promoting generalization of treatment gains has been developed, it is important that procedures that train ecologically relevant behaviors be developed. Toward this end, the indications for training component skills versus molar behavior patterns need to be identified. In the meantime, a pragmatic approach might be to train only those components that are necessary to permit successful training of the desired molar behavior, and to train on as wide of a variety of ecologically relevant molar behaviors as time permits.

The present literature would indicate that both restoration of function to a damaged system and the development of new functional systems are important in accounting for treatment gains. It would appear that interventions can involve either or both. Zihl's work on shrinking the size of patients' scotomas (Zihl & Von Cramon, 1979) exemplifies the former, while his work on training rudimentary visual appreciation (Zihl, 1980) inside of patients' scotomas would represent the latter.

Finally, it should be noted that as a discipline, we are far from constructing the much needed meta-theory of rehabilitation for brain injury (Diller & Gordon, 1981). While specific approaches to conceptualizing rehabilitation from strokes (Diller & Weinberg, 1977) and head injury (Long, Gouvier, & Cole 1984) have been offered, they are woefully in need of refinement and elaboration. Given the present status of this developing area, and the number of significant recent contributions, the outlook looks promising for further advances.

References

Bender, M. B., Fink, M., & Green, M. (1951). Patterns in perception simultaneous tests of face and hand. *Archives of Neurology and Psychiatry, 66,* 355-362.

Ben-Yishay, Y., Diller, L., Gerstmann, L., & Gordon, W. (1970). Relationship between initial competence and ability to profit from cues in brain damaged individuals. *Journal of Abnormal Psychology, 75,* 248-259.

Birch, H., Belmont, I., & Karp, E. (1967). Delayed information processing and extinction following cerebral damage. *Brain, 90,* 113-124.

Blanton, P. D., & Gouvier, W. D. (1986a) Cognitive retraining therapies with neurologically impaired patients. *The Behavioral Therapist, 3,* 47-50.

Blanton, P. D., & Gouvier, W. D. (1986b). Sex differences in visual information processing in nonneglecting right brain damaged subjects. Manuscript under editorial review, Louisiana State University and University of Alabama at Birmingham.

Bolger, J. (1981). Cognitive retraining: A developmental approach. *Clinical Neuropsychology, 4,* 66-70.

Bracy, O. (1982). *Cognitive rehabilitation programs for brain injured and stroke patients.* Indianapolis: Psychological Software Services, Inc.

Bracy, O. (1983). Computer based cognitive rehabilitation. *Cognitive Rehabilitation, 1,* 7-8.

Castro-Caldas, A., & Salgado, V. (1984). Right hemifield alexia without hemianopsia. *Archives of Neurology, 41,* 84-87.

Colombo, A., DeRenzi, E., & Gentilini, M. (1982). The time course of visual hemi-inattention. *Archives of Psychiatry and Neurological Sciences, 231,* 539-546.

Craine, J., & Gudeman, H. (1981). *The rehabilitation of brain functions: Principles, procedures and techniques of neurotraining.* Springfield, Illinois: Charles C. Thomas.

Diller, L., Ben-Yishay, Y., Gerstman, G., Goodkin, R., Gordon, W., & Weinberg, J. (1974). *Studies in cognition and hemiplegia.* New York: New York University Medical Center, Institute of Rehabilitation Medicine.

Diller, L., & Gordon, W. (1981). Interventions for cognitive deficits in brain-injured adults. *Journal of Consulting and Clinical Psychology, 49,* 822-834.

Diller, L., & Weinberg, J. (1977). Hemi-inattention in rehabilitation: The evolution of a rational remediation program. *Advances in Neurology, 18,* 63-82.

Drymalski, W. (1981). Cortical blindness. *Comprehensive Therapy, 7,* 13-18.

Gianutsos, R., Cochran, E., & Blovin, M. (1984). *Computer programs for cognitive rehabilitation, Vol. III.* Bayport, New York: Life Sciences Associates.

Gianutsos, R., Glosser, D., Elbaum, J., & Vroman, G. (1983). Visual perception in brain-injured adults: Multifaceted measures. *Archives of Physical Medicine and Rehabilitation, 64,* 456-461.

Gianutsos, R., & Klitzner, C. (1981). *Computer programs for cognitive rehabilitation.* Bayport New York: Life Sciences Associates.

Gianutsos, R., & Matheson, P. (1986). The rehabilitation of visual perceptual disorders attributable to head injury. In M. J. Meier, L. Diller, & A. R. Benton (Eds.), *Neuropsychological rehabilitation,* London: Churchill Livingstone.

Goldman, H. (1966). Improvement of double simultaneous stimulation perception in hemiplegic patients. *Archives of Physical Medicine and Rehabilitation, 47,* 681-687.

Gordon, W. A., Hibbard, M. R., Egelko, S., Diller, L., Shaver, M. S., Lieberman, A., & Ragnarsson, K. (1985). Perceptual remediation in patients with right brain damage: A comprehensive program. *Archives of Physical Medicine and Rehabilitation, 66,* 353-359.

Gouvier, W. D., Bua, B. G., Blanton, P. D., & Urey, J. R. (in press). Behavioral changes following visual scanning training: Observations of five cases. *International Journal of Clinical Neuropsychology.*

Gouvier, W. D., Cottam, G., Webster, J. S., Beissel, G. F., & Woffard, J. D. (1984). Behavioral interventions with stroke patients for improving wheelchair navigation. *International Journal of Clinical Neuropsychology, 4,* 186-190.

Gouvier, W. D., Bua, B. G., & Blanton, P. D. (1986). Cognitive retraining with brain damaged patients. In D. Wedding, A. Horton, & J. Webster (Eds), *The neuropsychology handbook: Clinical and behavioral perspectives,* New York: Springer-Verlag.

Gouvier, W. D., Webster, J. S., & Warner, M. S. (1986). Treatment of acquired visuoperceptual and hemi-inattentional disorders. *Annals of Behavioral Medicine, 8,* 15-20.

Heilman, K., Watson, R., & Valenstein, E. (1985). Neglect and related disorders. In K. Heilman & E. Valenstein (Eds.), *Clinical Neuropsychology* (2nd ed.). New York: Oxford, 243-293.

Hier, D. B., Mondlock, J., & Caplan, L. R. (1983). Recovery of behavioral abnormalities after right hemisphere stroke. *Neurology, 33,* 345-350.

Johnston, C. W., Sablow, D., & Johnson, M. (1986). Perceptual cognitive retraining in commissurotomy-induced hemialexia. Minneapolis MN, manuscript under editorial review.

Jones, R., Giddens, H., & Croft, D. (1983). Assessment and training of brain damaged drivers. *American Journal of Occupational Therapy, 37,* 754-760.

Kewman, D. G., Seigerman, C., Kintner, H., Chu, S., Henson, D., & Reeder, C. (1985). Simulation training of psychomotor skills: Teaching the brain-injured to drive. *Rehabilitation Psychology, 30,* 11-27.

Lawson, I. R. (1962). Visual-spatial neglect in legions of the right cerebral hemisphere. *Neurology, 12,* 23-33.

Lewinsohn, P., & Graf, M. (1973). A followup study of persons referred for vocational rehabilitation who have suffered brain injury. *Journal of Community Psychology, 1,* 57-62.

Long, C. J., Gouvier, W. D., & Cole, J. C. (1984). A model of recovery for the total rehabilitation of individuals with head trauma. *Journal of Rehabilitation, 50,* 39-45.

Luria, A. R. (1963). *Restoration of function after brain injury.* Oxford: Pergamon.

Luria, A. R. (1966). *Higher cortical functions in man.* New York: Basic Books Inc.

Luria, A. R., & Tsvetkova, L. S. (1964). The reeducation of brain damaged patients and its psychoeducational applications. In J. Helmuth (Ed.), *Readings in special education.* New York: Grune & Stratton.

Meerwaldt, J. D. (1983). Spatial disorientation in right handed infarction: A study of the speed of recovery. *Journal of Neurology, Neurosurgery, & Psychiatry, 46,* 426-429.

Merrill, M. K., & Kewman, D. G. (In press). Training of color and form identification in cortical blindness: A case study. *Archives of Physical Medicine and Rehabilitation.*

Reitan, R., & Davison, L. (1974). *Clinical neuropsychology: Current status and applications.* New York: Wiley.

Riddoch, M. J., & Humphreys, G. W. (1983). The effect of cuing on unilateral neglect. *Neuropsychologia, 21,* 589-599.

Savir, H., Michelson, I., David, C., Mendelson, L., & Najenson, T. (1977). Homonymous hemianopsia and rehabilitation in fifteen cases of CCI. *Scandinavian Journal of Rehabilitation Medicine, 9,* 151-153.

Sbordone, R. J. (1983). *Computer programs for neuropsychological testing and cognitive rehabilitation.* Fountain Valley, CA: RJ Sbordone, PhD, Inc.

Shubert, R., & Irwin, E. (1985). Louisiana Tech's tracking simulator. Engineering Tech Brief, NIHR Grant #G0083C0097, Ruston, Louisiana: Rehabilitation Engineering Center, Louisiana Tech University.

Sivak, M., Hill, C. S., Henson, D. L., Butler, B. P., Silber, S. M., & Olson, P. L. (1984). Improved driving performance following perceptual training in persons with brain damage. *Archives of Physical Medicine and Rehabilitation, 65,* 163-167.

Sivak, M., Olson, P. L., Kewman, D. G., Won, H., Henson, D. L. (1981). Driving and perceptual/cognitive skills: Behavioral consequences of brain damage. *Archives of Physical Medicine and Rehabilitation, 62,* 476-483.

Skilbeck, C. E., Wade, D. T., Hewer, R. L., & Wood, V. A. (1983). Recovery after stroke. *Journal of Neurology, Neurosurgery, & Psychiatry, 46,* 5-8.

Stanton, K. M., Pepping, M., Brockway, J. A., Bliss, L., Frankel, D., & Waggener, S. (1983). Wheelchair transfer training for right cerebral dysfunctions: An interdisciplinary approach. *Archives of Physical Medicine and Rehabilitation, 64,* 276-279.

Taylor, M. M., Schaeffer, N. J., Blumental, F. S., & Grissell, J. L. (1971). Perceptual training in patients with left hemiplegia. *Archives of Physical Medicine and Rehabilitation, 52,* 163-169.

Timmermans, S., Bouman, J., & Reed, P. (1986). The role of assessment and driving outcome for head injured individuals. Paper presented at the National Head Injury Foundation conference, November, Chicago, Illinois.

Torkelson, R. M., Jellinek, H. M., Malec, J. F., & Harvey, R. F. (1983). Traumatic brain injury: Psychological and medical factors related to rehabilitation outcome. *Rehabilitation Psychology , 28,* 169-174.

Trobe, J. D., Acosta, P. C., Krischer, J. P., & Trick, G. L. (1981). Confrontation visual field techniques in the detection of anterior visual pathway lesions. *Annals of Neurology, 10,* 28-34.

Webster, J. S., Jones, S., Blanton, P. D., Gross, R., Beissel, G. F., & Woffard, J. D. (1984). Visual scanning training with stroke patients. *Behavior Therapy, 15,* 129-143.

Weinberg, J., Diller, L., Gordon, W. A., Gerstman, L. J., Lieverman, A., Lakin, P., Hodges, G., & Ezrachi, O. (1977). Visual scanning training effect on reading related tasks in acquired right brain damage. *Archives of Physical Medicine and Rehabilitation, 58,* 479-496.

Weinberg, J., Diller, L., Gordon, W. A., Gerstmann, L. J., Lieberman, A., Lakin, P., Hodges, G., & Ezrachi, O. (1979). Training sensory awareness and spatial organization in people with right brain damage. *Archives of Physical Medicine and Rehabilitation, 60,* 491-496.

Weinberg, J., Piasetsky, E., Diller, L., & Gordon, W. (1982). Treating perceptual organization deficits in non-neglecting RBD stroke patients. *Journal of Clinical Neuropsychology, 4,* 59-75.

Young, G., Collins, D., & Hren, M. (1983). Effect of pairing scanning training with block design training in the remediation of perceptual problems in left hemiplegics. *Journal of Clinical Neuropsychology , 5,* 201-212.

Zihl, J. (1980). "Blindsight": Improvement of visually guided eye movements by systematic practice in patients with cerebral blindness. *Neuropsychologia, 18,* 71-77.

Zihl, J., & VonCramon, D. (1979). Restitution of visual functions in patients with cerebral blindness. *Journal of Neurology, Neurosurgery, & Psychiatry, 42,* 312-322.

8

The Remediation of Everyday Memory Deficits

Marsha M. Little

Memory deficits are the most frequently reported consequence of cerebral trauma (Levin, Benton & Grossman, 1982). They are associated with such conditions as head injury, cerebral tumor and infection, progressive degenerative disease, nutritional disorder and stroke. Not only are they a pervasive consequence of brain injury, but memory disorder is complex and very difficult to remediate. This is in part due to the complexity of human memory. The deficit may be in immediate, short- or long-term storage, and it may be modality or material specific, or the problem may be in either encoding, storage or retrieval of information.

When memory impairment occurs in people who have suffered such brain injuries, they and their families are likely to experience great difficulty in procuring treatment or even suggestions to help them deal with such a devastating problem, and the problems that result from this type of impairment in their everyday life. The much advertised programs observed in the media to improve memory are virtually useless for individuals who have suffered cerebral damage. These individuals need a program embedded in a protective environment and assistance from professionals specially trained in the field of rehabilitation (Prigatano, 1986).

Several questions remain unanswered regarding memory remediation in brain-damaged individuals. First, which strategies work and for which types of memory deficits do they work? Second, are brain-damaged individuals able to generalize the usage of such techniques to their everyday lives and practical memory problems? Third, how well do brain-injured individuals comply with learning and practicing the techniques, and how long are they maintained in daily life after initial training?

The purpose of this paper is to review the effectiveness of these memory retraining techniques and to offer further alternatives for intervention in memory disorder. However, in order to better understand the literature, one must first appreciate the historical antecedents of memory retraining, the multidimensionality of memory and assessment of memory impairment. Only then can the effectiveness of the visual imagery methods and verbal mnemonics be reviewed. Some alternatives to these strategies will be suggested including the use of memory aids or compensation strategies. Finally, special problems relevant to the remediation of memory such as modality-specificity and functional deficits will be discussed.

Overview of Memory

Types of Memory

A major question of those interested in memory has been how many kinds of memory are there? This section will attempt to summarize current views of memory by highlighting the distinctions of memory such as subtypes of memory stores, modality specificity of memory, and other dimensions in memory that are especially relevant to memory retraining. As with any other very brief overview, this will inevitably be a simplification and a more extensive account of current views of memory for the non-specialist can be read in such reviews as Baddeley (1982a).

As every introductory student learns, memory can be divided into at least three memory stores (Atkinson & Shiffrin, 1971). The first is sensory memory, which is of a very brief duration and can be further differentiated into iconic (visual), echoic (auditory) and haptic (tactile) memory. A breakdown in any one of these is often manifested as a perceptual or attentional deficit. The second type of memory is short-term or working memory, which lasts from a few seconds to a few minutes. Finally, the third type of memory is long-term or secondary memory which is usually manifest as slowed or impaired learning.

Memory can also be differentiated by modality specificity. Very often material is divided into verbal and visual information, but there are other kinds of specific memory, such as motor learning and procedural learning. It is important to assess strengths and weaknesses along these lines because it may be possible to capitalize on the clients strengths to compensate for his weaknesses. For example, in theory, the person with a verbal mem-ory deficit may be trained to use visual imagery strategies to remember new information (Jones, 1974; Wilson, 1982).

Memory can also be divided by semantic versus episodic content. Semantic memory refers to memory for knowledge or facts, like kinds of fruit or the state capitols. In contrast, episodic memory refers to events, such as dinner last evening or the context of learning. It is essentially autobiographical in nature.

Another distinct type of memory is procedural learning. It is manifested in classical conditioning acquisition of mirror writing or learning the Tower of Hanoi puzzle. It has been demonstrated that amnesic patients are able to learn such tasks, but are unable to relate how or where they learned it (Baddeley, 1982b).

The Structure of Memory

Memory can also be broken down into processing states, input, storage and retrieval. Input or encoding is comprised of attention, intention to learn, organization of information and levels and types of processing (Craik and Lockhart, 1972). Attention and intention are for the most part necessary for learning. Organization of information facilitates recall and new material is organized in terms of already existing memory stores. Craik and Lockhart (1972) demonstrated that levels of processing has a bearing on how well information is remembered: the more elaborate the processing, the greater the retention and recall.

The least understood processing state is that of storage. Little is known about the manner and location of information stored in the brain. The final processing state is that of retrieval. Two factors can influence retrieval, encoding specificity and encoding variability. In encoding specificity, retrieval is optimal when the retrieval context is the same as when the material was learned, and this includes context dependent and state-dependent memory. An example is retracing one's steps to remember something. Encoding variability involves with the generalization of information to another context. A way to reduce encoding specificity and enhance encoding variability is to practice a new skill in as many environments as possible (Prigatano, 1986).

It is important to understand that there can be a deficit in any of the memory stores or types, and in any of the processing states. Given such complexity it is essential that a good memory assessment be conducted before a remediation program is developed.

Memory Assessment

Given the complexity of human memory, a thorough assessment of memory ability is essential in order to develop a sufficiently specific retraining program. One of the main reasons for a thorough assessment is to identify specific memory deficits and to be used as a baseline to measure effectiveness of treatment. A good memory assessment must assess sensory, short and long-term functions. It must also include measures that can separate verbal and visual-spatial functions. Patients with lateralized damage will have different impairments in memory. Left hemisphere damaged patients profit more from non-language related retraining strategies and right hemisphere damaged patients profit more from language related strategies, or variants of them (Binder & Schreiber, 1980; Fordyce & Jones, 1980; Gasparrini & Satz, 1979; Jones, 1974). Care must be taken to determine if there is a modality specific memory deficit. Assessment can also identify functions that underlie specific deficits. For example, performance can be affected by non-related sensory deficits or poor motivation.

It is important to ascertain the extent to which a person's memory impairment affects everyday life. This can be accomplished by direct observation of the person's behavior in the rehabilitation setting or by means of relative and self-report questionnaires. Research has indicated that relative reports are significantly related to memory test results (Bennett-Levy & Powell, 1980; Brooks, 1979; Hermann & Neisser, 1978; Little & Williams 1985; Sunderland, Harris & Baddeley, 1983; Zelinski, Gelewski & Thompson, 1984). Memory diaries that record forgotten items have also been shown to be somewhat helpful (Wilson & Moffatt, 1984). The major advantage of everyday memory measures is that they can directly identify problems related to progress in treatment and enable one to ascertain specific problem areas in which to learn specific strategies.

Finally, in order to fully comprehend the extent of memory deficits, the assessment should be carried out within the context of a complete neuropsychological evaluation, including assessment of perceptual and language abilities, psychomotor and psychosensory abilities, attention, conceptual reasoning and general intelligence. If a person has impaired perceptual skills, for example, they may not accurately perceive the stimulus material and language impairment may limit comprehension of instructions or inability to express the answer. It is also important for the patient to be made aware of deficits (Prigatano, 1986; see also Gouvier & Warner, this volume). This awareness allows the patient to develop realistic goals, accept those deficits and eventually begin to develop and use compensation strategies.

The History of Memory Retraining

After World War II, the health care system was faced with the rehabilitation of many returning brain-injured soldiers. Prominent in this development was Goldstein (1942), who recognized three classes of symptoms that could underlie the mental or neuropsychological disturbances of these patients. He proposed one group of symptoms that were not a direct result of the damage to the brain, but were reflective of the person's ability to cope with his cognitive deficits in the environment. The second class were cognitive deficits directly resulting from damage to specific areas of the brain. The third class of symptoms resulted from an impairment of the "abstract attitude", and Goldstein suggested that many of the personality problems of brain injured patients really reflected this third class of difficulties. Shortly after, Zangwill (1947) proposed three principles useful in the rehabilitation of brain injured patients. These principles are 1) the use of compensation to get around a deficit, 2) the use of substitution to solve a problem that the brain is able to solve, but by different means, and 3) attempting to retrain the deficit. These three principles are the basis of modern rehabilitation, and most cognitive retraining methods center around either retraining a deficit or use of strengths to develop compensation strategies. Furthermore, they are often used directly in the remediation of memory impairments.

The first recorded mnemonic strategy is attributed to Simonides in 477 B.C. who, according to Cicero, was able to identify the corpses of noblemen crushed beyond recognition soon after a ceiling collapsed at a banquet. He was able to identify them by scanning his visual memory of the seating arrangement. Other methods for remembering are described by Cicero and Quintillian, such as the ancient method of loci (Yates, 1966). Some practical applications of these methods can be found in Furst (1944), Lorayne and Lucas (1974) and Luria (1968).

Verbal techniques also have a long history. For example, Peter Ramus, in the 16th century, developed a system for remembering by organizing information into a hierarchical tree (Ramus, 1578). Abstract concepts branched out into progressively more concrete instances. People who used this system argued that not as much additional information had to be learned in order to use this system as in visual imagery systems. In 1849, Brayshaw published a book, *Metrical Mnemonics,* incorporating 2000 dates and facts from physics, astronomy, history and geography into a selection of rhymes. One of the best known examples of such a rhyme helps one remember the number of days in the month: "Thirty days have September, April, June and November, when short February comes, all the rest have thirty-one." One of the best known anatomy mnemonics refers to the names of the cranial nerves: "On Old Olympia's Towering Top a Finn and German Vault and Hop" (olfactory, optic, oculomotor, trochlear, trigeminal, abducens, facial, auditory, glossopharyngeal, vagus, accessory and hypoglossal).

In the field of cognitive remediation, a central issue of retraining versus compensation needs clarification. Cognitive retraining or remediation of memory implies the "retraining" of brain tissue in other areas of the brain that are supposed to perform the lost function. In contrast, the use of memory aids is simply a way of supplementing memory functions, usually by adding an external memory store. Cognitive retraining is based on a neural model, inferring changes in neuronal mechanisms, like the rerouting of neural connections. In contrast, the use of memory aids is a form of functional compensation which is based on a behavioral model (Heilman & Valenstein, 1979). Instead of rerouting connections, the brain damaged person develops new solutions to problems using residual structures and functions. The theory of retraining was initially developed by Luria (1969). In general, it claims that the dynamic reorganization of the nervous system is promoted by specific therapy such as the retraining of memory.

It has been shown that when such methods are used by neurologically intact individuals, recall of specific information can be greatly enhanced (Atwood, 1971; Bower,

1970; Pavio, 1969). Given this apparent success, such techniques have been recently advocated as potential treatment approaches to the remediation of organic memory disorder. Several cognitive retraining packages have been offered to help in the rehabilitation of brain damaged adults, but the results of such treatment strategies are anecdotal and equivocal. One problem with determining the efficacy of such treatments is that few well controlled group studies have been done and even then, the groups have mixed etiologies making it difficult to determine the benefits of such treatments for particular individuals and particular types of brain damage. Another difficulty with existing studies is that the subjects are often many months post-trauma and are no longer impaired as assessed by neuropsychological tests.

Memory Remediation Strategies

There are several basic "rules of thumb" that should be taken into account whenever a cognitive retraining program is developed. Wilson (1981a, 1982) points out that behavioral strategies are especially useful in memory retraining because they are widely adaptable, and the goals are set in small and more easily attainable increments. Furthermore, assessment can be ongoing and perhaps most importantly, behavioral approaches have been shown to be effective in a wide range of behavior changes. Such a program includes certain basic stages including, 1) identification of each specific behavior to be changed, 2) specification of goals, 3) baseline measures of specified behavior, 4) formulation of a specific remediation strategy suited to the individual, 5) treatment plans, when, where and how often, etc., 6) evaluation of progress on a regular and frequent basis and, 7) change of procedures if necessary. Not only is a behavioral program likely to effect improvement on specific memory problems, but using this type of structured program allows the clinician to monitor treatment effectiveness, thus improving cost/effectiveness.

Several measures can be taken to maximize the benefits of a memory rehabilitation program. For example, if memory strategies capitalize on the patient's strengths rather than retraining deficits, there is greater likelihood of success. Similarly, understanding individual differences in learning ability and cognitive style and selecting strategies that most closely meld with these differences increases success. Given that generalization of strategies to everyday situation is a common problem with any cognitive retraining, thus, memory skill training should be integrated into as many modalities and settings as possible. For example, the same skills can be developed in speech, occupational and physical therapies. They might also be carried over into interactions with the nursing staff and taught to family members who will care for the patient after discharge.

Strategies for remediating memory impairment can be divided into five general categories which include retention, recall, internal, and external strategies and physical treatments (Wilson & Moffatt, 1984).

Retention Strategies

Retention or rehearsal strategies are basic mnemonics that most people use automatically, but in the brain-damaged person, automatic use of such strategies is impaired. An example of an automatic retention strategy is the repetition of phone numbers after just hearing them. Some forms of rehearsal are distributed practice, which has been shown to be more effective when rehearsal or practice sessions were shorter and more frequent. This is because with each session, the individual come with different experiences (e.g., mood and

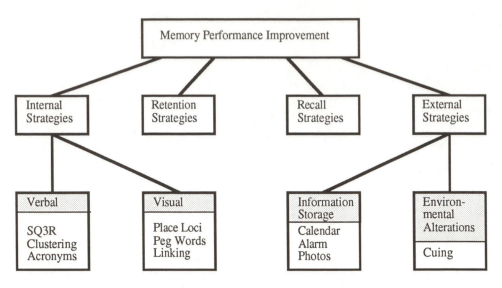

Figure 1. Memory Retraining Strategies.

physical surroundings) and therefore establishes more cues. If the sessions are kept short, fatigue is less likely to become an inhibiting factor (Baddeley, 1986).

Recall Strategies

There are several ways to enhance recall of information. Attempting to reinstate the conditions under which one learned information, serves to increase cues to facilitate recall (Baddeley, 1986). Bringing to mind the environment and mood or physical state existing when learning occurred helps facilitate memory. The difficulty with this strategy is that in brain-damaged individuals, memory for the context is also usually forgotten. Providing cues for the person can sometimes help facilitate recall. Teaching the person to look for surrounding cues can also eventually help memory.

Internal Strategies

Visual Imagery Techniques. Many studies have found that there is a greater capacity for visually encoded information and it is more resilient to forgetting than verbally encoded information (Haber, 1970; Nickerson, 1968; Sheppard, 1967). The elaborate visual memory capacity of humans allows them to recall or recognize a large amount of visual information. In addition, having the subject create vivid, highly associated visual images results in substantially increased recall in neurologically intact subjects (Atwood, 1969). It has also been suggested that bizarre and vivid images are more effective, but there has been little empirical evidence to support these claims. For example, Collyer, Jonides & Bevan (1972) studied a group of 80 normal subjects and found that bizarre, implausible scenes did not enhance the free recall of noun-verb-noun triplets. In fact, recall was enhanced by more plausible images. Similarly, Poon & Walsh-Sweeney (1981) found that logical interacting images were more effective in facilitating recall of paired associates than bizarre images in both young and older subjects. In addition, elderly subjects tended to resist the use of bizarre images.

Visual imagery forms the basis for several mnemonic techniques such as the Place-loci method, the Peg-word method, and the Link or Chaining method. Since these are the three major visual mnemonics used, they will be discussed separately.

The Place-loci Method. In order to make use of this system, the subject must be able to remember a series of geographical or architectural locations in a fixed order. Once this fixed order is learned, newly presented material can be learned by associating it with specific geographical locations or loci. It can later be recalled by retracing the path through the fixed order of loci and retrieving the objects. For example, if the subject had three chores to complete on a given day (e.g. buying milk, washing a shirt and painting a door), then the subject could associate a salient image from each chore (e.g. carton or milk, shirt, door) with three rooms in the house. The subject might imagine the following: a carton of milk in the middle of the vestibule, his shirt in an easy chair in the living room, and a door lying on the bed in the bedroom. In order to recall these chores, the subject need only visualize the vestibule, living room and bedroom and identify the object in each.

The Peg-word Method. This method makes use of a well learned series of visual objects paired with numbers. The information that is to be remembered is visualized interacting with an associated peg word forming a compound visual image. For example, if the first thing to be remembered in the morning is to take medication, a subject can visually pair a pill with a bun and imagine it sandwiched between the two halves of the bun. If the second thing is to start the coffee, he might visualize the coffee pot sitting inside an enormous shoe, etc. The subject can later recall this information by going through the number series and reconstructing the images paired with the peg words. A popular version of the Peg-word system is presented below:

one is a bun	six is sticks
two is a shoe	seven is heaven
three is a tree	eight is a gate
four is a door	nine is a vine
five is a hive	ten is a hen

The Linking or Chaining Method. This is the most straight-forward of all the visual mnemonic techniques. A memory chain is formed by linking the to-be-remembered items with interactive images or similar semantic or acoustic similarities. For instance, the first step of using the peg system uses the link system and is based on simple acoustical associations (e.g. one=bun).

Verbal Mnemonics. While the average adult often uses verbal mnemonics such as rhymes to remember information, they are probably poor generic techniques that can be used in many situations, especially by those who have memory disorders. All verbal strategies are predicated on the assumption that deeper processing of information insures better memory for that information (Craik & Lockhart, 1972). Since all of these methods are classification systems, they still require that the person remember even more information. Although they have not met with the same popularity as the visual imagery techniques, several verbal or non-visual strategies have been developed to retrain memory in brain damaged individuals.

One verbal strategy used to improve memory is putting new information into a sentence or story. An example is the "airplane list" developed by Higbee (1977) in which several new to-be-remembered words are inbedded in a silly story. Similarly, one can remember a fact by devising a mnemonic sentence for that fact. For example, the sentence "the id is hid" helps one remember that the id is unconscious, or as every musician knows, "every good boy does fine" helps one remember the names of the notes on the musical scale. Acronyms are favorites for remembering information, for example, GOAT stands for the Galveston Orientation and Amnesia Test and MADD represents Mothers Against Drunk Drivers. Finally, information can be put into a rhyme to facilitate recall, e.g. "thirty days hath September...".

Organization is another major method of using verbal information to facilitate memory. Various information can be sorted 1) by likes, 2) by importance as in an hierarchy or outline, 3) by proximity, to remember a phone number, 396-1710, you would encode it into three-ninety-six, seventeen, ten.

Note-taking was used in a study designed to facilitate memory for prose. Lewinsohn et al. (1977) trained a fifty year old anoxic man to decompose stories into a relatively small number of main ideas. He was to read the story, write down the main points and try to remember those. No data are offered to make comparisons of pre- and post-treatment performance, but the authors conclude that his memory was substantially improved.

An elaboration of this note taking method is the SQ3R or the PQRST method. This method is a study aid that has been shown to be efficacious for improving the performance of college students on recall tests (Robinson, 1970; Young & Gregga, 1973). The acronyms stand for five specific stages with which to approach the recall of prose. The brain damaged patient must be trained in each of these steps then taught to use the method as a whole.

1. **Skim/Preview**: Skim material in order to become familiar with it.
2. **Question;** On the basis of the preview, formulate key questions to be answered while reading the text.
3. **Read**; Read actively, attending to it and attempting to answer the questions asked above.
4. **Recite/State**; Repeat the information that has been read. ·
5. **Rehearse/Test**; Test oneself on the material, specifically answering the questions asked.

Any of the internal strategies described above take a great deal of time for a brain-damaged person to acquire. They also require some memory ability and a higher level of cognitive processes in order to be learned. For example, the place-loci and peg-word methods both require sequencing skills and purposeful planning to be used. Generalization of these strategies to everyday situations is not effective. Very often, if a patient must use one of these strategies in a short period of time, he becomes frustrated and cannot make use of the mnemonic. Finally, many brain-injured individuals, particularly those with diffuse damage, have difficulty initiating behavior. They also tend to be concrete or lack the "abstract attitude", making both visual and verbal mnemonics difficult.

External Strategies

Another method of ameliorating memory deficits in brain damaged patients is to initiate the use of memory aids as compensatory measures for a permanent memory disorder. The time and effort necessary to retrain a brain damaged person's memory may be far in excess of the benefit they derive from the use of such strategies. Therefore, it may be simpler and more efficacious to teach the use of compensation strategies and aids to expand their memory capacity to include an external store. Furthermore, external aids are face valid and it is easy for the patient to understand why these strategies will help. Many neurologically intact individuals routinely make use of such strategies in the form of lists, appointment books and diaries. Harris (1980) points out that even after memory retraining, many people prefer such memory aids.

There are many kinds of memory aids, and most brain damaged patients are likely to be able to profit from some combination of them to extend their memory capacity. A simple and effective way to help organize a persons's activities is to instruct them in the use of a calendar book. This strategy can even help keep the severely memory disordered person disoriented to time. For example, the person can be trained to tear off the corner of the page of the current date in order to locate the appropriate day. Once the current day is located the subject can determine what must by done on that particular day. This strategy can be extended to help the person remember past events by having the patient keep a diary. If the calendar book is large enough, the patient can jot down meaningful events on the appropriate dates. This enables rehearsal of the event at some future time and eventually most patients will be able to retrain the information if enough rehearsal is afforded.

An expansion of this method is to include the memory for names and faces by having the person take polaroid snapshots of people and record the name, date, and event (Williams, personal communication). This method provides a visual aid as well as verbal cues. Visual cues from the background also provide more information about the event. Many times providing one cue to an event can trigger many other aspects of the same event.

Making organized lists as memory aids is something most people do to help supplement their limited memory store. However, a difficulty with lists of activities is that while they indicate to a memory disordered person what they must do, they do not indicate when to do it. For example, if a list contains an entry that a person is supposed to see the doctor at 10 o'clock Tuesday morning, this may go unheeded if the person does not have a reminder to check the list at the right time. With the current availability of such devices as alarm watches however, this may be a minor problem. The individual can be trained to set the watch alarm at the appropriate times in the morning according to the daily agenda. The patient can be trained to look at the list or calendar when the alarm rings. Most of these watches also mark the hour with a beeping noise. As an alternative to setting an alarm, the individual can be trained to check the schedule every time the watch signals the hour. This system can be adapted for such useful purposes as training a person to self-administer medication.

A memory disordered person's environment can be organized in order to help them remember. Objects can be used to facilitate memory. For example, a hammer might be laid on the table to help the person to remember to hang a picture or keys might be left lying on the table by the front door so they are never lost. In addition, the nature of familiar surroundings and familiar faces tends to facilitate memory.

An advantage of using memory aids as an adjunct to memory training is that once the individual is trained to use them, they have a greatly enhanced memory capacity with numerous applications. In addition, the training necessary to implement the use of memory aids is simple compared to mnemonic strategies. Moreover, since the individual is trained to use these methods in everyday situations, generalization to other situations may be much easier. In the long run, they become generic problem solving strategies that serve to increase memory capacity.

Effectiveness of Memory Retraining

To date, a search of the literature offers 28 case studies of brain damaged patients for whom several of these methods have worked moderately well. However, their success must be qualified in that thus far, all of the subjects had full scale IQs in at least the low average range when reported. While this fact helps define a specific memory disordered subject, it limits the generalization of the treatment of the population that most clinicians see, since a large proportion of brain damaged individuals are left with significantly lower IQs. The group studies reported have demonstrated that patients with left brain damage do better when taught visual mnemonics and right brain damaged patients benefit more when taught to use verbal strategies for remembering (Haber, 1970; Nickerson, 1968; Sheppard, 1968).

Retention Strategies

Noting the effort required to use imagery techniques, Schacter (1980) suggested the use of spaced retrieval or retrieval practice technique (Bjork, 1979; Landauer & Bjork, 1978) under the assumption that retrieval has a powerful effect on the memorability of a bit of information and that it requires little cognitive effort. Subsequently, Schacter, Rich & Stampp (1985) conducted a study in which four patients with mixed etiologies were trained to use this technique in remembering names, origins, occupations and hobbies of eight people. First, with the experimenter cuing them when to retrieve information and then for the patient to initiate use of the strategy on their own. They found that in all four patients, there was a significant increase in the ability to recall the information but they qualify their results by stating that this technique is useful only when the amount of to-be-remembered material is relatively small, and only when the delay of time between treatment and assessment is relatively short.

Recall Strategies

Although cuing is a very common strategy used to retrain memory in most rehabilitation facilities, there has been no research conducted examining the efficacy of this strategy to date. More importantly, the possibility of self-cuing has not been investigated. Research is needed to investigate the possible use of cuing methods in a brain damaged population.

Visual Imagery Techniques

Recently, there has been an expanding body of literature examining whether the efficacy of imagery mediation demonstrated in normal subjects can be utilized in clinical populations. Several groups have been studied, including the elderly (Hulicka & Grossman, 1967; Poon & Walsh-Sweeney, 1981), educable mentally retarded (Lebrato & Ellis, 1974),

Korsakoff patients (Cermak, 1975; Binder & Schreiber, 1980), other amnesics (Kovner, Mattis & Goldmeier, 1983), and brain damaged individuals (Crosson & Buenning, 1984; Lewisohn, Danaher & Kikel, 1988; Lewisohn, Glasgow, Barrera, Donaher, Alperson, McCarty, Sullivan, Zeiss, Nyland & Rodriquez, 1977; Jones, 1974; Crovitz, Harvey & Ham, 1979; Jones-Gotman & Milner, 1978; Wilson, 1982; Gasparrini & Satz, 1979). Generally, the use of visual imagery resulted in moderate improvement on recall measures in all of these groups when compared to other forms of mediation. However, the question of clinically significant improvement and generalization of the strategy to everyday tasks have not been studied.

The effectiveness of the Place-Loci method has been established in normal subjects by Atwood (1969) and Bower (1979). However, it has been less successful in the treatment of a brain damaged subject who had difficulty learning the sequential lists of movements through the locations (Lewisohn, et al., 1977). In contrast, Robertson-Tchabo, Houseman and Arenberg (1976) report increased immediate recall of a word list using this method in elderly subjects but they showed no increase in recall on the delayed task and showed no generalization of this method to situations outside the laboratory.

Clearly, the effectiveness of the Place-loci method is influenced by several aspects of the learning situation. A subject must first be able to learn sequenced information as well as be able to visualize that information. A brain damaged subject may not be able to acquire such a complex series of tasks in order to remember.

The effectiveness of the Peg-word method has been investigated in a well controlled study of left hemisphere CVA patients who evidenced verbal memory deficits and at least mild aphasia by Gasparrini & Satz (1979). They found that a peg-word system was more effective than rote repetition with encouragement as well as showing that there was a significant improvement pre- and post-treatment. They also report a trend for the system to be effective when learning word lists and sentences. Patten (1972) reports four case studies of subjects with mixed etiologies including CVA and seizure disorder who benefited from the peg-word method. However, statistics were not presented to evaluate the degree of improvement. Lewinsohn et al. (1977) report memory retraining closed head injury patients utilizing the peg-word method. Memory enhancement failed in both these cases possibly because of difficulty in generating interacting imagery, both with the time necessary to construct them and in the quality of the images. When drawings were presented, they quickly faded from memory. Finally, Wilson (1982) presented a case of a right hemisphere CVA patient who was taught this method to learn a shopping list with 100% accuracy, but was unable to generalize this strategy to any other setting.

In all of these studies, generalization was a major problem. On follow up examinations all of the patients were neglecting to use the strategies in everyday, practical situations. Furthermore, Patten (1972) reports that of the seven patients initially selected for memory retraining procedures, three were not able to benefit even in the structured training setting, which further qualifies the practical efficacy of such strategies.

Moderately successful results have been obtained in two fairly well controlled group studies using the Linking or Chaining method with Korsakoff patients and recovering alcoholics. Cermak (1975) reports that visual linking was more beneficial in learning paired associates than cued or rote learning when a recognition measure was used but there was no difference between visual linking and cued verbal recall when a free recall task was used to measure success. Similar results were obtained by Binder and Schreiber (1980) who found that recovering alcoholics were able to profit from this technique even when the interacting images were not presented to them visually. Neither of these studies report pre-treatment data however, so the amount of improvement cannot been determined.

The linking method has also been studied in brain damaged individuals. Lewinsohn, Danaher & Kihel (1977) reported in a well controlled investigation of patients with mixed etiologies, mostly CVA's, that there was improved performance on a paired associate task after a thirty minute delay, but not after a delay of one week. Crovitz, Harvey & Horn (1979) present three case studies of brain damaged individuals who had difficulty using an imagery technique. They suggest that when given unlimited time in which to form idiosyncratic images, even if concrete, these patients can then benefit from such procedures. Still, their data is anecdotal and no objective measures were used to quantify the results.

Some case studies have been conducted in which the linking method has been used to promote recall of names and faces. Lewinsohn et al. (1977) report the case on an hypoxic patient who was able to improve this skill using the method devised by Lorayne & Lucas (1974). This method involves forming an image that linked the name with an outstanding facial characteristic. These conclusions were limited however, by the fact that only five face-name pairs were presented and especially "easy" names (e.g. Ms. Johnson, Mr. Armstrong) were used but the improvement was maintained, and the subject demonstrated good recall ten days after the learning trial. Glasgow, Zeiss, Barrera & Lewinsohn (1977) present the case of a 23 year old head trauma patient who was able to benefit from this procedure in a structured setting, but not in everyday situations.

Another way of linking words and images is to inbed them in a story. Crovitz (1979) used a technique based on mnemonic encoding techniques developed by Higbee (1977). A bizarre, novel storyline was developed linking ten items together. He found that in two brain damaged patients, no increase in performance was found, but when retrieval cues were offered, performance did improve. In an experimental study of patients with mixed etiologies, Kovner, Mattis & Goldmeier (1983) found that amnesics demonstrated improved ability to recall a twenty-item word list using this method. They suggest that the story line allows memory disordered patients to "chunk" the information and therefore to retrieve it later. Correspondingly, in a single case study of a closed head injured patient, Crosson & Buenning (1984) showed that a visual imagery technique of visualizing a story as it was read improved free recall for that story more than using no strategy or attempting to increase concentration with feedback. However, this technique was not better than asking questions throughout the story about salient items. Unfortunately, on a nine month follow-up, the patient was no longer using the strategies taught to him and there was a corresponding drop in performance.

In summary, visual imagery techniques have shown a modest effect in improving some individual's memory skills for structured material such as word lists. However, when stimulus material includes names and faces, there is less improvement. Names and faces can be remembered using a visualization strategy as long as there is a limited number and the names are easy to visualize, but in both instances, subjects failed to generalize the techniques to everyday functional memory tasks. Generalization of imagery techniques to remember prose are also deficient in effecting change in functional tasks. Without reminders to use the technique, patients did not continue to use it outside of the structured setting. Without reminders to use the technique, patients did not continue to use it outside of the structured setting. Furthermore, this technique seems to be dependent on cues for retrieval; when retrieval cues are not provided there is a substantial decrease in performance, which suggests that it is not the memory technique alone but the retrieval cues that are also crucial for remembering. Some possible explanations for the equivocal results obtained in these studies are that the methods are not standardized, patients with very different etiologies are included in the same studies, and some studies perform between group comparisons while others measure within group and individual comparisons. All of these methodological weaknesses lead to an equivocal summary of findings.

Verbal Mnemonics

In an early study of verbal mnemonic elaboration, Gianutsos & Gianutsos (1979) found that four brain damaged subjects improved to some extent when taught to use a set of words in a story to help remember. However, the findings are limited by the fact that one subject showed little improvement at all, one had only temporary improvement and two showed lasting improvement.

Lewinsohn et al (1977) used the PQRST technique with a 27 year old head injured man and found it to be very effective. Similarly, Glasgow et al. (1977) report its very successful use with a 22 year old head injured woman. In addition, both patients were able to generalize the use of this strategy to everyday situations. It muse be noted, however that both of these patients were several years post-trauma and had WAIS IQ scores that were in the high average range.

In general, little evidence is offered supporting the premise that verbal mnemonics are able to ameliorate memory disorder in brain damaged patients. No controlled group studies have been performed. In addition, most of the subjects studied were at least one year post-trauma and were neuropsychologically intact or demonstrated overall superior functioning, indicating that the patients may have been completely recovered. Therefore, it is difficult to generalize these results to all brain damaged subjects. For example, the PQRST or SQ3R method, in particular, requires the ability to carry out a sequence of steps, which requires the ability to use purposeful planning in the future, a quality that many brain damaged patients lack. This method may be limited to the relatively high functioning patient.

External Strategies

The use of such strategies is seriously neglected in brain damaged individuals. In reviewing the literature, only one study can be identified making use of a memory aid in a brain damaged individual and then this aid was modified to be used as a retraining procedure. This study was done by Lewinsohn et al. (1977), wherein an anoxic patient was taught to take notes about the main points in a story and then to remember those major facts by rehearsing them. Unfortunately, recall for the story was not assessed, nor was carry over to other situations. Although this is the only study attempted, it indicates that the use of memory aids is a viable alternative or addition to training in mnemonic strategies, such as visualization.

Other Recommendations

It is often advantageous to combine remediation strategies when developing a memory retraining program. The more methods used the more likely the information will be encoded. Similarly, the more modalities used to encode information such as writing, hearing and vocalizing the information, the more likely it is that the information will be retained. When at all possible, it is advisable to teach the skill in the setting in which it will be used. This alleviates the problem of generalization by furnishing a concrete use of the strategy. Finally, teaching a brain-injured individual to develop routines will facilitate memory. For example, checking an appointment book and a memory place at given intervals which might be set on an alarm watch will minimize missed appointments and forgetting to perform specific tasks. Perhaps most importantly, a memory disordered person must learn to de- velop a routine linked to time cues, which will in turn reduce disorientation to time.

The use of memory groups may be helpful in working with brain -injured patients. Besides the obvious cost and time efficiency of groups, there are many benefits that can only be gained from a group setting. For example, interacting with others with similar memory problems can result in mutual support and advice. An idiosyncratic approach for a specific memory problem may transfer and work for another patient. Further, compliance in the use of memory strategies and aids is facilitated by seeing others doing the same. When one person in the group enjoys success, the effect can be contagious, in that the others in the group are more likely to view the treatment as effective and motivation may be enhanced.

Summary

When faced with the choice of memory retraining strategies, several factors are important. A thorough neuropsychological assessment must be completed before one can determine the patient's specific deficits and how they are manifested in behavior. Since there are no adequate measures for evaluating disturbances in everyday information processing, this assessment should include a self-report or report by a significant other of memory difficulties in everyday situations because these are the problems for which the patient is seeking help. A key concept is that any memory retraining program must be individually designed to address these everyday problems. For example, a person who comes in with a presenting problem of difficulty remembering names and faces is probably not going to profit from the use of visual imagery to help remember word lists. Similarly, the same pa- tient will not benefit from the method of visual imagery to recall names and faces cited earlier by Lewinsohn et al. (1977), because it involves a great deal of energy and many procedural steps that also must be remembered. However, training this person to photograph recently introduced people and events and keep an album of these in a diary might be of much greater utility. Moreover, such a strategy gives the person immediate feedback as to the accuracy as well as a record of the face with the name to refer in the the future.

In general, the memory retraining strategies presented in the literature thus far have enjoyed moderate success, however, in virtually all case studies presented, subjects had full scale IQs in at least the low average ranges which limits generalization to more impaired population. To date, very little research has focused on the effectiveness of supplementary external memory aids used to extend a person's memory store. Thus, their efficacy is still unknown. It is suggested that using multiple strategies may be useful and the use of memory groups is encouraged to provide social and emotional support as well as retrain basic memory skills.

References

Atkinson, R.C. & Shiffrin, R.M. (1971). The control of short-term memory and its control processes, *Scientific American, 225*, 82-90.

Atwood, G. (1971). An experimental study of visual imagination and memory. *Cognitive Psychology, 2*, 290-299.

Baddeley, A.D. (1982a). *Your Memory: A user's Guide*. Harmondsworth, Middlesex: Penguin Books,

Baddeley, A.D. (1982b). Amnesia: a minimal model and an interpretation. In L. Cermak, *Human Memory and Amnesia*, Hillsdale, NJ: Lawrence Erlbaum Associates,

Baddeley, A.D. (1986). Memory theory and memory therapy. In B.A. Wilson and N. Moffatt (Eds.), *Clinical Management of Memory Problems*. Rockville, Maryland: Aspen Systems Corp.

Bennett-Levy, J. & Powell, G.E. (1980). The subjective memory questionnaire (SMQ): and investigation into the self-reporting of "real-life" memory skills, *British Journal of Social and Clinical Psychology, 19*, 177-183.

Binder, L.M & Schreiber, V. (1980). Visual imagery and verbal mediation as memory aids in recovering alcoholics. *Journal of Clinical Neuropsychology, 2*, 71-74.

Bjork, R. A. (1979). Retrieval practice. Presented to Conference on Developmental and Experimental Approaches to Memory, Ann Arbor.

Bower, G. H. (1970). Analysis of a mnemonic device. *American Scientist, 68*, 496-510.

Brayshaw (1849). *Metrical Mnemonics*. Yorkshire, England: Yorkshire Press.

Brooks, D. N. (1979). Psychological events after severe blunt head injury. Their significance and rehabilitation. In D.J. Osborne, M.M. Gruneberg, & J.R. Eiser. *Research in Psychology in Medicine, 2*, London: Academic Press.

Cermak, L. S. (1975). Imagery as an aid to retrieval for Korsakoff patients. *Cortex, 11*, 163-169.

Collyer, S. C., Jonides, J. & Brown, W. (1972). Images as memory aids: Is bizarreness helpful? *American Journal of Psychology, 85*, 31-38.

Craik, F.I.M. & Lockhart, R.S. (1972). Levels of processing: a framework for memory research, *Journal of Verbal Learning and Verbal Behavior, 11*, 671-684.

Crosson, B. & Buenning, W. (1984). An individualized memory retraining program after closed head injury: A single-case study. *Journal of Clinical Neuropsychology, 6*, 287-301.

Crovitz, H. (1979). Memory retraining in brain damaged patients. The airplane list. *Cortex, 15*, 131-134.

Crovitz, H. F., Harvey, M. T. & Horn, R. W. (1979). Problems in the acquisition of imagery mnemonics: Three brain damaged cases. *Cortex, 15*, 225-234.

Furst, B. (1944) *The Practical Way to a Better Memory*. New York: Grosset & Dunlap.

Gasparrini, B. & Satz, P. (1979). A treatment for memory problems in left hemisphere CVA patients. *Journal of Clinical Neuropsychology, 1*, 137-150.

Glasgow, R., Zeiss, R., Barrera, M., & Lewinsohn, P. (1977). Case studies on remediating memory deficits in brain damaged individuals. *Journal of Clinical Psychology, 33*, 1049-1054.

Goldstein, K. (1942). *Aftereffects of Brain Injury in War*. New York: Grune and Stratton.

Haber, R. N. (1970). How we remember what we see. *Scientific American, 222*, 104-112.

Harris, J. (1980). Memory aids people use: Two interview studies. *Memory and Cognition, 8*, 31-38.

Heilman, K. M., & Valenstein, E. (1979). *Clinical Neuropsychology*, New York/Oxford: Oxford University Press.

Hermann, D. & Neisser, U. (1978). An inventory of everyday memory experiences; in Gruneberg, M. M., Morris, P. and Sykes, R. (Eds.), *Practical Aspects of Memory*. London: Academic Press

Higbee, K. (1977). *Your Memory: How it Works and How to Improve It*. Englewood Cliffs, New Jersey: Prentice-Hall

Hulicka, J. & Grossman, J. (1967). Age group comparisons for the use of mediators in paired-associate learning. *Journal of Gerontology, 22*, 46-51.

Jones, M. K. (1974). Imagery as a mnemonic aid after left temporal lobectomy: contrast between material specific and generalized memory disorders. *Neuropsychologia, 12*, 21-30.

Jones-Gotman, M., & Milner, B. (1978). Right temporal lobe contribution to image mediated verbal learning. *Neuropsychologia, 16*, 61-71.

Kovner, R., Mattis, S., & Goldmeier, E. (1983). A technique for promoting robust free recall in chronic organic amnesia. *Journal of Clinical Neuropsychology, 5*, 65-71.

Landauer, T. K., & Bjork, R. A. (1978). Optimum rehearsal patterns and name learning. In K. M. Gruneaberg, P. E. Morris & R. N. Sykes (Eds.), *Practical Aspects of Memory*, New York: Academic Press.

Lebrato, M. T., & Ellis, N. R. (1974). Imagery mediation in paired-associate learning by retarded and nonretarded subjects. *American Journal of Mental Deficiency, 78*, 704-713.

Levin, H.S., Benton, A.L., & Grossman, R.G. (1982). *Neurobehavioral Consequences of Closed Head Injury.* New York: Oxford University Press.

Lewinsohn, P. M., Danaher, B. G., & Kikel, S. (1977). Visual imagery as a mnemonic aid for brain injured persons. *Journal of Consulting and Clinical Psychology, 45*, 717-723.

Lewinsohn, P. M., Glasgow, R. E., Barrera, M., Danaher, B. G., Alperson, J., McCarty, D. L., Sullivan, J. M., Zeiss, R. A., Nyland, J., & Rodriquez, M. P. P. (1977). Assessment and treatment of patients with memory deficits: initial studies. *Catalog of Selected Documents in Psychology, 7.*

Little, M.L. & Williams, J. M. (1984). Everyday Memory and Clinical Memory Tests. Paper presented at the Annual meeting of the National Academy of Neuropsychologists, San Diego, CA.

Lorayne, H., & Lucas, J. (1974). *The Memory Book.* New York: Ballentine.

Luria, A. R. (1968). *The Mind of a Mnemonist.* New York: Basic Books.

Luria, A. R. (1963). *Restoration of Function after Brain Injury.* New York: Mac Millan Publishing Co.

Nickerson, R. S. (1968). A note on long term recognition memory for pictorial material. *Psychonomic Science, ll*, 58.

Patten, B. M. (1972). The ancient art of memory - usefulness in treatment. *Archives of Neurology, 26 ,* 25-31.

Pavio, A. (1969). Mental imagery in learning and memory. *Psychological Review, 76*, 241-263.

Poon, L. W., & Walsh-Sweeney, L. (1981). Effects of bizarre and interacting imagery on learning and retrieval of the aged. *Experimental Aging Research, 7*, 65-70.

Prigatano, G. P. (1986) Cognitive retraining in perspective, In G.P. Prigatano (Ed.) *Neuropsychological Rehabilitation after Brain Injury.* Baltimore: Johns Hopkins University Press.

Ramus, P. (1578). *Scholae Retoricae.* Bale.

Robertson-Tchabo, E. A., Houseman, C. P., & Arenberg, D. (1976). A classical mnemonic for older learners: A trip that works! *Educational Gerontology, l*, 215-226.

Robinson, F. (1970). *Effective Study.* New York: Harper.

Schacter, D L. (1980). Imagery mnemonics, retrieval mnemonics, and the closed head injury patient. Presented at the Annual Meeting of the International Neuropsychological Society, San Francisco.

Schacter, D. L., Rich, S. A., & Stampp, M. S. (1985). Remediation of memory disorders: Experimental evaluation of the spaced-retrieval technique. *Journal of Clinical and Experimental Neuropsychology, 7*, 79-96.

Sheppard, R. (1967). Recognition memory for words, sentences and pictures. *Journal of Verbal Learning and Verbal Behavior, 6*, 156-163.

Sunderland, A., Harris, J., & Baddeley, A. D. (1983). Do laboratory tests predict everyday memory? A neuropsychological study, *Journal of Verbal Learning and Verbal Behavior, 22*, 341-357.

Wilson B. (1981a). A survey of behavioral treatments carried out at a rehabilitation center for stroke and head injuries. In Pewell, G. (Ed.), *Brain Function Therapy*, Aldershot: Gower Press,

Wilson, B. (1982). Success and failure in memory training following a cerebral vascular accident. *Cortex, 18*, 581-594.

Wilson, B., & Moffatt, N. (1984). *Clinical Management of Memory Problems*, Rockville, Maryland: Aspen.

Yates, F. A. (1966). *The Art of Memory.* London: Routledge & Kegon Paul

Zangwill, O. L. (1947). Psychological aspects of rehabilitation in cases of brain injury. *British Journal of Psychology, 37*, 60-69.

Zelinski, E.M., Gelewski, M. J., & Thompson, L. W. (1980). Do laboratory tests relate to self-assessment of memory ability in the young and old? In L. W. Poon, J. L. Fozard, L. S. Cermak, D. Arenberg & L. W. Thompson (Eds.), *New directions in memory and aging: Proceedings of the George Talland Memorial Conference.* Hillsdale, N. J.: J. Erlbaum.

9

Cognitive Rehabilitation: Psychosocial Issues

Mark T. Wagner and Marian B. Danse

Neuropsychological conditions which result in significant reversible cortical dysfunction represent a major challenge for rehabilitation specialists. Much of the early recovery of cognitive function seems to involve neurological reorganization (Bach-y-Rita, 1981); however, many nonorganic factors also appear to interact and influence the long term recovery course. To a great extent, the literature in this area has turned to a multidimensional perspective for determining outcome, as is evidenced by recent articles which have emphasized psychosocial factors (Jennett, Snoek, Bond & Brooks, 1981; Oddy, Coughlan, Typerman & Jenkins, 1985; Wagner, Williams & Long, 1984). Presently, the degree to which psychological and social changes influence recovery and eventual outcome is unclear, but appear as important in overall recovery as are the more obvious physical and cognitive impairments. In this chapter, factors which influence and the importance of psychosocial factors in cognitive rehabilitation during the recovery process will be discussed.

Epidemiology

The incidence of head injury and stroke help underscore the magnitude of the rehabilitation challenge that reversible cortical dysfunction patients represent to health care professionals. For example, head injury is considered the leading cause of brain damage in previously healthy individuals. In the National Head and Spinal Cord Injury Survey, the overall estimate of occurrence of head injury in 1974 corresponded to an estimated incidence of 200/100,000 for individuals that were first treated as inpatients (Kalsbeek, McLaurin, Harris, & Miller, 1980).

While head injury is a leading cause of brain damage in previously healthy young people, stroke is the most common serious neuropsychological disease in late adult life. The incidence of reported stroke varies widely depending on the source of the sample, the sample age distribution, composition, etc., but there are estimated to be 400,000 cases discharged from acute care hospitals annually (Wolf, Kannel, and Berter, 1984).

While rehabilitation is indicated for a large percentage of stroke and head injury patients, care is frequently limited to acute hospitalization. Following discharge from acute care facilities, many individuals with persisting neuropsychological deficits are left to their own devices during the chronic phase of recovery. The impact that these disabilities will have on individuals' everyday lives are largely unknown and ignored. This is probably due to a lack of research available on long-term outcome, and concomitantly, to the lack of facilities and funding available for treatment. Even for individuals who participate in some form of rehabilitation, recovery frequently involves alterations in individuals' emotional, vocational and/or social functioning.

Neuropsychological Consequences of Brain Injury

Historically, measures of brain damage have been used both the assess cerebral dysfunction and have been used for long-term treatment planning. In general, however, initial neurological measures of brain damage have limited utility in predicting outcome. For example, coma duration and post-traumatic amnesia have been used as initial indicators of severity of brain damage in closed head injury, but have been of questionable value in predicting long-term outcome (Gronwall, 1977; Russell & Smith, 1961). Similarly, although computerized tomographic (CT) scan imaging has been used to diagnose head injury and cerebral vascular accidents, the CT scan is also of limited utility in predicting outcome (Henley, Pettit, Todd-Pokropek, & Tubber, 1985). Therefore, it is not surprising that health care professionals have been restricted to making decisions about potential recovery and the everyday consequences of the lesion based on inadequate data.

Serial neuropsychological testing, on the other hand, has been found useful in more accurately delineating the behavioral and psychological consequences of cerebral dysfunction, and for more accurate predictions of outcome (Heaton & Pendleton, 1981). For example, Dikmen, Reitan and Temkin (1983) followed a series of adults who had mild to severe head injury in order to evaluate recovery of function. They found a broad range of simple and complex neuropsychological deficits, representing a diversity of behavioral performances, improving over an 18 month period. In another similar type of study, Mandleberg and Brooks (1975) serially evaluated severely head-injured patients using the Wechsler Adult Intelligence Scale (WAIS) as a dependent measure of recovery. They found that patients' Verbal subtest scores approached that of the comparison group within about one year following the injury while recovery of Performance subtest scores continued over three years. Lezak (1979) found similar patterns of recovery on memory tasks in closed-head injury patients which she followed over a three year period.

Serial assessment of stroke patients is less common, but recovery patterns are similar. For example, Sarno and Levita (1979) found persistent improvement in linquistic abilities in the first year post-stroke. Similarly, Chen and Ling (1985) reported approximately 84% of the patients they followed showed significant motor recovery of at least two grades in the hemiparetic limbs at a three year follow-up. Finally, Meier, Ettinger, and Arthur (1982) found significant recovery on multiple measures of cognitive and psychomotor functions at a 6 month follow-up. Additional recovery may have occurred, but the patients were not followed beyond the six month period.

While there are a number of factors which influence recovery of function such as initial severity of injury, the site of lesion, etc., the general finding in the literature indicates significant recovery of function following head injury or stroke. In particular, neuropsychological recovery of function occurs over an extended period of time, with wide variability in individual recovery curves, and when recovery plateaus is uncertain, but is generally thought to be within one to three years.

Psychosocial Consequences of Brain Injury

While serial assessment of neuropsychological recovery is valuable in treatment planning and counseling, bridging the gap between the patient's neuropsychological test performance and the patient's everyday functional abilities is a difficult task that, until recently, has been largely ignored in the literature. In part, this has been due to a preoccupation with diagnostic issues. An important extension of the recovery of function literature has to do with questions raised regarding the significance of neuropsychological deficits in predicting everyday functioning (Davis, 1983; Diller & Gordon, 1981; Heaton & Pendleton, 1981). In attempting to determine how physical, cognitive and emotional deficits influence everyday adjustment following brain injury, a number of authors have assessed the role of psychosocial issues involved in the recovery process. For example, McKinlay, Brooks, Bond, Martinage, and Marshall (1981) employed serial structured interviews to obtain information from a close relative about the patient's psychosocial changes following head injury. They found that emotional changes, poor memory, and subjective symptoms, such as fatigue and psychomotor retardation, were problems most frequently reported. Interestingly, complaints about physical symptoms were less common. Other authors have also found that psychosocial disabilities, such as anger, frustration, personality changes, decreased leisure activity, etc., resulting from head injury contributed more to overall disability than did neurological deficits (Bond, 1976; Jennett et al., 1981). These findings have also been confirmed in long-term follow-ups with patients that have been followed for up to a decade (Oddy et al., 1985; Wagner et al., 1984).

The psychosocial findings at follow-up in stroke patients are similar. Hamrin (1982) found that for all the patients they had studied, stroke had resulted in significant social isolation. In another study, mood disorders were investigated during a two-year longitudinal evaluation of stroke patients (Robinson, Starr, Kubos & Price, 1983). These authors found that approximately 50% of patients studied had experienced clinically significant depression. Finally, in the ongoing Framingham study, Labi, Phillips, and Gresham (1980), studied social reintegration of long-term survivors of documented, completed stroke. They found that with individuals who had already achieved satisfactory levels of physical function post stroke, a significant proportion manifested psychosocial disabilities such as decreased socialization outside the home, decreased interests, and disrupted family relationships. They felt that the impact of psychosocial factors during recovery is much more prolonged than was previously realized and argued for increased long-term social and psychological rehabilitation.

Social Consequences of Brain Injury

The impact that brain injury has on individuals' broader social readjustment to everyday life has also been investigated. Weddell, Oddy and Jenkins (1980) used an interview technique at two years post-head injury and found that patients who returned to work were no longer able to cope with their former jobs, had decreased interest in leisure activities, were more frequently bored, and had decreased social contacts. A follow-up of the same series indicated that the patients' physical and cognitive disabilities and their social relationships had not changed significantly over the seven year period (Oddy et al., 1985). Social isolation continued to be a major problem with about 50% of the patients having only very limited contact with friends. Romantic relationships were likewise adversely affected. The authors speculated that these patients' failure to rebuild their social lives was due, in part, to a lack of a network of friends, the lack of goals, the lack of opportunities to show off competence, and the absence of any source of social identity or status.

To specifically investigate the role of social factors involved in recovery from head injury, Wagner, Williams and Long (1986) used a social network analysis technique. At long-term follow-up, it was found that head-injured individuals had fewer friends, fewer social contacts, and more enmeshed social networks when compared to control subjects and were significantly more dissatisfied with their social situation. A regression analysis revealed that social factors were highly predictive of overall outcome. That is, the better the quality of the social network, the more globally successful outcome is likely to be. Interestingly, it was not tangible social support, per se, which was most valued by the brain-injured individuals, but rather, intangible support such as belongingness, promotion of self-esteem, and support of self-confidence which seemed to foster a positive outcome during the chronic phase of recovery.

During recovery from brain damage, psychosocial issues such as depression, decreased socialization, decreased self-worth, impaired family relations, personality change, and apathy are common psychological reactions during the second six months following brain injury and set the stage for the eventual outcome. Even in cases where there is complete or near complete physical recovery, estimates of negative psychosocial sequelae range from 25 to more than 50% (Espmark, 1973; Klonoff & Thompson, 1969; Labi et al., 1980; Robinson et al., 1983). Presumably, because of unrealistic recovery expectations and reduced neuropsychological capacities, many patients fail to live up to their expectations in both their work and/or domestic environments and often suffer repeated social failures (Ford, 1976; Long & Gouvier, 1982; Wagner et al., 1984). Ford (1976) argued that this leads to a social breakdown of work and family life, increasing frustration, loss of confidence, and finally, disintegration of psychosocial functioning, thus significantly impairing overall outcome.

Psychosocial Issues in Rehabilitation

Albrecht (1976) has argued that one of the anomalies of modern medicine is that patients, families, and medical staff are not prepared to address the consequences of chronic medical conditions. This is because chronic disability requires a reorientation of roles by the individuals, families, and friends, which is clearly outside the domain of current medical practice. However, the cognitive, emotional and physical consequences of brain injury force individuals into a situation where many old behavior patterns and role expectations may not be appropriate and into a situation in which patients must reconstruct both their personal and social identity. This "reconstruction" process takes place through the patient's social interaction with family, friends and co-workers. The successfulness of the readjustment process appears to be a critical factor in successful long-term outcome. Having considered the magnitude of the psychosocial problems secondary to brain injury, it is worthwhile to critically evaluate the efficacy of current rehabilitative treatment methods from a psychosocial perspective.

Psychosocial Aspects of Physical Rehabilitation

Most multidisciplinary physical rehabilitation programs tend to be quite narrow in their focus and emphasize very pragmatic issues of daily living such as bathing, ambulation, toileting, homemaking, etc. Generalization of treatment effects are usually limited to one or two home visits, to test the patient's ability to function outside the institution. Follow-up is likewise limited to nonexistent. The cognitive and emotional sequelae of brain injury, on the other hand, are less obvious and are easily overlooked during the course of rehabilitation. In part, this is due to the structure of the rehabilitation setting and the temporal stage of recovery. For example, during rehabilitation, patients live in a highly structured environment where roles are clearly defined and expectations of behavior are delineated. The day is occupied by a busy schedule and outside support is probably near its peak. Visitors are frequent and supportive. Physical recovery and functional gains are rapid during the early stages, and everyday cognitive and emotional demands are at a minimum. However, as time progresses, a whole new set of issues become apparent. Following discharge, patients and family must make major social adjustments. Concurrently, cognitive deficits become much more apparent in the unstructured environment of the home and community. Complex role demands of the family, of friends, and possibly of work associates emerge. It is during this phase that the medical community usually relinquishes its responsibility of the patient: it is at this point that patients are at risk for psychosocial deterioration.

Cognitive Rehabilitation

In response to this type of scenario, an important extension of rehabilitation services has been developed. Cognitive rehabilitation has gained popularity as a long-term treatment approach. Cognitive rehabilitation may include patients who require some restoration of physical function, but has a particular focus on remediation of cognitive functioning.

From a theoretical perspective, the idea of restitution of lost cognitive function is very appealing. The effects might be widespread. For example, by treating an identified central neuropsychological deficit, a whole range of behavioral deficits and subsequent social impairments might be improved. Nonetheless, in several reviews of the literature on individualized treatment for remediation of cognitive deficits, authors have concluded that as studies become more clinically relevant, the results become less convincing (Miller, 1980; Wagner, 1982). Part of the problem is that research on remediation of cognitive function has taken place largely in the laboratory, or within institutional settings, using laboratory or psychometrically derived techniques. Generalizations to everyday functioning has been a secondary concern. Because of the limited success of such techniques, some authors questioned if it is sufficient to teach a skill or improve performance on psychometric tests, or is the goal to improve daily functioning (Diller & Gordon, 1981). These issues have not been resolved in the literature and certainly deserve further research attention.

Unidimensional Cognitive Rehabilitation Techniques

Examples of direct cognitive rehabilitation techniques for the treatment of perceptual, memory, and intellectual deficits are relatively sparse, however, cognitive remediation techniques for the treatment of language deficits secondary to aphasia have a much longer history and have been more adequately researched. In general, there has been an evolution away from direct individualized retraining of lost cognitive function, toward methods which emphasize compensatory techniques in the social environment. From a neurological point of view, this evolution in the treatment technique makes sense. For example, cognitive retraining techniques aimed at direct restoration of lost function secondary to tissue destruction, rely on a theory of equipotentiality in which cortical areas nor normally involved in language production begin to assume a new function (Bach-y-Rita, 1981; Luria, 1963). On the other hand, cognitive rehabilitation techniques which utilize compensatory mechanisms in the social environment rely on an underlying neurological theory in which intact cortical areas are recruited enabling the individual to compensate for a deficit by performing the task in different ways (Luria, 1963).

An example of traditional cognitive retraining of lost language function for the treatment of aphasia involves stimulus-response tasks designated to elicit discrete language functions, such as auditory comprehension or word retrieval (Schuell, 1964). This approach to cognitive rehabilitation is quite popular and is, in theory, similar to techniques currently being employed by many occupational therapists and neuropsychologists (Gianutsos, 1981). However, the outcome of this type of treatment approach has been generally poor (Miller, 1980; Prigatano, 1986; Sarno & Levita, 1979).

Wepman (1972) and Chapey (1981) on the other hand, have used divergent language tasks with aphasics to facilitate communication rather than discrete language skills. This type of cognitive remediation technique utilizes compensatory strategies and is based on neurological theory in which intact cortical tissue is utilized for the task. The emphasis is on improving existing functions and employing alternative strategies which are designed to improve functional abilities. Similarly, Davis and Wilcox (1981) developed a compensatory strategy for the treatment of aphasia which approximates "real life" communication in the natural environment. Multimodal communication strategies, such as gesturing, and interactive conversation are used to facilitate functional communication skills rather than linguistic accuracy with the aphasic patient. Generalization is also fostered by instructing family and spouse in the technique. Finally, Lubinski (1981) provides an example of how cognitive remediation can be expanded into the psychosocial realm by incorporating aspects of the patient's environment into the therapy. She has developed a Profile of the Communication Environment of the Aphasic Adult, which samples the patient's everyday communication opportunities and everyday barriers which inhibit successful communication. The idea is based on reciprocal interaction in which the brain-injured individual is thought not only to act on the environment but also to be influenced by his or her impact on the environment. From a cognitive remediation standpoint, the indirect approach appears to be more clinically effective than direct cognitive retraining methods. This may be because the indirect approach does not seem to require major neural reorganization of the nervous system for recovery of lost cognitive function and instead, facilitates intact compensatory strategies.

The trend in speech therapy has been away from direct cognitive retraining of lost linguistic abilities toward a broader compensatory training and psychosocial approach. It would seem that the experiences of speech therapists employing cognitive retraining techniques might aid in the development of individual cognitive remediation techniques by neuropsychologists.

Multidimensional Cognitive Rehabilitation Techniques

One other major treatment approach to cognitive rehabilitation which has been milieu therapy. Historically, physical competence was considered the only measure of successful rehabilitation. More recently, however, multidimensional factors such as cognitive, emotional and social aspects of the individual have been incorporated more significantly into rehabilitation programs with in- and out-patient cognitive rehabilitation programs becoming more popular. In recent years, outcome data is beginning to emerge from cognitive rehabilitative programs which have emphasized the milieu approach. In terms of specific direct remediation of cognitive deficits, the results have been generally disappointing; however, psychosocial factors have improved significantly with treatment. For example, Ben-Yishay and Diller (1981) used a modular treatment program employing three major components: 1) cognitive retraining, 2) group therapy focusing primarily on role playing, and 3) community activities. At the conclusion of this study, results showed limited improvement in psychometrically evaluated cognitive functioning, but have shown significant improvement in awareness of the injury, acceptance of their situation, and an increase in activity level. Similarly, a cognitive rehabilitation program developed by

Prigatano, Fordyce, Zeiner, Roueche, Pepping, and Wood (1984) focused on neuropsycho-logical deficits as the primary target, but also placed equal emphasis on emotional states accompanying the cognitive impairment. Awareness and acceptance issues were also addressed by both patient and family. Results of the program demonstrated modest but statistically reliable improvements in cognitive functioning. The impact that his had on everyday functioning was not determined. However, treatment did result in substantial improvement in interpersonal skills and a reduction of emotional distress. The authors reported that typically, individuals showed a willingness to use compensatory methods to get around their deficits and concluded that one of the most important benefits of the program was improvement in psychosocial functioning (Prigatano, 1986).

The experimental research investigating the specificity and plasticity of the central nervous system has stimulated a variety of innovative techniques which have tremendous clinical implications. Individualized cognitive remediation techniques, however, have demonstrated only small statistically significant effects and generalization to the everyday environment has been questionable. Psychosocial or milieu interventions, on the other hand, appear to have significant clinical effects.

Psychological Value of Cognitive Rehabilitation

While direct cognitive retraining techniques, such as stimulus-response aphasia therapy, abstract cognitive reasoning exercises, memory retraining exercises, etc., may have limited value in terms of specific restoration of function, such techniques may have other therapeutic benefits. For example, cognitive remediation exercises serve two major purposes. Firstly, from a psychological perspective, such exercises help illustrate to the patient that a deficit actually exists. Awareness of the deficit is a key part of the treatment process because, before any progress can be made, the patient must be aware that something is wrong. Secondly, awareness that something is wrong frequently gives way to significant reactive depression. Therefore, cognitive exercises give the patient the sense that they have some control over the recovery process. This is an important therapeutic ploy as this process helps to re-orient the patient away from the traditional medical model, where he/she is the passive recipient of treatment, to a rehabilitative model in which the patient is an active member responsible for his/her own recovery. At this point, the therapist and the patient can begin working on compensatory strategies with a specific intent of reducing the effect the deficit has on the patient's everyday functioning in his/her environment.

Both individualized cognitive remediation techniques and milieu approaches seem to directly or indirectly address some of the initial emotional issues. From a psychosocial standpoint it is not surprising that the milieu approach to cognitive rehabilitation produces results that appear more clinically promising than the direct remediation of cognitive functions (Ben-Yishay & Diller, 1981; Prigatano et al., 1984). Milieu therapy incorporates a strong social factor emphasizing compensatory strategies. However, while the milieu approach to cognitive rehabilitation offers significant advantages over individualized direct retraining techniques, it is often not enough to treat patients in a rehabilitation setting with the hope that the effects will generalize. Because social factors outside the rehabilitation setting are powerful determinants of behavior, they can frequently undo significant treatment gains. For example, adverse secondary psychological reactions which emerge during the chronic phase of recovery, as the individual struggles with complex personal and social restructuring, can negatively influence their adaptation to the environment (Wagner et al, 1986).

For this reason, several neuropsychological processes are important to comprehensive rehabilitation from a psychosocial standpoint. Firstly, secondary emotional reactions to the brain injury must be addressed in the early stages of recovery. Secondly, psychological reactions which emerge during the chronic phase of recovery secondary to so-cial readjustment are equally as important. From an idealistic standpoint, these deficits should be assessed and treated in the individual's natural social environment.

Broader Social Issues in Rehabilitation

Sussman (1976) has addressed the psychosocial problem of rehabilitation from a broader sociological perspective and offers an interesting theoretical ideas. He has argued that rehabilitation services should be built into the individual's own environment. In doing so, professionals and consultants could provide general care and treatment in the patient's home with the family. He argued that the utility of this approach becomes more evident if one accepts that the family and extended kin network is viable as a potential therapeutic milieu. Frequently, family networks can provide care at a cost lower than institutions if appropriate "incentives" and physical support systems are provided. This would require political and economic reallocation of institutional resources. Incentives could include cash payments, subsidized funds for remodeling to accommodate the disabled member, tax write-offs, special social services such as patient-sitting, transportation and shopping assistance. Further, options for leisure, recreation, and vocational activities could be similarly subsidized and perhaps incorporated into the architectural design of multi-family dwellings. Sussman (1976) concludes that such incentives could provide reciprocal rewards and bring chronic care rehabilitation back into the household, neighborhood, and community.

Conclusion

In summary, it was the purpose of this chapter to outline the major challenge that reversible cortical dysfunction places on rehabilitation specialists. Recovery is far more complicated than neurological reorganization. Persisting cognitive and physical deficits have a major impact on both the individual's readjustment to the social outcome. Currently, physical rehabilitative techniques largely ignore not only cognitive, but psychosocial issues, particularly as they impact on long-term recovery. Cognitive rehabilitation techniques begin to address psychosocial issues as factors influencing the ultimate level of overall recovery but ultimately fall short.

There are clearly no simple solutions to these problems. Further research is needed to delineate the magnitude and subtle aspects of the psychosocial complications which follow brain injury as well as how these affect ultimate outcome. Additionally, experimental interventions which treat everyday rehabilitation problems in the everyday environment, are also warranted.

The authors wish to express their appreciation to Carol Cusson and Linda Glaser for their assistance in the preparation of this manuscript.

References

Albrecht, G.L.. (1976). *The sociology of physical disability and rehabilitation.*   Pittsburg: University of Pittsburgh Press.

Bach-y-Rita, P. (1981). Brain plasticity as a basis of the development of rehabilitation procedures for hemiplegia. *Scandinavian Journal of Rehabilitation Medicine, 13,* 73-83.

Ben-Yishay, Y. & Diller, L. (1981). Rehabilitation of cognitive and perceptual deficits in people with trau - matic brain damage. *International Journal of Rehabilitation Research, 4,* 208-210.

Bond, M. R. (1976). Assessment of psychosocial outcome of severe head injury. *Acta Neurochir, 34,* 57-70.

Chapey, R. (1981). The assessment of language disorders in adults. In R. Chapey (Ed.) *Language intervention strategies in adult aphasia.* Baltimore: Williams & Wilkins.

Chen, Q. & Ling, R. (1985). A 1-4 year follow-up study of 306 cases of stroke. *Stroke, 16,* 323-327.

Davis, G. A. (1983). *A survey of adult aphasia.* Englewood Cliffs, NJ: Prentice-Hall.

Davis, G.A. & Wilcox, M.J. (1981). Incorporating parameters of natural conversation in aphasia treatment. In R. chapey (Ed.). *Language intervention strategies in adult aphasia.* Baltimore: Williams & Wilkins.

Dikmen, S., Reitan, R.M. & Temkin, N.R. (1983). Neuropsychological recovery in head injury. *Archives of Neurology, 40,* 333-328.

Diller, L. & Gordon, W.A. (1981). Interventions for cognitive deficits in brain-injured adults. *Journal of Consulting and Clinical Psychology, 49,* 822-834.

Espmark, S. (1973). Stroke before 50: A follow-up study of vocational psychological adjustment. *Scandinavian Journal of Rehabilitation Medicine* (Suppl. 2), 3-81.

Finger, S. (1978). *Recovery from brain injury.* New York: Plenum Press.

Ford, B. (1976). Head injuries: What happens to survivors. *Medical Journal of Australia, 1,* 603-605.

Gianutsos, R. (1981). *Handbook: Computer programs for cognitive rehabilitation.* Bayport, New York: Life Sciences Associates.

Gronwall, D. (1977). Paced auditory serial addition task: A measure of recovery from concussion. *Perceptual and Motor Skills, 44,* 367-373.

Hamrin, E. (1982). One year after stroke: A follow-up of an experimental study. *Scandinavian Journal of Rehabilitation Medicine, 14,* 111-116.

Heaton, R. & Pendleton, M. (1981). Use of neuropsychological tests to predict adult patients' everyday func - tioning. *Journal of Consulting and Clinical Psychology, 49,* 807-821.

Henley, S., Pettit, S., Todd-Pokropek, A., & Tubber, A. (1985). Who goes home? Predictive factors in stroke recovery. *Journal of Neurology, Neurosurgery, and Psychiatry, 48,* 1-6.

Jennett, B., Snoek, J., Bond, M.R., & Brooks, D.N. (1981). Disability after severe head injury: Observations of the use of the Glasgow Outcome Scale. *Journal of Neurology, Neurosurgery, and Psychiatry, 44 ,* 285-293.

Kalsbeek, W.D., McLaurin, R. L., Harris, B.H., & Miller, J.D. (1980). The National Head Injury and Spinal Cord Injury Survey: Major findings. *Journal of Neurosurgery, 53,* (Suppl.), 19-31.

Klonoff, H. & Thompson, G.B. (1969). Epidemiology of head injuries in adults: A pilot study. *Canadian Medical Association Journal, 100,* 235-241.

Labi, M.L., Phillips, T.F., & Gresham, G.E. (1980). Psychosocial disability in physically restored long-term stroke survivors. *Archives of Physical Medicine and Rehabilitation, 61,* 561-565.

Lezak, M.D. (1979). Recovery of memory and learning functions following traumatic brain injury. *Cortex, 15,* 63-72.

Long, C. J. & Gouvier, W.D. (1982). Neuropsychological assessment of outcome following closed-head injury. In. R.N. Malatesha & L.C. Hartlage (Eds.) *Neuropsychology and cognition.* Boston: Martinus Nighoff.

Lubinski, R., (1981). Speech, language and audiology programs and home health care agencies and nursing homes. In D.S. Beasley, & G.A. Davis (Eds.) *Aging: Communication processes and disorders.* New York: Grune & Stratton.

Luria, A.R. (1963). *Restoration of function after brain trauma.* London: Pergamon Press.

Mandleberg, J.A. & Brooks, D.N. (1975). Cognitive recovery after severe head injury. *Journal of Neurology, Neurosurgery and Psychiatry, 38,* 1121-1126.

McKinlay, W.W., Brooks, D.N., Bond, M.R., Martinage, D., & Marshall, M.M. (1981). The short-term outcome of severe blunt head injury as reported by relatives of the injured persons. *Journal of Neurology, Neurosurgery, and Psychiatry, 44,* 527-533.

Meier, M.J., Ettinger, M.G., & Arthur, L. (1982). Recovery of neuropsychological functioning after cerebrovascular infarction. In R.N. Malatesha & L.C. Hartlage (Eds.). *Neuropsychology & cognition*, Boston: Martinus Nighoff.

Miller, E. (1980). Psychological intervention in the management and rehabilitation of neuropsychological impairments. *Behavior Research and Therapy, 18*, 527-535.

Oddy, M., Coughlan, T., Typerman, A., & Jenkins, D. (1985). Social adjustment after closed head injury: A further follow-up seven years after injury. *Journal of Neurology, Neurosurgery, and Psychiatry, 48* 564-568.

Prigatano, G.P. (1986). *Neuropsychological rehabilitation after brain injury* . Baltimore: John Hopkins University Press.

Prigatano, G.P., Fordyce, D.J., Zeiner, H.K., Roueche, J.R., Pepping, M., & Wood, M.C. (1984). Neuropsychological rehabilitation after closed head injury in young adults. *Journal of Neurology, Neurosurgery and Psychiatry. 47*, 505-513.

Robinson, R.G., Starr, L.B., Kubos, K.L., & Price, T.R. (1983). A two-year longitudinal study of post-stroke mood disorders: Findings during the initial evaluation. *Stroke, 14*, 736-741.

Russell, W.R. & Smith, A. (1961). Post-traumatic amnesia in closed head injury. *Archives of Neurology, 5* , 19-29.

Sarno, M.T. & Levita, E. (1971). Natural course of recovery in severe aphasia. *Archives of Physical Medicine and Rehabilitation, 52*, 175-178.

Schuell, H.M., Jenkins, J.J., & Jimenez-Pabon, E. (1964). *Aphasia in adults*. New York: Harper & Row.

Sussman, M.B. (1976). The disabled and the rehabilitation system. In G.L. Albrecht (Ed.) *The sociology of physical disability and rehabilitation*. Pittsburgh: University of Pittsburgh Press.

Wagner, M.T. (1982). *Cognitive rehabilitation: An annotated bibliography*. Unpublished manuscript, Department of Psychology, Memphis State University, Memphis, TN.

Wagner, M.T., Williams, J.M., & Long, C.J. (1984). Assessment of the long-term effects of head injury. Paper presented at the annual meeting of the International Neuropsychological Society, San Diego, CA.

Wagner, M.T., Williams, J.M., & Long, C.J. (1986). The influence of social support on the recovery from head injury. *Journal of Clinical and Experimental Neuropsychology, 8*, 142.

Weddell, R., Oddy, M., & Jenkins, D. (1980). Social adjustment after rehabilitation: A two-year follow-up of patients with severe head injury. *Psychological Medicine, 10*, 257-263.

Wepman, J.M. (1972). Aphasia Therapy: A new look. *Journal of Speech & Hearing Disorders, 37*, 203-214.

Wolf, P.A., Kannel, W.B., & Verter, J. (1984). Cerebrovascular diseases in the elderly: Epidemiology. In M.L. Albert (Ed.). *Clinical neurology of aging*. New York: Oxford Press.

10

Cognitive Stimulation in the Home Environment

Thomas A. Novack, Thomas F. Bergquist, Gerald Bennett, and Donna Hartley

The rehabilitation of brain impaired individuals, particularly traumatically brain injured persons, has been expanding in terms of breadth and duration in the past several years. One example of this expansion is the growing emphasis on cognitive retraining for such individuals. The last 15 years have seen a tremendous investment of effort and monies in developing cognitive retraining programs, sometimes utilizing state-of-the-art technology, such as personal computers (Gianutsos, Glosser, Elbaum, & Vromen, 1983; Lynch, 1982; Ben-Yishay & Diller, 1983; Adamovitch, Henderson, & Auerbach, 1985). Numerous reports, most often case studies, have been published addressing the application of cognitive retraining programs (Rao & Bieliauskas, 1983; Crosson & Buenning, 1984; Gianutsos, 1981; Crovitz, 1979; Malec & Questad, 1983; Fowler, Hart, & Sheehan, 1972; Glasgow, Zeiss, Barbera & Lewinsohn, 1977; Jaffe & Katz, 1975). Although firm conclusions are not warranted based on case studies, the growing number of case reports and findings from group studies (Gasparinni & Satz, 1979; Jones, 1974; Weinberg, Piasetsky, Diller, & Gordon, 1982; Prigatano, Fordyce, Zeiner, Roueche, Pepping, & Wood, 1984) suggest that cognitive retraining programs are effective in specific areas. The neglect syndrome (Heilman, Watson, & Valenstein, 1985), commonly manifested as hemispatial neglect, appears to be amenable to remediation using structured behavioral techniques (Webster, Jones, Blanton, Gross, Beissel, & Wofford, 1984; Weinberg, Diller, Gordon, Gerstman, Lieberman, Lakin, Hodges, & Ezrachi, 1977). In fact, Gordon and his colleagues (Gordon, Hibbard, Egelko, Diller, Shaver, Lieberman, & Ragnarsson, 1985) have formulated a comprehensive retraining program for disorders related to right hemisphere dysfunction with successful results in the rehabilitation setting. Remediation of memory dysfunction has also been addressed in several reports (Jones, 1974; Glasgow et al., 1977; Gianutsos, 1981; Crosson & Buenning, 1984), although the evidence of success in this area is not as consistent as in the area of visual imperception. Added to the experiences of neuropsychologists in cognitive retraining are the contributions of individuals practicing aphasia therapy and occupational therapy, which also involve cognitive remediation. In fact, some would assert that aphasia therapy represents the most basic and well-established of the approaches to cognitive retraining.

It is not surprising that in developing, and now implementing, cognitive retraining programs there has been a strong emphasis on professionalism . In many respects, application of such programs is viewed as a professional endeavor, that is, accomplished by individuals with special training and education. This professionalism as regards cognitive retraining is manifested in several ways. First, cognitive retraining is surfacing with increasing frequency as a topic of professional meetings and journal articles. Second, in marketing, rehabilitative treatment facilities often refer specifically to cognitive retraining programs provided by professional staff, such as neuropsychologists. Third, other professions have identified neuropsychologists as providing cognitive retraining services, and referrals for such services are increasing. Finally, an increasing number of professionals are seeking training in cognitive retraining approaches, as suggested by the number of training seminars being offered every year.

Limitations of a Professional Approach To Cognitive Retraining

While professional emphasis in the area of cognitive retraining has been beneficial in terms of development and efficient dissemination of techniques, there are also inherent drawbacks to such an approach.

Number of Professionals Available

Based on a Glasgow Coma Scale score of 12 or less on arrival at the emergency room, there are approximately 35,000 individuals in the United States who survive moderate to severe closed head injury each year given a population estimate of 422,000 new cases of head injury per year (Kalsbeek, McLaurin, Harris, & Miller, 1980; Kraus, 1980). Since these individuals survive well past their injury in most cases, there is a cumulative population of several hundred thousand traumatically brain injured (TBI) persons in the United States. While cognitive retraining seems to be most commonly utilized with TBI persons, the potential need for such retraining among other patient groups should not be overlooked. In fact, positive results using cognitive retraining programs have been reported consistently with persons having cerebrovascular accident (CVA), of whom there are approximately 300,000 surviving each year in the United States (Toole, 1979). Added to this are individuals with neoplasm, infectious diseases, and other brain illnesses.

There are a limited number of professionals capable of providing such services to the multitude of individuals who might benefit. At the time of this writing there are approximately 200 individuals certified in neuropsychology by the American Board of Professional Psychology, while the clinical neuropsychology division of the American Psychological Association has approximately 2,000 members. Clearly, neuropsychology alone cannot fulfill the need for cognitive retraining. The number of licensed Master's level speech therapists (approximately 40,000) is heartening, but less than 8% of those individuals work in rehabilitation settings, based on American Speech and Hearing Association records. In sum, the existing professional community is insufficient in number to cope with the existing need for cognitive retraining.

Number of Possible Contact Hours

The number of possible contact hours between brain-injured individuals and professionals implementing cognitive remediation programs must be considered. Given present-day case loads in most settings, the professional who is able to spend an hour a day with a brain-impaired person is indeed fortunate. However, the impact of one hour of intensive cognitive stimulation can be minimized based on what occurs during the remaining waking hours. When the brain-impaired person is in an inpatient rehabilitation facility, the other waking hours are often highly structured, providing sufficient stimulation. However, once the person is discharged, appointments with rehabilitation professionals often diminish in frequency, and a stimulating environment is no longer assured. The potential lack of structure and stimulation in the post-discharge phase is particularly disturbing, since it is clear that brain-impaired persons in general require structure and externally generated stimulation in order to perform at a suitable level during the early recovery phase (Ben-

Yishay & Diller, 1983; Malec, 1984). Without such structure and stimulation, brain-impaired individuals are often prone to passive activities, such as watching television, which are of minimal value for cognitive recovery. In sum, it is not clear that periodic professional appointments are sufficient to ensure maximal results in cognitive rehabilitation of the brain-impaired person.

Generalization from Office to Home

The generalization of gains in cognitive remediation activities to the injured person's everyday environment and activities of daily living is of paramount importance to the justified continuation of cognitive remediation programs. Unfortunately, this has not been fully addressed in the literature. From a scientific perspective, it is distressing to encounter the heavy marketing of cognitive retraining programs with insufficient attention to the evaluation of concrete benefits. In fact, there is evidence to suggest that gains in cognitive retraining are not stable, and do not generalize to the everyday environment (Lewinsohn, Danaher, & Kikel, 1977; Wilson, 1982; Levin, Benton, & Grossman, 1982). In some respects, it is illogical to think that training confined to an office space, which may involve materials that are not otherwise available, will significantly influence performance in a totally different environment with different stimulus cues. To generate maximum benefit, training exercises should take place in environments where the change is desired, which, in the case of brain-impaired persons, is often the home.

Expense of Treatment

The cost of a cognitive remediation program, particularly if extended over several months, can be quite high and must be borne by the brain-impaired individual, his/her family, or their representatives. Companies providing health insurance have generally been hesitant about covering cognitive retraining services. Insurance companies are in the unenviable position of having to weigh the possible benefits of any treatment against the expense involved. Unfortunately, the cost efficiency of cognitive retraining programs has not been sufficiently addressed by the professional community, leaving insurance companies in a quandary which they must resolve on their own.

It should not be overlooked that third-party payment for cognitive retraining programs is a luxury which many brain-impaired individuals do not have. Given the segment of the population often affected by TBI (Rimel & Jane, 1983), it is not uncommon to encounter persons with no health insurance or extremely limited coverage. Realistically, such persons are likely to receive only limited professional guidance and contact. For such individuals an alternative to professional cognitive retraining seems to be a necessity.

Cognitive Recovery As Time Limited

Implementing cognitive retraining programs as a professional endeavor in a rehabilitation setting carries with it a subtle implication that cognitive recovery is time limited. That is, there is an implication that once formal cognitive retraining is at an end, so is cognitive recovery. Fortunately, professionals familiar with recovery from brain injury would accurately contest this view. However, the public in general may be more susceptible to such subtle implications, which could in the long term carry more weight than the attitudes of professionals. The concept of rehabilitation as solely a professional endeavor entails an extremely narrow focus, which psychology as a profession has worked to overcome for many years. We realize now that physical rehabilitation is only one aspect of recovery from brain injury and that cognitive recovery may continue even after physical recovery has stabilized. Considering we have worked so diligently to overcome a narrow definition of rehabilitation, it would be unfortunate for us to be engaging in activities which serve to support that narrow definition by encouraging a time-limited view of recovery.

Cognitive Intervention as a Professional Concern

When presenting cognitive retraining as a professional endeavor, there is an implication that in order to aid someone with cognitive recovery, one has to have a graduate degree and years of experience. It is not uncommon to hear the phrase, "the doctor knows best," which typifies the conception of the lay person that their input is non-essential. In fact, the input of family members is extremely important in that these individuals are most familiar with the brain-impaired person and are likely to be spending the most time with him/her. As professionals who have limited personal contact with patients, we are dependent on the family in most cases to follow through with goals set during formal reha- bilitation. It is reasonable to expect that the common sense judgment which forms the basis of professional decisions in formal rehabilitation, can also be employed by family members.

In sum, the picture of cognitive retraining as an endeavor of professionals will be increasingly difficult to uphold if such techniques are to be broadly applied to the brain-impaired population. As noted above, in the interest of promoting the notion that recovery does not end with formal rehabilitation, and that progress is not limited to contact with professional providers, we may wish to avoid promoting cognitive retraining as a solely professional endeavor. What is needed, and which already exists in some respects, is a means of utilizing paraprofessionals to promote cognitive recovery. This is already accomplished, to some extent, when a cognitive retraining program is developed by a neuropsychologist or speech therapist and carried out by other staff members in a rehabilitation setting. The scope of paraprofessional involvement, however, could extend beyond this. Specifically, the brain-impaired person's family members, who are often underutilized in the rehabilitation setting, could be utilized as paraprofessionals in promoting cognitive recovery.

Family Involvement in Cognitive Recovery

Just a few years ago the role of family members in rehabilitative treatment was minimal. In fact, the presence of family members was often considered detrimental to the injured person's rehabilitation, to the point that families were asked to leave the premises during treatment. One rationale for this attitude was that the presence of families increased the dependency of the brain-impaired person, thus circumventing the goals of rehabilitation. Unfortunately, the end result of such action was that families often lacked awareness of what had been accomplished during the inpatient stay, and, partly as a result, rehabilitation goals were circumvented after discharge, when rehabilitation staff could have minimal impact upon the situation. In recent years there has been an increasing emphasis on family involvement in the rehabilitation process (Adamovitch et al., 1985; Rosenthal & Muir, 1983). This promotes the conception that rehabilitation is not a time-limited process, and that family members can influence the patient's recovery. In addition, there is a realization that dependency issues can best be dealt with by staff in the rehabilitation setting. Training family members as paraprofessionals requires that they be encouraged to attend therapies at least periodically and participate in the care and treatment of their family member. Literally, this allows family members to get to know the brain-impaired person's deficits and capabilities. Consequently, the family is much better prepared to deal with the brain-impaired person at the time of discharge than would otherwise be the case.

Issues Important to Family Involvement

From the outset, several factors are important in considering the suitability of any particular family for training as paraprofessionals. First is the availability of family members for training purposes. Unfortunately, there are cases in which family members are unable or unwilling to participate in rehabilitative care. It should be noted that families who initially refuse to participate in rehabilitative care may warm to the idea over time, particularly if their input is valued. From our experience it is a rare occasion when family members totally divest themselves of a brain-impaired person. A second factor to be considered in training families as paraprofessionals is their degree of awareness of the deficits associated with the brain injury. While it has often been stressed that the brain-impaired person needs to be aware of deficits prior to remediation, it is equally important that the family have a consistent and accurate view of the existing deficits. Disagreement over deficits undermines cooperation between professionals and family members to the detriment of the brain impaired person. Regular attendance at therapy sessions, even if only weekly or biweekly, often serves to alleviate this sort of problem, as the family members are able to see what the difficulties are in the rehabilitation setting. A third factor to consider is the overall stability of the family. It is often most efficient and practical to designate one or two persons who will be trained as paraprofessionals and responsible for home stimulation activities. There must be some assurance that these individuals, once trained, will be available to the brain-impaired person on a regular basis. This does not mean that these persons must always provide the home stimulation activities themselves, but that they must be in a position to at least direct those who will be involved. The designated family member can also serve as a contact person for professional follow-up in the future. Finally, because cognitive remediation is in many ways an educational endeavor, it is important to ascertain the family's attitude toward education overall. For instance, to maximize generalization, it is important for families to recognize the importance of repetition, consistency, reinforcement, and levels of training.

Qualifications as to Family Involvement in Rehabilitation

In considering the active involvement of family members in the rehabilitation setting and the expectation that such family members continue rehabilitative care after discharge, several concerns need to be addressed. It would be erroneous to assume that what is being proposed here is that family members replace rehabilitation professionals. Realistically, family members will not provide the same quality or extent of service that can be obtained through professional rehabilitation settings. With specific reference to cognitive remediation, it is apparent that families will not have the same expertise as neuropsychologists in developing and implementing cognitive remediation programs. For this reason, it may be misleading to think that the aim of utilizing families as paraprofessionals is for them to develop and implement sophisticated cognitive retraining programs, although some families may be capable of this. A more realistic aim is that the family be able to implement techniques as suggested by rehabilitation professionals, such as neuropsychologists. As such, it may be more appropriate to view the family's endeavors as focusing on *cognitive stimulation* of the brain impaired person, which implies a lesser degree of organization and consistency than is associated with a formal *cognitive retraining* program. This does not mean that the family's endeavors will be ineffective; in our experience it is unnecessary to implement a sophisticated cognitive retraining program in order to promote cognitive recovery. It should be kept in mind that the use of families as paraprofessionals as suggested here first and foremost is intended to discourage the brain-impaired individual from engaging in extremely passive activities which have very little impact on cognitive recovery. Even if only a minimum of active stimulation can be promoted by the family, that is an obvious benefit as compared to more passive activities.

In addition to the question of whether family members can provide quality services, the question has been raised as to whether family members are emotionally capable of providing such services to brain impaired persons. Studies focusing on family members of brain-impaired individuals suggest that they experience a great deal of stress and that emotional disorders, such as depression, are fairly common (Lezak, 1978; Oddy, Humphrey, & Uttley, 1978; Brooks & McKinlay, 1983). For instance, the incidence of psychiatric illness among family members of TBI persons is estimated to be 30 to 40 percent at any one time, twice the rate for the general population (Livingston, Brooks, & Bond, 1985). Such factors could easily impair the capacity of family members to implement a cognitive stimulation program. Research results also indicate that perceived stress tends to increase over time, at least into the first year after onset of brain injury, and there is a strong association between subjective complaints of the impaired persons and the stress level of relatives (Brooks & McKinlay, 1983; Livingston et al., 1985). It is our perception, albeit subjective, that one reason for the increasing distress of family members over time is the family's evolving perception that very little can be done about behavioral and cognitive problems associated with brain injury. During this phase of recovery there is often a lack of purpose and direction to aid the family in setting goals and establishing a daily routine. Guiding families through home stimulation activities can help alleviate some of their distress by providing a sense of direction and purpose to their rehabilitation activities.

An ongoing study at the Spain Rehabilitation Center (SRC), which can be discussed in preliminary terms, suggests that family members are able to view the disability of their relative in an objective fashion. For instance, given an objective instrument, such as The Rappaport Disability Rating Scale (RDRS; Rappaport, Hall, Hopkins, Belleza, Berrol, & Reynolds, 1977), 13 family members of TBI persons were able to gauge disability levels very accurately as compared to ratings provided by professionals. Ratings of disability severity based on RDRS scores were very similar for families and professionals at the time of patient admission and discharge. Our experience indicates that obtaining such ratings on patient admission provides an excellent medium for discussion of deficits and possible goals. Preliminary findings from the same study also indicate that only 2 of 13 family members were clinically depressed based on the Beck Depression Inventory (Beck, Rush, Shaw, & Emory, 1979) at the time of patient admission, while only 1 of 13 were in this range at the time of discharge. On follow-up, approximately three months post-discharge, none of the 13 family members, who had primary responsibility for the brain-impaired person, were depressed. This argues against the notion that family members would be unable to effectively participate in rehabilitation due to denial of deficits or emotional distress.

Development of Home Stimulation Programs

In developing a home stimulation program several factors are of importance. First, cooperation and motivation of the brain impaired person will be maximal if the tasks comprising the program are inherently interesting. This may seem so basic as to be unworthy of mention; however, it is easy to fall into the trap of being technically rigorous, at the expense of fun for those involved. In addition, it should be recognized that practice of tasks focusing on areas of cognitive deficit, even if the tasks are interesting, may be aversive to brain-impaired persons after a period of time. Some variability in specific cognitive areas addressed is a necessity; building self-esteem by periodically focusing on areas of strength for the brain-impaired person is a good counterpart to remediation of deficits. For instance, individuals working to overcome visuo-spatial deficits may find language-oriented tasks a refreshing diversion.

The level of interest of the brain impaired person is only one consideration; the interest of family members must also be addressed. If the family finds the stimulation tasks boring, the potential for consistent implementation is diminished. This is particularly important since it is often the family that dictates daily activities. Realistically, the need for consistency and repetition emphasized in formal cognitive retraining does not always generalize well to the home situation. In sum, the more interesting and fun an activity, the more likely it will be employed in a home stimulation program.

Another factor that is of importance to many families is that the materials required by the program be easily accessible and inexpensive. In this respect, recommendations for computer-generated tasks may be of little utility, particularly in rural or impoverished settings. In our experience materials available in the home and supplements, are often sufficient.

To maximize implementation, a cognitive stimulation program should be easily comprehensible. Even sophisticated families may find overwhelming a program involving multiple levels with numerous qualifications as to application and parameters as to progression. While such detail is desired in the professional and research settings, it is unrealistic to expect families to rigidly adhere to such guidelines. This does not mean that all attempts to promote levels of training should be abandoned; rather the levels should be few and fairly concrete.

Finally, working with families to develop a daily schedule of activities for the brain-impaired person may be beneficial. A time for cognitive stimulation activities can thus be set aside, as can times for activities, such as ambulation and self-care, suggested by other therapists. The time allotted for cognitive stimulation should be tailored to the recovery level of the brain-impaired person. For instance, early in recovery, relatively short episodes, such as 15 minutes several times a day, should be encouraged while at a later stage, concentrated efforts over the span of an hour can be expected. The tasks comprising the cognitive stimulation program need to reflect the potential variability in daily time allotment. Thus, tasks requiring extensive preparation and which cannot be resumed after a hiatus may not be suitable. In addition, tasks that are fairly easy to implement and which require little, if any, material are more likely to be utilized on the spur of the moment when a few minutes may be available.

Through our rehabilitation center, trials involving home stimulation programs have been underway for several months. To clarify what is being discussed, segments of the most recent revision of the home stimulation program are presented in Appendix A. Part or all of this program has been presented to families of TBI persons undergoing rehabilitation with training and discussion related to the tasks recommended. There are several tasks under each major section with varying stages of difficulty for each task. The difficulty levels were developed subjectively based on experiences with brain-injured individuals. When discussing the stimulation program, family members are encouraged to ask questions and consider modifications as their experiences warrant with the aim of increasing their investment in the program.

While the development of home stimulation programs is dependent on the ingenuity of professionals and family members for the most part, it would be unfortunate to overlook commercially available aids in this endeavor. Specifically, this refers to popular games which are readily available in stores. While games such as chess, checkers, and cards were not developed as cognitive retraining instruments, they may be quite suitable as a means of stimulation. Also, to be marketable, games must be inherently interesting, which means they may be more likely to be used and enjoyed by the family. In many cases, rules governing games may need to be modified, depending on the cognitive deficits of the brain-impaired person. For instance, time constraints and motor speed requirements may need to be liberalized due to problems in the person's ability to attend and concentrate. Our experience is that playing games also serves an important social function in that such activities are appropriate outside the home. In addition, playing games may be an important avenue of contact with children, who may otherwise by unsure of how to relate to the brain-injured person. A listing of commercially available games with some potential uses is provided in Appendix B.

Published materials are also available that can be of help to professionals and families in developing home stimulation programs. Academic workbooks have progressed beyond simple arithmetic and writing to focus on skills such as visual discrimination, sequencing, and problem-solving, to name a few. Educational publishers provide a wealth of such materials, often at differing levels of mastery. As is the case with games, educational workbooks were not developed for stimulation of brain-impaired individuals, but there is no reason they cannot be applied in that area. Such materials are available through educational supply stores which cater to school teachers. Fortunately, there is also a growing body of published material focusing specifically on the stimulation of brain-impaired individuals. Carter, Caruso, and Languirand (1984) have written a remediation manual which serves as a cognitive skills workbook. Craine and Gudeman (1981) have provided an extensive listing of stimulation activities broken down into component skills and modalities involved. In most cases the materials required are readily available, but there is no attempt to present tasks in a hierarchial fashion. In addition, texts available in the area of aphasia therapy (e.g., Brubaker, 1982; Kilpatrick & Jones, 1977; Kilpatrick, 1979), which provide suggestions for cognitive stimulation activities, should not be overlooked.

Conclusions

The professional community cannot adequately fulfill the need for cognitive retraining as generated by enormous numbers of brain-impaired persons. Furthermore, focusing on professional involvement as the primary mode of treatment for cognitive deficits carries with it implications which may be detrimental to the concept of rehabilitation over the long term. Ultimately, irrespective of the degree or duration of professional treatment received, the responsibility for the brain-impaired person rests with his/her family in most cases. While rehabilitation specialists have come to realize the importance of the family, there have been few attempts to systematize and direct the contribution of the family in the recovery process. Seeking family involvement in the recovery process by treating them as paraprofessionals acknowledges their involvement and directs family efforts. Realistically, the ability of family members to implement a cognitive stimulation program will vary. Also, the impact of such programs on patient outcome, are, as yet, unclear. Studying such issues represents a significant research challenge.

References

Adamovitch, B.B., Henderson, J.A., & Auerbach, S. (1985). *Cognitive rehabilitation of the closed head injured patients: A dynamic approach.* San Diego: College-Hill Press.

Beck, A.T., Rush, A.J., Shaw, F.F., & Emery, G. (1979). *Cognitive therapy of depression.* New York: Guilford Press.

Ben-Yishay, Y., & Diller, L. (1983). Cognitive remediation. In M. Rosenthal, E.R. Griffith, M.R. Bond, & J.D. Miller (Eds.). *Rehabilitation of the head injured adult.* Philadelphia: F.A. Davis.

Brooks, D., & McKinlay, W. (1983). Personality and behavioral change after severe blunt head injury - a relative's view. *Journal of Neurology, Neurosurgery, and Psychiatry, 46,* 336-344.

Brubaker, S.M. (1982). *Sourcebook for aphasia: A guide to family activities and community resources.* Detroit: Wayne State University Press.

Carter, L.T., & Caruso, J.L. (1984). *The thinking skills workbook: A cognitive skills remediation manual for adults (2nd ed.).* Springfield: Charles C. Thomas.

Craine, J.F., & Gudeman, H.E. (1981). *The rehabilitation of brain functions, principles, procedures, and techniques of neurotraining.* Springfield: Charles C. Thomas.

Crosson, B., & Buenning, W. (1984). An individualized memory retraining program after closed-head injury: A single-case study. *Journal of Clinical Neuropsychology, 3,* 287-301.

Crovitz, H. (1979). Memory retraining in brain-damage patients: The airplane list. *Cortex, 15,* 131-134.

Fowler, R., Hart, J., & Sheehan, M. (1972). A prosthetic memory: An application of the prosthetic memory concept. *Rehabilitation Counseling Bulletin, 16,* 80-85.

Gasparrini, B., & Satz, P. (1979). A treatment for memory problems in left hemisphere CVA patients. *Journal of Clinical Neuropsychology, 1,* 80-85.

Gianutsos, R. (1981). Training the short- and long-term verbal recall of a postencephalitic amnesic. *Journal of Clinical Neuropsychology, 3,* 143-153.

Gianutsos, R., Glosser, D., Elbaum, J., & Vroman, G. (1983). Visual imperception in brain-injured adults: multifacted measures. *Archives of Physical Medicine and Rehabilitation, 64,* 456-461.

Glasgow, R., Zeiss, R., Barbera, Jr., M. & Lewinsohn, P. (1977). Case studies on remediating memory deficits in brain-damaged individuals. *Journal of Clinical Psychology, 33,* 1049-1054.

Gordon, W., Hibbard, M., Egelko, S., Diller, L., Shaver, M., Lieberman, A., & Ragnarsson, K. (1985). Perceptual remediation in patients with right brain damage: A comprehensive program. *Archives of Physical Medicine and Rehabilitation, 66,* 353-359.

Heilman, K.M., Watson, R.T., and Valenstein, E. (1985). Neglect and related disorders. In K.M. Heilman and E. Valenstein (Eds.). *Clinical Neuropsychology* (2nd ed.). New York: Oxford University Press.

Jaffe, P., & Katz, A. (1975). Attenuating anterograde amnesia in Korsakoff's psychosis. *Journal of Abnormal Psychology, 84,* 559-562.

Jones, M. (1974). Imagery as a mnemonic aid after left temporal lobectomy: Contrast between material-specific and generalized memory disorders. *Neuropsychologia, 12,* 21-30.

Kalsbeek, W.D., McLaurin, R.L., Harris, B.S., & Miller, J. (1980). The national head and spinal cord injury survey: Major findings. In D.W. Anderson and R.L. McLaurin (Eds.) *Report on the National Head and Spinal Cord Injury Survey (Special Supplement). Journal of Neurosurgery, 53 ,* 513-531.

Kilpatrick, K. (1979). *Therapy guide for the adult with language and speech disorders, Volume II: Advanced stimulus materials.* Akron: Visiting Nurse Service, Inc.

Kilpatrick, K., & Jones, C.L. (1977). *Therapy guide for the adult with language and speech disorders Volume I: A selection of stimulus materials.* Akron: Visiting Nurse Service, Inc.

Kraus, J.F. (1980). Injury to the head and spinal cord: The epidemiological relevance of the medical literature published from 1960-1978. *Journal of Neurosurgery (Suppl.), 53,* 3-10.

Levin, H.H., Benton, A.L., & Grossman, R.G. (1982). *Neurobehavioral consequences of closed head injury.* New York: Oxford University Press.

Lewinsohn, P., Danaher, B., & Kikel, S. (1977). Visual imagery as a mnemonic aid for brain-injured persons. *Journal of Consulting and Clinical Psychology, 5,* 717-723.

Lezak, M.D. (1978). Living with the characterologically altered brain injured patient. *Journal of Clinical Psychiatry, 39*, 592-598.

Livingston, M., Brooks, D., & Bond, M. (1985). Patient outcome in the year following severe head injury and relatives' psychiatric and social functioning. *Journal of Neurology, Neurosurgery, and Psychiatry, 48*, 876-881.

Malec, J. (1984). Training the brain-injured in behavioral self-management skills. In B.A. Edelstein and E.T. Couture (Eds.) *Behavioral assessment and rehabilitation of the traumatically brain damaged.* New York: Plenum.

Malec, J. & Quesdad, K. (1983). Rehabilitation of memory after craniocerebral trauma: Case report. *Archives of Physical Medicine and Rehabilitation, 63*, 436-438.

Oddy, M., Humphrey, M., & Uttley, D. (1978). Stresses upon the relatives of head-injured patients. *British Journal of Psychiatry, 133*, 507-513.

Prigatano, G., Fordyce, D., Zeiner, H., Roueche, J. Pepping, M., & Wood, B. (1984).Neuropsychological rehabilitation after closed head injury in young adults. *Journal of Neurology, Neurosurgery, and Psychiatry, 47*, 505-513.

Rao, S., & Bieliauskas, L. (1983). Cognitive rehabilitation two and one-half years post right temporal lobectomy. *Journal of Clinical Neuropsychology, 4*, 313-320.

Rappaport, M., Hall, K., Hopkins, K., Belleza, T., Berrol, S., & Reynolds, G. (1977). Evoked brain potentials and disability in brain-damaged patients. *Archives of Physical Medicine and Rehabilitation, 58*, 333-338.

Rimel, R.W., & Jane, J.A. (1983). Characteristics of the head-injured patient. In M. Rosenthal, E.R. Griffith, M.R. Bond, J.D. Miller (eds.) *Rehabilitation of the head injured adult.* Philadelphia: F.A. Davis.

Rosenthal, M., & Muir, C.A. (1983). Methods of family intervention. In M. Rosenthal, E.R. Griffith, M.R. Bond, & J.D. Miller (Eds.) *Rehabilitation of the head injured adult.* Philadelphia: F.A. Davis.

Toole, J. (1979). *Diagnosis and management in stroke.* Dallas: American Heart Association.

Webster, J., Jones, S., Blanton, P., Gross, R., Beissel, G., & Woffard, J. (1984). Visual scanning training with stroke patients. *Behavior Therapy, 15*, 129-143.

Weinberg, J., Diller, L., Gordon, W., Gerstman, L., Lieberman, A., Lakin, P., Hodges, G., & Ezrachi, O. (1977). Visual scanning training effects on reading-related tasks in acquired right brain damage. *Archives of Physical Medicine and Rehabilitation, 58*, 479-486.

Weinberg, J., Piasetsky, E., Diller, L. & Gordon, W. (1982). Treating perceptual organization deficits in nonneglecting RBD stroke patients. *Journal of Clinical Neuropsychology, 4*, 59-75

Appendix A

Examples of Home Stimulation Activities

Attention and Concentration

Task I--Shell Game

Stage I--Materials: Two clear glasses and a marble. Directions: Turn the glasses upside down, placing the marble underneath one with the trainee watching. Ask the trainee to point to the glass containing the marble. Once this has been accomplished move the glasses and ask the trainee to indicate once again. Repeat several times.

Stage II--Materials: Two identical opaque containers and a marble. Directions: Same as Stage I. At this stage the trainee can no longer see the marble in the container. On repetitions, slowly increase the amount of time spent moving the containers.

Stage III--Materials: Three or more opaque containers and one marble. Directions: Same as previous stages.

Stage IV--Materials: Three or more opaque containers and two or more distinctly colored marbles. Directions: Place all marbles under separate containers with the trainee watching. Ask the trainee to identify where each colored marble may be found. Move the containers about and ask again. Repeat several times, increasing the amount of time spent moving the containers.

Task 2--Cancellation Tasks

Stage I--Materials: An 8x11 sheet of white paper with the letters K B L Z B O Y across the middle in large print. Directions: Ask the trainee to mark out all the B letters. This could be done with shapes (e.g., square, triangle, circle, hexagon, etc.) and numbers. Repeat several times with different sequences and search letters (or shapes or numbers).

Stage II--Materials: An 8x11 sheet with two rows of letters (shapes, numbers), smaller print. Directions: Same as Stage I. Repeat with variations in the material.

Stage III--Materials: An 8x11 sheet of paper with three or more rows of letters (shapes, numbers). Directions: Same as Stage II.

Stage IV--Materials: An 8x11 sheet with several rows of upper and lower case letters. Directions: Tell the trainee to mark out a single letter, both upper and lower case. Repeat with varied material.

Stage V--Materials: An 8x11 sheet with several rows of upper and lower case letters (or numbers) in which particular patterns are imbedded (e.g., the letters I N Q or the number sequence 2 8 7). Directions: Ask the trainee to cancel the sequence whenever encountered. Repeat with varied material.

Stage VI--Materials: An 8x11 sheet with several rows of letters in which three-letter words are imbedded (e.g., I P H O G Q Z). Spacing must be equal throughout. Directions: Ask the trainee to find the words.

Task 3--Time Sense

Materials for all stages: Stopwatch and score pad.

Stage I--Directions: Give the stopwatch to trainee with instructions to start the watch when told and stop it at ten seconds. Then tell the trainee to start the watch. Repeat with variations in time up to one minute. When the trainee can stop the watch within one to two seconds of goal consistently, move on to Stage II.

Stage II--Directions: The trainee should not be allowed to see the stopwatch. The trainee is asked to tell the trainer when ten seconds have passed since the stopwatch was started. Counting out loud should be encouraged at first. Repeat with variations in the time span up to two minutes. With increasing time, a wider span of error should be anticipated. For every 10 seconds of time span, 1.5 seconds variation should be allowed. Thus, for 30 seconds as the goal, a response by the trainee between 25.5 and 34.5 seconds would be acceptable.

Stage IV--Directions: Same as for Stage III except that the trainer is to fill in the time with conversation, questions, etc. The trainee must try to keep track of the passing seconds despite these distractions. A larger range of error is acceptable; two seconds for every 10 seconds of time span. So for 30 seconds as a goal, a response between 24 and 36 seconds is acceptable.

Task 4--Number Sequences

Materials for all stages: Pencil and paper.

Stage I--Directions: Ask the trainee to say or write the numbers one to 10 in sequence. If either of these is difficult, present the 10 numbers written on individual squares of paper and ask the trainee to order the numbers by sight. Repeat several times, increasing the number span if the trainee succeeds. The trainer could also use the alphabet, days of the week, and months of the year for sequencing in this manner.

Stage II--Directions: Ask the trainee to sequence numbers by odd, even, or 10s (e.g., count by odd numbers, count by even numbers, count by 10s). Begin by providing the initial four digits in the sequence, either written or spoken, for the trainee. Repeat several times, altering the directions (e.g., odd vs even) and the starting point. When consistent success is evident, go on to Stage III.

Stage III--Directions: Provide the trainee with the first four digits of a sequence in which a set number is added or subtracted each time (e.g., 3 - 7 - 11 - 15). Instruct the trainee as to the steps to be taken (e.g., add 4 on each time) and ask the trainee to continue the sequence. Repeat with variations.

Stage IV--Directions: Same as Stage III except that the trainer does not specify the operation to be employed (e.g., don't tell the trainee to add 4 each time). This requires that the trainee figure out what has to be done.

Stage V-- Directions: Same as Stage IV except that operations can now include multiplication, exponentiation, or any other reasonable mathematical operation. At this stage the trainer might also employ other sequences, particularly the alphabet (e.g., call out every third letter of the alphabet).

Stage VI-- Directions: Ask for sequences in reverse order (e.g., count backwards from 20, name the alphabet backwards, name the months of the year backwards). Counting backwards by three or some other variation would also be suitable.

Motor Speed

Task I--Finger Tapping

Materials for all Stages: Preferably a typewriter or home computer with a keyboard.
Stage I--Directions: Ask the trainee to tap a single key on the board as rapidly as possible for ten seconds with one finger of the preferred hand. Score is the number of letters typed. Allow 20 seconds of rest and repeat. Do this five times. If a typewriter is not available, have the trainee tap the table with one finger and count the taps. Repeat this cycle with several individual fingers on both hands.
Stage II-Directions: Have the trainee tap two keys with two fingers on the same hand, alternating between the keys, for 10 seconds. Allow a rest period and repeat. Change fingers and/or hands after five trials.
Stage III--Directions: Have the trainee alternate between tapping two keys, one with a finger from the left hand, the other with a finger on the right hand. Repeat as instructed in Stages I and II.
Stage IV--Directions: Using four fingers of the right hand have the trainee press four keys in sequence for 30 seconds. Repeat several times, then try the left hand. Introduce variations in the sequence.

Task 2--Nuts and Bolts

Materials for all Stages: 25 nuts and 25 matching bolts approximately one inch long. Three empty shoe boxes. If nuts and bolts are not available, any two small items could be used (e.g., buttons, paper clips, coins).
Stage I--Directions: Place the nuts in one box and place an empty box approximately 12 inches away. Using the right hand, ask the trainee to place nuts one at a time into the empty box. After some practice assess speed by allowing 30 seconds to transfer. Score is how many nuts are transferred in that time. When one hand is fatigued, switch to the other hand.
Stage II--Directions: Place all the nuts in one box. Arrange two empty boxes on each side of the full box, about 12 inches away. Ask the trainee to place individual nuts in empty boxes, alternating between the two. If the trainee stops alternating provide a reminder. Assess speed as in Stage I. When one hand tires, switch to the other hand.
Stage III--Directions: Place three boxes in a row with full box in middle, as in Stage II. Ask trainee to transfer nuts one at a time using both hands simultaneously. The left hand is to fill the box on the left. Time and score as in Stages I and II.
Stage IV--Directions: Arrange boxes as in Stage III. Place both nuts and bolts in center box. Using the left hand, the trainee is to place the nuts in the box on the left, and with the right hand place the bolts in the box on the right. Correct errors when they occur. Encourage the use of both hands simultaneously and look for approximately equal numbers of items in each box. Periodically switch the task: right hand for nuts, left hand for bolts. Time for 60 seconds.
Stage V--Directions: Place nuts in one box and bolts in another. Instruct the trainee to pick up a bolt with one hand and a nut with the other and screw the nut on the bolt a few turns (just enough so they do not come apart). The completed assembly is to be placed in the remaining empty box. Allow practice and then time for 60 seconds. As performance improves increase the time allotted to two minutes, then three, etc.

Constructional - Spatial

Task I--Centering

Materials for all stages: Paper and pencil.

Stage I--Directions: Draw straight line on the paper and ask the trainee to mark each end of the line with perpendicular lines. Correct any errors. Then ask the trainee to mark the center of the line. Provide feedback and repeat, varying the length of lines.
Stage II--Directions: Draw a straight line on the paper and ask the trainee to divide it into thirds. Provide feedback and repeat. Vary the length of the line, number of divisions (e.g., fourths, fifths), and the orientation of the line (vertical, diagonal, horizontal).
Stage III--Directions: Draw an enclosed figure (e.g., circle or square) and ask the trainee to place a dot in the center of the figure. Repeat with varying figures of different sizes.
Stage IV--Directions: Draw a square and ask the trainee to divide the square into four equal portions using intersecting lines. Then ask the trainee to place a dot at the center of each of the smaller squares. Repeat with varying size squares. As performance improves, make the division more demanding. For instance, ask for six or nine squares created by intersecting lines.

Task 2--Right-Left Orientation

Stage I--Directions: Have the trainee identify body parts on the right and left. For instance ask him/her to touch the right ear. Provide guidance if necessary.
Stage II--Materials: A front view drawing or picture of a person, including both arms and legs. Directions: Holding the picture in front of the trainee, ask the trainee to point out the pictured persons' right and left features (which are opposite to the trainee's right and left). If there is some confusion, reverse the drawing so that the pictured person's right and left correspond to the trainee's. If necessary, keep reversing in this fashion.
Stage III--Directions: Ask the trainee to identify right and left body parts on trainer with the trainer sitting next to the trainee and facing the same direction.
Stage IV--Directions: Ask the trainee to identify right and left body parts on the trainer with the trainer sitting and facing the trainee.
Stage V--Directions: Ask the trainee to touch body parts in a specific manner. For instance, ask the trainee to touch his/her left ear with the right hand or the right leg with the left heel.

Task 3--Connecting the Dots

Materials for all Stages: Two pieces of paper with multiple nine-dot squares on each (see below).

```
.  .  .

.  .  .

.  .  .
```

Stage I--Directions: The trainer draws a line connecting two of the dots in one square. Using another sheet, the trainee duplicates the line on a nine-dot square. Repeat several times using a new square each time and different dots.
Stage II--Directions: The trainer connects two dots and then a third in a continuous line. The trainee duplicates this. Repeat several times using a new square each time. When performance is accurate on three consecutive trials, connect four dots. Do not let the lines

cross. Ask the trainee to duplicate. As performance allows, keep connecting more dots but without crossing lines. Initially, allow the trainee to see the standard as it is drawn. As this is mastered, the trainee can be presented with complete designs.

Stage III--Directions: Connect at least four dots and cross lines. Ask the trainee to duplicate. As performance warrants, the trainer may increase the number of dots connected. To add complexity, the number of dots in the square can be increased.

Task 4--Locating Squares

Materials: For Stages I to V a sheet of paper with multiple 3x3 square matrices (like a tic-tac-toe grid) marked horizontally with letters and vertically with numbers will be required.

Stage I--Directions: Ask the trainee to point to the squares under the letter B and then to the squares in row 2. Do this for other columns and rows.

Stage II--Directions: Ask the trainee to point to the intersection of row 2 and column B. Encourage the use of a finger for pointing as a means of structuring the task. Do the same thing for other columns and rows.

Stage III--Directions: Point at a square and ask the trainee to provide the row number and column letter (for example, row 1, column C).

Stage IV--Directions: Give the trainee a row number and column letter and ask him/her to place an "X" in the proper square.

Stage V--Directions: Play TIC-TAC-TOE with the trainee providing only coordinates which the trainee must fill in (for example, "I select 3B").

Stage VI--Materials: Increase the number of squares by adding new rows and columns to the grid labeling each by number or letter. Directions: Continue to ask the trainee to locate squares given coordinates.

Stage VII--Materials: A 10x10 grid labeled as above. Directions: Each player locates "ships" on the grid out of sight of the other player. For instance, one ship could be several squares positioned in a row, column, or diagonally. The size and number of ships can be varied. Each player is then to take turns in trying to guess the location of the other person's ships given three guesses per turn. If a player provides the coordinates of an opponent's ships, the opponent indicates this by saying "hit." When all squares comprising a particular ship are guessed, the ship is considered sunk. The player who sinks all his/her opponent's ships wins. This game can be made more complex by adding more rows and columns.

Stage VIII--Materials: Television listing for one day. Directions: An everyday task involving visual search is reading a television schedule. You must first locate the time on the listing and then look for the program and channel. Provide a listing of a time and channel and ask what program will be aired (e.g., "What will come on Channel 4 at 8:00 pm?). You can make a list of such questions and let the trainee work alone.

Task 5--Drawing Figures

Materials for all Stages: Colored pencils and unlined paper.

Stage I--Directions: With the trainee watching, the trainer draws a shape beginning with the most simple, such as a horizontal or verticle line, circle, square, or triangle. Given a different color pencil, the trainee is to trace the edge of the figure. Repeat several times varying the figure. As performance allows, the figure may become more complex, such as a hexagon, octagon, etc.

Stage II--Directions: Have the trainee shadow trace figures. For best results the original page with figures to be traced should be taped to the table with a clean sheet of paper taped over the top.

Stage III--Directions: Provide dotted outlines of figures on a clean sheet with the expectation that the trainee fill in the figures. The more dots provided the easier the task. For greatest complexity, a dot at each vertex of the figure is all that should be provided.

Stage IV--Directions: Ask the trainee to copy figures on a clean sheet, matching the standard in terms of size and orientation. Once geometric shapes are mastered, move on to drawing of objects, such as a house, automobile, tree, etc.

Stage V--Directions: The trainee should draw geometric figures to command, that is, without a standard from which to copy. Once geometric shapes are mastered, the drawing of objects to command can be attempted.

Task 6--Puzzles

Stage I--Materials: Two- to four-piece flat puzzles. These can be manufactured by cutting up pictures from magazines. Directions: Initially show the completed puzzle to the trainee and dismantle in his/her presence. Have the trainee assemble, with guidance if necessary. If the trainee is performing well, present him/her with the dismantled pieces, never having seen the completed puzzle.

Stage II--Materials: Flat puzzles with varying numbers of pieces, up to 100. Directions: Allow the trainee to assemble the puzzle. If the puzzle comes with a picture of the completed product, allow this to be used for guidance.

Stage III--Materials: Building blocks of varying sizes. Directions: The trainer builds two dimensional constructions (e.g., towers, walls) which the trainee is asked to duplicate with the trainer's standard in full view. Repeat with varying constructions.

Stage IV--Materials: Same as Stage III. Directions: The trainer uses blocks to make three dimensional constructions (e.g., a pyramid, a "house"). With this standard in view the trainee is to duplicate. Repeat with increasing complexity in the construction. For instance, the construction need not be symmetrical.

Task 7--Mazes

Materials: Paper and pencil mazes of varying complexity which may be purchased at an educational supply store or some newstands.

Directions: Have the trainee attempt the mazes, beginning with the simplest. Initially it may be necessary for the trainer to draw an exit line and the trainee trace the line. As performance warrants, go on to more complex mazes.

Task 8--Map Location

Stage I--Materials: Hand drawn map of the neighborhood. Directions: With the trainee's pen at "home" on the map, give directions which the trainee will follow with the pen. For instance, tell the trainee to go east and turn right on a particular street. Repeat with trainee starting at home and vary directions.

Stage II--Materials: A map as in Stage I with stores and other important locations included and colored pencils. Directions: Direct the trainee to get from home to important locations using different colored pencils for each location. On actual excursions outside the home, ask the trainee to direct the way. It may be helpful to bring along the map.

Stage III--Materials: City map. Directions: Point out two locations on the map and have the trainee determine the shortest route between the two.

Stage IV--Materials: Road atlas of the United States. Directions: Ask trainee to designate a route between points in two cities, including interstate highways and city thoroughfares.

Language Skills

The following tasks are intended for persons who are able to communicate through language at a basic level by comprehending, speaking, reading, or writing.

Task I--Word Search

Given an array of letters, the person is to underline words.

Stage I--Materials: Write four letters with a three-letter word inserted (Example: PDOG). Directions: Ask the trainee to underline the word. Generate as many letter sequences with inserted words as possible.

Stage II--Materials: Write four letters with a three-letter word inserted in reverse (Example: XTAC). Directions: Ask the trainee to underline the word. Generate as many sequences as possible to provide practice.

Stage III--Materials: A four by four (4x4) block of letters with a word inserted on each row. Example:

T	A	G	H
P	A	N	D
X	W	H	Y
P	I	N	A

Directions: Ask the trainee to underline each word.

Stage IV--Materials: Four by four block as in Stage III but with words presented vertically. Directions: Ask trainee to circle words.

Stage V--Materials: Four by four block as in Stage III but with words reversed in each row. Directions: Ask trainee to underline words.

Stage VI--Materials: Four by four letter block as in Stage III with words presented in any format; rows, columns, or reversed. Directions: Ask trainee to circle words.

Stage VII--Directions: Increase the complexity of the task by adding rows and columns of letters and presenting longer words.

Task 2--Crossword Puzzles

Crossword puzzles of varying difficulty are available through newsstands and educational supply stores. It may be appropriate to begin with simpler puzzles intended for children and work up to more complex puzzles.

Task 3--Hangman

Materials: Paper and pencil.

Stage I--Directions: The trainer thinks of a word and draws spaces corresponding to the number of letters (Example: _ _ _). A scaffold with noose is also drawn. The person is then given chances to guess letters in the word. If a letter in the word is guessed, that space is filled in. If the letter is not in the word, then a body part (for example, head, trunk, arm) is added to the figure on the scaffold. The challenge is to guess the word before the man on the scaffold is complete and thus "hung." Provide a definition of the word being sought and write down letters guessed within sight of the person.

Stage II--Directions: Same as above except a definition of the word is not provided. Write down letters guessed by the person. This prevents duplication of guesses.

Stage III--Directions: Same as above but do not provide definitions and do not write down guesses.

Task 4--Fill in the Blank

Stage I--Directions: A sentence is provided with a space for a missing word. The sentence with the missing word is accompanied by a picture to which the sentence refers (Example: picture of a red ball with the sentence "The color of the _____ is red.")

Stage II--Directions: No picture is provided but the missing word is easily determined in the context of the sentence. (Example: "The color of grass is _____.")

Stage III--Directions: Sentences are provided with multiple blanks which can be filled by more than one word. (Example: "_____, _____, and _____ are some of the animals that can be seen at the zoo.")

Reasoning/Problem Solving

Task 1--Locating Information in the Newspaper

Materials: Local newspaper

Stage I--Directions: Ask the trainee about information from the front page, such as headlines, the date, and name of the paper.

Stage II--Directions: Ask the trainee to locate sections of the paper, such as sports, business, and classified ads.

Stage III--Directions: Ask for specific information without indicating the section in which it can be found. For instance, ask for the score of baseball games (or any seasonal sport), movies showing in town, and weather information (low temperature, high temperature, etc.)

Stage IV--Directions: Ask for specific information involving a decision. For instance, you are interested in buying a car, such as a foreign small car, for a given price and ask the trainee to provide a list of cars for sale that meet the criteria.

Task 2--Ordering Numbers

Materials: Small pieces of paper with a number written on each.

Stage I--Directions: Give the trainee three numbers and ask him/her to arrange in order from lowest to highest.

Stage II--Directions: Start with three numbers to be arranged and then hand the trainee other numbers, one at a time, to be inserted in the sequence.

Stage III--Directions: Given three numbers, ask the trainee what the numbers have in common (for instance, odd or even, multiples of each other, or another common number).

Task 3--Problem Situations

Materials: Paper and pencil.

Stage I--Directions: Provide a written list of steps involved in a simple task, such as brushing teeth. For example:

> Brush teeth
> Take out toothpaste and toothbrush
> Put toothpaste on toothbrush

Ask the trainee which comes first, second, and so forth.

Stage II--Directions: Ask the trainee how to go about more complex tasks, such as scrambling eggs, or changing a tire on a car. Ask for details about what is done. If an important step is left out, ask the trainee where it should go.

Stage III--Directions: Present problem situations in which decisions are required and no clear sequence of behavior is evident. For instance, ask the trainee how he/she would respond to running out of gas in the car, finding that he/she had no money while standing at the cash register of a store, losing his/her wallet, being lost in a new city, being improperly dressed at a formal party.

Task 4--Reasoning from General to Specific

Materials: Paper and pencil.

Stage I--Directions: Given a general heading (such as tools, animals, plants, countries, occupations, foods, sports), ask the trainee to generate as many items in that area as possible. If the trainee is stumped, hints are permissible. For instance, in generating the names of animals you could advise the trainee to think of the zoo or the farm. For foods you could suggest thinking of the grocery store.

Stage II--Directions: Same as Stage I except the possible responses to the general heading are more limited. For instance, asking which sports involve running, use of balls, water contact, use of a racquet, more or less than five players, or physical contact between players. This involves a decision process in which the trainee must rule out inappropriate items.

Stage III--Directions: Tell the trainee that you bought something at the grocery store and that he/she must figure out what it is by asking questions. Encourage the trainee to ask very general questions at first (for example, "Is it a vegetable?" or "Is it a meat?") rather than very specific questions (such as, "Is it a cucumber?"). Once more general questions are answered more specific questions can be asked. Initially, allow as many questions as necessary. After the trainee has guessed correctly on a few items, start to limit the number of questions allowed the trainee, starting with 30, then down to 20, then to 15.

Task 5--Categorization

Stage I--Materials: A list of 30 items each belonging to one of three categories (for example, food, furniture, clothing). Directions: Ask the trainee to sort the items according to category. If the trainee is unable to determine the categories, they may be provided.

Stage II--Materials: A list of 30 items all from the same general category but which can be subdivided (for example, a list of food items that can be divided into meats, vegetables, and

dairy products). Directions: Ask the trainee to sort the items into three categories but do not specify the categories.
Stage III--Materials: A listing of paired items that have something in common (for example, chair-couch, steak-pork, book-newspaper). Directions: Ask the trainee what each pair of items have in common. Ask for more than one answer if possible (for example, a book and a newspaper are both written and both are made of paper).

Task 6--Budgeting

Materials: Make up a budget with entries for each month in the following areas: rent, food, electricity, car.
Stage I--Directions: Ask the trainee during which month a particular expenditure (such as for electricity) was highest (or lowest).
Stage II--Directions: Ask for yearly totals of expenditures in all areas. Alter the amount spent in each category and add other categories (for example, entertainment, clothing).
Stage III--Directions: Ask the trainee to determine how much money would be required each month to live within the budget. Break this down further into weekly income and finally hourly wage. Include consideration of taxes at a rate of 10 percent.

Appendix B

Popular Games Suitable for Cognitive Stimulation

The following is an alphabetical list of games that are commercially available which could be used in a cognitive stimulation program. This list is by no means comprehensive. The manufacturer of the game is provided after each entry (unless the game is available through several manufacturers) along with a listing by number of the cognitive skills required. The number coding of cognitive skills is as follows:

1. **Perceptual accuracy** - All games require perceptual (usually visual) accuracy to some extent but some focus on accuracy as a goal.
2. **Spatial organization** - Games requiring, as a basic focus, organization of material in two or three dimensions are given this designation.
3. **Perception-motor functioning** - Basically this entails fine motor functioning or motor speed when it represents a primary component of the game.
4. **Verbal skills** - Games addressing the generation of words or other verbal material.
5. **Arithmetic skills** - Games in which basic arithmetic plays a central role, including the handling of money.
6. **Convergent problem-solving** - The emphasis here is on piecing together solutions in a step-wise fashion, an essential component to effective strategy.
7. **Divergent problem-solving** - Flexibility in approach is the hallmark. In other words, diverging from step-by-step solutions to generate new strategies.
8. **Sequencing** - This is often a component of convergent and divergent problem-solving but, in some cases, is a goal in itself.
9. **Memory** - All games require ongoing monitoring and recall as part of the game process but some games focus on memory itself, that is, the ability to retrieve information from for long-term storage.

The complexity of the games varies a great deal and is very difficult to rate in a consistent fashion. However, even complex games can be made more simple by altering rules, such as by removing special cards and liberalizing time constraints. For instance, the game Uno (International) can be simplified by removing all special cards, such as Draw Four and Reverse.

Aggravation (Lakeside) - 6
Bargain Hunter (Milton Bradley) - 5,6
Bed Bugs (Milton Bradley) - 3
Boggle (Parker Brothers) - 4,7
Chess - 2,6,7
Connect Four (Milton Bradley) - 1,6
Erector Sets - 2,3,6
Foursight (Lakeside) - 2,7
Lego - 1,2,3
Lincoln Logs (Playskool) - 1,2,3
Lotto (Edu-Cards)
   Farm Lotto - 1,6
   Go-Together Lotto - 1,6
   Object Lotto
   Zoo Lotto - 1,6
   The World About Us Lotto - 1,6
Models, plastic replica - 1,2,3,8
Mhing (Suntex) - 6,7,8
Othello - 2,6
Parcheesi (Selchow & Righter) - 6
Pay Day (Parker Brothers) - 5,6
Perquacky (Lakeside) - 4,7,9
Pic Up Stik (Steven) - 3
Rage (International) - 6,8
Sabotage (Lakeside) - 6,7
Scrabble - 2,4,7,9
Sorry (Parker Brothers) - 6
Toss Across (Ideal) - 3
Tripoley - 1,8
Verbatim (Lakeside) - 4,7,9
Word War (Whitman) - 4,6,7,9
Yahtzee (Milton Bradley) - 5,6

Backgammon - 2,5,6
Battleship (Milton Bradley) - 2,6
Bingo - 2
Checkers - 2,6
Clue (Parker Brothers) - 6
Dominoes - 1,2
Etch-A-Sketch (Ohio Art) - 2,3
Gridlock (Ideal) - 1,2,6
Life (Milton Bradley) - 5,6
Lite-Brite (Hasbro) - 1,2,3
Luck Plus (International) - 1,5
Mastermind (Pressman) - 2,6
Memory Original (Milton Bradley) - 2,9
   -Animal Families (Milton Bradley) - 2,9
   -Fronts & Backs (Milton Bradley)- 2,9
   -Step by Step (Milton Bradley)- 6,8
Monopoly (Parker Brothers) - 5,6
Mystery Mansion - 6
Paint-by-numbers - 1,2,3
Password (Milton Bradley) - 4,6,9
Pente (Parker Brothers) - 2,6
Picture Tri-Ominoes (Pressman) - 1
Racko (Milton Bradley) - 8
Risk (Parker Brothers) - 2,6,7
Scotland Yard (Milton Bradley) - 2,6,8
Smath (Pressman) - 2,5,6
Think & Jump (Pressman) - 2,6
Tri-Ominoes (Pressman) - 1
Uno (International) - 1,8
Whodunit (Selchow & Righter) - 6
Word Yahtzee (Milton Bradley) - 4,7,9

Part Three: Pediatric Cognitive Rehabilitation

11

The Neuropsychology of Children's Learning Disorders

Gurmal Rattan and Raymond S. Dean

Early theories of children's learning disabilities were modeled largely upon acquired language and speech disorders in adults. These explanations ranged from "functional ret-rogression" or a return to an earlier stage of development (Jackson, 1874), to the hypotheses that letter reversals were associated with confused dominance of cortical hemispheres (Orton, 1937). For the most part, these early notions of children's learning disorders were attributed to anomalies of the central nervous system (Critchley, 1964; Orton, 1937).

Inferences drawn about specific cortical dysfunctions for children with learning disabilities were based upon the similarity of symptoms with those presented by adults with documented neurological damage. That is to say, although particular behavioral patterns may well be reliable predictors of adult brain lesions, the assumption that these behaviors observed in children reflect underlying anomalies of the central nervous system are tenable at best. Indeed, patterns of behavior used to infer cortical damage in adults may be more heuristically related to an interaction of developmental and environmental variables with children (Dean, 1985). The failure to appreciate the neurological differences between children and adults may be responsible for early overzealous attempts to explain all children's learning problems in terms of neurological dysfunctions (e.g., Strauss & Lehtinen, 1948).

A discussion of the behavioral characteristics associated with learning disabilities was attempted at various times during the early 1960's (see Strother, 1972 for a review). At this point it was recognized that diversity in symptoms, etiology, and treatment of children's learning problems precluded a unitary nosological classification. Instead, clinical judgment was recommended in diagnosing the disorder (Kirk & Becker, 1963). It was further argued that the term "dyslexia" be considered a distinct learning disability and as such, it was portrayed as a unitary syndrome with a genetically based etiology (Critchley, 1964). Dsylexic symptoms without a genetic base were acknowledged, but a consensus concerning its etiology proved problematic. Overall, the 1960's were marked by an attempt to provide consistency in the definition of learning disabilities.

Difficulties in establishing diagnostic criterion for learning disabilities continue to exist. This problem in diagnosis seems related to the tenuousness of a single syndrome to represent the full spectrum of learning disorders. The utility of a diagnostic syndrome for learning disabilities would serve to identify children displaying behaviors with a common underlying etiology or similar deficits. Difficulties arise, however, since the behaviors presented by these children are varied. For example, symptoms such as hyperactivity, distractability, attentional deficits, poor impulse control, irritability, clumsiness, etc. may be presented by children with learning, behavioral, emotional, and neurological problems.

Discussion of a single versus multiple syndrome paradigm of learning disabilities is portrayed in a running commentary between Vellutino (1979) and Satz (Fletcher & Satz, 1979). Vellutino (1979) suggested a unitary notion of reading disabilities based upon an underlying linguistic deficit. He argued that since discrimination of letters or words is not due to visual acuity difficulties, reading errors may more appropriately be attributed to phonological, semantic, and syntactic attributes. In this regard, a linguistic as opposed to a perceptual deficit hypothesis was seen to best fit a large data base offered by Vellutino and his associates (Vellutino, Smith, Steger, & Kaman, 1975; Vellutino, Steger, & Kandel, 1972).

In contrast, Satz and his colleagues (Satz, Taylor, Friel, & Fletcher, 1978) present evidence favoring distinct subtypes of reading disorders with an underlying developmental component. Basing their hypothesis on longitudinal research, Satz pointed to the fact that younger children with reading problems (ages 5-8) are more likely to present with sensorimotor-perceptual deficits which are expressed in errors of copying and correctly reading letters and words. After age eight, however, disabled readers were shown to display deficits in higher-order linguistic skills which are exhibited in lower verbal comprehension. For a review of the subtleties of each argument, the reader is referred to Vellutino, Steger, Moyer, Harding, and Niles (1977) and Fletcher and Satz (1979). Consistent with the multiple syndrome paradigm of learning disabilities, numerous descriptive labels have been introduced (e.g., hyperkinetic syndrome, developmental clumsiness, perceptual-motor handicap, congenital aphasia, and others) (Benton, 1974; Gubbay, Ellis, Walton, & Court, 1965; Stewart, Pitts, Craig, & Dierag, 1966).

Definition

Initial attempts to assess the behavioral, emotional, linguistic and cognitive characteristics of learning disabled children stemmed, in part, from the work of Strauss and his associates (Strauss, 1944; Strauss & Kephart, 1955; Strauss & Lehtinen, 1947). The impetus for this research largely resulted from the need to develop individual remedial programs.

With the enactment of Federal Legislation (PL 94-142), criteria for classifying a child as learning disabled became more uniform in public schools throughout the United States. In general, most states define a learning disabled child as exhibiting a severe deficit in perceptual, integrative or expressive process which adversely affects learning ability. The disorder is seen to reflect deficits in processes or skills (e.g., listening, thinking, talking, reading, writing, spelling or arithmetic) while excluding learning problems due to other handicapping conditions (e.g., visual, hearing, motoric handicaps, mental retardation, emotional disturbance and the like). Under this definition, eligibility criteria would require a severe discrepancy between normal or near normal intelligence and academic achievement in the areas of reading decoding and comprehension, written expression, expressive language, mathematic reasoning/calculations or listening comprehension. Normal or near normal cognitive ability on a measure of intelligence (e.g., Wechsler Intelligence Scale for Children-Revised)(WISC-R) would require a score of 90 or above on either the Verbal or Performance Scales (Clements, 1966). This required ability-achievement discrepancy is usually operationalized as two or more academic years below grade placement.

The American Psychiatric Association (DSM III, 1980) classifies learning disabled children under the rubric of Specific Developmental Disorders (e.g., Reading Disorders). Criteria for classification requires that reading deficits of one-to-two years that cannot be accounted for by chronological age, mental age or inadequate schooling. Further descriptive information about etiology, prevalence, and treatment programs is not presented.

Although the ability-achievement discrepancy notion of learning disabilities as proposed by Bateman (1965) has served as the mainstay for classifying learning disabled children, there remains much disagreement regarding its utility (e.g., Algozzine, Forgnone, Mercer, & Trifiletti, 1979; Ysseldyke & Algozzine, 1979). Parenthetically, provisions of special education are predicated on the assumption that symptoms or academic deficiencies may be eliminated with remedial help.

Epidemiology

An accurate epidemological estimate of learning disabilities is difficult to establish. Clearly, if what characterizes a learning disability is disputed, so must any estimate of its morbidity. Indeed, the heterogeneity of behavioral characteristics presented by learning disabled children preclude an accurate estimation of the disorder.

These concerns, notwithstanding, epidemological estimates indicate that from 10-15% of the school-aged population have some form of learning disorder (Gearheart, 1980). Rutter, Tizard, and Whitmore (1970) report the results of an epidemological study examining the number of educationally handicapped children on the Isle of Wight in Britain. Approximately 2300 children on the Island between the ages of 9-12 years were administered a series of educational, psychological, medical, and neurological tests. One rationale for such an undertaking was to obtain an unbiased estimate of the types and frequency of children's reading disorders without the confounding effect of self-selection. Reading "backwardness" was defined as 2 years 4 months below a child's chronological age. Reading "retardation" on the other hand was seen as a delay of 2 years 4 months or more based on a level predicted from the child's age and performance on a short form of the Wechsler Intelligence Scale for Children (WISC) (Yule, 1967). Generally, it was found that reading backwardness was associated with disorders in neurological, motoric, speech, and other developmental functions while reading retardation was associated more with deficits in speech and language development (Yule & Rutter, 1976). Statistically, 7.9% of all children in the catchment area were considered to have learning deficits while 16.1% were labelled multiply handicapped.

With emphasis on learning disorders, Myklebust and Boshes (1969) assessed over 2000 third and fourth grade learning disabled children throughout the United States. All subjects had an intelligence score of 90 or above on either the Verbal or Performance subscales of the WISC. Children in this study were considered learning disabled if their learning quotient (LQ) (reading age divided by expectancy age times 100) was less than 90 on verbal and nonverbal tasks. Although this was not an epidemological study per se, results were similar to the Rutter et al (1975) study. More specifically, Myklebust and Boshes (1969) found that 15% of these children were achieving below their measured ability. Of these, 7.5% showed signs of neurological involvement.

When sex differences are examined, males far exceed females in frequency of learning difficulties. D'Amato, Dean, and Rattan (1986) for example, evaluated the referral patterns for 1332 children presenting with learning difficulties in the schools. A ratio of some 3.5:1 was reported for males to females. Indeed, it appears that males are more at risk for expressive and receptive language difficulties than female cohorts (Dean, 1982).

When the number of learning disabled children receiving special education was evaluated, Silverman and Metz (1973) found that only 1.4%-2.6% of underachievers were actually receiving such services. This was significantly below the 15% empirically shown by Myklebust and Boshes (1969). The above discrepancy in special education services may well be explained better by socio-political factors than differences in incidence. Concomitantly, it seems that the epidemiology of learning disabilities is more influenced by political and economic concerns than any risk factors.

Etiology

As one would assume by the foregoing, no single statement can be made regarding the etiology of learning disabilities (Dean, 1978, 1982; Gaddes, 1980; Pirozzolo & Harrel, 1985). Underlying causes of these disorders have been attributed to a number of physiological, sociological and environmental factors (Dean, 1985; Gaddes, 1976, 1980; Obrzut & Hynd, 1983). When neurophysiological factors are examined for groups of learning disabled children, significantly greater numbers of neurological anomalies have been reported for these children when compared to normal cohorts. For example, convolutions on the right hemisphere appear earlier than those of the left hemisphere for learning disabled children. More specifically, Chi, Dooling, and Gilles (1977) have reported that the gryi and sulci around the Sylvanian fissures develop earlier in the right side. This was confirmed by computerized tomographic (CT) studies of subjects with developmental dyslexia who were found to have larger right parieto-occipital regions. This is in contrast to larger left parieto-occipital regions found for normal individuals (Hier, LeMay, Rosenberger, 1978; Bosenberger & Hier, 1980). Galaburda and Kemper (1979) report a histological examination of a dyslexic subject who was found to have mild cortical dysplasias through the left hemisphere on autopsy. Disordered cellular architecture may well have adverse affects on the language areas in the brain of some learning disabled children (Galaburda, 1986). Similarly, other post-mortem examinations of dyslexic brains have reported abnormal convulutions of both parietal lobes and thin corpus callosum fibers (Drake, 1969). Additionally, the language areas of the left hemisphere have been found to be symmetrical in size to the right side. The above notwithstanding, nearly one-fourth of all "normal" brains do not have typical patterns of asymmetry while a small percentage have been shown to have a reversed asymetrical pattern with the right hemisphere being larger than the corresponding left hemisphere (Lansdell, 1980). Therefore, while brain symmetry cannot be viewed as a causal determinant of learning disabilities, it does present an interesting neurological perspective.

A relationship between immune disorders, left handedness, and learning disabilities has also been reported (e.g., Geschwind & Beham, 1984). Autoimmunity occurs when the immune system begins attacking the body's own tissues and results in disorders such as rheumatoid arthritis, lupus erythematosus, and myasthenia gravis. Geschwind and Beham (1984) observed an increased incidence of learning problems and immune disorders among the relatives of learning disabled children. In a subsequent study, these researchers reported that normal left handers also had a higher incidence of migraines, allergies, dyslexia, stuttering, skeletal malformation, and thryoid disorder than would be expected in the general population (Geschwind & Behan, 1984). The increased incidence between sinistrality and immune disorders was explained by abnormal testosterone activity in utero.

Other physiological factors such as malnutrition have been reported to result in reduced brain size and intellectual functioning (Stoch & Symthe, 1968). Prolonged nutritional deprivation results in permanent cognitive deficiencies and has been shown to adversely affect verbal, nonverbal intelligence functions, and auditory-visual integration (Cravioto, De Licardie, & Birch, 1966). Such studies investigating neurodevelopmental abnormalities in nutritionally deprived children clearly suggest compromised cognitive functions. Moreover, these deficiencies have been shown both on neuropsychological tests and on experimental procedures (e.g., dichotic listening and split visual-field research Kimura, 1967; Speery, 1974).

Sociological or environmental causes of learning disabilities are considerably more difficult to establish. It seems to be generally recognized that factors such as inadequate or inappropriate instructions, poor role models, motivational factors, personal aspirations, and low socio-economic status contribute significantly to a child's academic performance (see Hallahan & Cruickshank, 1973). From the history of normal and disabled readers, it was found that extrinsic factors such as birthdate between July and December are associated with learning disabilities (Donofrio, 1977). In this regard, boys have been shown to be influenced to a significantly greater extent than girls by the season of birth (Di Pasquale, Morcle, & Flewelling, 1980). Using correlational information, Badian (1984) found that the season of birth and the birth month temperature (exceeded 71 degrees F) played a significant role in predicting boys with identifiable reading disorders. Idiosyncratic relationships between learning disabilities and environmental variables may well be attributed to the variability of characteristics in learning disabled children (Eisenberg, 1978).

Utility of a Neuropsychological Assessment

Interest in the neuropsychological assessment of school-aged children has increased geometrically during the past two decades (Gaddes, 1980, 1983; Knights & Bakker, 1976). As a diagnostic tool, neuropsychological assessment has also been useful in delineating cognitive strengths/weaknesses, processing preference patterns (simultaneous-sequential), and the identification of suspected neurological disorders for learning disabled children. In reference to the latter point, Gaddes (1983) argued convincingly for the inclusion of a neuropsychological assessment for all special education children in light of the fact that 2% of school aged children present with "hard" signs of neurological disorders.

Although a complete neuropsychological examination has been proposed as an aid to remedial planning (Hynd & Obrzut, 1981; Kaufman, 1979), the WISC-R has served as the mainstay in assessing cognitive strengths and weaknesses. Moreover, the WISC-R has been shown on a number of occasions to offer the most salient measure of neurological dysfunction in children (Dean, 1985). In light of this fact, the utility of lengthy neuropsychological examinations such as the Halstead-Reitan Neuropsychological Test Battery (HRNB) it has been questioned if HRNB measures provide orthogonal information from the WISC-R. In this regard, a recent effort was made to assess the orthogonal information offered by the HRNB when administered in conjunction with the WISC-R. Using multivariate methods, D'Amato, Gray, and Dean (1986) showed that all but 10% of skills measured by WISC-R were redundant with the HRNB. It was apparent from these data that additional unique information is indeed offered by the HRNB for functions involving spatial speed of operations, spatial memory, and developmental tasks. In a further effort to assess neuropsychological aspects, each subtest of the WISC-R was regressed on tests of the HRNB (Rattan, Rattan, Gray, & Dean, 1986). The sample consisted of 1074 children between the ages of 9-14 years diagnosed by the public schools as learning disabled. Results showed that the amount of shared variability (R^2) ranged from a low of .04 between HRNB subtests and the Vocabulary subtest of the WISC-R to a high of .17 between HRNB and the Arithmetic subtest. In general, HRNB measures which explained the most variability in WISC-R subtests consisted of the Tactual Performance Test (TPT) - total time, Speech-Sounds Perception, Seashore Rhythm, TPT-memory, and Trail Making-B (time). From the relatively small amount of skill-overlap between the WISC-R and HRNB, inclusion of the latter as a part of an assessment battery has the potential of adding information to the understanding of the learning disabled child.

Subtyping of Learning Disabilities

The subtyping of children's learning disabilities arose from a need to provide differential remediational treatments, distinguish between learning disabled and other groups such as mentally retarded and low achievers, and gain a better theoretical understanding of the disorder (Epps, Ysseldyke, Algozzine, 1985). A number of attempts have been made to use measures of the HRNB to identify specific subtypes of learning disorders (e.g., Denckla, 1972; Doehring & Hoshko, 1977; Fisk & Rourke, 1979; Mattis, French & Rapin, 1975; Morris, Blashfield, & Satz, 1981). The majority of studies in the area include measures of psychomotor skills, visual-perceptual and visual-spatial skills, receptive and expressive language functions along with integration and synthesis of auditory or visual information, abstract reasoning and problem solving strategies. The aims of subtyping include the isolation of diagnostic markers, enhanced matching of remedial strategies, and the investigation of etiological factors for individual subtypes.

Early attempts at subtyping learning disorders utilized a clinical approach. This involved a variety of tests administered and *a priori* criteria used to classify learning difficulties. As an example, Mattis et al (1975) classified 82 reading disabled children into subtypes, labelled language disorders, articulo-graphomotor dyscoordination, and visual-perceptual disorder. A cross-validation of these subtypes resulted in a correct classification of 78% of the sample (Mattis, 1978). Other researchers (e.g., Denckla, 1972) using a clinical approach obtained similar subtypes to those of Mattis et al. (1975) but a large proportion of the sample (70%) could not be adequately classified according to the established criteria. Differential results using this research paradigm may be explained by self-selection to clinic settings and the subjective nature of classification criteria.

Other subtyping methods have focused on multivariate techniques (e.g., Fisk & Rourke, 1979; Morris et al., 1981). These techniques have involved Q-factor and cluster approaches. Q-factor techniques involve the analysis of relationships between subjects in contrast to the traditional correlations between tests. The resultant factors describe groups of children in relation to loadings on specific tests or skill areas. In using this technique, similar subtypes of learning disorders have been identified across studies. In one early attempt, Doehring and Hoshko (1977) studied a sample of 34 children and adolescents aged 8-17 years who were attending a summer reading program. The results of this investigation were interpreted as showing three distinct subtypes. The first group was characterized by poor oral reading, the second by slow matching of spoken and written letters, while children in the third group had deficits in matching of spoken and write words. To examine the generalizability of these subtypes, Doehring and Hoshko (1977) administered the same tests to 31 children who had learning problems or were mentally retarded. Results of this cross-validation study showed that the second and third subtypes noted above were also found for the mixed handicapped group. Petrauska and Rourke (1979) also employed Q-factor techniques and reported three distinct subtypes of reading disorders in a sample of 133 poor readers. The subjects ranged in age from 7-9 years and were drawn from a large clinic sample of children referred for a neuropsychological assessment. Results from their analysis indicated that the first subtype was characterized by deficits in auditory-verbal and language-related skills with adequate visual-spatial and eye-hand coordination abilities. This subtype was similar to the language disorder subtype of Doehring and Hoshko (1977). The second group was characterized by problems in sequencing while the third subtype was identified by deficits in verbal retentive and expressive language skills. To examine developmental aspects of these subtypes, Fisk and Rourke (1979) administered 44 measures to 264 learning or perceptually handicapped children in three age groups. The subtype for the youngest group (9-10 years) was differentiated from the other subtypes by deficits on tests of finger localization, perception of numbers written on fingertips and mild to moderate deficiencies in auditory-verbal processing and psycholinguistic skills. The second group (11-12 years) was typified by moderate to severe deficiencies in auditory-verbal and language related skills with well developed visual-spatial and eye-hand coordination. This subtype was similar to the language disorder subtype of Mattis et al. (1975). Subtype C primarily characterized the older group (13-14 years) and was similar to subtype A but with more prominent deficits in perception of numbers written on fingertips. The youngest age group did not load on subtype C suggesting an age-specific subtype. In total, 80% of the sample was correctly classified as belonging to one of three groups.

Although similarities in subtypes can be found across studies, a caveat is presented in accepting the validity of studies using Q-factor techniques. Most investigators suggest a ratio of subjects to tests of 10:1 when using multivariate techniques in order to preserve the assumption of random sampling without taking undue advantage of chance variations (Nunnally, 1978). In this regard, Doehring and Hoshko (1977) administered 31 tests to 34 subjects, a ratio of approximately 1:1. Although the language disorder subtype was similar to that found by Petrauskas and Rourke (1979) and Fisk and Rourke (1979), one needs to question the extent to which consistency of results may be a function of common methodology. Fisk and Rourke (1979), for example, used a ratio of approximately 6:1 while Petrauskas and Rourke (1979) employed a subject to test ratio of 8:1. In view of the less than 10:1 ratio of subject to tests, the chances of obtaining spurious factor structures is greatly increased (Nunnally, 1978). The advantage of using Q-factor technique as a taxonomic procedure will certainly need to be interpreted with caution. In addition, the generalizability of such results is limited by the fact that most of the samples were drawn from "clinic" populations.

A good deal of research which seeks to subtype children's learning disabilities has used formal cluster analytic techniques (e.g., Morris, Blashfield, & Satz, 1981). Cluster analysis is considered to be a quasi-statistical classification technique which classifies subjects according to either their pattern or level of responses across an array of variables. The grouping of subjects is based upon the criteria of increased homogeneity within groups and decreased overlap between the groups.

Morris et al. (1981) presented a detailed and well executed study to demonstrate the use of cluster analysis. The subjects in this study consisted of 89 white males identified as learning disabled based upon low achievement levels. Four tests in total were used to assess abstract verbal conceptualization, expressive verbal abilities, visual-motor and visual-spatial abilities. A cluster analysis, using a hierarchical agglomerative method was used to determine the number of groups available from the data. The resulting six clusters were then subjected to an iterative partitioning method to reduce within and increase variance between clusters. This latter procedure reduced the number of clusters to five by eliminating the "outliers." The last and perhaps most critical procedure used in this study was a cross-validation of the results. This procedure is necessary in order to determine the stability of the obtained cluster solution. Without such a validation, the results may be due to random variations or a finding unique to a specific clustering technique. In validating the above subtypes, Morris et al. (1981) found that 11% of the sample was misclassified when alternate hierarchical clustering methods were employed, 15% when a split-design was used, and 4% when additional subjects were added to the original sample before the data was reclustered. The above cross-validation results are certainly encouraging when compared to the large number of children misclassified using a clinical subtyping methodology.

Although a number of advantages exist for cluster techniques which recommend them, a caveat, however, relates to the subjective nature in deciding the similarity and clustering methods to be used. As noted above, 11% of the sample changed classification as a function of the clustering method employed. One needs to seriously consider validation procedures useful in assessing the extent to which derived cluster solutions are generalizable and thus of clinical merit.

From longitudinal (Satz, Taylor, Friel, & Fletcher, 1978; Spreen & Haaf, 1986) and cross-sectional (Fisk & Rourke, 1976) studies of learning disabilities, it is apparent that age-related changes in skill deficits are evident for learning disabled children. Satz et al. (1978) conducted a follow-up of children from kindergarten to grade six and found that the younger children were more likely to present with reading process deficits such as sensorimotor and cross-model integration than older children who had greater difficulty in conceptual-linguistic skills. Spreen and Haaf (1986) in a longitudinal study, assessed children at a mean age of 10 years and later at age 24 years on a variety of neuropsychological and achievement measures. Subtypes identified as visuo-perceptual, articulo-graphomotor, and linguistic were found early on. However, at follow-up some 14 years later, only the visuo-perceptual and articulo-graphomotor subtypes remained, with the linguistic subtype was no longer evident. Similarly, Fiske and Rourke (1979) found that subtype C which was marked by deficits in fingertip number writing was present for the older age group (13-14 years) but absent for the youngest age group (9-10 years). The above studies suggest the types of learning deficits children experience may well be related to age. Such changes could be expected on the bases of neurophysiological maturation, compensation for the central nervous system due to early cerebral insult, and effects of remediation programs.

Classification of children's learning disabilities has also been attempted on the basis of emotional or behavioral aspects. McKinney (1984) administered the Classroom Behavior Inventory in addition to intelligence and achievement measures to 59 first and second grade learning disabled children. A hierarchical cluster analysis produced four subtypes. Subtype I comprised 33% of the sample and was characterized by average verbal skills and deficits in sequential and spatial tasks. Behaviorally, this group was noted to have deficits in independence and task-orientation. They were viewed by the teachers as more considerate and less hostile than the other two groups. A second subtype (10%) had the most severe academic deficits and were rated the lowest on all behavioral scales. These children were viewed to be less considerate and more hostile than the other groups. Similar to group one, a third group (47%) was found to have mild impairment in achievement, but behaviorally they were differentiated by their extroverted behavior. This third group was similar to the second in the level of hostility and inconsiderateness. A final group (10%) did not show behavioral deficiencies but were characterized by poorer academic performance than group one or three. The above classifications were subsequently replicated by McKinney (1984) using still another rating scale.

In summary, the research on subtyping is still in its infancy. Lack of similar subtypes between studies can be attributed to a variety of methodological factors. Specifically, studies have used 1) a limited range of neuropsychological measures, 2) samples were primarily gleaned from clinics which were not representative of the population, 3) few cross-validation procedures to determine the similarity of results, 4) samples too small to properly consider multivariate techniques, and 5) failed to consider emotional aspects of children's functioning. In view of the monumental task of delineating the etiological factors underlying the multiple syndrome conceptualization of learning disabilities, results of subtyping studies are encouraging.

Emotional Factors of Learning Disabilities

Much of the neuropsychological research in the area of learning disabilities has focused on cognitive aspects of functioning (e.g., Fisk & Rourke, 1979; Lyon & Watson, 1981; Satz & Morris, 1981). Research for the most part has failed to consider socio-emotional and behavioral concomitants of learning disorders. Several researchers, however, have presented data suggesting that learning disabled children in addition to cognitive problems are also at risk for emotional disturbance (Bender, 1985a, 1985b; McKinney & Feagan, 1983). Indeed, several studies have reported that learning disabled children have increased feelings of insecurity and depression (Stevenson & Romney, 1984). In one recent study, 14% of a sample of 103 learning disabled children were found to be clinically depressed on the Children's Depression Inventory (Stevenson & Romney, 1984). Symptoms presented by the depressed children in the sample consisted of a low self-esteem, emotional withdrawal, detachment, and emotionally labile. McConaughy and Ritter (1986) recently assessed social competence and behavioral problems in learning disabled boys between 6-11 years with the Child Behavior Checklist. The results indicated that these children significantly lacked social skills, had fewer social contacts with friends and organizations, and participated less in social activities when compared to a normative sample. Emotional disturbance for learning disabled children is not surprising in view of the fact that these children must cope with an environment where few opportunities exist for success. Such children present a unique challenge to psychologists since it is often untenable to consider skill remediation apart from the child's emotional response to failure (Dean & Rattan, 1986).

Repeated failure at any level of skill development may have emotional implications for a child's future functioning. As an example, the initial stage of learning to read requires different neurological processes (e.g., letter/word recognition) than those required at a later stage (e.g., reading comprehension). Taken together, although the task expectations change as the child advances through the educational system, the emotional reactions of children with learning problems may be very similar.

The high frequency with which children diagnosed as learning disabled also display maladaptive emotional problems has been well documented (Dean, 1981; Stevenson & Romney, 1984). Many of the negative reactions to academic failure may be presented in seemingly unrelated behaviors (e.g., conduct disorder, hyperactivity, withdrawal, somatic complaints, school phobia, etc.) (Paul & Epanchin, 1982; Stevenson & Romney, 1984). Such behaviors may be the result of the development of maladaptive response sets as the learning disabled child attempts to cope with the stress of school failure (Bender, 1985a, 1985b; Dean & Rattan, 1986; McKinney & Feagans, 1983). It is not clear whether a pre-disposition to withdrawal is a precursor to early academic difficulties or if learning deficits are compounded by acquired emotional reactions. The truth may be in a subtle interaction of both. It seems apparent that neither neuropsychological nor emotional difficulties can be approached in isolation when planning a treatment. Meaningful remediation of disorders must address the cognitive-emotional interaction.

There is a paucity of research that has assessed the behavioral sequelae of learning disabled children's attempts to cope with failure. Recently, Dean and Rattan (1986) in-vestigated the ways in which learning disabled and normal learners cope with obvious failure. Groups of normal and disabled readers were presented with extremely difficult words to decode after they had read simple words. Sixty learning disabled children were randomly assigned to either a failure (learning disabled-stressed, LDS) or non-failure (learning disabled-non-stressed, LDN) group. Thirty children without specific or generalized learning problems comprised the normal group. The stimulus materials consisted of 20 mastery words which were characterized as being one grade level below the child with the lowest reading level. The stress words on the other hand were chosen from a list that were one grade level above the highest achieving child from any group. The order of stimulus presentation was such that all three groups initially received 5 mastery words followed by 5 stress words for the LDS and normal groups while the LDN received an additional 5 mastery words. All groups then received 10 mastery words. Following presentation of each word, the subject was asked to read the word and then given appropriate feedback (i.e., "that is correct" or "that is wrong"). When words were read incorrectly, no corrective feedback was provided.

Analysis of data showed that the three groups did not differ significantly ($p > .05$) in the initial words read correctly indicating mastery across groups. As predicted, children in the LDS scored significantly lower ($p < .001$) than normal and LDN children on the post-test. The normal and LDN groups, on the other hand, did not differ significantly in the number of post-words read correctly.

These results suggested that learning disabled children under the stress of failure experience difficulty recovering. Children in the LDS group often responded recklessly and exhibited behaviors inappropriate for the setting. Thus it appears that when confronted with failure, many children with histories of learning deficiencies develop aversive reactions to school related tasks. This behavior pattern could be understood as a phobic reaction to academic tasks. Such aversive reactions may extend beyond the immediate learning task to a creation of negative emotional reaction to subject areas where failure was previously experienced. Therefore, what may appear to be an early cognitive processing difficulty may well lead to a failure-aversion-behavioral maladjustment response set in coping with the stress of failure.

Systematic desensitization is a behavioral approach shown to be successful in modifying phobic responses. Once an individual's hierarchy of fear to stimuli are identified, positive reinforcing stimuli are then paired with events that initially produced the negative reactions (see Wolpe, 1969). This approach has been successful in modifying children's phobic responses to a large number of stimuli (Bandura, 1977; Meichenbaum, 1971). Indeed, such an *in vivo* approach would seem to hold promise with learning disabled children in reducing underlying aversive reactions to academic studies while rewarding academic attempts. It should simultaneously work to remediate academic skills while desensitizing the associated emotional aspects of the learning deficit.

Integrating Emotional and Neuropsychological Factors

Neuropsychological assessment has been shown to be of some utility in treatment planning with learning disabled children. A number of authors have reported success in programs which assess the child's neuropsychological strengths and focus upon them in treatment (Gaddes, 1975; Golden, 1978; Hartlage, 1975; Hynd & Obrzut, 1981; Rourke, 1976; Reynolds, 1981). Indeed, a number of remedial reading programs using a individualized neuropsychological strength approach have been shown to produce significant achievement gains over more traditional approaches (Hartlage, 1975; Hartlage & Lucas, 1973). These results stand in contrast to deficit oriented intervention programs based upon psycholinguistic training (Kirk & Kirk, 1971), sensory-integration (Ayres, 1972), and perceptual training (Frostig, 1975) which have generally not proven effective in remediating school related achievement. In addition to methodological problems (Hartlage, 1975), these programs have failed to consider the emotional concomitants interacting with childrens learning. Interestingly, relatively few investigators have addressed emotional factors in planning intervention programs (Bandura, 1977; Kazdin, 1974).

As mentioned above, it has become apparent that children with histories of classroom failure may retain aversive reactions to specific academic tasks even after obvious success (Lange, 1977). With this as a backdrop, it would seem that children with disorders in learning may benefit from an approach which focuses on neuropsychological strengths while attempting to modify negative emotional responses. The remainder of this chapter reports an experimental treatment program built on these underpinings with the treatment goals of: 1) academic remediation, 2) desensitization of negative emotional reactions, and 3) development of appropriate classroom behaviors were approached simultaneously. Sessions that focused on academic skills were structured in a manner so as to simultaneously desensitize the child's emotional reactions and reinforce appropriate coping behaviors.

Each learning disabled child in this project was administered a complete neuropsychological battery as shown in Appendix A. This examination was used to define the child's neuropsychological strengths to be used in therapy and as an aid in defining a hierarchy of remedial tasks for each child along an approach-avoidance continuum. Children in the program choose rewards from an individually prescribed personal learning hierarchy according to the level of both task difficulty and aversion to the task (see Appendix B). Near the top of the task-based hierarchy was placed salient academic skills which were basic to remediation. Concomitant with these tasks was thought to be the avoidance behavior generated as a result of past failure. The levels of a child's learning hierarchy ranged from the most obvious academically related task to simply talking with the clinic educator. As noted from the sample hierarchy for William C (Appendix B), the child can be involved anywhere along the approach-avoidance continuum and is differentially reinforced according to the aversiveness of the task. It should also be noted that children were reinforced both for success at a given level and for attempting higher levels on the hierarchy. The construction of each child's learning hierarchy was structured using a task analytical approach. In effect, this approach is related to a systems analysis philosophy, in which selected aspects of an input-through-output model are established for each child. Another feature of the program was structuring of the 45 minute session from nine five-minute periods. Thus, for each five minute interval the child would chose a given level of the hierarchy. In this way, the patient perceived control over each remedial session.

In summary, this program was thought to retain as many of the desirable qualities of the neuropsychological examination while considering emotional aspects and how the individual child best learned new material. Indeed, the neuropsychological evaluation provided an understanding of how the child best processes information and allowed focus on individual strengths. The pretreatment neuropsychological assessment also allowed the therapist to follow the program.

After some eight months of treatment, children were found to have made significant gains over their initial achievement scores when compared to two control groups. Children in the experimental group significantly improved in specific academic skills, rated classroom behavior, and the ability to respond consistently even after obvious failure. These results were interpreted as support for this program in remediating academic deficits while improving the child's ability to cope with the stress of their academic disability. Interestingly, gains in achievement and emotional functioning were as clear as the lack of differences between groups in the post measure in neuropsychological functioning. Other than marginal improvements in auditory discrimination, the therapy did little to improve actual neuropsychological deficits. Thus, this program was seen as having potential of allowing children to compensate for neuropsychological deficits in an environment which often provides little positive feedback.

Conclusions

The neuropsychology of children's learning disorders remains obscure. The early naive comparison of adult neurological sequelae to children exhibiting functional learning disorders may well be responsible for the present confusion. Indeed, the direct application of brain-behavior relationships established with adults to children is tenable. The translative problems relate to the continuing autonomical and functional changes in the brain which occur throughout elementary-school years. These developmental aspects become even more complex when one considers the exquisite influence of environment on an immature organism. Although most serious reviews of the literature on children's learning disorders have rejected early overzealous attempts to portray all children's learning problems in terms of neurological morbidity, confusion remains in defining the complex interaction of neurology, environment, and emotions. Our present primitive understanding of such disorders is attributed, in part, to diagnostic schemes which continue to portray learning disorders as a single nosological entity. Although some forms of children's learning problems clearly have a neurological etiology, these are often obscured in quixotic attempts to offer a single syndrome.

In the wake of such confusion, it is hardly surprising to find reactionary moves to embrace atomistic approaches to children's behavior. However, recent attempts to isolate neuropsychological constellations indicative of specific subtypes are encouraging (e.g.,

Dean, 1983; Fisk & Rourke, 1979).   Research which considers developmental and emotional aspects in conjunction with traditional measures of neuropsychological function hold considerable promise in defining individual syndromes. Indeed, it is apparent that chil-dren retain an emotional reaction to school-failure which may be as problematic as the original neuropsychological impairment. So too, future attempts at subtyping must address changes in the locus of the dysfunction that is consistent with the child's neurological development.

Of interest from a treatment perspective, data exist favoring a neuropsychological perspective which goes beyond the diagnoses of impairment to the structuring of educational programs that maximize the patient's functional strengths. Recent interventions which focus on the combination of neuropsychological strengths and the child's emotional response to failure have been shown to significantly improve academic achievement. Interestingly, such procedures seem to have little effect on the patient's neuropsychological functioning, but rather, they may provide the child with methods of compensating for specific processing disorders. These data also stress the importance of considering emotional factors in any treatment approach to children's learning disorders.

References

Algozzine, B., Forgnone, C., Mercer, C. D., & Trifiletti, J. J. (1979). Toward defining discrepancies for specific learning disabilities. *Learning Disabilities Quarterly, 2*, 25-31.

Ayres, A. J. (1972). *Sensory integration and learning disorders.* Los Angeles: Western Psychological Services.

Badian, N. A. (1984). Reading disability in an epidemiological context: Incidence and environmental correlates. *Journal of Learning Disabilities, 17*, 129-136.

Bandura, A. (1969). *Principles of behavior modification.* New York: Holt, Rinehart & Winston.

Bandura, A. (1977). Self-efficacy: Toward a unifying theory of behavior change. *Psychological Review, 84*, 191-215.

Bateman, B. (1965). An educator's view of a diagnostic approach to learning disorders. In J. Hellmath (Ed.), *Learning disorders* (Vol. 1). Seattle: Special Child Publications.

Bender, W. N. (1985 a). Differential diagnosis based on task-related behavior of learning disabled and low-achieving adolescents. *Learning Disability Quarterly, 8*, 261-266.

Bender, W. N. (1985 b). Differences between learning disabled and non-learning disabled children in temperament and behavior. *Learning Disability Quarterly, 8*, 11-18.

Benton, A. L. (1964). Developmental aphasia and brain damage. *Cortex, 1*, 40-52.

Chi, J. G., Dooling, E. C., & Gilles, I. H. (1977). Gyral development of the human brain. *Annals of Neurology, 1*, 86-93.

Clements, S. D. (1966). *Minimal brain dysfunction in children.* NINDB Monograph No. 3, U.S. Department of Health, Education and Welfare, Washington, D.C.

Cravioto, J., DeLicordie, E. R., & Birch, H. G. (1966). Nutrition, growth and neurointegrative development: An experimental and ecologic study. *Pediatrics, 38*, 319-372.

Critchley, M. (1964). *Developmental dyslexia.* Springfield, IL: C. C. thomas.

D'Amato, R. C., Dean, R. S., & Rattan, G. (1986). A study of psychological learning problem referrals by grade level and gender. Manuscript submitted for publication.

D'Amato, K. R. C., Gray, J. W., & Dean, R. S. (1986). *A comparison between intelligence and neuropsychological functioning.* Manuscript submitted for publication.

Dean, R. S. (1978). The use of the WISC-R in distinguishing learning disabled and emotionally disturbed children. *Journal of Consulting and Clinical Psychology, 46*, 381-382.

Dean, R. S. (1982). Neuropsychological assessment. In T. R. Karatochwill (Ed.), ʹ(Vol. 2). HIllside, NJ: Lawrence Erlbaum.

Dean, R. S., & Rattan, A. I. (1986). Measuring the effects of failure with learning disabled children. Manuscript submitted for publication.

Denckla, M. B. (1972). Clinical syndromes in learning disabilities: The case for "splitting" vs. "lumping". *Journal of Learning Disabilities, 5*, 401-406.

Di Pasquale, G. W., Maule, A. D., & Flewelling, R. W. (1980). The birthdate effect. *Journal of Learning Disabilities, 13,* 234-238.

Doehring, D. G., & Hoshko, I. M. (1977). Classification of reading problems by the Q-technique of factor analysis. *Cortex, 13,* 281-294.

Donofrio, A. F. (1977). Grade repetition: Therapy of choice. *Journal of Learning Disabilities, 10,* 349-351.

Drake, W. E. (1969). Clinical and pathological findings in a child with a developmental learning disability. *Journal of Learning Disability, 1,* 9-25.

Eisenberg, L. (1978). Definitions of dyslexia: Their consequences for research and policy. In A. L. Benton & D. Pearl (Eds.). *Dyslexia: An appraisal of current knowledge.* New York: Oxford University Press.

Epps, S., Ysseldyke, J. E., & Algozzine, B. (1985). An emphasis of the conceptual framework underlying definitions of learning disabilities. *Journal of School Psychology, 23,* 133-144.

Fisk, J. L, & Rourke, B. P. (1979). Identification of subtypes of learning disabled children at three age levels: A neuropsychological, multivariate approach. *Journal of Clinical Neuropsychology, 1,* 289-310.

Fletcher, J. M., & Satz, P. (1979). Unitary deficit hypotheses of reading disabilities: Has Vellutino led us astray. *Journal of Learning Disabilities, 12,* 22-26.

Frostig, M. (1975). The role of perception in the integration of psychological functions in W. H. Cruickshank & D. P. Hallahan (Eds.), *Perceptual and learning disabilities in children,* (Vol. 1). Syracuse: Syracuse University Press.

Gaddes, W. H. (1976). Prevalence estimates and the needs for the definition of learning disabilities. In R. M. Knights & D. J. Bakker (Eds.). *The neuropsychology of learning disorders.* Baltimore: University Park Press.

Gaddes, W. H. (1980). *Learning disabilities and brain function: A neuropsychological approach.* New York: Springer-Verlag.

Gaddes, W. H. (1985). *Learning disabilities and brain function: A neuropsychological approach* (rev. ed.). New York: Springer-Verlag.

Galaburda, A. M. (1986). Developmental dyslexia: A review of biological interaction. *Annals of Dyslexia, 35,* 21-33.

Galaburda, A. M., & Kemper, T. L. (1979). Cytoarchitectonic abnormalities in developmental dyslexia: Case studies. *Annals of Neurology, 6,* 94-100.

Gearheart, B. R. (1980). *Special education for the 80's.* St. Louis: C. V. Mosby.

Geschwind, N., & Behan, P. (1982). Left handedness: Association with immune disease, migraines, and developmental learning disorders. *Proceedings of the National Academy of Sciences, USA 79,* 5097-5100.

Geschwind, N., & Behan, P. (1984). Laterality, hormones, and immunity. In N. Geschwind & A. M. Galaburda (Eds.) *Cerebral dominance: The biological foundation.* Cambridge, MA: Harvard University Press.

Golden, C. J. (1978). *Diagnosis and rehabilitation in clinical neuropsychology.* Springfield, IL: C. C. Thomas.

Gubbay, S. S., Ellis, E., Walton, J. N., & Court, S. D. (1965). Clumsy children, a study of apraxic and agnostic deficits in 21 children. *Brain, 88,* 295-312.

Hallahan, D. P., & Cruickshank, W. M. (1973). *Psycho-educational foundations of learning disabilities.* Englewood Cliffs: Prentice-Hall.

Hartlage, L. C. (1975). Neuropsychological approaches to predicting outcomes of remedial education strategies for learning disabled children. *Pediatric Psychology, 3,* 23-28.

Hartlage, L. C. & Lucas, D. G. (1973). Group screening for reading disability in first grade children. *Journal of Learning Disabilities, 6,* 48-52.

Hier, D. B., LeMay, M., & Rosenberger, P. B. (1978). Developmental dyslexia. *Archives of Neurology, 35,* 90-92.

Hynd, G. W., & Obrzut, J. E. (1981). School neuropsychology. *Journal of School Psychology, 19,* 45-50.

Jackson, J. H. (1874). On the duality of the brain. Medical Press, 1-19. Reprinted in J. Taylor (Ed.), *Selected writings of John Hughlings Jackson,* (Vol. 2). Hodder 7 Stoughton: London. 1932.

Kaufman, A. S. (1979). *Intelligent testing with the WISC-R.* New York: John Wiley & Sons.

Kazdin, A. E. (1974). Covert modeling, model similarity, and reduction of avoidance behavior. *Behavior Therapy, 5,* 325-340.

Kimura, D. (1967). Functional asymmetry of the brain in dichotic listening. *Cortex, 3,* 163-178.

Kirk, S. A., & Becker, W. (Eds.) (1963). *Conference on children with minimal brain impairment.* Urbana: University of Illinois.

Knights, R. M., & Bakker, D. J. (1976). *The neuropsychology of learning disorders: Theoretical approaches .* Baltimore, MA: University Park Press.

Landsell, H. (1980). Theories of brain mechanisms in minimal brain dysfunctions. In H. E. Rie & E. D. Rie (Eds.), *Handbook of minimal brain dysfunction: A critical review*. New York: Wiley & Sons.

Lyon, R. & Watson, B. (1981). Empirically derived subgroups of learning disabled readers: Diagnostic characteristics. *Journal of Learning Disabilities, 14,* 256-261.

Mattis, S. (1978). Dsylexia syndromes: A working hypothesis that works. In A. L. Benton & D. Pearl (Eds.). *Dyslexia: An appraisal of current knowledge*. New York: Oxford University Press.

Mattis, S., French, J., & Rapin, I. (1975). Dyslexia in children and young adults: Three independent neuropsychological syndromes. *Developmental Medicine and Child Neurology, 17,* 150-163.

McConaughy, S. H., & Ritter, D. R. (1986). Social competence and behavioral problems of learning disabled boys aged 6-11. *Journal of Learning Disabilities, 19,* 39-45.

McKinney, J. D. (1984). The search for subtypes of learning disability. *Journal of Learning Disabilities, 17,* 43-50.

McKinney, J. D. & Feagans, L. (1983). Adaptive classroom behavior of learning disabled students. *Journal of Learning Disabilities, 16,* 360-367.

Meichenbaum, D. H. (1971). Examination of model characteristics in reducing avoidance behaviors.. *Journal of Personality and Social Psychology, 17,* 298-307.

Morris, R., Blashfield, R., & Satz, P. (1981). Neuropsychology and cluster analysis: Potential and problems. *Journal of Clinical Neuropsychology, 3,* 79-99.

Mykleburt, H. R., & Boshes, B. (1969). *Final report, minimal brain damage in children*. Department of Health, Education, and Welfare. Washington, D.C.

Nunnally, J. (1978). *Psychometric theory*. (2nd ed.). New York: McGraw-Hill.

Obrzut, J. E., & Hynd, G. W. (1983). Implications of neuropsychology for learning disabilities. *Journal of Learning Disabilities, 16* 532-533.

Orton, S. T. (1937). *Reading, writing, and speech problems in children*. New York: W. W. Norton.

Paul, J. L., & Epanchin, B. C. (1982). *Emotional disturbance in children*. Columbus, OH: Bell & Howell.

Petrauska, R., & Rourke, B. (1979). Identification of subgroups of retarded readers: A neuropsychological multivariate approach. *Journal of Clinical Neuropsychology, 1* 17-37.

Pirozzolo, F. J., & Harrell, W. (1985). The neuropsychology of learning disabilities. In L. C. Hartlage & C. F. Telzrow (Eds.), *The neuropsychology of individual differences*. New York: Plenum.

Rattan, A. I., Rattan, G., Gray, J. W., & Dean, R. S. (1986). *Construct specificity of WISC-R subtests as predicted by the Halstead-Reitan Neuropsychological Test Battery*. Paper presented at the meeting of the National Academy of Neuropsychologists, Las Vegas, NV.

Reynolds, C. R. (1981). Neuropsychological assessment and the habilitation of learning: Considerations in the search for the aptitude and treatment interaction. *School Psychology Review, 10,* 343-349.

Rosenberger, P. B. & Hier, D. B. (1980). Cerebral asymmetry and verbal intellectual deficits. *Annals of Neurology, 8,* 300-304.

Rourke, B. P. (1976). Issues in the neuropsychological assessment of children with learning disabilities. *Canadian Psychological Review, 17,* 89-102.

Rutter, M. J., Tizard, & Whitmore, K. (1970). *Education, health and behavior*. London: Longmans.

Satz, P., & Morris, R. (1981). Learning disability subtypes: A review. In F. J. Pirozzolo M. C. Wittrock. (Eds.) *Neuropsychological and cognitive processes in reading*. New York: Academic Press.

Satz, P., Taylor, G., Friel, J., & Fletcher, J. (1978). Some developmental and predictive precursors of reading disabilities: A six-year follow-up. In A. L. Benton & D. Pearl (Eds.), *Dyslexia: An appraisal of current knowledge*. New York: Oxford University Press.

Silverman, L. J., & Metz, A. S. (1973). Number of pupils with specific learning disabilities in local public schools in the United States: Spring 1970. *Annals of the New York Academy of Sciences, 205,* 146-157.

Spreen, O., & Haaf, R. (1986). Empirically derived learning disability subtypes: A replication attempt and longitudinal patterns over 15 years. *Journal of Learning Disabilities, 19,* 170-180.

Speery, R. W. (1974). Lateral specialization in the surgically separated hemispheres. In F. O. Schmitt & F. G. Wordens (Eds.), *The neurosciences: Third study program*. New York: Wiley & Sons.

Stevenson, D. T., & Romney, D. M. (1984). Depression in learning disabled children. *Journal of Learning Disabilities, 17,* 579-582.

Steward, M. A., Pitts, F. N., Craig, A. G., & Dierof, N. (1966). The hyperactive child syndrome. *American Journal of Orthopsychiatry, 36,* 861-867.1

Stock, M. B., & Smythe, P. M. (1968). Undernutrition during infancy, subsequent brain growth and intellectual development. In N. S. Scrimshaw & J. E. Gordon (Eds.) *Malnutrition, learning and behavior*. Cambridge, MA: MIT Press.

Strauss, A. A. (1944). Ways of thinking in brain-crippled deficient children. *American Journal of Psychiatry, 100,* 639-647.

Strauss, A. A., & Kephart, N. C. (1955). *Psychopathology and education of the brain-injured child.* (Vol. 2). New York: Grune & Stratton.

Strauss, A. A., & Lehtinen, L. E. (1947). *Psychopathology and education of the brain-injured child.* New York: Grune & Stratton.

Strother, C. R. (1972). Minimal cerebral dysfunction: An historical overview. *Annals of the New York Academy of Science, 205,* 6-17.

Vellutino, F. R., Smith, H., Steger, J. A., & Kaman, M. (1975). Age differences and the perceptual deficit hypothesis. *Child Development, 46,* 493-497.

Vellutino, F. R., Steger, B. M., Moyer, S. C., Harding, C. J., Niles, J. A. (1977). Has the perceptual deficit hypothesis led us astray? *Journal of Learning Disabilities, 10,* 375-385.

Wolpe, J. (1969). *The practice of behavior therapy.* New York: Pergamon.

Ysseldyke, J. E., & Algozzine, B. (1979). Perspective on assessment of learning disabled students. *Learning Disability Quarterly, 2,* 3-13.

Yule, W., & Rutter, M. (1976). Epidemiology and social implications of specific reading retardation. In R. M. Knights & D. J. Bakker (Eds.). *The neuropsychology of learning disorders.* Baltimore: University Park Press.

Appendix A

Neuropsychological/Psychological Test Battery

Ability	Instrument
General Ability (Multiple Abilities)	Wechsler Intelligence Scale for Children--Revised
Basic Skills in Mathematics/ Expressive Language	Wide Range Achievement Test (Mathematics & Spelling)
Basic Skills in Reading	Peabody Individual Achievement Test (Reading Recognition & Comprehension)
Motor Development	Halstead--Reitan Finger Oscillation and Grip Strength
Sensory Perception-- Tactile, Auditory, & Visual	Reitan Sensory--Perceptual Examination
Cerebral Lateralization	Lateral Preference Schedule
Speech/Language	Aphasia Screening Test
Non-verbal Learning/ Psychomotor Coordination	Tactual Performance Test
Gross Coordination	Balance Hopping
Fine Coordination	Toe Tapping Finger Sequencing Hand Patting
Praxis	First-Edge-Palm Alternating Hand Postures Finger Localization
Emotional School Functioning	Achenback Teacher's Questionnaire
Home/School Functioning	Devereux Behavior Rating Scales
Personality	IPAT--Children's Personality Questionnaire

Appendix B

Hierarchy of Tasks

Name: William C., Age: 8 years 3 months

Activity	Tokens	Achievement Necessary
1. Phonetic learning and practice	15	90% success
2. Oral reading	10	90% success
3. Listen to cassette story for comprehension	6	90% success
4. Create story given initial sentence	3	4 grammatical correct sentences
5. Talk with therapist about reading problems	2	
6. Talk with therapist about anything	1	
7. Leave the session	0	

Structure: Forty-five minute session divided into nine five-minute intervals. Patient chooses activity for each interval.

Tokens
  45 tokens = 10 cents or a coke
  30 tokens = 5 cents or five pieces of candy
  15 tokens = one piece of candy
200 tokens = trip to auto show
300 tokens = surprise present

12

The "So What?" Question: Intervention with Learning Disabled Children

Cathy F. Telzrow

Converging data indicate special education has little impact on the amelioration of learning disabilities. In fact, those factors most closely associated with positive outcomes for persons identified as having learning disabilities as children are not related to educational interventions at all. Schonhaut and Satz (1983), for example, reviewed 18 studies examining outcome for LD populations, and concluded that socioeconomic status (SES) was one of the best predictors of success. These data suggested LD children from high SES families were more likely to achieve at higher scholastic levels; to graduate from post-secondary programs; and to find and maintain employment. Similar findings were reported by Compton (1984), who compared the achievement, social adjustment, and job experience of 114 randomly selected LD students with their non-LD siblings 10 years post diagnosis. Family support and socioeconomic status, as well as IQ and psychosocial functioning, were reported to be predictive of academic, social, and job success.

In addition to these studies, which suggest factors that cannot be attributed to direct educational intervention (e.g., IQ and family SES) are most closely associated with success for LD youngsters, are others which have shown characteristics associated with learning disabilities in children persist into adulthood. Buchanan and Wolf (1986) reported 33 LD adults studied continued to demonstrate low motivation, distractibility, and poor organization. Similar observations were conveyed by Denckla (1985), who reported children with attention deficit disorder have continuing difficulties as adults, including problems forming and maintaining social relationships and having job and home stability. In a study of dyslexic adults who received special education as children, neuropsychological patterns characteristic of LD youngsters were identified, including higher Performance than Verbal IQ's, relatively superior performance on tasks requiring spatial as opposed to sequential processing, and achievement patterns that favored the arithmetic>reading>spelling profile frequently observed in dyslexics (Frauenheim & Heckerl, 1983). Similar findings were reported by McCue, Shelly, Goldstein, & Katz-Garris (1984), who described the neuropsychological characteristics of 25 young adults with learning disabilities. These authors also found a Performance greater than Verbal Wechsler IQ pattern, as well as deficits in written language skills, although oral language skills were considered to be adequate. Additional studies provide further support for the similarity of neuropsychological processing patterns in LD children and adults (Cordoni, O'Donnell, Ramaniah, Kurtz, & Rosenshein, 1981; McCue, Shelly, & Goldstein, 1986).

Data such as these suggest learning disabilities represent lifelong afflictions that to date, have been influenced little, if at all, by sometimes aggressive special education interventions. The following section will propose some possible reasons for the failure of special education to ameliorate learning disabilities in identified individuals.

Possible Reasons Why the LD-non-LD Gap Doesn't Narrow

Insufficient Time on Task

One hypothesis for the failure of special education to close the gap between regular and LD pupils is that insufficient time is devoted to the instructional process. In a study describing the attendance of handicapped pupils in 14 special education resource rooms, Sullivan and McDaniel (1983) reported 22% of resource room contacts were missed. This is the equivalent of a youngster missing one day per week of special education instruction. The authors reported half these contacts were missed because of student absence, one-fourth because of competing activities, such as field trips and school assemblies, and another quarter due to teacher absences or scheduling conflicts. This study suggests that even in instances where LD children have been identified and scheduled into appropriate special education programs, more than a fifth of the time these interventions are not delivered because of student or teacher absences or systemic problems, such as scheduling conflicts or failure to provide substitutes for absent special education teachers.

A second line of research with regard to the insufficient time on task hypothesis is related to evidence that mildly handicapped children may require more time to learn than the average child. According to this theory, achievement is defined as the ratio between time needed to learn and the time actually spent in learning (Carroll, 1984; Kavale & Forness, 1986). Mildly handicapped children may require more than the average amount of time needed to learn (Gettinger, 1984). When they are not afforded this extra time, but instead are moved along in the educational system with their average achieving peers, the gap between their level of achievement and that of their peers increases (Anderson, 1984; Gerber, 1986; Kavale & Forness, 1986).

The work of Shinn (1986) would seem to lend some credence to this hypothesis. In an analysis of the achievement of mildly handicapped children, the vast majority of whom were learning disabled, Shinn (1986) found significant amounts of learning indeed occurred during the time interval studied. However, the rate of learning was slower than the norm, and hence not sufficient to narrow the gap between these youngsters and their non-handicapped peers. Indeed, the author reported, "In most cases, *the differences in reading performance grew significantly larger, not smaller*" (Shinn, 1986, p. 55, author's emphasis).

Special Education Isn't Special

Despite the fact that educators assert the need for "special" education for a variety of handicapped children, increasing evidence suggests the instruction that occurs in special education classrooms is not particularly special at all (Shinn, 1986). Swanson (1984) examined the types of instruction delivered in special and regular classrooms in eight different schools. While he found there were some significant differences between the two types of instruction (e.g., LD teachers were more likely to verbalize steps in sequential processes and to ask other than yes/no questions), *neither* the LD nor the regular teachers engaged in strategy-oriented or metacognitive types of instruction recommended by specialists in learning, particularly for LD students (e.g., Graham & Freeman, 1985; Lewis, 1983;

Sheinker, Sheinker, & Stevens, 1984). Other data suggesting special education isn't special were reported by Neely and Lindsley (1978), in an elaborate study of teaching strategies and student achievement for a special education cooperative. The authors concluded, "the same teaching strategies were used in special education as in regular education" (p.436).

Real Learning Disabilities Cannot be Ameliorated

A third hypothesis which may explain the failure of special education to narrow the LD-non-LD gap is that this goal is unrealistic, since learning disabilities are pervasive, lifelong disorders. The Association for Children with Learning Disabilities (ACLD) adopted a description of learning disabilities in 1984, and provided a rationale for this definition in 1986 ("ACLD Description," 1986). In this description, it is asserted that "throughout life, the condition can affect self esteem, education, vocation, socialization, and/or daily living activities" (p.15). Similar sentiments are expressed by others. Zigmond (1979), for example, reflected, "remediation of dyslexia may be a contradiction in terms" (p. 445). Frauenheim and Heckerl (1983) noted "within the field of learning disability, there seems to be only limited awareness or acceptance that some learning disabled individuals may not achieve functional literacy skills" (p. 345). Certainly the work cited earlier, in which a number of different authors described persisting neuropsychological difficulties in adults who had learning disabilities as children, seems to support the conclusion that learning disabilities are lifelong afflictions.

In his presidential address to the Division of Neuropsychology of the American Psychological Association, Boll (1984) emphasized the importance of the dynamic interaction of neuropsychological and environmental variables. This approach to the interpretation of assessment data and the development of rehabilitation strategies would appear to be especially relevant for children (e.g., Bolter & Long, 1985), particularly in cases of great subtlety and complexity, such as specific learning disabilities. In this section, three hypotheses have been proposed to explain the failure of special education to narrow the gap between LD and non-LD students. It seems reasonable to assume that all these hypotheses are operative to some degree, and in fact these variables no doubt interact with one another in a complex manner. The next section will describe the major systemic deterrents to the amelioration of learning disabilities in special education programs within the public schools, followed by a section outlining proposed changes to mitigate the negative effects of these systemic factors on LD remediation.

Major Systemic Deterrents to Successful Intervention for Learning Disabilities in Public Schools

The System: Schedules, Field Trips, Assemblies, Carnegie Units

Public school systems are inherently systematic. They are characterized by a structured set of requirements that in many cases detracts from the optimal delivery of special education. A few examples are listed in the title of this section. Class schedules and Carnegie units (the required numbers and types of courses necessary for high school graduation) often hamstring creativity in delivering special education for children with unique learning needs. Field trips, assemblies, and a variety of personally valuable, but non-academic activities (e.g., athletic practice, band and orchestra rehearsals, photo sessions for yearbooks) too often occupy a major part of the school day, resulting in substantially reduced time for academic learning. Available data suggest that somewhat less than two-thirds of the elementary school day is devoted to instructional activity, with the remaining time spent in recess, lunch, and teacher-controlled, non-instructional time (Burns, 1984). For LD children, this reduced time on task is especially detrimental, as these youngsters quite likely require more than the average amount of time to learn (Kavale & Forness, 1986). And yet despite their need for more time to learn, evidence suggests LD children may be exposed to less instructional time: one study reported as few as 27 minutes per day are devoted to reading activities (Zigmond, Vallecorsa & Leinhardt, 1980).

Overemphasis on Independent Work

Many special education classrooms incorporate a large amount of independent drill and rehearsal. LD children are scheduled for periods of time at the Language Master, in Frostig materials, at listening centers, and on workbook papers (e.g., Strother, 1985). One rationale offered for this practice is that it permits teachers to interact with each pupil individually while others are occupied in learning activities. The fallacy in this argument relates to evidence that direct instruction, characterized by teacher-led lessons in small groups rather than one-to-one contexts, is associated with greater gains for mildly handicapped students (e.g., Gersten, 1985). It seems many special education teachers have interpreted the P.L. 94-142 mandate requiring each student to have an Individual Education Program (IEP) to mean one-to-one instruction. However, as several experts have noted (e.g., Polloway, Cronin, & Patton, 1986; Wang, 1980, 1984), individual instruction may just as aptly pertain to individual planning and appraisal of pupil progress, with actual teaching delivered in groups of children. Furthermore, greater increases in achievement have been demonstrated for students who engage in teacher-directed, small-group instruction than in one-to-one teaching, accompanied by independent drill (e.g., Polloway, Cronin, & Patton, 1986). In short, LD pupils have unique difficulty benefitting from independent work, and emphasis on this as a teaching strategy may be counterproductive.

Persistence in Employing Unsuccessful Interventions

Some types of interventions are not effective, or at best minimally effective, when employed with certain types of LD students. However, there is a tendency among special education teachers to persist in the use of these techniques in the belief they ultimately will pay off. Often teachers explain their steadfast persistence in the use of these nonproductive techniques by asserting students "have to learn it sometime". Such an explanation is frankly puzzling: it is as though teachers believe students are being intentionally contrary in not learning to write, spell, or compute. The case of a youngster with pure dysgraphia illustrates this attitude. Handwriting and spelling represented extraordinary chores for this student. His mother had introduced the use of a typewriter for him at home, and found his written work improved. When she inquired about the feasibility of his using the classroom's computer to learn word-processing, the teacher replied he wouldn't always have access to a computer, and he'd have to learn to write sooner or later. When one extends her analogy to children who cannot walk, the absurdity becomes clear.

Delay in Introducing Compensatory Techniques

The above problem--that of persisting in the use of unsuccessful interventions--is directly related to the next one, delay in introducing compensatory techniques. Increasingly, experts in learning disabilities recognize the importance of altering approaches for students so they can acquire information and convey what they know without reading and writing

(Kutsick, 1982; Minskoff, 1982; Zigmond, 1979). Children whose teachers introduce such enabling devices as calculators, computers, word-processors, and tape-recorders are able to make progress in overall objective of education--learning. Children whose reading deficit is so extreme that acquiring information via independent reading is unlikely can learn content material via taped texts. Youngsters like the one described above whose specific dysgraphia prevents them from engaging in the mechanical task of writing may learn principles of composition through the use of an assistive device such as a word-processor. The belief that the introduction of such compensatory techniques will provide a "crutch" for students, thus interfering with their drill in the difficult area, does not appear to be justified. It does appear true, however, that delaying the use of devices and techniques that can enable students to progress in the overall objective of learning can have detrimental effects on their achievement.

Fragmentation of Instruction

Increased specialization in educational delivery has both advantages and disadvantages, but for handicapped pupils, the latter are paramount. Some LD students interact with as many as 10 different educators per week, each emphasizing a discrete skill or concept which bears little apparent relationship to those taught by the other nine. Seeing relationships between these discrete areas of learning and maintaining sight of the "big picture" are difficult tasks for all children to master. Such difficulties are magnified for LD students, who have been reported to have unique difficulty in problem solving and making generalizations (e.g., Lewis, 1983). Departmentalization, often occurring as early as the primary grades, may interfere with optimal educational delivery for learning disabled children.

These deterrents to employing successful interventions for LD children are largely faults of the educational system. Despite the best of intentions on the part of individual teachers, who often display astute sensitivity to the appropriate educational needs of students, the "system" prevails. While "standards" are maintained, this ostensible compliance is a farce: often even severely learning disabled students are enrolled in difficult required courses, while receiving hours of tutoring to coach them through examinations over concepts and material they do not comprehend. Although "standards" are not compromised, the pupil in question learns nothing. For LD populations, significant changes in the delivery of special education is imperative.

General Characteristics of Model LD Programs

Many of the problems in delivering appropriate interventions to LD children noted above require systemic approaches to change. The following general characteristics of model LD programs appear central to the goal of narrowing the LD-non-LD gap. These general program characteristics are viewed as important for all LD children, regardless of the expression of their disabilities.

Increased Engaged Time on Task

As noted above, much data suggest the time needed to learn for LD students is longer than that of non-handicapped pupils. Model intervention programs for these pupils need to incorporate increased time for learning, with necessary repetition until mastery is obtained (Gersten, 1985; Lewis, 1983; Tarver, 1986). Too often, systemic problems alluded to above make this impossible. On the average, students miss seven hours of core classroom instruction per week because of special education pull-out programs (Kimbrough & Hill, 1983), then miss more than 20% of resource room contacts because of student and teacher absences and interfering activities (Sullivan & McDaniel, 1983). Even when children are in class, the amount of time in direct, teacher-controlled instruction is alarmingly small (Burns, 1984; Leinhardt, Zigmond, & Cooley, 1981; Zigmond, Vallecorsa, & Leinhardt, 1980). In a recent visit to the well-organized classroom of a veteran teacher, this author was astounded (and the teacher clearly distressed) to find she spent 25 minutes of class time collecting money from students for lunch, for the sale of PTA calendars, for United Way, and for a class picnic. Such disruptions are unfair to all children; yet handicapped children, with their need for greater amounts of time to learn, are especially vulnerable to the negative effects of such diversions from instructional activities.

Another concern is that even time devoted to teacher-controlled instruction may be less than it appears because students may not be engaged in the learning process (e.g., Anderson, 1984; Stallings, 1980). This may be especially true for LD students, who may "require more instructional effort or more powerful instructional techniques, or both" (Gerber, 1986, p.2). Data such as these suggest major changes in the ways in which public schools conceive and deliver special education to handicapped pupils may be necessary. Examples are the consideration of such controversial ideas as self-contained classrooms (perhaps in regular education settings with special education assistants) and extended school days or school years.

High Levels of Structure and Teacher-Directed Instruction

Learning disabled children often have difficulty organizing themselves. In addition, independent learning activities have not been shown to be as effective for such children as teacher-directed instruction. Optimal educational interventions for LD children adapt many of the strategies used by successful cognitive retraining programs. Features of such programs include a detailed task analysis of stated objectives, with instruction focused on teaching behavioral components of the overall goal; systemic cuing and shaping; the application of appropriate reinforcements; instruction to mastery levels; and continuous monitoring of pupil progress (Gersten, 1986; Lewis, 1983; Polloway, Epstein, Polloway, Patton, & Ball, 1986; Tarver, 1986). Other evidence suggests training LD students to use metacognitive techniques to monitor their attention and behavior (Brown & Alford, 1984); to enhance reading comprehension (Chan & Cole, 1986); and to persist in task completion (Carlton, Hummer, & Rainey, 1984) is an effective strategy for moving toward the goal of self-management, shown to be related to successful achievement (Wang, 1984).

Immersed Curricula

LD children do not perceive relationships and make generalizations easily (Gelzheiser, Solar, Shepherd, & Wozniak, 1983; Sheinker et al., 1984). As a result, an immersed curriculum which can provide these kinds of linkages for pupils is necessary in model LD programs. In such an approach, concepts and ideas acquired in reading would be employed in other content areas, such as science and social studies. Spelling and vocabulary lessons would be derived from content area texts, and children would be helped to conceptualize history by studying literary and scientific achievements of a particular historical period. Generalization training in a variety of areas of academic and social learning would be incorporated automatically. Educational delivery systems that utlize self-contained classrooms as opposed to a departmentalized model may be better suited to implementing these strategies.

Ongoing Pupil Appraisal with Appropriate Adjustments in Instruction

While annual reviews are a routine part of special education programs, the manner in which the student's program is altered as a result of the annual review is less well defined. Too often, when a pupil does not attain the longterm objectives on his or her IEP, these goals are simply listed again for the following year, without modification of either the goals or the strategies used to attain them. Model LD programs must incorporate ongoing pupil appraisal, with concomitant adjustment in the objectives or instructional strategies to avoid the fatal trap of perseverating on ineffective interventions (Fuchs & Fuchs, 1986; Shinn, 1986; Wesson, Skipa, Sevcik, King, & Deno, 1984).

Emphasis on Functional and Social Skills Curricula

Many LD children may not attain proficiency in basic skill areas such as reading, computation, or composition (e.g., Frauenheim & Heckerl, 1983; Zigmond, 1979). However, by introducing the judicious use of compensatory techniques, students may use these as assistive devices to become functionally independent (Hartlage & Telzrow, 1983; Minskoff, 1982). Functional independence refers to the ability to live independently, to find and maintain employment, and to engage in pleasurable recreational activities. Overemphasis on the acquisition of basic academic skills with little or no progress, accompanied by delay in introducing compensatory strategies, may produce LD graduates who are neither educationally independent nor functionally independent. Model LD programs must keep sight of the major goal of education--to help students become independent adults--and help achieve this objective.

Related to functional independence is the concept of social skills training. Many LD students have impaired social skills. They have been reported to participate in fewer activities and be less socially involved than average youngsters (McConaughy & Ritter, 1986). Some LD students have been said to misperceive facial expressions and verbal comments, to misinterpret social cues, and frequently to be awkward in social interactions (Denckla, 1983; Schumaker & Hazel, 1984; Weintraub & Mesulam, 1983). Social skills deficits have been demonstrated across settings and raters, and are present in both interpersonal (e.g., expressing feelings, accepting authority) and task-related areas (Gresham & Reschly, 1986). Acquisition of appropriate social skills has been reported to be associated with success while in school (Gresham, 1985), as well as following graduation (Compton, 1984). Hence, attention to instructing students in a variety of social skills, including those necessary for functioning in a large, complex public school, is an essential ingredient in special education programs.

Neuropsychologically Based Interventions

Finally, model LD programs must incorporate intervention techniques and strategies that are suited to the neuropsychological strengths and weaknesses of individual children. Increasingly, we are becoming aware that learning disabilities, while representing a vague syndrome which shares certain features in common, are often unique in the expression of specific deficits (e.g., McKinney, 1984; Rourke, 1985). Perhaps this conclusion is demonstrated most clearly in the work of Kavale and Nye (1985-86), who conducted a meta-analysis of over 1,000 studies of the characteristics of LD students. The authors examined 38 variables across four domains, defined as linguistic, achievement, neuropsychological, and social/behavioral. Kavale and Nye reported they could correctly classify 75% of LD students, although no clear distinguishing factors were identified. The authors concluded, "there is more than one type of LD and no uniform pattern of deficits. Consequently, uniform conceptualizations of LD that stressed deficits in a single domain are inadequate for describing LD in general and can explain only a limited number of LD cases" (p. 457).

If we believe, and there now appears to be general consensus among most experts on this point, that learning disabilities are of several different types, then it seems reasonable that interventions must be specific to the pattern of deficits exhibited. The following section will address the issue of neuropsychologically based interventions in greater detail.

Illustration of Neuropsychologically Based Interventions

In addition to the systemic changes in special education delivery that are important for all LD children, specific intervention strategies that are derived from a careful analysis of neuropsychological strengths and weaknesses are necessary for optimal achievement. This section will describe a model of neuropsychologically based interventions and illustrate its use via two case studies of children with specific learning disabilities.

Intervention Continuum Model

The literature about intervention describes three approaches to teaching children: a) a remediation of deficits approach, which identifies missing skills and teaches them; b) a capitalization of stengths approach, which describes intraindividual strengths and uses these as the basis for instruction; and c) a compensatory approach, which teaches techniques to circumvent weaker areas (Cronbach & Snow, 1977). The remediation of deficits approach is the most direct, and the most reasonable for many children. However, such an approach to intervention is problematic for children who are neurologically impaired, including those with subtle dysfunction such as may be expressed in specific learning disabilities. Such children, for example, often have unique difficulty acquiring basic skills of word recognition or phonetic analysis that may be emphasized in a remediation of deficits approach. Thus for LD children, some alternative instructional approach is recommended.

The model advocated by the author is one that has been described in greater detail elsewhere (Hartlage & Telzrow, 1983) and will be reviewed briefly. This model incorporates both the capitalization of stengths and the compensatory approaches in an intervention continuum. One extreme of the continuum works best with children who are bright, who have discrete rather than pervasive learning disabilities, who are motivated to invest themselves in interventions, and who are in situations where they get a great deal of support both at home and at school. This point on the continuum utilizes a capitalization of strengths approach, so that by taking advantage of their preserved abilities, such children can acquire expected educational skills. Often these techniques can be provided in a regular classroom by a teacher who is knowledgeable about and sensitive to neuropsychological processing strengths and weaknesses. As a result, it is the least restrictive option for children. While sometimes such students require LD tutoring or assistance in a special education resource room for those discrete areas where they are having unique difficulty, the attainable goal for children at this point on the continuum is educational independence.

The other extreme on the continuum is for youngsters who exhibit severe learning disabilities or whose problems are pervasive. They typically require intensive interventions that necessitate a significantly modified program. Since it is unusual for such modifications to be manageable in regular classroom settings, these youngsters may require more restrictive educational environments, such as self-contained special education classrooms, or perhaps even special schools. The goal of educational independence for such children probably is not realistic (e.g., Frauenheim & Heckerl, 1983; Zigmond, 1979). However, through thoughtful application of compensatory techniques, such children may become what this author (Telzrow, 1985) has described as functionally independent with assistive devices. Hence, with the aid of compensatory techniques to assist them in basic skills areas, these individuals can learn to live independently, to obtain and maintain employment, and to enjoy recreational activities.

Case Study Illustrations

Case 1: Pure Dysgraphia. The first case is that of a 13-year-old young man with a rather discrete learning disability known as pure developmental dysgraphia (e.g., Gaddes, 1985). Although of superior intelligence and possessing excellent reading and math skills, this young man has unique difficulty with handwriting, spelling, and written language skills (Table 1). Neuropsychological testing is significant for lateralized weakness implying dysfunction in the left hemisphere. There is a family history of similar learning disabilities involving the two brothers of his mother. Both parents have advanced degrees: his father is an attorney, his mother a teacher.

Followed by the author since he was in fourth grade, this young man has received LD tutoring for approximately one-half hour per day while attending regular education classes. At the author's suggestion, the use of a word-processor was introduced in fifth grade, and all parties have reported a significant increase in both the quantity and the quality of his written work since that time. In addition to the assistive device of the word-processor, which he uses for virtually all written assignments, this young man has benefitted from a few other educational modifications. The first is time. He requires much more than the average amount of time to organize and produce his written work. Often he organizes his thoughts orally, before beginning to write, and his mother reports he paces and talks to himself while preparing a written assignment. Consequently, his teachers give him assignments in advance of other students so that he can meet deadlines successfully. A second adjustment requires the use of a proofreader to correct spelling errors. To date, this young man has not found the use of specific spelling correction packages on the word-processor to be helpful: although his spelling his improved over the years, his errors are too numerous and too discrepant from the correct spellings to make the use of such a strategy practical. His teachers have permitted him to use a proofreader--typically one of his parents--on preliminary drafts of his written work, incorporating these corrections into the final product.

This case illustrates the least restrictive point on the continuum. This young man is bright, motivated, has support and understanding both at home and at school, and has discrete learning problems. By capitalizing on his strengths (e.g., his preserved oral language skills) he has been able to progress in written expression. His teachers have been able to accommodate necessary modifications in the regular classroom, and LD tutoring has instructed this youngster in many of the strategies necessary for organizing written work. It is expected that, while spelling and handwriting will remain problematic for him, this young

Table 1

Case 1: Pure Dysgraphia

	Age = 11-0	Age = 13-0		Age = 11-0	Age=13-0
Wechsler Intelligence Scale					
For Children (Revised)					
Verbal IQ	133	127			
Performance IQ	121	117			
Full Scale IQ	130	125			
Information	13	14	Picture Completion	12	15
Similarities	18	14	Picture Arrangement	16	13
Arithmetic	11	12	Block Design	14	13
Vocabulary	16	16	Objects Assembly	12	11
Comprehension	18	16	Coding	11	10
Digit Span	15	12			
Test of Written Language (TOWL)					
Vocabulary	14	9	Style	10	12
Thematic Maturity	9	10	Thought Units	6	
Spelling	6	7	Handwriting	4	3
Word Usage	10	11			
Boder Test of Reading/Spelling Patterns					
Reading Level	7.3		9.2		
Quotient	125		111		
Known Words					
Spelled Incorrecltly	0		10%		
Unknown Words					
Spelled as GFE's	10%		30%		
Trail Making Test					
A /B	12 sec/45 sec		11 sec/22 sec		
Aphasia Screening Test					
Construction Dyspraxia			Construction Dyspraxia		
Spelling Dyspraxia			Spelling Dyspraxia		
Dysgraphia			Dysgraphia		
Left-Right Confusion					
Finger Oscillation					
Left/Right Hand(10 sec)	42 taps/33 taps		51 taps/36 taps		

man will become sufficiently proficient through his use of modifications to pursue his goal of a college education and a career in forestry.

Case 2. Developmental Language Disorder. The second case is one of a 6-year-old youngster with a history of delayed language and behavior problems (Table 2). At the time of initial evaluation by the author, this child was unable to manage in a first grade classroom, and much concern had been expressed about his unusual, often bizarre behaviors. Examples of such behavior included inability or refusal to follow directions; inappropriate play, including aggressive behavior; and, most notably, a tendency to respond to others' questions or conversations in what his mother referred to as "gibberish"--i.e., English words, but of a nonsensical nature, such as reciting a nursery rhyme or describing a plot from a television program. This child's father and his uncle (i.e., the father's brother) were described as demonstrating speech and language problems requiring therapy as children. Both parents have advanced degrees: the father is an engineer, the mother an indexer of math and science textbooks.

Evaluation of this youngster resulted in a pattern of scores suggesting a significant developmental language disorder. On nonverbal tasks in an individual test situation, this youngster appeared clam, well-focused, thoughtful, and able to monitor his work carefully. His scores on such tasks (e.g., Leiter and WISC-R Performance Scale) were significantly above average. In contrast, when verbal tasks were introduced, particularly those requiring him to process a syntactically and semantically complex sentence, such as on the WISC-R Information and Comprehension subtests, his responses were often tangential and sometimes frankly bizarre. His performance on the Token Test for Children most closely resembled the average performance of 3 to 3 1/2 year old children. When introduced to groups of children, where the demands for sorting out and processing verbalizations increased, his behavior deteriorated further.

This youngster's developmental language disorder most closely resembles the semantic-pragmatic type described by Rapin and Allen (1983). Many of his unusual behaviors that others had observed, including his bizarre conversations, appeared to be related to his inability to use language in a socially meaningful way. Hence, he often ignored pragmatic rules such as turn-taking and beginning and ending conversations appropriately.

With the cooperation of an open and flexible educational staff, a significantly modified program was developed for this youngster. Initially he was removed from the regular first grade classroom, which represented such a confusing milieu for him, and received all academic instruction in a learning disabilities classroom, in an individual, small-group setting. It was planned for him to be reintegrated into the regular classroom in a careful, systemic fashion when his auditory processing and language skills were sufficiently well developed to make such a transition successful. He received individual language therapy three days per week, where the initial emphasis was placed on following directions and responding to questions. Additional language interventions were planned cooperatively between the LD teacher and the speech pathologist. Additionally, an expert in social skills training consulted with the LD teacher to plan and implement a program for appropriate behavior and to assist with generalization training in realistic settings (e.g., on the playground).

This case illustrates a somewhat more restrictive point on the intervention continuum than Case 1. This second youngster displays a fairly severe, pervasive language disorder

Table 2

Case 2: Developmental Language Disorder

Leiter International Performance Scale			
Age	6-9	IQ	115
Mental Age	7.8		

Wechsler Intelligence Scale For Children (Revised)			
Information	4	Picture Completion	14
Similarities	12	Picture Arrangement	11
Arithmetic	7	Block Design	15
Vocabulary	9	Object Assembly	11
Comprehension	2	Coding	8
Verbal IQ	80	Performance IQ	112

K-ABC Achievement Battery	SS	%	
Faces & Places	95	37	
Arithmetic	87	19	
Reading/Decoding	85	16	
Total	85	16	

Developmental Test of Visual Motor Integration (Berry VMI)		
Raw Score	14	Standard Score = 16, %=95
Age Equivalent	7-3	

Token Test For Children	Raw Score	Standard Score
I	6	438
II	1	457
III	6	488
IV	3	492
V	2	480
Total	18	473

Child Behavior Checklist - Parent	T-scores		T-scores
I Anxious	76	VI Social Withdrawn	70
III Uncommunicative	75	VII Hyperactive	80
IV Obsessive-Compulsive	77	VIII Aggressive	73

which has impaired his ability to understand and use language meaningfully and to manage in age-appropriate social settings. Significant modifications in his educational program, requiring the expertise of several specialists working in concert, are necessary to respond to this youngster's unique needs.

Summary

Consideration of the interplay of neuropsychological and environmental variables is a necessary prerequisite for the rehabilitation of learning disabilities in children. This chapter has described a variety of systemic deterrents to implementing successful interventions for LD children, and has outlined several programmatic features that evidence suggests are essential for narrowing the LD-non-LD gap. Finally, an intervention continuum model, which incorporates information about the nature and severity of neuropsychological impairment when planning educational programs, was described and illustrated via two case studies. While the goal of total remediation of learning disabilities probably is not realistic, implementation of such a model may maximize the potential of these youngsters.

References

ACLD description: Specific learning disabilities. (September-October, 1986). *ACLD Newsbriefs*, No. 166, 15-16.

Anderson, L.W. (1984). An introduction to time and school learning. In L.W. Anderson (Ed.), *Time and school learning* (pp. 1-12). New York: St. Martin's Press.

Attention disorder--crime link dispelled. (1985). *APA Monitor, 16*(11), 16.

Boll, T.J. (1984, August). *Developing issues in neuropsychology*. Presidential address to the Division of Neuropsychology, American Psychological Association, Toronto, Canada.

Bolter, J.F., & Long, C.J. (1985). Methodological issues in research in developmental neuropsychology. In L.C. Hartlage & C.F. Telzrow (Eds.), *Neuropsychological aspects of individual differences: A developmental perspective* (pp. 41-59). New York: Plenum.

Brown, R.T., & Alford, N. (1984). Ameliorating attentional deficits and concomitant academic deficiencies in learning disabled children through cognitive training. *Journal of Learning Disabilities, 17*, 10-16.

Buchanan, M., & Wolf, J.S. (1986). A comprehensive study of learning disabled adults. *Journal of Learning Disabilities, 19*, 34-38.

Burns, R.B. (1984). How time is used in elementary school: The activity structure of classrooms. In L.W. Anderson (Ed.), *Time and school learning* (pp. 91-127). New York: St. Martin's Press.

Carlton, G., Hummer, T., & Rainey, D. (1984). Teaching learning disabled children to help themselves. *The Directive Teacher, 61*, 8-9.

Carroll, J.B. (1984). The model of school learning: Progress of an idea. In L.W. Anderson (Ed.), *Time and school learning* (pp. 15-45). New York: St. Martin's Press.

Chan, L.K.S., & Cole, P.G. (1986). The effects of comprehension monitoring training on the reading competence of learning disabled and regular class students. *Remedial and Special Education, 7*(4), 33-40.

Compton, C. (1984, February). *Living with learning disabilities: A ten-year follow-up study*. Paper presented at the meeting of the National Association for Children with Learning Disabilities, New Orleans.

Cordoni, B.K., O'Donnell, J.P., Ramaniah, N.V., Kurtz, J., & Rosenshein, K. (1981). Wechsler Adult Intelligence score patterns for learning disabled young adults. *Journal of Learning Disabilities, 14*, 404-407.

Cronbach, L.J., & Snow, R.E. (1977). *Aptitudes and instructional methods*. New York: Irvington Publishers.

Denckla, M.B. (1983). The neuropsychology social-emotional learning disabilities. *Archives of Neurology, 40*, 461-462.

Frauenheim, J.G., & Heckerl, J.R. (1983). A longitudinal study of the psychological and achievement test performance in severe dyslexic adults. *Journal of Learning Disabilities, 16*, 339-347.

Fuchs, L.S., & Fuchs, D. (1986). Curriculum-based assessment of progress toward long-term and short-term goals. *The Journal of Special Education, 20*, 69-82.

Gaddes, W.H. (1985). *Learning disabilities and brain function: A neuropsychological approach* (2nd Ed.). New York: Springer-Verlag.

Gelzheiser, L.M., Solar, R.A., Shepherd, M.J., & Wozniak, R.H. (1983). Teaching learning disabled children to memorize: A rationale for plans and practice. *Journal of Learning Disabilities, 16*, 421-425.

Gerber, M.M. (1986, February). Cognitive-behavioral training in the curriculum: Time, slow learners, and basic skills. *Focus on Exceptional Children*.

Gersten, R. (1985). Direct instruction with special education students: A review of evaluation research. *The Journal of Special Education, 19*, 41-58.

Gettinger, M. (1984). Measuring time needed for learning to predict learning outcomes. *Exceptional Children, 51*, 244-248.

Graham, S., & Freeman, S. (1985). Strategy training and teacher- vs. student-controlled study conditions: Effects on LD students' spelling performance. *Learning Disabilities Quarterly, 8*, 267-274.

Gresham, F.M. (1985). Best practices in social skills training. In A. Thomas & J. Grimes (Eds.), *Best practices in school psychology* (pp. 181-192). Kent, OH: National Association of School Psychologists.

Gresham, F.M., & Reschly, D.J. (1986). Social skill deficits and low peer acceptance of mainstreamed learning disabled children. *Learning Disability Quarterly, 9*, 23-32.

Hartlage, L.C., & Telzow, C.F. (1983). The neuropsychological bases of educational intervention. *Journal of Learning Disabilities, 16*, 521-528.

Kavale, K.A., & Forness, S.R. (1986). School learning, time and learning disabilities: The disassociated learner. *Journal of Learning Disabilities, 19*, 130-138.

Kavale, K.A., & Nye, C. (1985-86). Parameters of learning disabilities in achievement, linguistic, neuropsychological, and social/behavioral domains. *The Journal of Special Education, 19*, 443-458.

Kimbrough, J.M., & Hill, P.T. (1983, September). *Problems of implementing multiple categorical education programs.* (Available form Rand Publications Department, 1700 Main St., P.O. Box 2138, Santa Monica, CA 90406-2138).

Kutsick, K. (1982). Remedial strategies for learning disabled adolescents. *Academic Therapy, 17*, 329-335.

Leinhardt, G., Zigmond, N., & Cooley, W.W. (1981). Reading instruction and its effect. *American Educational Research Journal, 18*, 343-361.

Lewis, R.B. (1983). Learning disabilities and reading: Instructional recommendations from current research. *Exceptional Children, 50*, 230-240.

McConaughy, S.H., & Ritter, D.R. (1986). Social competence and behavioral problems of learning disabled boys aged 6-11. *Journal of Learning Disabilities, 19*, 39-45.

McCue, P.M., Shelly, C., & Goldstein, G. (1986). Intellectual, academic and neuropsychological performance levels in learning disabled adults. *Journal of Learning Disabilities, 19*, 233-236.

McCue, M., Shelly, C., Goldstein, G., & Katz-Garris, L. (1984). Neuropsychological aspects of learning disability in young adults. *The International Journal of Clinical Neuropsychology, 6*, 229-232.

McKinney, J.D. (1984). The search for subtypes of specific learning disability. *Journal of Learning Disabilities, 17*, 43-50.

Minskoff, D.H. (1982). Training LD students to cope with the everyday world. *Academic Therapy, 17*, 311-316.

Neely, M.D., & Lindsley, O.R. (1978). Phonetic, linguistic, and sight readers produce similar learning with exceptional children. *The Journal of Special Education, 12*, 423-441.

Polloway, E.A., Cronin, M.E., & Patton, J.R. (1986). The efficacy of group versus one-to-one instruction: A review. *Remedial and Special Education, 7*(1), 22-30.

Polloway, E.A., Epstein, M.H., Polloway, C.H., Patton, J.R., & Ball, D.W. (1986). Corrective reading program: An analysis of effectiveness with learning disabled and mentally retarded students. *Remedial and Special Education, 7*(4), 41-47.

Rapin, I., & Allen, D.A. (1983). Developmental language disorders: Nosologic considerations. In U. Kirk (Ed.), *Neuropsychology of language, reading, and spelling* (pp. 155-184). New York: Academic Press.

Rourke, B.P. (Ed.) (1985). *Neuropsychology of learning disabilities: Essentials of subtype analysis.* New York: Guilford.

Schonhaut, S., & Satz, P. (1983). Prognosis for children with learning disabilities: A review of follow-up studies. In M. Rutter (Ed.), *Developmental neuropsychiatry* (pp. 542-563). New York: Guilford.

Schumaker, J.B., & Hazel, J.S. (1984). Social skills assessment and training for the learning disabled: Who's on first and what's on second? I. *Journal of Learning Disabilities, 17*, 422-431.

Sheinker, A., Sheinker, J.M., & Stevens, L.J. (1984, September). Cognitive strategies for teaching the mildly handicapped. *Focus on Exceptional Children, 17*(1), 1-15.

Shinn, M.R. (1986). Does anyone care what happens after the refer-test-place sequence: The systematic evaluation of special education program effectiveness. *School Psychology Review, 15*, 49-58.

Stallings, J. (1980). Allocated academic learning time revisited, on beyond time on task. *Educational Researcher, 9*, 11-16.

Strother, D.B. (1985, December). Adapting instruction to individual needs: An electric approach. *Phi Delta Kappa*, 308-311.

Sullivan, P.D., & McDaniel, E.A. (1983). Pupil attendance in resource rooms as one measure of the time on task variable. *Journal of Learning Disabilities, 16*, 398-399.

Swanson, H.L. (1984). Does theory guide teaching practice? *Remedial and Special Education, 5*(5), 7-16.

Tarver, S.G. (1986). Cognitive behavior modification, direct instruction and holistic approaches to the education of students with learning disabilities. *Journal of Learning Disabilities, 19*, 368-375.

Telzrow, C.F. (1985). The science and speculation of rehabilitation in developmental neuropsychological disorders. In L.C. Hartlage & C.F. Telzrow (Eds.), *Neuropsychological aspects of individual differences: A developmental perspective* (pp. 271-307). New York: Plenum.

Wang, M.C. (1980). Adaptive instruction: Building on diversity. *Theory into Practice, 19*, 122-128.

Wang, M.C. (1984). Time-use and the provision of adaptive instruction. In L.W. Anderson (Ed.), *Time and school learning* (pp. 167-203). New York: St. Martin's Press.

Weintraub, S., & Mesulam, M.M. (1983). Developmental learning disabilities of the right hemisphere. *Archives of Neurology , 40*, 463-468.

Wesson, C., Skiba, R., Sevcik, B., King, R.P., & Deno, S. (1984). The effects of technically adequate instructional data on achievement. *Remedial and Special Education, 5*(5), 17-22.

Zigmond, N. (1979). Remediation of dyslexia: Discussion. In A.L. Benton (Ed.), *Dyslexia: An appraisal of current knowledge* (pp. 437-448). New York: Oxford University Press.

Zigmond, N., Vallecorsa, A., & Leinhardt, G. (1980). Reading instruction for students with learning disabilities. *Topics in Language Disorders, 1*(1), 89-98.

13

Learning Disabilities and Hyperactivity: Implications for Research and Clinical Assessment

Lisa A. Wolfe, Aleida K. Inglis, and Randolph W. Parks

The longstanding association between hyperactivity and learning problems has resulted in much confusion regarding the identification and characteristics of these diagnoses. Recently, a number of studies have attempted to compare children with hyperactivity, children with learning disabilities, and children with both disorders in order to gain more understanding about each of these diagnoses. Unfortunately, because the definitions of these disorders have always been vague, these studies themselves often succumb to various methodological problems. This paper provides a brief overview of the literature comparing learning disabled and hyperactive children, raises some of the main methodological problems, and offers suggestions for future research.

Methodological Issues

Definitional Problems

The most widely accepted definition of learning disability, first proposed by the National Advisory Committee on Handicapped Children in 1968 and later instituted by Congress, states:

> "Specific learning disability" means a disorder in one or more of the basic psychological processes involved in understanding or in using language, spo - ken or written, which may manifest itself in an imperfect ability to listen, think, speak, read, write, spell, or to do mathematical calculations. The term includes such conditions as perceptual handicaps, brain injury, minimal brain dysfunction, dyslexia, and developmental aphasia. The term does not include children who have learning problems which are primarily the result of visual, hearing, or motor handicaps, of mental retardation, of emotional disturbance, or of environmental, cultural, or economic disadvantage. (Federal Register, 1977, p. 65083)

As many authors have pointed out, however, several problems surround this definition. It relies on criteria of exclusion, leaving undefined the conditions constituting learning disabilities (e.g. "basic psychological processes") and instead specifying what learning disability is not (Schere, Richardson, & Bialer, 1980). Many researchers criticize the definition's over-emphasis on etiology. Schere et al. (1980) write that the definition "would exclude children with learning problems 'which are primarily the result of . . . mental retardation and of emotional disturbance,' leaving it to the expert to determine when such factors are the 'primary causes' of the learning problems. The problem arises from the fact that the behaviors delineated by the definition and the etiologies specified as exclusion factors are so inextricably interwoven as to preclude the designation of a particular etiology as a 'primary cause' of behavioral disabilities" (p. 6).

Hyperactivity as defined in DSM-III (1980) represents a special case of attention deficit disorder--a high level of inattention and impulsivity--accompanied by excessive motor activity. Similarly, deficits in one or more facets of attention are considered to play a key role in disturbed learning processes (see Dykman, Ackerman, Holcomb, & Boudreau, 1983; Keogh & Margolis, 1976; Routh, 1979; Tarver & Hallahan, 1974 for reviews). Both disorders, in addition, present more commonly in boys than in girls (Lambert & Sandoval, 1980).

Hence, if children with attentional deficits who have difficulty learning can be considered "learning disabled", then hyperactive children may very well constitute a subset of these children. However, researchers often do not acknowledge that learning disabilities comprise many subtypes, and often clump subjects simply labeled as "learning disabled" into one sample. Furthermore, studies often do not specify the procedure used to diagnose children as learning disabled. Many studies use a discrepancy between expected achievement test scores and IQ as indicative of a learning disability. But this definition is not in keeping with the federal guidelines as it does not necessarily include neuropsychological impairment; a child may perform poorly on the achievement test for other reasons, such as insufficient motivation.

Even when a discrepancy between achievement test scores and IQ is used as the basis for diagnosis, researchers have not agreed on what achievement test cut-off point to use to label a child as learning disabled. Some researchers employ a cut-off at the 25th percentile of the Wide Range Achievement Test for children with an IQ of at least 90 to determine whether the child is learning disabled. Halperin et al. (1984) contend that this cut-off permits the inclusion of children who are only mildly handicapped, performing less than one year below grade level, as learning disabled.

Sampling Strategies

Research indicates that the diagnoses of LD and hyperactivity frequently overlap. Studies of hyperactive (HA) children estimate that 40-50% exhibit signs of LDs (Cantwell & Satterfield, 1978; Hinton & Knights, 1971; Lambert & Sandoval, 1980; Weiss, Minde, Werry, Doublas, & Nemeth, 1971). Silver (1981) discovered 92% of a sample of 95 HA and/or distractible children to have learning disabilities, and 91% of 110 LD children to be HA and/or distractible. Weinberg and Rehmet (1983) found that 35-40% of new students entering a learning disabilities program over four years, out of a total 167 students, were hyperactive or both hyperactive and depressed. Ross (1976) cautions that studies may inflate the rate of hyperactivity among LD children, because the LD child with hyperactivity is more likely to stand out in the classroom as having behavioral and learning problems than is the LD child without hyperactivity.

On the other hand, Ackerman, Oglesby, & Dykman (1981) claim that mixed HA-LD subjects were harder to identify for their study than were pure HA and pure LD types. They maintain that had Cantwell and Satterfield (1978) used Rutter's standard--stressing underachievement based on age--to classify subjects as LD instead of a standard based on both age and IQ, more of Cantwell and Satterfield's HA subjects would have fallen into the normal range for achievement. Staton and Brumback (1981) diagnosed 92 out of 178 children, referred to an educational diagnostic center for learning or behavioral problems, as having specific LDs. Seventy-eight children were HA, but hyperactivity was not present to a significantly greater extent in the LD children than in the non LD children. Al the children in this study, however, manifested various school problems; hence both the LD and non LD subjects in this sample--though not significantly different from each other--may have displayed more hyperactivity than the general population.

Hence, data concerning the overlap of hyperactivity and learning disabilities is strongly biased according to the sampling procedures used. In addition, studies that compare hyperactive children with learning disabled children are subject to sampling biases. For example, when HA-LD children are culled from a larger original sample of hyperactive subjects, (e.g. Halperin et al., 1984), differences are less likely to emerge than when LD children are screened for hyperactivity and then compared to pure hyperactive types. If subjects come from child guidance clinics or the like, than those who are categorized as LD are likely to exhibit behavioral problems as well, and will appear to hyperactive or other behaviorally disturbed children.

Cognitive Processes in HA and LD Children

Keogh (1971) offered three hypotheses to account for the predominance of learning problems in HA children: 1) both LDs and hyperactivity stem from a common underlying condition such as neurological dysfunction; 2) the nature and extent of the HA child's motor activity interferes with the attentional processes required for learning; 3) the disturbed, speeded-up decision-making processes of the HA child impede learning. Keogh states that these three hypotheses are neither exhaustive nor mutually exclusive and reviews evidence showing the role of each of these processes in contributing to learning problems in HA children.

In order to clarify the relationship between LD and hyperactivity, several studies have investigated cognitive differences between distinct groups of these children. Such differences have been mainly investigated on the level of attention and its composite functions. A problem in comparing studies of attention arises from the different definitions and measures of attention employed by various investigators. Keogh and Margolis (1976), on the basis of a review of the literature, summarized attention in terms of three broad, interactive functions: coming to attention (settling down and focusing attention), decision-making (reflective versus impulsive cognitive style), and maintaining attention.

Sustained Attention

Several studies point to problems in impulse control and in maintaining attention among LD children as compared to controls (Douglas, 1972, 1974, 1980; Keogh & Donlon, 1972). Douglas and her colleagues, however, differentiate between the specific deficits of HA children and of LD children. They postulate that whereas HA children suffer from impaired attentional processing and poor inhibitory control, LD children sustain impaired processing of auditory or visual information, a receptive language deficit, or a reading disability, to which attentional deficits are secondary.

A handful of studies suggest that HA children encounter more problems in impulse control and in sustaining attention than do HA-LD children (Anderson, Halcomb, & Doyle, 1973; Dykman et al, 1971) and pure LD children (Brown & Wynne, 1984). But in a study comparing 22 mixed HA-LD children to 62 pure HA children, the mixed group performed more poorly on the Matching Familiar Figures Test, a measure of cognitive impulsivity (Halperin, Gittelman, Klein, & Rudel, 1984), in contrast to the findings of Anderson et al. (1973) Mixed HA-LD boys also made more errors than non HA-LD boys on this test, although the difference did not reach statistical significance (Copeland & Weissbrod, 1983). In another study by Dykman and his colleagues, 20 pure HA boys were described as "more able than willing" to sustain attention as compared to 20 pure LD boys; the HA boys' lack of "tolerance for a problem" led to their poor performance (Dykman, Ackerman, & Oglesby, 1979). The HA boys, however, achieved insight in concept formation more rapidly than did LD and control boys. The 20 LD boys manifested passivity and rule-boundedness in learning, with problems in both selective and sustained attention. Yet in still another study on the effects of methylphenidate on attention, four groups of male HA, reading-disabled (RD), HA-RD, and non-hyperactive attention deficit disordered subjects did not differ on a cognitive battery assessing various aspects of attention, during any of the pretreatment, placebo, or drug phases (Ackerman, Dykman, Holcomb, & McCray, 1982).

Selective Attention

Studies of selective attention, which refers to the ability to focus on a particular stimulus against background distraction, have yielded even more inconsistencies. Tarver and Hallahan (1974) concluded from a review of the literature that LD children exhibit more distractibility than controls on embedded figures tasks, but that LD children do not succumb to distractions such as flashing lights and extraneous color cues. One source of such findings no doubt derives from the differential discriminative abilities of various tasks (Harvey, Weintraub, & Neale, 1984), although other post-hoc explanations have been offered, such as Browning's (1967) hypothesis. Browning's (1967) and Tarver and Hallahan's (1974) statements that the bright light distractors actually assist the LD child in discrimination tasks, however, are compatible with the notion that the easier distractibility tasks, using lights and noise, may discriminate less well between clinical and normal groups than do task of intermediate difficulty such as embedded figures tasks.

LD children fared worse than HA children on a task of selective attention in Dykman et al's (1979) study. This set of researchers also found LD children to evince selective attention deficits in a later study, on a task requiring children to discover the correct cue from up to a dozen stimuli (Dykman, Holcomb, Oglesby, & Ackerman, 1982). McIntyre, Murray, and Blackwell (1981) compared 12 LD, 12 HA-LD, 12 HA boys, and control groups for each type on a visual search task tapping selective attention. They found that both the LD and the HA-LD groups performed worse than their respective control groups, but that the HA group did not significantly differ from its control group. The investigators interpreted their results as supporting Ross' (1976) theory that deficits in selective attention characterize LD children but not HA children. Examination of the means of the three clinical groups, however, reveals the performance across tasks of the HA group to fall in between the means of the LD and the HA-LD group. The performances of the three groups, therefore, may have been more similar than appeared at first glance. The lack of a significant difference between the HA group and its control group alone does not justify the authors' conclusion, especially in light of the small sample sizes. Brown and Wynne (1984) uprooted no differences between pure LD children and pure HA children and normal controls on a similar visual search task, the Children's Embedded Figures Test. Halperin et al (1984) also detected no differences between HA-RD and pure HA children on this task.

Conceptual Abilities

In Dykman et al.'s (1979) study, HA boys achieved insight in concept formation more rapidly than did LD and control boys, while the LD boys manifested passivity and rule-boundedness in learning. A comparison of HA-LD and non HA-LD boys on various conceptual tasks revealed similar performance between these groups, though both performed more poorly than non LD controls (Copeland & Weissbrod), 1983). On one conceptual style task, the HA-LD subjects employed a less mature strategy than did the non HA-LD boys.

Physiological Studies

The abnormalities exhibited by LD children in sustaining attention surface on the level of physiology as well, such as in measures of heart rate and skin conductance. Dykman et al. (1983) state, in their review of the literature on physiological correlates of LDs, that these measures index in LD children an inability or unwillingness to sustain attention, and inertia in shifting from inner to outer involvement in evaluating the significance of stimuli and in becoming appropriately alert. Dykman et al also remark that whereas differences on psychological measures nearly always emerge between clinical groups and controls, measures taken during baseline responses to stimuli rarely net differences between clinical groups.

Ferguson, Simpson, and Trites (1976) obtained no consistent differences among HA subjects, divided into good and poor drug responders, and non HA-LD subjects, on resting levels of heart rate and skin conductance, or on patterns on heart rate and skin conductance during an orienting and reaction time procedure. Delameter, Lahey, and Drake (1981) also uncovered no differences between HA-LD and non HA-LD subjects on basal heart rate and skin conductance levels or on phasic responses to tones during a habituation and a discrimination task. Dykman and his coworkers found that basal autonomic levels did not statistically distinguish HA, RD, HA-RD, and control boys, although controls exhibited heart rate deceleration in anticipation of reward more consistently than did the clinical groups, especially the HA group (Dykman, Ackerman, Oglesby, & Holcomb, 1982).

On the other hand, Dykman and his colleagues have contrasted hyperactive LD children with hypoactive LD children and noted the slower reaction times and slower cardiac acceleration response during orientation in the latter group (Dykman et al., 1971; Ackerman, Dykman, & Peters, 1977). These observations, according to this set of researchers, support the conception of the non HA-LD child as a passive, over-inhibited learner, in contrast to the HA child who lacks inhibition and is impulsive and easily distracted.

Socio-emotional Factors

The various problems in self-esteem and social relations of the LD child have been extensively studied (see Bryan & Bryan, 1981, for a review), but less work has focused on specific differences between HA and LD children in facing these problems. Ottenbacher

(1979) asked teachers to rate 64 LD and 12 MBD pupils on the Hyperactivity Rating Scale (Spring, Bluden, Greenberg, & Yellin, 1977). The pattern of scores for these children did not resemble the pattern typical of HA children, who peak on restlessness, distractibility, work fluctuation, and impulsivity and excitatory categories. The LD children were instead characterized by poor motor coordination, low perseverance, and social withdrawal.

Aggression

Learning disabilities have been associated with aggression and conduct disorder (see Lane, 1980 for a review), and some studies have compared ratings of aggressive behavior among HA, LD, and mixed HA-LD groups. Such studies can help determine whether aggressive behavior in LD children can be traced to the presence of hyperactivity in these subjects.

In several studies, parents rated HA boys as more aggressive on the Conners (1969) scale than pure LD boys, mixed HA-LD boys, and controls (Ackerman, Dykman, & Oglesby, 1983; Ackerman, Elardo, & Dykman, 1979; Ackerman et al., 1981). Halperin et al (1984), however, found no significant differences between pure HA and HA-LD children on Conners teacher ratings or on psychiatrist ratings of aggression. These inconsistencies may partly stem from the use of different criteria to classify LD subjects, as well as different sampling methods. Since Halperin et al. (1984) obtained their HA-LD subjects from a sample originally categorized as hyperactive, their two groups were apt to be more similar.

Anxiety

In addition to having more behavior problems, HA-LD children in an Israeli study scored higher on an anxiety scale than did non HA-LD children (Margalit & Arieli, 1984). Ackerman et al. (1979) found that 20 HA subjects were rated as more anxious than 20 LD subjects, and both were more anxious than controls, on the Conners scale. In another study, however, no differences emerged on anxiety between HA, RD, HA-RD children and children with attention deficit disorder (Ackerman et al., 1983). Halperin et al. (1984) also found no differences on teacher ratings of anxiety between HA and HA-RD children.

Other Psychiatric Disorders

HA children may run a higher than average risk for other psychiatric disorders as adults. Borland and Heckman (1976) found upon follow-up of 20 HA boys that four were sociopathic and five had "nervous problems" for which they had sought treatment; while none of their brothers had incurred such problems. But Silver (1981) comments that because this study did not consider whether the subjects were also learning disabled, the adult findings could be traced either to hyperactivity or to unrecognized learning disabilities. Manuzza and Gittelman (1984) followed up 24 HA boys, 12 HA girls, and 24 male controls as adolescents. Again, no statement about possible learning disabilities was offered. When compared to the controls, the male probands presented with more attention deficit disorder and other DSM-III diagnoses, especially substance use disorder and conduct disorder.

LD children with hyperactivity may develop other psychiatric disorders as a direct result of the learning disabilities, or as a result of associated hyperactivity underlying both learning and emotional problems, as Rutter, Graham, and Yule (1970) have hypothesized with reading retardation. Moreover, hyperactivity or distractibility themselves can result from other problems such as anxiety or depression (Silver, 1981). Hyperactivity, learning disabilities, and other disorders no doubt interact with each other in many complex ways.

Summary

In sum, HA children not only often display learning disabilities, but LD and HA children exhibit problems in various aspects of attention and show similar corresponding patterns in physiological arousal. The exact differences between children with learning disabilities only, children with hyperactivity only, and children with both disorders remain unclear, and findings on these groups are inconsistent. LD and HA children also demonstrate various other behavioral difficulties. HA children, whether learning disabled or not, appear to pose more problems than pure LD children. Although a handful of studies suggest that HA children are more aggressive than LD children, studies need to use clear-cut definitions of learning disability and less biased sampling procedures to verify these results. An ideal way to select LD and HA subjects might be to draw them from a regular school population, but most children with such problems should have already been identified and placed in special programs. Selection of LD and HA-LD children from special education programs would probably serve as a less biased method for comparison than selection of these types from a larger group already identified as hyperactive.

Perhaps the greatest need in the field of LD/HA research, however, is a set of consistently used measures to determine the behavioral and cognitive aspects of each of these conditions. At the present time, several measures appear in widespread use, some more successfully than others. The Conners scale (Conners, 1962) is frequently used to assess activity level. Ideally, teacher and parental ratings, physician diagnoses, and laboratory measures should be employed in conjunction when assessing hyperactivity. To detect the presence of "specific learning disability", many researchers have looked at the discrepancy between IQ level and achievement test scores in specific skill areas (e.g., reading, spelling, mathematics). Although the measures mentioned delineate some of the essential elements of hyperactivity and learning problems, they leave many skill areas unexamined. A more comprehensive method of evaluation of such children is needed.

In order to carefully diagnose a learning disability, in keeping with the more original framework of research on brain dysfunction, a thorough neuropsychological work-up should be conducted. This battery should include an analysis of WISC-R subtest scatter patterns, rather than a single measure of discrepancy between WRAT and IQ scores. Ideally, other tests of attention, visuospatial and motor skills, and language abilities should be included as well. The use of a broad-based neuropsychological test battery for the assessment of a wide variety of cognitive skills would provide teachers and clinicians with important information to better describe the nature of each child's problems, and to help determine what remedial materials and strategies would be most useful.

References

Ackerman, P. T., Dykman, R. A., & Oglesby, D. M. (1983). Sex and group differences in reading and attention disordered children with and without hyperkinesis. *Journal of Learning Disabilities, 16,* 407-415.

Ackerman, P. T., Dykman, R. A., & Peters, J. E. (1977). Teenage status of hyperactive and non-hyperactive learning disabled boys. *Journal of Abnormal Child Psychology, 7,* 91-99.

Ackerman, P. T., Elardo, P. T., & Dykman, R. A. (1979). A psychosocial study of hyperactive and learning disabled boys. *Journal of Abnormal Child Psychology, 7*, 91-99.

Ackerman, P. T., Oglesby, D. M., & Dykman, R. A. (1981). Contrast of hyperactive, learning disabled, and hyperactive-learning disabled boys. *Journal of Clinical Child Psychology, 10*, 168-173.

American Psychiatric Association (1980). *DSM-III: Diagnostic and Statistical Man ual of Mental Disorders.* (3rd ed.) APA, Washington, D.C.

Anderson, R. P., Halcomb, C. G., & Doyle, R. B. (1973). The measurement of attentional deficits. *Exceptional Children, 39*, 534-539.

Bender, L. (1942). Postencephalitic behavior disorders in children. In Neal, J. B. (Ed.) *Encephalitis: A clinical study.* New York: Grune & Stratton.

Borland, B. L. & Heckman, H. I. (1976). Hyperactive boys and their brothers. *Archives of General Psychiatry, 27*, 414-417.

Brown, R. T. & Wynne, M. E. (1984). Attentional characteristics and teacher ratings in hyperactive, reading disabled, and normal boys. *Journal of Clinical Child Psychology, 13*, 38-43.

Browning, R. M. (1967). Hypo-responsiveness as a behavioral correlate of brain-damage children. *Psychological Reports, 20*, 251-259.

Bryan, T. H. & Bryan, J. H. (1978). Some personal and social experiences of learning disabled children. In Keogh, B. (Ed.), *Advances in special education.* Greenwich, CT: JAI Press.

Conners, C. KI., (1969). A teacher rating scale for use in drug studies with children. *American Journal of Psychiatry, 126*, 884-888.

Copeland, A. P. & Weissbrod, C. S. (1983). Cognitive strategies used by learning disabled children: Does hyperactivity always make things worse? *Journal of Learning Disabilities, 16*, 473-477.

Dalameter, A. M., Lahey, B. B., & Drake, L. (1981). Toward an empirical subclassification of 'learning disabilities': A psychophysiological comparison of 'hyperactive' and 'nonhyperactive' subgroups. *Journal of Abnormal Child Psychology, 9*, 65-77.

Douglas, V. I. (1972). Stop, look, & listen: The problem of sustained attentional and impulse control in hyperactive and normal children. *Canadian Journal of Behavioral Science, 4*, 259-282.

Douglas, V. I. (1980). Higher mental processes in hyperactive children: Implications for training. In Knights, R. M. & Bakker, D. J. (Eds.), *Rehabilitation, treatment, and management of learning disorders.* Baltimore: University Park Press.

Dykman, R. A., Ackerman, P. T., Clements, S. D. & Peters, J. E. (1971). Specific learning disabilities: An attentional deficit syndrome. In Myklebust, H. R. (Ed.), *Progress in learning disabilities*, Vol. 2. New York: Grune & Stratton.

Dykman, R. A., Ackerman, P. T., Holcomb, P. J., & Boudreau, A. Y. (1983). Physiological manifestations of learning disability. *Journal of Learning Disabilities, 16*, 46-53.

Dykman, R. A., Ackerman, P. T., & Oglesby, D. M. (1979). Selective and sustained attention in hyperactive, learning-disabled, and normal boys. *Journal of Nervous and Mental Disease, 167* , 288-297.

Dykman, R. A., Ackerman, P. T., Oglesby, D. M., & Holcomb, P. J. (1982). Autonomic responsivity during visual search of hyperactive and reading-disabled children. *Pavlovian Journal of Biological Science, 17*, 150-157.

Dykman, R. A., Holcomb, P. J., Oglesby, D. M., & Ackerman, P. T. (1982). Electrocortical frequencies in hyperactive, learning and disabled, mixed, and normal children. *Biological Psychiatry, 17*, 675-685.

Federal Register (1977). Vol. 42, no. 250, Thursday, December 29.

Ferguson, H. G., Simpson, S. & Trites, R. L. (1976). Psychophysiological study of methylphenidate responders and nonresponders. In Knights, R. M. & Bakker, D. J. (Eds.), *The neuropschology of learning disorders.* Baltimore: University Park Press.

Halperin, J. M., Gittelman, R., Klein, D. E., & Rudel, R. G. (1984). Reading-disabled hyperactive children: A distinct subgroup of attention deficit disorder with hyperactivity? *Journal of Abnormal Child Psychology, 12*, 1-14.

Harvey, P. D., Weintraub, S., & Neale, J. M. (1984). Distractibility in learning-dis abled children: The role of measurement artifact. *Journal of Learning Disabilities, 17*, 234-236.

Hinton, G. G. & Knights, R. M. (1971). Children with learning problems: Academic history, academic prediction, and adjustment three years after assessment. *Exceptional Children, 37*, 513-519.

Keogh, B. K. (1971). Hyperactivity and learning disorders: Review and speculation. *Exceptional Children, 38*, 101-109.

Keogh, B. K. & Donlon, G. (1972). Field independence, impulsivity, and learning disabilities. *Journal of Learning Disabilities, 5*, 331-336.

ambert, N. M. & Sandoval, J. (1980). The prevalence of learning disabilities in a sample of children considered hyperactive. *Journal of Abnormal Children Psychology, 8*, 33-50.

ane, B. A. (1980). The relationship of learning disabilities to juvenile delinquency: Current status. *Journal of Learning Disabilities, 13*, 425-434.

Manuzza, S. & Gittelman, R. (1984). The adolescent outcome of hyperactive girls. *Psychiatry Research, 13*, 19-29.

Margalit, M. & Arieli, N. (1984). Emotional and behavioral aspects of hyperactivity. *Journal of Learning Disabilities, 17*, 374-376.

McIntyre, C. W., Murray, M. E., & Blackwell, S. L. (1981). Visual search in learning disabled and hyperactive boys. *Journal of Learning Disabilities, 14*, 156-158.

Ottenbacher, K. (1979). Hyperactivity and related behavioral characteristics in a sample of learning disabled children. *Perceptual and Motor Skills, 48*, 105-106.

Ross, A. O. (1976). *Psychological aspects of learning disorders and reading disorders*. New York: McGraw-Hill.

Routh, D. K. (1979). Activity, attention, and aggression in learning disabled children. *Journal of Clinical Child Psychology, 8*, 183-187.

Rutter, M., Graham, P., & Yule, W. (1970). *A neuropsychiatric study in childhood*. Lavenham, Suffolk, England: Labenham Press.

Schere, R. A., Richardson, E., & Bialer, I. (1980). Toward operationalizing a psychoeducational definition of learning disabilities. *Journal of Abnormal Children Psychology, 8*, 5-20.

Silver, L. B. (1981). The relationship between learning disabilities, hyperactivity, distractibility, and behavioral problems: A clinical analysis. *Journal of the American Academy of Child Psychiatry, 20*, 385-397.

Spreen, O. (1981). The relationship between learning disability, neurological impairment, and delinquency. *Journal of Nervous and Mental Disease, 169*, 791-799.

Spring, D., Bluden, D., Greenberg, L., & Yellin, A. (1977). Validity and norms of a hyperactive rating scale. *Perceptual and Motor Skills, 52*, 323-332.

Staton, R. D. & Brumback, R. A. (1981). Non-specificity of motor hyperactivity as a diagnostic criterion. *Perceptual and Motor Skills, 52*, 323-332.

Tarver, S. G. & D. P. Hallahan (1974). Attention Deficits in Children with Learning Disabilities: A review. *Journal of Learning Disabilities, 7*, 560-569.

Weinberg, W. A. & Rehmet, A. (1983). Childhood affective disorder and school problems. In Cantwell, D. P. & Carlson, G. A. (Eds.), *Affective disorders in childhood and adolescence: An update*. New York: Spectrum.

Weiss, G., Minde, K., Werry, J. S., Douglas, V., & Nemeth, E. (1971). Studies on the hyperactive child: VII. Five-year follow-up. *Archives of General Psychiatry, 24*, 409-414.

14

Cognitive Training with Brain-Injured Children: General Issues and Approaches

Tina L. Brown and Sam B. Morgan

In the traditional view, the neuropsychologist's primary clinical role was in diagnosis and assessment of disorders associated with brain damage or dysfunction. As the title of this book suggests, the role has evolved to include more and more participation in the development of treatment programs based on neuropsychological knowledge and theory. Along with this increasing emphasis on treatment, there has been a growing interest in the study of childhood disorders from a neuropsychological perspective. Titles of recent books, such as *Child Neuropsychology* (Rourke, Bakker, Fisk, & Strang, 1983) and *Developmental Neuropsychiatry* (Rutter, 1983), attest to this interest. As with adult neuropsychology, work in this burgeoning specialty of child neuropsychology has extended beyond diagnosis to the development of specific educational and therapeutic programs based on neuropsychological models (Hartlage & Telzrow, 1984; Satz & Fletcher, 1981).

In this chapter we discuss general issues concerning remediation of deficits that children may have as a result of brain injury. We address, in turn, the emerging role of the neuropsychologist in such training, the need for a developmental, idiographic perspective, and general neuropsychological and cognitive strategies for training of brain-damaged children. Particular emphasis is given to those approaches directed toward the development (or re-development) of cognitive functions impaired by brain damage. Our intent is not to outline the specifics of different training methods but rather to stress general strategies with their underlying rationales and advantages and disadvantages. While we focus on training of children with known brain damage, we include strategies that are based to some extent on work with learning disabled children presumed to have underlying cerebral dysfunction that may or may not be associated with clear brain damage. Indeed, there is substantial overlap in remedial strategies for the two groups because both show many of the same skill deficits at the behavioral level. For more thorough discussion of assessment and treatment techniques with learning disabled children, however, we refer the reader to the chapters by Dean and Telzrow in this book.

The Neuropsychologist's Role in Training and Remediation
with the Brain-Injured Child

The general goal of remediation or training with the brain injured person is to help the person acquire the behavioral repertoire needed to solve problems or perform tasks that seem difficult or impossible after the brain injury (Diller & Gordon, 1981). Children with brain damage suffer from a multiplicity of problems that require services of an interdisciplinary team. Rehabilitation would include not only special educational techniques directed toward cognitive impairments and associated academic deficits but also interventions provided by other disciplines such as speech pathology and physical therapy (Diller & Gordon, 1981). In such training regimens, the clinical neuropsychologist can contribute by developing spe - cific procedures to remediate higher cortical functions and corresponding cognitive skills impaired by brain damage. Further, the neuropsychologist can help in planning treatments for behavioral and emotional problems secondary to the damage. By providing a functional analysis of behavioral and cognitive strengths and weaknesses in the brain injured child, the neuropsychologist can help to coordinate various rehabilitation specialists in retraining deficits and helping the child adjust to life changes brought about alterations in CNS functioning (Satz & Fletcher, 1981). Based upon neuropsychological and other test results, the neuropsychologist can help determine realistic goals for intervention with the ultimate goal of helping the child to attain as normal and independent functioning as possible (Miller, 1980). Perhaps the most important contribution that the neuropsychologist can make, however, is through development and empirical validation of models for treatment of the behavioral and cognitive problems of brain-injured children.

The Need for a Developmental, Idiographic Approach

Child neuropsychology attempts to elucidate brain-behavior relationships in the developing human brain. Such study entails certain complications that distinguish it from the investigation of the mature brain (Rourke, Bakker, Fisk, & Strang, 1983). Foremost among these complications is the developmental variable. The developing child has a constantly changing nervous system that confounds the study of neuropsychological functions and the effects of brain injury on these functions. With adults we interpret the effects of brain damage on the assumption that all neuropsychological skills have already reached full development. With children, however, we must view the effects of brain injury in light of the age of the child and the level and type of previously acquired skills. In older children who sustain brain injury, there may be considerable loss of skills already acquired. In younger children, however, fewer skills have been acquired, so the damage may have more implications for future development; in addition to possibly causing some loss of already existing skills, it may prevent or delay the child's acquiring certain skills at the expected age.

Because of this critical developmental dimension, the treatment models used with brain damaged adults may be inappropriate with brain damaged children. Adults are typically rehabilitated with the goal of achieving a return to an already acquired capacity, hence the terms "cognitive retraining" or "rehabilitation." This goal of restoring lost functions applies to some brain-injured children, especially those who suffer the injury at an older age. With younger brain-damaged children, however, training often focuses on abilities that are still in the process of development--abilities that may be delayed or impaired by the brain damage. For this reason, we feel that the term "cognitive training" more accurately describes the psychological and educational interventions used with brain damaged children.

In developing cognitive training programs for brain injured children, the neuropsychologist must adopt an idiographic approach based on the distinctive characteristics of each child. Such as individualized approach is essential because "brain damage" is a generic term that refers to CNS injury that can occur through diverse agents, including diseases (e.g., encephalitis, tumors), toxic substances (e.g., lead, radiation), anoxia and head injury (Boll & Barth, 1981; Rutter, Chadwick, & Shaffer, 1983). Further, such damage can vary along dimensions of severity, location, and specificity. Moreover, the cognitive and behavioral effects of the damage vary substantially from child to child, even with comparable etiologies (Rutter, Chadwick, & Shaffer, 1983; Telzrow, 1985). Brain-injured children show a diversity of characteristics that include general intellectual impairment (Levin, Benton, & Grossman, 1982), specific deficits on neuropsychological tests, especially on measures of speeded motor performance (Bawden, Knights, & Winogron, 1985), memory disorders (Levin & Eisenberg, 1979a, 1979b), and behavioral and emotional problems (Shaffer, 1974; Rutter, 1977).

In assessing the brain-injured child for treatment, the neuropsychologist must take into account not only the features of the lesion but such variables as the child's experiential history and social environment, age and stage of cognitive development, level of pre-injury functioning, current adaptive abilities, and motivational, behavioral, and personality factors. All of these factors play a role in determining the child's functional level and response to training. The age and corresponding developmental level of the child are particularly important considerations not only in assessing the effects of the damage but also in developing an appropriate remedial program (Boll & Barth, 1981; Golden, 1981; Rourke, Bakker, Fisk, & Strang, 1983). In order to determine whether an actual deficit exists, the clinician, of course, should know basic norms for motor, perceptual, and speech development in children. In some cases the brain-injured child may "grow out" of a presumed deficit because it was not really a deficit in the first place.

Because children vary a great deal from one cognitive stage to the next in their ability to process and interpret information, the particular cognitive developmental stage of the child must be considered and the intervention tailored to that stage (Cohen & Schleser, 1984). This is especially critical with cognitive interventions that require certain levels of cognition. One cannot assume that the approach that works with the older child is appropriate for the younger one.

The clinician should also be familiar with stages of neuropsychological development--that is, the age ranges within which certain neuropsychological systems become functional (Golden, 1981). A deficit due to early brain damage may appear at a later age because the involved skill may be part of a system that has not yet become functional at the time of the damage. For example, Golden (1981) proposes that the tertiary sensory system (located primarily in the parietal lobe and responsible for cross-modality integration) does not become psychologically active until the child is 5-8 years old. Hence, a child who is injured in this area at two years may appear normal until elementary school tasks (e.g., reading) demand the use of this system.

Rourke et al. (1983) stress the importance of the variable of age in evaluating the brain-impaired child's potential for remediation and recovery of functions. As a general rule, younger children have greater opportunity to recover from brain damage and to respond to remedial programs than do older children. One reason for this is that the younger brain shows more plasticity and less differentiation in functions that the older brain. Infants, for example, who have their left hemispheres removed soon after birth develop language functions in their right hemisphere; that is, the right hemisphere takes over functions typically subserved by the left hemisphere (Dennis & Kohn, 1975). However, older children (i.e., 9 or 10 years of age and above) who have suffered extensive damage to the left hemisphere do not show nearly so dramatic a take-over by the right hemisphere. On the other hand, under certain circumstances the child who sustains brain impairment at an older age may show better training potential than one with early damage. Rourke et al. (1983) note that the child who suffers damage at a later age (i.e., late childhood or adolescence) has a longer learning history and thereby may have more premorbid learned engrams to rely on in a remedial program (provided, of course, the engrams are intact). When the damage affects a primary sensory or perceptual system (e.g., visual, auditory, tactile), the prognosis is probably better for children who sustain damage at an older age.

For a thorough discussion of factors that should be considered in assessing the brain-impaired child's remedial needs and remediable capacities, the reader is referred to Rourke et al. (1983). These factors include information gained from neuropsychological assessment, variables related to the known or hypothesized brain lesion, the demands of the child's environment, and availability of remedial resources. Foremost in the assessment information is child's general capacity for adaptation as reflected by general measures of intelligence and adaptive skills. Rourke et al. (1983) propose that, as a general rule, the child with higher general adaptational capacity has a better prognosis, responds to a wider range of remedial approaches, and shows more insight into his or her problems. The neuropsychological assessment should also give the child's particular pattern of strengths and weaknesses as well as the type and number of neuropsychological systems impaired, degree of impairment, quality of strengths, and premorbid learned engrams that are intact.

Rourke et al. (1983) also specify variables that should be considered regarding the brain damage. These include the known or suspected cause of the lesion, the level and extent of the lesion, the age at which the lesion was sustained and the chronicity of the lesion (Rourke et al., 1983). Further, immediate and long range demands of the child's environment should be assessed in terms of learning and work expectations as well as social interactions. In evaluating remedial resources, one should consider the family's role in remediation, the availability of specialized therapists and programs, and the child's own motivational level. Moreover, there would be the need for someone to coordinate the remedial plan. As noted previously, the child neuropsychologist may play a role in the coordination when several disciplines are involved.

An idiographic perspective allows the neuropsychologist to appreciate variable patterns of impairment as well as differential recovery and response to treatment (Finger & Stein, 1982). Brain injured children present differing levels and constellations of impairments that are mediated by age and other variables just reviewed. In designing remedial approaches, such as those discussed in the subsequent sections of this chapter, the neuropsychologist must consider the child's individual pattern of neuropsychological strengths and weaknesses within the context of these interacting variables.

Neuropsychological Issues and Approaches to Training

In applying neuropsychological approaches to remediation of cognitive deficits in brain-injured children, we need to proceed in empirical fashion with some measure of skepticism. The term "neuropsychological" has a euphonious, scientific ring, and neuropsychological approaches to assessment and treatment are becoming increasingly popular in psychology and related disciplines (as evidenced, for example, in the large attendance at neuropsychological workshops). There is the danger of simplistic theorizing and premature or uncritical acceptance of such techniques on the basis of construct validity or even face validity in the absence of empirical validity. Such a situation occurred with the "perceptual training" movement of the 1960s, when a number of remedial programs were adopted on the premise that certain underlying perceptual "processes" had to first be remediated before the learning disabled child could learn to read or write (Mann, 1971). Some writers (e.g., Sandoval & Haapanen, 1981) have recently cautioned against the similar application of neuropsychological models to educational programs without appropriate empirical verification. In a similar vein, Rourke et al. (1983) has stressed that there are still more questions than answers in the area of remediation of brain-related deficiencies in children.

In discussing approaches to training with brain-injured children, then, we must acknowledge at the start that empirical evaluation of these proposed strategies has only recently begun. The approaches presented should be viewed as theoretically based methods that need further experimental validation with children with brain damage or dysfunction.

Deficit-Oriented versus Strength-Oriented Training

In developing a remedial program for the brain-impaired child, one often has to decide whether the remedial program should focus on direct training (or retraining) of deficient skills or indirect training through substitution of intact or well-developed skills for the deficient skills.

Golden and Anderson (1979) have derived from Luria's theory (1973) four major ways to rehabilitate a child with brain injury: 1) direct retraining of the lost skill; 2) substitution of alternate basic skills for the lost skill; 3) substitution of more complex skills for the lost skill; and 4) changing the environment. The first approach, of course, is deficit-oriented, while the second two are variations of a strength-oriented strategy. The last approach is beyond the scope of our discussion since it relates more to environmental engineering (i.e., adapting the environment of the child to circumvent the child's handicaps) than to training of the child.

Deficit-Oriented Training

According to Golden and Anderson (1979), direct retraining can either involve retraining the injured area itself or substituting another part of the brain for the injured area. If damage to the area is only partial, the child might recover the involved skill with intensive training in the form of repeated practice of the skill. If the damage to the area is more extensive, another part of the brain may take over the involved skill. This "take over" could occur in two ways. First, in functions normally controlled by one hemisphere, the opposite hemisphere, if intact, could take over the function if the brain injury occurs early enough; this is unlikely, however, with later injuries. Second, in complex skills that involve both hemispheres, the intact hemisphere may take over the function of the injured hemisphere.

However, direct retraining has advantages and disadvantages. The major disadvantage is that this approach is directed toward the child's weakness, which makes it, in many ways, a more difficult and slower approach. The child will seemingly make less progress than with other methods because he or she is required to develop a deficient or absent skill rather than use an already developed skill. Direct retraining requires more patience on the part of the child, parents, and teacher or therapist; they must all be willing to settle for long-term, modest goals rather than quick, dramatic improvements. The child must accept the fact that he or she must work harder than other children and practice tasks that appear "childish" because they are so basic. The primary advantage of direct retraining is that it may help the child to eventually remedy deficits and function at as normal a level as possible given the limitations of the injury, general motivation, and intelligence of the child. This approach offers the child more alternatives later in life since there is not a glaring deficit in the child's skills.

According to Golden and Anderson (1979) direct retraining is more appropriate with highly delimited disorders and with younger children, who are less likely to perceive the tasks as childish and more likely to respond to tangible and social reinforcers. With older children and cases involving massive injuries, however, this approach is contraindicated.

Rourke et al. (1983) note a number of reasons for developing and using a remedial plan that attacks directly the child's neuropsychological weaknesses. The age of the child is a critical consideration. Younger children, that is, below 9 or 10 years of age, would be expected to respond better to this strategy than older children primarily because of the greater capability of the younger child's brain for reorganization. Further, older children with long-term neuropsychological deficits often have acquired a behavioral style compatible with their pattern of neuropsychological abilities; this style may be deeply ingrained and resistant to change. The child, for example, with substantial deficits in auditory-linguistic areas may have developed an adaptive and learning style that relies heavily on visual processing and bypasses the deficient areas. A younger child is less likely to have developed a style to circumvent the weakness and more likely to respond positively to therapy directed at the weaknesses.

Rourke et al. (1983) also recommend attacking the child's observed and predictable neuropsychological weaknesses as early as possible after the damage occurs, especially when limited areas of the brain have been affected. The longer the treatment is delayed, the greater the chance that the deficits will become entrenched and less responsive to intervention. With immediate intervention, such problems might be averted. The weakness-oriented strategy would also be advisable when the brain dysfunction is circumscribed but associated with a broad range of unfavorable behavioral consequences. A child with fine motor impairment, for example, might experience self-consciousness and a deep sense of failure because he or she is unable to perform many task required in the classroom. A motor training program may help the child to avoid such emotional and behavioral problems. In addition, remediation of specific deficits might yield secondary benefits in other skill areas.

Rourke et al. (1983) suggest that programs directed at deficits might also be appropriate when the child has only mild adaptive weaknesses and a good repertoire of well-developed psychological strengths. Such a program should be stopped, however, if the child shows strong resistance or fails to progress. The weakness-oriented strategy might be suitable, too, when there is a high probability that the child's neuropsychological deficits will respond well to remediation. Some evidence suggests, for example, that motor problems consequent to brain damage respond well to an intensive remedial program (Chadwick, Rutter, Shaffer, & Shrout, 1981). Finally, when the child has two few neuropsychological strengths to compensate for a critical neuropsychological deficit, a program directed at the weakness might be employed. Such would be the case with children who have brain impairments that are highly generalized.

Rourke et al. (1983) point out that most remedial programs should include at least some component that directly attacks the weakness. In some cases, it may be the core strategy and in others it may be one part of a complicated remedial plan.

Strength-Oriented Training

As noted previously, Golden and Anderson (1979) propose that a strength-oriented program can be approached in two ways. One approach involves the substitution of more basic skills for lost skills, with simpler skills being put together to make up a more complex skill. For example, injuries to the frontal lobe cause impairment of planning skills, decision-making ability, and organizational ability. In dealing with such an impairment, a child could be taught to use reading skills in following a list, or to memorize or write sets of instructions to follow.

The other approach involves substituting more complex skills for the lost skill, thereby making a basic skill a part of a more complex process. A child with auditory-linguistic deficits, for example, might be taught to read by associating intact phonemic sounds with letters felt by hand and then associating the tactile letters with corresponding visual ones. This specific technique, according to Golden and Anderson (1979), would only work with children with isolated impairment in auditory-verbal areas of the brain. The strategy of substituting more complex skills for the lost skill is difficult to apply because it requires the formation of complex chains through practice of separate skills. It is most useful with children with limited injuries that render the first approach unusable.

Rourke et al. (1983) discuss a number of factors to consider in deciding whether to use a strength-oriented approach. Older brain-impaired children (i.e., in late childhood and early adolescence) often respond more positively to a remedial program that capitalizes on their neuropsychological strengths. As noted previously, such children may resist a program directed at their weaknesses, especially when they have experienced repeated failures in the weak areas. The strength-oriented program may even be appropriate for younger children who show marked emotional resistance to training that challenges their weaknesses. Such a program may also be suitable for children of different ages who have neuropsychological deficits that are resistant to remediation. For example, aphasic children with severe language deficits may be more responsive to a "total communication" program that capitalizes on strengths in nonverbal communication.

Rourke et al. (1983) stress that a program using the child's strengths will open options for general cognitive development that might otherwise be unavailable. Further, such a program is appropriate when the child shows salient deficits while having an intact area of functioning. For example, the child with intact verbal functions might be taught to "talk through" tasks in nonverbal areas where he may be impaired. Finally, Rourke et al. suggest that a strength-oriented approach might be used to further enhance already well-developed capacities, allowing the child to maintain confidence and motivation.

In concluding our discussion of the relative merits of deficit-oriented and strength-oriented strategies, we should emphasize that few remedial programs would use exclusively one or the other. Most programs probably would use a mixture of the two, with the degree of emphasis on one or the other being determined by the considerations just reviewed.

Neuropsychological Approaches to Remediation of Academic Skills

In using a neuropsychological approach in training brain-injured children, we should avoid focusing on attempts to remedy underlying neurological dysfunctions without evaluating whether we are developing skills that make a difference in the child's life. Golden and Anderson (1979) suggest that the task content of the program be pertinent to academic demands, strengthening not only neuropsychological abilities but also relevant academic skills. In determining priorities, one should remember that limited, concentrated attention in one single area typically yields better results. In order to assure early success and high motivation from the child, parent, and teacher, one should start with the most basic deficits that are educationally relevant and most readily remediable for the particular child.

The most relevant educational skills, of course, are reading, writing, and arithmetic. Hartlage (1981) has proposed a neuropsychological model, based on three basic working assumptions with associated treatment implications, for strength-oriented remediation of these skills. Although developed for learning disabled children in general, the model has applicability to brain-injured children with learning deficits.

The first assumption is that reading skill, particularly involving auditory sequencing, phonetic analysis, and comprehension, is primarily localized in posterior regions of the dominant (almost always left) cerebral hemisphere. Some early reading skills, however, may be dependent on posterior areas of the right hemisphere, especially those skills involving whole word recognition and visual word matching. The training implication is that if the right hemisphere is functioning more efficiently than the left, the child would more likely benefit from nonphonetic instruction based on visuospatial cues. Conversely, a child with a stronger (or more intact) left hemisphere would more likely profit from an approach based on phonetic analysis and reading for comprehension rather than on individual word revisualization. Early training might involve, for example, initial teaching alphabet for the former child and phonics for the latter, with a gradual shift in both cases to synthesis and comprehension as basic reading skills are learned. For the young child with marked right-hemisphere impairment, aural comprehension approaches (such as tape-recording reading material) can be used to circumvent the visual-spatial deficit.

The second working assumption is that computation may be dependent on either hemisphere, depending on complexity of the material and the particular neuropsychological skills involved. Mathematics involving language and sequential logic is more dependent on the left hemisphere, while that requiring spatial perception and visualization of two-dimensional problems depends more on the right hemisphere. For the child with a strong left hemisphere, teaching would emphasize math instructions that use concepts, language formulation, or sequential logic. This child's strengths would include algebra and computer programming. For the child with a strong right hemisphere, math instruction might employ visually oriented modes such as flash-cards and two-dimensional problems. Such a child might be expected to do better on computational problems and geometry.

The third working assumption is that spelling is basically an aspect of language and strongly depends on the left hemisphere. Although the learning of simple printing in very young children depends heavily on the right hemisphere, the left hemisphere assumes more and more involvement in later writing and spelling. The child with a strong left hemisphere, then, would be expected to respond well to the early introduction of linguistic aids to spelling. On the other hand, the child with a strong right hemisphere would be more likely to profit from an approach involving rote copying, visual aids, and use of whole words instead of a sequential approach.

While Hartlage's (1981) model is oriented toward learning disabilities and primarily based on neuropsychological research on learning disabled children, it offers a conceptual basis for developing strength-oriented training programs for children whose brain injury has resulted in learning deficits of one type or another. The model also provides a theoretical source for specific hypotheses that might be tested in research with brain-injured children. Whether the treatment implications derived from the model have validity for treatment of such children is an empirical question that can only be answered with further research.

Other writers have drawn on neuropsychological models for approaching classification and remediation of academic deficits associated with brain dysfunction. Most of the classification systems apply most directly to developmental learning disorders presumed to have a neurological basis but not necessarily associated with a history of brain damage. Nevertheless, as with Hartlage's (1981) model, these systems have implications for assessment and remediation of learning disabilities that may arise from brain damage.

From a developmental neuropsychological perspective, reading disability, or dyslexia, is generally classified into three types: auditory-linguistic, visual-spatial, and mixed (Boder, 1973; Pirozzolo, 1981; Telzrow, 1985). The auditory-linguistic type, which is by far the most common, is associated with impairment in the left hemisphere; the visual-spatial with impairment in the right hemisphere; the mixed with impairment in both hemispheres. Most writers (e.g., Hartlage & Telzrow, 1983; Pirozzolo, 1981) advocate a strength-oriented approach to remediation of these deficits, although the efficacy of this approach has not been clearly validated in well-controlled studies with learning disabled or brain-damaged children. According to this approach, children with the auditory-linguistic reading impairments would respond best to remediation emphasizing their intact visual-spatial skills (that is, using visual or graphic representations) whereas children with visual-spatial impairments would respond best to a "phonics" approach. A strength-oriented approach with children with mixed disorders would be more difficult because such children would have fewer strengths to capitalize on.

Using an even more direct neuropsychological approach to remediation, recent studies have explored the effects of hemispheric-specific stimulation on the reading performance of boys with two types of dyslexia, one type being associated with the right hemisphere and the other with the left hemisphere (Bakker, Moerland, and Goekoop-Hoefkens, 1981; Bakker & Vinke, 1985). The technique involved visual field stimulation to activate the "weak" hemisphere, thereby involving it more in reading. The results revealed that both groups showed significantly improved reading skills and that training-induced electrical changes in brain symmetry correlated with changes in measures of reading accuracy and speed. Further research is needed to determine whether this technique of direct hemispheric stimulation is feasible and effective with brain-injured children who have deficits associated with one or the other hemisphere.

There have been recent attempts to classify spelling and arithmetic disabilities into neuropsychological subtypes that can be related to remedial programs (Rourke, 1983; Sweeney & Rourke, 1985; Strang & Rourke, 1985). Rourke (1983) distinguishes between two types of disabled spellers: the "phonetically accurate" speller (who has relatively intact auditory and verbal skills but impaired visual perception and memory) and the "phonetically inaccurate" speller (who has relatively intact non-verbal skills but impaired language skills including reading). Sweeney and Rourke (1985) present a thorough discussion of remediation implications for the two types. The remedial approach for the child of the former type should generally be directed toward developing the deficient visual-perceptual skills through "right hemisphere" strategies. For the child of the latter type, the initial approach should involve intensive training in auditory analysis and synthesis of words to be learned; if the child fails to respond, an intensive sight-word strategy is recommended.

Arithmetic disabilities have only recently received attention in the child neuropsychological literature. Arithmetic is not based on any one underlying ability but is made up of highly complex skills based on hierarchically ordered subskills. As noted above in the discussion of Hartlage's (1981) model, different parts of the brain are involved, depending on the nature of the task. For a thorough discussion of neuropsychological subtypes of arithmetic disorders and suggestions for remediation, the reader is referred to Strang and Rourke (1985).

Behavioral and Cognitive Approaches

In addition to developing strategies for remediation of academic deficits associated with brain damage, the clinical neuropsychologist can play a role in developing treatments for adaptive and behavioral problems secondary to brain damage. Behavior therapy is considered the most effective form of treatment for many childhood disorders ranging from enuresis to hyperactivity to autism (Morris & Kratochwill, 1983). In developing programs for the brain-injured child, whether the program be directed at educational, or adaptive deficits, it makes sense to integrate principles of behavior therapy with neuropsychological knowledge and theory. Indeed, as Telzrow (1985) has stressed, the most effective treatment programs with both brain-injured children and adults are those that are highly behavioral.

Behavior therapy encompasses a diversity of techniques ranging from traditional behavior modification based on the systematic use of consequences to more recently developed cognitive behavioral techniques such as self-instruction and modeling (Aaron, 1981; Meichenbaum & Goodman, 1971). Training programs for brain-injured children and adults have successfully employed behavioral principles such as cuing, shaping, generalization, and positive reinforcement (Bolger, 1982). Salzinger and Feldman (1970) have demonstrated that parents of brain-injured children can be taught operant conditioning principles which allow them to design and carry out effective behavior modification programs based on functional analysis of the children's behavior.

With the rise of cognitive psychology, many behaviorists began to modify and expand their views. Rather than focusing exclusively on the modification of overt behavior, behavioral psychologists began to view internal thought processes as scientifically legitimate targets and mechanisms for change (Kendall & Braswell, 1985; Meichenbaum, 1977; Meyers & Craighead, 1984). Educational settings correspondingly began to emphasize programs to develop cognitive or thinking skills in children.

Cognitive psychology prompted the expansion of behavior therapy to such areas as modeling, problem-solving, self-control, and self-instruction training. Modeling, or observational learning, refers to the child's learning through viewing another's behavior. The major factors that influence modeling are the cognitive processes of attention and retention (Meyers & Craighead, 1984). Problem-solving involves the learning of certain "thinking" skills that will enhance the child's overt ability to deal with problems. In self-control, behavior is changed by modifying covert thought processes and increasing the role of internal factors in the control of one's behavior; self-control mechanisms include self-monitoring, self-evaluation, and self-reinforcement.

Self-instruction training, developed in the early 1970's by Meichenbaum (Miechenbaum & Goodman, 1971; Miechenbaum, 1976, 1977), includes teaching individuals to produce internally generated self-statements and to talk to themselves in a self-guiding fashion. Miechenbaum drew from writings of Luria (1959; 1961) and Vygotsky (1962) who suggested that during development the child's behavior is initially under the verbal control of the social environment of adults but gradually comes under the control of the child. The child's control is achieved first through overt speech and later through covert speech (Meyers & Craighead, 1984). Based on Luria's model of verbal and motor development, Meichenbaum and Goodman (1971) developed a self-instruction program to teach impulsive children how to control their own behavior. In the procedure the instructor first modeled the overt behavior and the appropriate self-statements; then the child imitated the target behavior while first self-instructing aloud, then whispering, and finally covertly rehearsing the self-statements. This method has proven to be a successful treatment for decreasing aggression, reducing hyperactivity and impulsivity, decreasing fear, improving academic performance, and training social competence in children (Meyers & Craighead, 1984; Kendall & Braswell, 1985).

In view of their effectiveness with behavioral and learning problems in children in general, cognitive behavioral approaches show promise for use in the treatment of the behavioral disturbances, adaptive deficits, and learning disabilities found in the brain-damaged child. Most of the research to date on these approaches has been done with behavior disordered and learning disabled children who do not necessarily have demonstrable brain damage. Nevertheless, the techniques have been found to work on specific problems also shown in brain-injured children--problems such as impulsivity, hyperactivity, attention deficits, and learning disabilities.

Miechenbaum (1976) developed a cognitive-functional approach to the study of learning disabled children. This approach includes both a task analysis and psychological analysis of cognitions (i.e., self-statements and images) that subjects use in order to perform a task. Brain-damaged children perform poorly because they produce negative self-statements, task-irrelevant thoughts, and anxiety-engendering ideas that interfere with adequate performance. Miechenbaum (1976) proposed that children with brain damage have a poorer self-concept than "normal" children. This poor self-concept is manifested in the child's internal dialogue as he approaches and performs a task, and is especially evident when he experiences frustration and failure. Achieving behavioral change and performance improvement requires more than just making the child aware of the self-statement. For improvements to occur, the child must view the negative self-statements and task-irrelevant thoughts as reminders to use the task-appropriate strategies taught in therapy. Miechenbaum (1976) has demonstrated that the learning-impaired child can learn adaptive, task-facilitative thinking processes through self-instructional training. By teaching the child to talk to himself or herself differently, one can change the child's thinking.

Kaufman and Kaufman (1979) found that cognitive training using nonacademic tasks not only improved efficiency on nonacademic tasks but also improved academic performance in children with or without learning deficits. These authors offered three key suggestions for cognitive training. First, the child should be guided in approaching the task at hand and encouraged to verbalize the use of successive strategies. It is more important to teach the child these strategies than to train the child on specific tasks. Thus the method of training is more important than the actual content of tasks used for training. These methods, however, are even more successful in improving academic performance when applied directly to school learning tasks. Second, these techniques can be used in a regular classroom to benefit all students. The average student's performance improved, but not to the extent that the below average student improved. Third, the training should involve material that is intrinsically interesting, fun, and nonthreatening.

More recent research applying cognitive behavioral techniques to learning disabled children has yielded some similarly encouraging findings. Montague and Bos (1986), for example, found that a cognitive strategy was effective in facilitating verbal math problem-solving in learning disabled adolescents. Further, maintenance and generalization of the strategy were evident. Rooney, Polloway, & Hallahan (1985) demonstrated that two cognitive behavioral procedures--self-monitoring of attention and self-monitoring of academic accuracy--were effective in improving the performance of low-functioning learning disabled students.

One problem commonly found in children with brain damage is motor impairment, particularly on speeded tasks (Bawden, Knights, & Winogron, 1985). Cognitive activities such as verbalization and mental rehearsal of various sequences of a movement pattern have been studied for their effects on motor training in the brain-impaired child (Haskell, Barrett, & Taylor, 1977). Most of the results would indicate that these techniques are successful in improving motor performance significantly beyond gains shown with physical practice alone.

In reviewing the efficacy of cognitive training with learning disabled children, Keogh and Hall (1984) note that findings are discrepant and even conflicting. One reason for this, of course, is the heterogeneity of the population. Nevertheless, these authors feel that self-monitoring and self-recording techniques can be effective with learning disabled children. Although the durability of effects from self-monitoring methods has been impressive, the range of skilled behavior affected is limited. All in all, Keogh and Hall conclude that learning disabled children are good candidates for programs that stress the formation of organizational plans and strategies.

While research supports the efficacy of cognitive behavioral techniques with children with learning and behavior problems, we cannot, of course, assume that the results would necessarily apply to children with clear brain damage. With brain damage the behavioral and cognitive deficits may not be nearly so specific as in learning disabilities where, by definition, the child is of normal intelligence and without marked emotional problems. Moreover, the brain-damaged child's impairment may be such that the meta-cognitive skills essential to this approach cannot be readily learned. In fact, research findings have consistently shown brain damaged children to be more neuropsychologically and intellectually impaired than learning disabled children (Selz & Reitan, 1979a, 1979b).

Summary and Conclusions

In this chapter we have reviewed general issues and approaches in cognitive training of brain-injured children. We have stressed the need for the child neuropsychologist to adopt a developmental, idiographic perspective in assessing children and planning their training programs. Foremost in this view is an appreciation of developmental variables that bear critically on interpretation of brain damage and development of remedial training for children of different ages. Recognizing that brain damage occurs in different ways with different results, we have emphasized the need for individualized training based on the child's own particular pattern of deficits and resources.

The neuropsychological approaches for remediation that we have reviewed are based largely on developmental considerations (such as age) and models of brain function. While the approaches draw upon general empirical findings regarding neuropsychological functions, they still need to be empirically tested for their utility in remediation with brain-impaired children. In short, the approaches appear to have construct validity but lack demonstration of predictive validity.

The question of predictive validity is a complicated one that goes beyond demonstrating the effectiveness of a given strategy in remediating brain impairments in children. It extends to comparing the relative effectiveness of different techniques with different types of impairments with children of different ages. In order to study how treatment effectiveness varies as a function of child factors such as type of impairment and age, we need, as Rourke et al. (1983) have suggested, to proceed systematically by carefully measuring the effects of well-defined treatments with homogeneous groups. In the past, the uncontrolled nature of the treatment as well as the heterogeneous composition of the groups has created difficulty in assessing treatment effects. Children with clear brain damage may respond differently to a given treatment than children with learning dysfunction without demonstrable damage. Further, we have to consider the differential response of children with different types of damage or dysfunction, not to mention the complications imposed by the age variable alone.

As we have noted, behavioral approaches using operant conditioning principles have been shown to be an effective component of training programs with brain-injured children. The results thus far with cognitive behavioral strategies are promising, although most of the work has been done with children with learning and behavior problems not necessarily associated with brain damage. As with the neuropsychological techniques, there is the need to further evaluate the effectiveness of these cognitive techniques with clearly defined groups of brain-injured children of varying ages.

Whether the approach is based upon a behavioral or neuropsychological model or a combination of both, the ultimate goal of any training program with brain-injured children is to help them adapt as normally as possible to the demands of everyday life. Perhaps the most crucial issue, then, in assessing interventions with brain-injured children is that of generalization and maintenance of training. The evaluation of training strategies should extend to an assessment of how well the learned skills are integrated and maintained in the child's natural environment (Satz & Fletcher, 1981). With most of the approaches that are used with brain-damaged children, this question still awaits a definitive answer.

References

Aaron, P. C. (1981). Diagnosis and remediation of learning disabilities in children: A neuropsychological key approach. In G. W. Hynd & J. E. Obrzut (Eds.), *Neuropsychological assessment and the school-aged child* (pp. 303-334). New York: Grune and Stratton.

Bakker, D. J., & Vinke, J. (1985). Effects of hemisphere-specific stimulation in brain activity and reading in dyslexics. *Journal of Clinical Neuropsychology 7,* 505-525.

Bakker, D. J., Moerland, R., & Goekoop-Hoetkens, M. (1981). Effects of hemisphere-specific stimulation on the reading performance of dyslexic boys: A pilot study. *Journal of Clinical Neuropsychology, 3,* 155-159.

Bawden, H. N., Knights, R. M., Winogron, H. W. (1985). Speeded performance following head injury in children. *Journal of Clinical and Experimental Neuropsychology 7,* 39-54.

Boder, E. (1973). Developmental dyslexia: A diagnostic approach based on three atypical reading-spelling patterns. *Developmental Medicine and Child Neurology, 15,* 630-687.

Bolger, J. P. (1982). Cognitive retraining: A development approach. *Clinical Neuropsychology, 4,* 66-70.

Boll, T. J., & Barth, J. T. (1981). Neuropsychology of brain damage in children. In S. B. Filskov & T. J. Boll (Eds.), *Handbook of clinical neuropsychology* (pp. 418-452). New York: John Wiley and Sons.

Chadwick, O., Rutter M., Shaffer, D., & Shrout P. E. (1981). A prospective study of children with head injuries: IV. Specific cognitive deficits. *Journal of Clinical Neuropsychology, 3,* 101-120.

Cohen, R., & Schleser, R. (1984). Cognitive development and clinical interventions. In A. W. Meyers & W. E. Craighead (Eds.), *Cognitive behavior therapy with children* (pp. 45-68). New York: Plenum Press.

Dennis, M., & Kohn, B. (1985). Comprehension of syntax in infantile hemiplegics after cerebral hemidecortication: Left hemisphere superiority. *Brain and Language, 2,* 472-482.

Diller, L., & Gordon, W. A. (1981). Interventions for cognitive deficits in brain-injured adults. *Journal of Consulting and Clinical Psychology, 49,* 822-834.

Finger, S., & Stein, D. G. (1982). *Brain damage and recovery: Research and clinical perspectives,* New York: Academic Press.

Glenwick, D. S., & Jason, L. A. (1984). Locus of intervention in child cognitive behavior therapy: Implications of a behavioral community psychology perspective. In A. W. Meyers & W. E. Craighead (Eds.), *Cognitive behavior therapy with children* (pp. 129-162). New York: Plenum Press.

Golden, C. J. & Anderson, S. (1979). *Learning disabilities and brain dysfunction: An introduction for educators and parents.* Illinois: C. C. Thomas.

Golden, C. J. (1981). The Luria-Nebraska Children's Battery: Theory and formulation. In G. W. Hynd & J. E. Obrzut (Eds.), *Neuropsychological assessment and the school-age child* (pp. 277-302). New York: Grune and Stratton.

Hartlage, L. C. & Telzrow, C. F. (1983). The neuropsychological basis of educational intervention. *Journal of Learning Disabilities, 16,* 521-528.

Hartlage, L. C. & Telzrow, C. F. (1984). Neuropsychological basis of educational assessment and programming. In P. E. Logue & J. M. Schear (Eds.), *Clinical neuropsychology; A multidisciplinary approach* (pp. 297-313). Illinois: Charles C. Thomas.

Hartlage, L. C. (1981). Neuropsychological assessment techniques. In C. R. Reynolds & L. Gutkin (Eds.), *Handbook of School Psychology* (pp. 296-320). New York: John Wiley and Sons.

Haskell, S. H., Barrett, E. K., & Taylor, H. (1977). *The education of motor and neurologically handicapped children.* New York: John Wiley and Sons.

Kaufman, D. & Kaufman, P. (1979). Strategy training and remedial techniques. *Journal of Learning Disabilities, 12,* 416-419.

Kendall, P. C. & Braswell, L. (1985). *Cognitive behavioral therapy for impulsive children.* New York: Guilford Press.

Keogh, B. K. & Hall, R. J. (1984). Training with learning disabled pupils. In A. W. Meyers & W. E. Craighead (Eds.), *Cognitive behavior therapy with children* (pp. 163-191). New York: Plenum Press.

Levin, H. S. & Eisenberg, H. M. (1979b). Neuropsychological outcome of closed head injury in children and adolescents. *Child's Brain, 5,* 281-292.

Levin, H. S. Benton, A. L., & Grossman, R. G. (1982). *Neurobehavioral consequences of closed head injury.* New York: Oxford.

Luria, A. R. (1959). The directive function of speech in development and dissolution. *Word, 15,* 341-352.

Luria, A. R. (1961). *The role of speech in the regulation of normal and abnormal behaviors*. New York: Liveright.

Luria, A. R. (1973). *The working brain: An introduction to neu ropsychology*. New York: Basic Books, Inc.

Mann, L. (1971). Perceptual training revisited: The training of nothing at all. *Rehabilitation Literature, 32,* 322-335.

Meichenbaum, D. (1976). Cognitive-functional approach to cognitive factors as determinants of learning disabilities. In R. M. Knights & D. J. Bakker (Eds.), *The neuropsychology of learning disability; theoretical approaches* (pp. 423-442). Baltimore: University Park Press.

Meichenbaum, D. (1977). *Cognitive-behavior modification; An inte grative approach*, New York: Plenum Press.

Meichenbaum, D., & Goodman, J. (1971). Training impulsive children to talk to themselves: A means of developing self-control. *Journal of Abnormal Psychology, 77,* 115-124.

Meyers, A. W. & Craighead, W. E. (1984). Cognitive behavior therapy with children: A historical, conceptual, and organizational overview. In A. W. Meyers & W. E. Craighead (Eds.), *Cognitive behavior therapy with children* (pp. 1-17). New York: Plenum Press.

Miller, E. (1980). Psychological intervention in the management and rehabilitation of neuropsychological impairments. *Behavior Research and Therapy, 18,* 527-535.

Montague, M., & Bos, C. S. (1986). The effect of cognitive strategy training on verbal math problem solving performance of learning disabled adolescents. *Journal of Learning Disabilities, 19,* 26-33.

Morris, R. J., & Kratochwill (Eds.) (1983). *The practice of child therapy*. New York: Pergamon Press.

Pirozzolo, F. J. (1981). Language and brain: Neuropsychological aspects of developmental reading disability. *School Psychology Review. 10,* 350-355.

Rooney, K., Polloway, E. A., & Hallahan, D. P. (1984). The use of self-monitoring procedures with low IQ learning disabled students. *Journal of Learning Disabilities, 18,* 384-389.

Rourke, B. P. (1983). Reading and spelling disabilities: A developmental neuropsychological perspective. In U. Kirk (Ed.), *Neuropsychology of language, reading, and spelling,* (pp. 204-234). New York: Academic Press.

Rourke, B. P., Bakker, D. J., Fisk, J. L., & Strang, J. D. (1983). *Child neuropsychology; An introduction to theory, research, and clinical practice*. New York: Guilford Press.

Rutter, M. (1977). Brain-damage syndromes in childhood: Concepts and findings. *Journal of Child Psychology and Psychiatry, 18,* 1-21.

Rutter, M. (Ed.). (1985). *Developmental neuropsychiatry*, New York: Guilford Press.

Rutter, M., Chadwick, O., & Schaffer, D. (1983). Head injury. In M. Rutter (Ed.), *Developmental neuropsychiatry* (pp. 83-111). New York: Guilford Press.

Salzinger, K., Feldman, R. S., & Portnoy, S. T. (1970). Training parents of brain injured children in the use of operant conditioning procedures. *Behavior Therapy, 1,* 4-23.

Sandoval, J., & Haapanen, R. M. (1981). A critical commentary on neuropsychology in the schools. *School Psychology Review, 10,* 389-393.

Satz, P., & Fletcher, J. M. (1981). Emergent trends in neuropsychology: An overview. *Journal of Consulting and Clinical Psychology, 49,* 851-865.

Selz, M., & Reitan, R. M. (1979a). Neuropsychological test performance of normal, learning disabled, and brain-damaged older children. *Journal of Nervous and Mental Diseases, 5,* 298-302.

Selz, M., & Reitan, R. M. (1979b). Rules for neuropsychological diagnosis: Classification of brain function in older children. *Journal of Consulting and Clinical Psychology, 51,* 406-413.

Shaffer, D. (1974). Psychiatric aspects of brain injury in childhood: A review. In S. Chess & A. Thomas (Eds.), *Annual progress in child psychiatry and child development*. New York: Brunner Mazel.

Strang, J. E., & Rourke, B. P. (1985). Arithmetic disability subtypes: The neuropsychological significance of specific arithmetical impairment in childhood. In B. P. Rourke (Ed.), *Neuropsychology of learning disabilities: Essentials of subtype analysis,* (pp. 167-183). New York: Guilford Press.

Sweeny, J. E., & Rourke, B. P. (1985). Spelling disability subtypes. In B. P. Rourke (Ed.), *Neuropsychology of learning disabilities; Essential of subtype analysis* (pp. 147-166). New York: Guilford Press.

Swift, M. S., & Spivack, G. (1974). Therapeutic teaching: A review of teaching methods of behaviorally troubled children. *Journal of Special Education, 8,* 281-289.

Telzrow, C. F. (1985). The science and speculation of rehabilitation in developmental neuropsychological disorders. In L. C. Hartlage & C. F. Telzrow (Eds.), *The neuropsychology of indi vidual differences; A developmental perspective*. New York: Plenum Press.

Vygotsky, L. (1962). *Thought and language*. New York: Wiley.

Subject Index

Activities of daily living, 45, 50, 99-100
Algebra, 224
Aphasia, 143
Assessment
    computers in, 112
    of depression in children
    functional/adaptive, 144
    of memory, 125
    neuropsychological, 15-18
    practice effects in, 99
    qualitative, 16-17
    resource, 43-45
    sensory system, 111
    serial, 140
    skill, 43-45
    of stengths, 118
Behavior therapy, 12, 226-227
Cancellation training, 113
Carnegie units, 193
Case reports
    learning disability, 199-200, 201-202
    severe head injury, 35, 50-54
Cerebral vascular accident, 109, 141
Child Behavior Checklist, 181
Cluster analysis, 179
Cognitive abilities
    and emotional factors
    assessment of, see Assessment
    deficits in, 3
    premorbid, 45, 96
Cognitive Behavior Rating Scales
    (CBRS), 49
Cognitive behavior therapy, see
    Behavior therapy
Cognitive retraining
    of block design, 113
    with children, 217-229
        development and, 218-219
        ideographic approach, 218-220
        working assumptions, 232
    computers in, 31, 80-92, 100
    cost-benefit, 36-37, 68, 151
    critical periods in, 100
    deficit vs strength oriented, 221-222
    direct, 31
    of driving, 116
    effectiveness, 31-32, 64-66,
        132-134, 217
    generalization of, 47, 116, 127, 133,
        144, 151, 197
    home-based, 154-156

    games as, 156, 169
    groups, 136, 145
    implementation, 100, 118, 151,
        154-155
    of language, 43, 143-144, 149, 183
    marketing, 151
    of memory, 123-137
    in the natural environment, 98, 197
    role in rehabilitation, 43-54
    specific tasks, 159-169
    termination of, 100
    theories of, see Neuropsychological
        theories
    visual imagery and, 132
Coma, 3 (see also Recovery)
Comparative psychology, 61
Compensatory strategies, 144, 194-195
Computer-assisted instruction, 86
    effectiveness of, 88-89
Computers, see Cognitive Retraining,
    Assessment
Cortical blindness, 110, 114-115
Denial of illness, 3, 145
Depression, 5, 7
    influence on cognitive ability
        see Cognitive abilities
    assessment of, see Assessment
Diaschesis, 49-50 (see also Recovery)
Double Simultaneous Stimulation (DSS),
    110, 113
Dyslexia, see Learning disability
Education of patient and family, 118
Electroencephalogram (EEG), 6
Everyday abilities, 43-45, 99, 125 (see
    also Assessment)
Fragmentation of instruction, 195
Halstead-Reitan Test Battery, 177-178
Head Trauma, 3 (see also Recovery)
    mild, 82
    prognosis in, 5, 18-21
Hemi-fovial perceptual disturbance, 109
Hemi-inattention, 109, 111, 113-114
History, 13-14, 26-27
    social, 14-15
Hyperactivity, 207-211
    impulse control and, 210, 226
    methylphenidate treatment of, 210
    selective attention and, 210
Immersed curricula, 196-197
IQ, 5, 8-9 (see also Wechsler Adult
    Intelligence Scale, Assessment)

Learning Disability, 173-185, 191-206
    (*see also* Hyperactivity)
    aggression and, 212
    attention and, 209-210
    computer tomography and, 176
    diagnostic criteria, 173-175
        208-209, 213
    dyslexia, 225
    emotional factors and, 181-183
    epidemiology, 175-176
    etiology, 176-177
    gender differences, 175-176
    hyperactivity and, *see* Hyperactivity
    immune disorders and, 176
    longitudinal studies of, 180
    malnutrition, 177
    model treatment programs, 195-196
    neurological basis, 173, 176, 180,
        211, 218
    neuropsychological assessment of,
        177-178, 185
    psychiatric factors, 212-213
    public schools and, 194-196
    Rutter's standard, 208-209
    subtyping, 178-181, 191-192,
        224-225
    task analysis and, 184
    treatment effectiveness of, 191
Learning Quotient, 175
Letter reversals, 173
Linking, 129
Matching Familiar Figures Test, 210
Methodological issues in evaluation of
        treatment, 95-105
    component control, 103
    internal validity, 96, 104-105
    placebo effects, 101
    research designs, 103-105
    spontaneous recovery, 101, 112
    waiting list control, 103
Minnesota Multiphasic Personality
        Inventory (MMPI), 9
Modeling, *see* Behavior therapy
Money search test, 118
Motor impairment, 227
Neglect, 109
Neuropsychological theories, 57-70
    Piagetian, 61
    information-processing, 62
    of memory, 123-126
Neurodevelopment, 30
Occupational therpay, 149
Orientation, 3
Paraprofessionals, 46, 152

Peg-word method, 129
Perceptual training, 183, (*see also*
        Cognitive retraining)
Place-loci method, 129
Plasticity, 220
Post Traumatic Amnesia, 3-6, 79
Premorbid abilities, *see* Cognitive abilities
Process approach, 63
Professional training, 152
Professionalism, 149
PQRST method, 130
Psychotherapy, 10-11, 31, 38
Q-factor techniques, 178
Reading, 176 (*see also* Learning
        disability)
Recall strategies, 128
Recovery
    biological potential of, 29
    from closed head injury, *see* Head
        Trauma
    emotional factors in, 82
    patterns of, 79-81, 140
    psychosocial aspects of, 3-7,
        139-146
    spontaneous, 112
    stages of, 3-5
Rehabilitation (see also Recovery,
        Cognitive retraining)
    cognitive, 13-15, 81-83, 143
    environmental predictors of, 20-21,
        97, 193
    family role in, 11-13, 152-153
    goals of, 43, 46-47, 83, 100, 143
        154, 217
    physical, 142
    principles of, 125
    psychiatric factors and, 38, 154
    resources management in, 48
Reorganization of cognitive functions, 45,
        57
Retention strategies, 127
Retraining, *see* Cognitive retraining
Right hemisphere injury, 109
Self-instruction, *see* Behavior therapy
Skill training, 47 (*see also* Cognitive
        retraining)
Social networks, 141-142
Special education, 192-193
Spelling, 224
Stroke, *see* Cerebral vascular accident
SQ3R method, 130
Systematic desensitization, 183
Tangible social support, *see* Social
        networks

Therapeutic milieu, 33
Third-party payment, 181
Television games, 85
Verbal mnemonics, 135
Visual scanning training, 113
Visual field cut, 111 (*see also* Neglect)
Wechsler Intelligence Scale for Children,
    176
Wechsler Adult Intelligence Scale, 99,
    140
Wheelchair navigation skills, 113-114
Wide Range Achievement Test, 208
Work Trial, 34-36, 48-49
Writing, 224